THE CANON OF SCRIPTURE

F. F. BRUCE

INTERVARSITY PRESS
DOWNERS GROVE, ILLINOIS 60515

© 1988 F. F. Bruce

Published in the United States of America by InterVarsity Press, Downers Grove, Illinois, with permission from Chapter House Ltd., Glasgow, Scotland.

InterVarsity Press is the book-publishing division of InterVarsity Christian Fellowship, a student movement active on campus at hundreds of universities, colleges and schools of nursing. For information about local and regional activities, write Public Relations Dept., InterVarsity Christian Fellowship, 6400 Schroeder Rd., P.O. Box 7895, Madison, WI 53707-7895.

Distributed in Canada through InterVarsity Press, 860 Denison St., Unit 3, Markham, Ontario L3R 4H1, Canada.

Cover illustration: Jerry Tiritilli

ISBN 0-8308-1258-X

Printed in the United States of America

Library of Congress Cataloging-in-Publication Data

Bruce, F. F. (Frederick Fyvie), 1910-
    The canon of scripture/F. F. Bruce.
      p.   cm.
    Bibliography: p.
    Includes index.
    ISBN 0-8308-1258-X
     1. Bible—Canon.   I. Title.
    BS465.B78 1988
    220.1'2—dc19
                                  88-29206
                                        CIP

---

17   16   15   14   13   12   11   10   9   8   7   6   5   4   3   2
99   98   97   96   95   94   93   92   91   90   89

TO THE DEPARTMENTS
OF HUMANITY AND GREEK
IN THE UNIVERSITY OF ABERDEEN
FOUNDED 1497
AXED 1987
WITH GRATITUDE FOR THE PAST
AND WITH HOPE
OF THEIR EARLY AND VIGOROUS RESURRECTION

CONTENTS

PREFACE

When I taught in the University of Manchester I lectured in alternate years on the Text and Canon of the Old Testament and the Text and Canon of the New Testament. My lectures on the text, I hope, served the needs of the students who listened to them, but they do not call for further publication. The subject-matter of my lectures on the canon, however, has continued to engage my attention, as regards both its historical aspect and its relevance today.

It will be plain in what follows that I am more concerned about the New Testament canon than about the Old Testament canon. The collapse of the century-old consensus on the Old Testament canon — namely, that the process of canonization is indicated by the traditional threefold division of books in the Hebrew Bible — has been underlined in two important works of recent date: Roger Beckwith's *The Old Testament Canon of the New Testament Church* and John Barton's *Oracles of God*. Attacks have been made on the consensus on the New Testament canon — namely, that its main structure was substantially fixed by the end of the second century. It continues to stand, however, because it is supported by weighty evidence, as is shown in Bruce Metzger's magnificent work on *The Canon of the New Testament*. When a consensus is attacked, it has to be carefully reassessed, and that is all to the good: there is no point in pretending that we know more than we do.

With works like those mentioned now available, it may be asked,

9

what need is there for this book? Perhaps the author needs to get it out of his system, but it may justify its appearance as an attempt to communicate the present state of knowledge to a wider public.

I am most grateful to the University of London for permission to reproduce my Ethel M. Wood Lecture (1974) as Appendix 1, and to the *Epworth Review* and its editor, the Revd John Stacey, for permission to reproduce my A. S. Peake Memorial Lecture (1976) as Appendix 2.

My first introduction to this subject was effected through the original edition of *The Text and Canon of the New Testament*, by my revered teacher Alexander Souter, Regius Professor of Humanity in the University of Aberdeen. My indebtedness to him and to the Department over which he presided with high distinction, together with its sister Department of Greek, is acknowledged in the dedication.

F.F.B.

ABBREVIATIONS

GENERAL

ANF	The Ante-Nicene Fathers (Eerdmans)
AV/KJV	Authorized/King James Version (1611)
BJRL	*Bulletin of the John Rylands (University) Library*
CBQ	*Catholic Biblical Quarterly*
CHB	*Cambridge History of the Bible*, I–III (Cambridge, 1963–70)
Cod(d).	Codex (Codices)
CSEL	Corpus Scriptorum Ecclesiasticorum Latinorum (Vienna)
DB	*Dictionary of the Bible,* I–IV, ed. W. Smith (London, ²1893)
DCB	*Dictionary of Christian Biography*, I–IV, ed. W. Smith and H. Wace (London, 1877–87)
EQ	*Evangelical Quarterly*
E.T.	English translation
FGNTK	Forschungen zur Geschichte des neutestamentlichen Kanons, I–IX, ed. T. Zahn (Leipzig, 1881–1929)
GCS	Die griechischen christlichen Schriftsteller (Berlin)
Hist. Eccl.	*Ecclesiastical History* (Eusebius, Sozomen)
HTR	*Harvard Theological Review*
JBL	*Journal of Biblical Literature*
JBR	*Journal of Bible and Religion*
JTS	*Journal of Theological Studies*
LXX	Septuagint (pre-Christian Greek version of OT)
Mart. Pal.	*Martyrs of Palestine* (Eusebius)
MS(S)	manuscript(s)

11

MT	Masoretic text (of Hebrew Bible)
NCB	New Century Bible
NEB	New English Bible (1961, 1970)
NIGTC	New International Greek Testament Commentary
NIV	New International Version (1978)
NovT Sup	Supplement(s) to *Novum Testamentum*
NPNF	Nicene and Post-Nicene Fathers (Eerdmans)
n.s.	new series
NT	New Testament
NTS	*New Testament Studies*
OT	Old Testament
PG	*Patrologia Graeca* (ed. J.-P. Migne)
PL	*Patrologia Latina* (ed. J.-P. Migne)
RSV	Revised Standard Version (1952, 1971)
Strom.	*Stromateis (Miscellanies)*, by Clement of Alexandria
Sup.	Supplement(s)
s.v.	*sub vocabulo* = 'under the word'
TB	Babylonian Talmud
TDNT	*Theological Dictionary of the New Testament,* I–X, ed. G. Kittel and G. Friedrich, E. T. by G. W. Bromiley (Eerdmans, 1964–76)
TNTC	Tyndale New Testament Commentaries
TS	Texts and Studies (Cambridge University Press)
TU	*Texte und Untersuchungen*
UCCF	Universities and Colleges Christian Fellowship
VTSup	Supplement(s) to *Vetus Testamentum*
ZNW	*Zeitschrift für die neutestamentliche Wissenschaft*
ZTK	*Zeitschrift für Theologie und Kirche*

MANUSCRIPTS

A	Codex Alexandrinus (in British Museum, London)
Aleph	Codex Sinaiticus (in British Museum, London)
B	Codex Vaticanus (in Vatican Library, Rome)
D	Codex Bezae (in Cambridge University Library)
D^P	Codex Claromontanus (in Bibliothèque Nationale, Paris)
G^P	Codex Boernerianus (in Sächsische Landesbibliothek, Dresden)
P	*Papyrus*
P^{45}	Chester Beatty papyrus codex of Gospels and Acts
P^{46}	Chester Beatty papyrus codex of Pauline epistles and Hebrews
P^{47}	Chester Beatty papyrus codex of Revelation

ABBREVIATIONS

P^{52}	Rylands Library papyrus fragment of John 18
P^{72}	Bodmer papyrus codex of 1 and 2 Peter and Jude
P^{75}	Bodmer papyrus codex of Luke and John
P. *Fouad* 266	Cairo papyrus fragment of Deut. 31–32 (LXX)
P. *Oxy.*	Oxyrhynchus Papyri
P. *Ryl.* 458	Rylands Libary papyrus fragment of Deut. 23–28 (LXX)
Q	Qumran: a number preceding Q indicates the numbered cave in which the MS was found
4Qflorilegium	Biblical anthology from Qumran Cave 4
4QLXX Lv^a	Fragment of Leviticus (LXX) from Qumran Cave 4
4QLXX Lv^b	Another fragment of Leviticus (LXX) from Qumran Cave 4
4QLXX Num	Fragment of Numbers (LXX) from Qumran Cave 4
7QLXX Ex	Fragment of Exodus (LXX) from Qumran Cave 7
7QLXX Ep Jer	Fragment of Letter of Jeremiah from Qumran Cave 7
CD	Book of the Covenant of Damascus (two main MSS in Cairo; some fragments from Qumran Cave 4)
8Hev XII gr	MS of Minor Prophets in Greek from Wadi Hever

PART ONE

INTRODUCTION

CHAPTER ONE

HOLY SCRIPTURE

THE WORD 'CANON'

When we speak of the canon of scripture, the word 'canon' has a simple meaning. It means the list of books contained in scripture, the list of books recognized as worthy to be included in the sacred writings of a worshipping community. In a Christian context, we might define the word as 'the list of the writings acknowledged by the Church as documents of the divine revelation.'[1] In this sense the word appears to have been first used by Athanasius, bishop of Alexandria, in a letter circulated in AD 367.[2]

The word 'canon' has come into our language (through Latin) from the Greek word *kanōn*.[3] In Greek it meant a rod, especially a straight rod used as a rule; from this usage comes the other meaning which the word commonly bears in English—'rule' or 'standard'. We speak, for example, of the 'canons' or rules of the Church of England. But a straight rod used as a rule might be marked in units of length (like a modern ruler marked in inches or centimetres); from this practice the

---

[1] R. P. C. Hanson, *Origen's Doctrine of Tradition* (London, 1954), pp.93, 133; *cf* his *Tradition in the Early Church* (London, 1962), p.247.

[2] See pp.71, 78, 79, 208f.

[3] The Greek word was probably borrowed from the Semitic word which appears in Hebrew as *qāneh,* 'reed, 'rod'. From the same origin come Latin *canna* and Eng. 'cane'.

Greek word *kanōn* came to be used of the series of such marks, and hence to be used in the general sense of 'series' or 'list'. It is this last usage that underlies the term 'the canon of scripture'.

Before the word 'canon' came to be used in the sense of 'list', it was used in another sense by the church—in the phrase 'the rule of faith' or 'the rule of truth'.[4] In the earlier Christian centuries this was a summary of Christian teaching, believed to reproduce what the apostles themselves taught, by which any system of doctrine offered for Christian acceptance, or any interpretation of biblical writings, was to be assessed. But when once the limits of holy scripture came to be generally agreed upon, holy scripture itself came to be regarded as the rule of faith. For example, Thomas Aquinas (*c* 1225–1274) says that 'canonical scripture alone is the rule of faith'. From another theological perspective the Westminster Confession of Faith (1647), after listing the sixty-six books of the Old and New Testaments, adds: 'All which are given by inspiration of God, to be the rule of faith and life.'[5] These words affirm the status of holy scripture as the 'canon' or 'standard' by which Christian teaching and action must be regulated. While the 'canon' of scripture means the *list* of books accepted as holy scripture, the other sense of 'canon'—*rule* or *standard*—has rubbed off on this one, so that the 'canon' of scripture is understood to be the *list* of books which are acknowledged to be, in a unique sense, the *rule* of belief and practice.

The question to be examined in the following pages is: how did certain documents, and these only, come to receive this recognition? Who, if any one, decided that these, and no others, should be admitted to the list of the holy scriptures, and what were the criteria which influenced this decision?

PEOPLE OF THE BOOK

Many religions have sacred books associated with their traditions or their worship. There was a once-famous series of volumes entitled *The Sacred Books of the East*.[6] But Jews, Christians and Muslims have come

---

[4] See p. 150, 179.

[5] Thomas Aquinas, *On the Gospel of St. John*, Lesson 6 on John 21 (*sola canonica scriptura est regula fidei*, perhaps '. . . *a* rule of faith'); Westminster Confession of Faith, 1, § 2.

[6] The 55 volumes, originally under the general editorship of Friedrich Max Müller, appeared between 1879 and 1924 (Oxford: Clarendon Press).

to be known as 'people of the book' in a special sense. This is a designation given repeatedly in the Qur'ān to Jews and Christians. Among 'people of the book' the 'book' has a regulative function: conformity to what the book prescribes is a major test of loyalty to their religious faith and practice.

For Jews the 'book' is the Hebrew Bible, comprising the Law, the Prophets and the Writings (from the initials of these three divisions in Hebrew the Bible is often referred to among Jews as the *TeNaKh*).[7] For Christians it is the Hebrew Bible, which they call the Old Testament (amplified somewhat in certain Christian traditions),[8] together with the New Testament. Muslims recognize the Hebrew Bible, the *tawrat* (the Arabic equivalent of Heb. *tôrāh*, 'law'), and the Christian New Testament, the *injīl* (from Gk. *euangelion*, 'gospel'), as earlier revelations of God, but these find their completion in the revelation given through the Prophet, the *Qur'ān* (literally 'recitation' or 'reading'), the 'book' *par excellence*.

THE TWO TESTAMENTS

Our concern here is with the Christian Bible, comprising the Old and New Testaments. The word 'testament' in English normally means a will (someone's 'last will and testament'); but this is not the sense in which it is used of the two parts of the Christian Bible. Our word 'testament' comes from Latin *testamentum*, which similarly means a will, but in this particular context the Latin word is used as the translation of the Greek word *diathēkē*. This Greek word may indeed mean a will,[9] but it is used more widely of various kinds of settlement or agreement, not so much of one which is made between equals as of one in which a party superior in power or dignity confers certain privileges on an inferior, while the inferior undertakes certain obligations towards the superior. It is used repeatedly in both Old and New Testaments, both in the Greek translation of the Hebrew Bible and in the original Greek of the New Testament. It is usually rendered by our word 'covenant', and its most distinctive usage relates to an agreement between God and human beings. Here, of course, there can be no question of an agreement between equals.

---

[7] This word is an acronym, formed of the initial letters of *Tôrāh* ('law', 'direction'), N^e*bî'îm* ('prophets') and K^e*tûbîm* ('writings'), the names given to the three divisions (see p. 29).

[8] See pp. 47f.   [9] See p. 181.

In the earliest books of the Old Testament God makes a covenant with Noah and his descendants (Gen. 9:8–17), and again with Abraham and his descendants (Gen. 15:18; 17:1–4). The external token of the covenant with Noah was the rainbow; the external token of the covenant with Abraham was the rite of circumcision. Later, when Abraham's descendants (or at least one important group of them) had migrated to Egypt and were drafted into forced labour gangs there, God remembered his covenant with Abraham and brought about their deliverance. Having left Egypt under the leadership of Moses, they were constituted a nation in the wilderness of Sinai. Their national constitution took the form of a covenant into which the God of their fathers entered with them, making himself known to them by his name Yahweh.[10] The terms of this covenant were, very simply, 'I will be your God, and you shall be my people.' Yahweh undertook to make various kinds of provision for them; they undertook to worship him exclusively and to obey his commandments. These undertakings were recorded in a document called 'the book of the covenant'. According to the narrative of Exodus 24:4–8,

> Moses wrote all the words of Yahweh. And he rose early in the morning, and built an altar at the foot of the mountain, and twelve pillars, according to the twelve tribes of Israel. And he sent young men of the people of Israel, who offered burnt offerings and sacrificed peace offerings of oxen to Yahweh. And Moses took half of the blood and put it in basins, and half of the blood he threw against the altar. Then he took the book of the covenant, and read it in the hearing of the people; and they said, 'All that Yahweh has spoken we will do, and we will be obedient.' And Moses took the blood and threw it upon the people, and said, 'Behold the blood of the covenant which Yahweh has made with you in accordance with all these words.'

This narrative is summarized in the New Testament, in Hebrews 9:18–20, where the covenant thus ratified is qualified as 'the first covenant'. This is because the writer to the Hebrews sets it in contrast with the 'new covenant' promised in Jeremiah 31:31–34. Over six hundred years after the ratification of the covenant of Moses' day at the foot of Mount Sinai, the prophet Jeremiah announced that, in days to come, the God of Israel would establish a new covenant with his people to replace that which he had made with the Exodus generation

[10] See Ex. 3:7–15.

when he 'took them by the hand to bring them out of the land of Egypt' (Jer. 31:31–34). That ancient covenant made the divine will plain to them, but did not impart the power to carry it out; for lack of that power they broke the covenant. Under the new covenant, however, not only the desire but the power to do the will of God would be imparted to his people: his law would be put within them and written on their hearts. 'In speaking of a new covenant', says the writer to the Hebrews, 'he treats the first as obsolete' (Heb. 8:13). And he leaves his readers in no doubt that the new covenant has already been established, ratified not by the blood of sacrificed animals but by the blood of Christ, a sacrifice which effects not merely external purification from ritual defilement but the inward cleansing of the conscience from guilt.

This interpretation of the promise of the new covenant is fully in line with Jesus's own words. During the evening before his death, sitting with his disciples round the supper-table, he gave them bread and wine as memorials of himself. When he gave them the wine, according to Mark's record, he said, 'This is my blood of the covenant (my covenant blood), which is poured out for many' (Mark 14:24). The echo of Moses' words, 'Behold the blood of the covenant. . .', can scarcely be missed. That the covenant associated with the blood of Jesus (his voluntary offering himself up to God) is Jeremiah's new covenant is implied; the implication is explicit in Paul's record: 'This cup is the new covenant in my blood'(1 Cor. 11:25).[11]

Each of these covenants—the ancient covenant of Sinai and the new covenant inaugurated by Jesus—launched a great spiritual movement. Each of these movements gave rise to a special body of literature, and these bodies of literature came to be known in the Christian church as 'the books of the ancient covenant' and 'the books of the new covenant'. The former collection came into being over a period of a thousand years or more; the latter collection has a more inaugural character. Its various parts were written within a century from the establishment of the new covenant; they may be regarded as the foundation documents of Christianity. It was not until the end of the second century AD that the two collections began to be described, briefly, as the Old Covenant (or Testament) and the New Covenant (or Testament). These short titles are attested in both Greek and Latin almost simultaneously—in

---

[11] Paul's is the earliest written record we have (AD 55): it preserves the words of institution as he learned them shortly after his conversion. Mark's record (put in writing c AD 65) reproduces the words as they were transmitted along another line.

Greek, in the works of Clement of Alexandria;[12] in Latin, in the works of Tertullian of Carthage.[13]

It has been suggested that the expression 'the New Covenant (or Testament)' is first used to denote a collection of books in AD 192, in an anti-Montanist work in Greek by an unknown writer, addressed to the Phrygian bishop Avircius[14] Marcellinus, from which Eusebius quotes some extracts. This work speaks of 'the word of the new covenant of the gospel, to which nothing can be added by any one who has chosen to live according to the gospel itself and from which nothing can be taken away'.[15] It is unlikely, however, that this is a reference to the New Testament in our sense of the term;[16] the anonymous writer is a little disturbed by the possibility that his own work might be viewed as an addition to 'the word of the new covenant of the gospel'.

A CLOSED CANON

The words 'to which nothing can be added...and from which nothing can be taken away', whatever they precisely meant in this context, seem certainly to imply the principle of a *closed* canon. There are some scholars who maintain that the word 'canon' should be used only where the list of specially authoritative books has been closed; and there is much to be said in favour of this restrictive use of the word (a more flexible word might be used for the collection in process of formation), although it would be pedantic to insist on it invariably.

Such language about neither adding nor taking away is used in relation to individual components of the two Testaments. To the law of Deuteronomy, for example, the warning is attached: 'You shall not add to the word which I command you, nor take from it' (Deut. 4:2; *cf* 12:32). A fuller warning is appended to the New Testament Apocalypse: 'I warn every one who hears the words of the prophecy of this book: if any one adds to them, God will add to him the plagues described in this book, and if any one takes away from the words of the

[12] See p. 188.   [13] See p. 180.   [14] Also spelt Abercius (Gk. *Aberkios*).
[15] *Hist. Eccl.* 5.16.3.
[16] At one time W. C. van Unnik thought that this might indeed be the earliest surviving instance of the phrase 'New Covenant' or 'New Testament' (Gk. *kainē diathēkē*) to denote a collection of writings ('De la règle *mēte prostheinai mēte aphelein* dans l'histoire du canon', *Vigiliae Christianae* 3 [1949], pp. 1–36; later, however, he had second thoughts on this ('*Hē kainē diathēkē*—a Problem in the Early History of the Canon', *Studia Patristica* = *TU* 79 [1961], pp. 212–227, especially p. 218).

book of this prophecy, God will take away his share in the tree of life and in the holy city, which are described in this book' (Rev. 22:18 f.).[17]

The author of the *Didachē* (an early manual of church order) echoes the warning of Deuteronomy when he says, 'You shall not forsake the commandments of the Lord, but you shall keep the things you received, "neither adding nor taking away".'[18] Around the same time (end of the first century AD) Josephus uses similar language about the Hebrew scriptures: 'Although such long ages have now gone by, no one has dared to add anything to them, to take away anything from them, or to change anything in them.'[19] This language can scarcely signify anything other than a closed canon.[20]

LITURGICAL RECOGNITION

The status of the scriptures is symbolically acknowledged in various traditions of public worship. Special veneration is paid to the scrolls of the law in a synagogue service as they are carried from the holy ark, where they are kept, to the *bimah,* from which they are read to the congregation. In the liturgy of the Orthodox Church the gospel book is carried in procession, and the reading from it is preceded by the call: 'Wisdom! All stand; let us hear the holy gospel.' The veneration thus paid to the gospel book is not paid to the materials of which it is composed nor to the ink with which it is inscribed, but to the Holy Wisdom which finds expression in the words that are read. In the Catholic liturgy the gospel is treated with comparable veneration and the reading from it is preceded and followed by special prayers. In the Anglican communion service the people stand while the gospel is read, and when it is announced they commonly say, 'Glory to Christ

---

[17] It is immaterial for our present purpose whether this warning comes from the seer of Patmos or from an editor of his work.

[18] *Didachē* 4.13.

[19] *Against Apion,* 1.42.

[20] See p.32. Similar language about neither adding nor subtracting occurs in the *Letter of Aristeas,* 311 (see p.44), where, after the translation of the Pentateuch into Greek, a curse was pronounced, 'in accordance with custom, on any one who should make any alteration, either by adding anything or changing in any way whatsoever anything that was written or leaving anything out'; also twice in Irenaeus (*Against Heresies,* 4.33.8; 5.30.1.)—on the latter occasion as a warning to those who reduce the number of the beast (Rev. 13:18) by 50 so as to read 616 (perhaps the first, but certainly not the last misuse of the warning of Rev. 22:15 f. to inhibit the proper exercise of textual criticism). See also Athanasius (p.79).

our Saviour', while at its conclusion, when the reader says, 'This is the gospel of Christ', they respond, 'Praise to Christ our Lord.'

In churches of the Reformed order (such as the Church of Scotland and other Presbyterian churches throughout the world) the first formal action in a service of public worship takes place when the Bible is carried in from the vestry and placed on the reading desk. Someone, of course, must carry it (the beadle, perhaps, or 'church officer'), but the person who does so has no liturgical significance (even if, in earlier days, he thought it proper to 'magnify his office'); it is the Bible that has liturgical significance. The Bible is followed at a respectful distance by the minister. And why? Because he is the *minister*—that is to say, in the original sense of the term, the 'servant' of the Word. No letters indicating academic achievement or public honour can match in dignity the letters V.D.M., appended to the pastor's name in some Reformed churches—*Verbi Divini Minister,* 'servant of the Word of God.' When the time comes in the service for the audible reading of the Bible, this lesson is underlined by the introductory exhortation: 'Let us hear the Word of God.'

It is from the contents, the message, of the book that it derives its value, whether we think of the gospel in particular or the Bible as a whole. It is therefore important to know what its contents are, and how they have come to be marked off from other writings—even holy and inspired writings. That is the point of examining the growth of the canon of holy scripture.

PART TWO

OLD TESTAMENT

CHAPTER TWO

THE LAW
AND THE PROPHETS

JESUS' APPEAL TO THE
HEBREW SCRIPTURES

The Christian church started its existence with a book, but it was not to the book that it owed its existence. It shared the book with the Jewish people; indeed, the first members of the church were without exception Jews. The church owed its distinctive existence to a person — to Jesus of Nazareth, crucified, dead and buried, but 'designated Son of God in power . . . by his resurrection from the dead' (Rom. 1:4). This Jesus, it was believed, had been exalted by God to be universal Lord; he had sent his Spirit to be present with his followers, to unite them and animate them as his body on earth. The function of the book was to bear witness to him.

Jesus, according to all the strata of the gospel tradition, regularly appealed to the Hebrew scriptures to validate his mission, his words and his actions. According to Mark, he began his ministry in Galilee with the announcement: 'The time is fulfilled, and the kingdom of God is at hand' (Mark 1:14). This was the good news which he proclaimed, inviting his hearers to believe it. Those of them who were familiar with the book of Daniel can scarcely have missed the reference in his words to the prophecy in that book concerning a coming day in which 'the God of heaven will set up a kingdom which shall never be destroyed' (Dan. 2:44 *cf* 7:14, 18, 27). The kingdom was to be bestowed on 'the saints of the Most High'; Daniel in vision saw how 'the time came when the saints received the kingdom' (Dan. 7:22). The implication of Jesus' announcement was that this time had now arrived. So, according to another evangelist, he encouraged his disciples with the assurance: 'it is the Father's good pleasure to give you the kingdom' (Luke 12:32). What was actually involved in this kingdom was spelled out in his teaching (especially his parables) and in his general ministry.

Luke records how, in the synagogue of his home town Nazareth, Jesus set out the programme of his ministry by reading from Isaiah 61:1f. the declaration of the unnamed prophet that God, by placing his Spirit on him, had anointed him 'to preach good news to the poor, . . . to proclaim release to the captives and recovering of sight to the blind, to set at liberty those who are oppressed, to proclaim the acceptable year of the Lord' (Luke 4:18f.). His reading of those words was followed by the announcement: 'Today this scripture has been fulfilled in your hearing' (Luke 4:21). This emphasis on scripture characterized Jesus' ministry right on to the time when (again according to Luke) he appeared in resurrection to his disciples and assured them that his suffering and rising again, together with the consequent proclamation of the gospel to all the nations, formed the subject-matter of what was 'written' (Luke 24:46f.).

The church's use of those writings was based on Jesus' use of them: as his followers searched them further, they discovered increasingly 'in all the scriptures the things concerning himself' (Luke 24:27). The Old Testament, as Christians in due course came to call these writings, was a book about Jesus. Here was the church's Bible. Here was the Bible of the Jewish people also; but so differently did the two communities read the same writings that, for practical purposes, they might have been using two different Bibles instead of sharing one.[1]

THE CANON OF THE OLD TESTAMENT

Our Lord and his apostles might differ from the religious leaders of Israel about the meaning of the scriptures; there is no suggestion that they differed about the limits of the scriptures. 'The scriptures' on whose meaning they differed were not an amorphous collection: when

[1] See 63–67.

they spoke of 'the scriptures' they knew which writings they had in mind and could distinguish them from other writings which were not included in 'the scriptures'. When we speak of 'the scriptures' we mean 'the sacred writings' as distinct from other writings: to us 'scripture' and 'writing' are separate words with distinct meanings. But in Hebrew and Greek one and the same word does duty for both 'writing' and 'scripture': in these languages 'the scriptures' are simply 'the writings'—that is to say, 'the writings' *par excellence*. As we shall see, sometimes this involves a measure of ambiguity: does the word in this or that context mean 'scripture' in particular or 'writing' in general?[2] But when 'the scriptures' or 'the writings' are mentioned, there is usually no ambiguity. Similarly in English 'the book' can be used in a special sense (indicated perhaps by the tone of voice or by the use of a capital initial) to denote the Bible—the Book as distinct from all other books.

The books of the Hebrew Bible are traditionally twenty-four in number, arranged in three divisions. The first division is the *Tôrāh* ('law' or 'direction'), comprising the five 'books of Moses' (Genesis, Exodus, Leviticus, Numbers, Deuteronomy). The second division is the *Nᵉbî'îm* ('prophets'): it is further subdivided into the four Former Prophets (Joshua, Judges, Samuel, Kings) and the four Latter Prophets (Isaiah, Jeremiah, Ezekiel, and the Book of the Twelve Prophets)[3]. The third division is called the *Kᵉtûbîm* ('writings'): it comprises eleven books. First come the Psalms, Proverbs and Job; then a group of five called the *Mᵉgillôt* or 'scrolls' (Song of Songs, Ruth, Lamentations, Ecclesiastes, Esther); finally Daniel, Ezra-Nehemiah (reckoned as one book), Chronicles.[4] This is the arrangement regularly followed in printed editions of the Hebrew Bible.

One of the clearest and earliest statements of these three divisions

[2] Compare the ambiguity at the beginning of 2 Tim. 3:16. Does *graphē* here mean 'scripture' (in the special sense) or 'writing' (in the general sense)? If the former (which is more probable), the translation is 'Every scripture is divinely inspired (God-breathed) and profitable...'; if the latter, the translation is 'Every divinely inspired writing is also profitable...'.

[3] The twelve prophets are those commonly called the Minor Prophets—not because they are less important, but because the books bearing their names are so much shorter than those of the 'Major Prophets' (Isaiah, Jeremiah, Ezekiel).

[4] These twenty-four books are identical with the thirty-nine of the Protestant Old Testament; the difference in reckoning arises from counting the twelve ('minor') prophets separately and dividing Samuel, Kings, Chronicles and Ezra-Nehemiah into two each.

and their respective contents comes in a *baraitha* (a tradition from the period AD 70–200) quoted in the Babylonian Talmud, in the tractate *Baba Bathra*.[5] This tradition assigns inspired or authoritative authors to all twenty-four books, and discusses their order. The order of the five books in the first division is fixed, because they are set in a historical framework in which each has its chronological position; this is true also of the four Former Prophets. But the order of the books in the Latter Prophets and in the Writings was not so firmly fixed. This is inevitable when separate scrolls are kept together in a container. It is different when a number of documents can be bound together in a volume of modern shape—a codex, to use the technical term. Here the first must precede the second and the second must precede the third, whether there is any logical or chronological basis for that sequence or not. The codex began to come into use early in the Christian era, but even after its introduction religious conservatism ensured that the Jewish scriptures continued for long to be written on scrolls. If the eleven books making up the Writings—or, to take one subdivision of them, the five *M^egillôt*—were kept in one box, there was no particular reason why they should be mentioned in one order rather than another.

But it cannot be by accident that, in the traditional arrangement of the books, Chronicles follows Ezra-Nehemiah. This is a quite unnatural sequence, which could not have been adopted without some substantial reason. Ezra-Nehemiah takes up the history of Israel where Chronicles leaves off, whether or not Ezra-Nehemiah was originally part of the same work as Chronicles—'the work of the Chronicler', as it is often called.[6] Practically every edition of the Old Testament, therefore, apart from the Hebrew Bible (and versions which follow its order), makes Ezra-Nehemiah come immediately after Chronicles (which is the logical and chronological sequence). Why then should the Hebrew Bible place Chronicles after Ezra-Nehemiah, which is properly the sequel to Chronicles? One answer to this question is that, when the canon of Old Testament scripture was in course of formation, Chronicles was 'canonized' (included in the canon) *after* Ezra-Nehemiah. There is no firm evidence that this is how it happened, but

---

[5] *Baba Bathra* 14b–15a.

[6] For arguments against the customary view that Ezra-Nehemiah was an integral part of the work of the Chronicler see H. G. M. Williamson, *Israel in the Books of Chronicles* (Cambridge, 1977); see also the balanced discussion in D. J. A. Clines, *Ezra, Nehemiah, Esther*, NCB (London/Grand Rapids, 1984), pp. 1–24.

it is difficult to think of a more probable answer.

There is evidence that Chronicles was the last book in the Hebrew Bible as Jesus knew it. When he said that the generation he addressed would be answerable for 'the blood of all the prophets, shed from the foundation of the world', he added, 'from the blood of Abel to the blood of Zechariah, who perished between the altar and the sanctuary' (Luke 11:50f.). Abel is the first martyr in the Bible (Gen. 4:8); Zechariah is most probably the son of Jehoiada, who was stoned to death 'in the court of Yahweh's house' because, speaking by the Spirit of God, he rebuked the king and people of Judah for transgressing the divine commandments (2 Chron. 24:20–22). Zechariah (c 800 BC) was not *chronologically* the last faithful prophet to die as a martyr; some two centuries later a prophet named Uriah was put to death in Jerusalem because his witness was unacceptable to King Jehoiakim (Jer. 26:20–23). But Zechariah is *canonically* the last faithful prophet to die as a martyr, because his death is recorded in Chronicles, the last book in the Hebrew Bible.[7]

How old is the threefold division? It is widely believed, and perhaps rightly, that it is referred to for the first time by the grandson of Jeshua Ben Sira when, shortly after emigrating from Palestine to Alexandria in Egypt in 132 BC, he translated his grandfather's book of wisdom (commonly called Ecclesiasticus or Sirach[8]) from Hebrew into Greek. Repeatedly in the prologue to his translation he speaks of his grandfather as a student of 'the law and the prophets and the other books of our fathers', 'the law itself, the prophecies and the rest of the books'. Here we may indeed have a reference to the Law, the Prophets and the Writings. But it is just possible to understand that Ben Sira is being described as a student of the holy scriptures (the law and the prophets) and of other Jewish writings not included among the scriptures.[9]

There is one place in the New Testament which may reflect the threefold division. In Luke's account of the appearance of the risen Lord to his disciples in Jerusalem, they are reminded how he had told

[7] If the quotation from 'the Wisdom of God' (Luke 11:49) goes on to '. . . between the altar and the sanctuary' in verse 51, the chronological evidence for the position of Chronicles as the last book in the Bible is unaffected. But probably RSV is right in making the quotation end with '. . . persecute' at the end of verse 49; the emphasis on 'this generation' is characteristic of Jesus' own style. Matthew's reference to 'Zechariah the son of Barachiah' in his parallel passage (Matt. 23:35) is a problem on its own, but the Zechariah of 2 Chronicles 24:20–22 is most probably meant.

[8] *Sirach* is a Greek spelling of *Sira*, the (Hebrew) name of the author's father.

[9] See J. Barton, *Oracles of God* (London, 1986), p.47.

them 'that everything written about me in the law of Moses and the prophets and the psalms must be fulfilled' (Luke 24:44). Here 'the psalms' might denote not only the contents of the Psalter[10] but also the whole of the third division — the Writings — of which the Psalter was the first book. We cannot be sure of this; in any case, the Hebrew scriptures are more often referred to in the New Testament as 'the law and the prophets'. Jesus said that the golden rule sums up 'the law and the prophets' (Matt. 7:12); Paul claims that God's way of righteousness set forth in the gospel which he preaches is attested by 'the law and the prophets' (Rom. 3:21). No problem was felt about including books of the third division among the 'prophets': David is called a prophet in Acts 2:30, Daniel in Matthew 24:15, and even Job, by implication, in James 5:10f.

Sometimes the whole Hebrew Bible, or any part of it, is referred to as 'the law': in John 10:34 Jewish disputants are told that part of Psalm 82 is 'written in your law'; in 1 Corinthians 14:21 a quotation from Isaiah 28:11f. is similarly said to be written 'in the law', while in Romans 3:10–19 a chain of quotations from the Psalms and Isaiah is included in 'whatever the law says'. Less often the whole collection is described as 'the prophets': when Jesus on the Emmaus road spoke of the two disciples' being so 'slow of heart to believe all that the prophets have spoken' (Luke 24:25), it is plain from the context that Moses is included among 'the prophets' (he was, in fact, the greatest of them).

THE EVIDENCE OF JOSEPHUS

A rather different threefold division of the same books is mentioned by Josephus, the Jewish historian, in the first volume of his treatise *Against Apion*, written in the nineties of the first century AD. Josephus contrasts the reliable sources for early Jewish history with the many conflicting accounts of origins given by Greek historians:

> We have not myriads of books, disagreeing and conflicting with one another, but only twenty-two, containing the record of all time, and justly accredited.
> Of these, five are the books of Moses, containing the laws and

[10] The Psalter was a specially rich source of gospel 'testimonies' (OT texts fulfilled in the gospel story), not least because the portrayal of the righteous sufferer (e.g. Pss. 22:1; 69:4, 9, 21) was believed to anticipate the experiences of Jesus.

the history handed down from the creation of the human race right to his own death. This period falls a little short of three thousand years. From the death of Moses to the time of Artaxerxes, who was king of Persia after Xerxes, the prophets who followed Moses have written down in thirteen books the things that were done in their days. The remaining four books contain hymns to God and principles of life for human beings.

From Artaxerxes to our own time a detailed record has been made, but this has not been thought worthy of equal credit with the earlier records because there has not been since then the exact succession of prophets.[11]

When he says that since Artaxerxes' time there has been no exact succession of prophets, Josephus does not mean that the gift of prophecy itself died out. He mentions its exercise among the Essenes,[12] he says that the Jewish ruler John Hyrcanus I (134–104 BC) was divinely enabled 'to foresee and foretell the future',[13] and he claims to have had the gift himself.[14] But in the period between Moses and Artaxerxes (465–423 BC) he appears to envisage an unbroken succession of prophets, guaranteeing the continuity and trustworthiness of the records which they were believed to have produced.

When Josephus speaks of twenty-two books,[15] he probably refers to exactly the same documents as the twenty-four of the traditional Jewish reckoning, Ruth being counted as an appendix to Judges and Lamentations to Jeremiah. His three divisions might be called the Law, the Prophets and the Writings. His first division comprises the same five books as the first division in the traditional arrangement. But his second division has thirteen books, not eight, the additional five being perhaps Job[16], Esther, Daniel, Chronicles and Ezra-Nehemiah. The four books of the third division would then be Psalms, Proverbs, Ecclesiastes and the Song of Songs. It is impossible to be sure, because he does not specify the books of the three divisions one by one.

It is unlikely that Josephus's classification of the books was his own;

---

[11] Josephus, *Against Apion* 1.38–41.

[12] Josephus, *Antiquities* 13.311; 15.373–379.

[13] Josephus, *Antiquities* 13.300.   [14] Josephus, *Jewish War* 3.351–354.

[15] The total of 22 may have been arranged so as to correspond with the number of letters in the Hebrew alphabet; see p.73, 78, 90.

[16] Job is perhaps reckoned among 'the prophets' in Sirach 49:9 (Hebrew) and James 5:10f.

he probably reproduces a tradition with which he had been familiar for a long time, having learned it either in the priestly circle into which he was born or among the Pharisees with whose party he associated himself as a young man.

DISCUSSIONS AT JAMNIA

About the same time as Josephus wrote his work *Against Apion*, the Hebrew scriptures were among various subjects debated by the rabbis who set up their headquarters at Jabneh or Jamnia in western Judaea, under the leadership of Yohanan ben Zakkai, to discuss the reconstruction of Jewish religious life after the collapse of the Jewish commonwealth in AD 70.[17] Jewish life had to be adapted to a new situation in which the temple and its services were no more. So far as the scriptures are concerned, the rabbis at Jamnia introduced no innovations; they reviewed the tradition they had received and left it more or less as it was.[18] It is probably unwise to talk as if there was a Council or Synod of Jamnia which laid down the limits of the Old Testament canon.

They discussed which books 'defiled the hands'[19]—a technical expression denoting those books which were the product of prophetic inspiration. One had to wash one's hands after handling them, just as one did after 'defiling' the hands (whether materially or ritually). One might explain this practice in terms of Mary Douglas's 'purity and danger';[20] but by the time we are dealing with the idea may simply have been that if people had to wash their hands every time they touched a sacred book they would be deterred from handling it casually.[21]

At any rate, the rabbis at Jamnia discussed whether certain books

[17] There are many references in the Mishnah and later rabbinical compilations to the discussions of the sages (including pre-eminently Yohanan ben Zakkai) in the 'vineyard of Jabneh' in the generation following AD 70. See J. P. Lewis, 'What do we mean by Jabneh?' *JBR* 32 (1964), pp. 125–132.

[18] Their 'discussions have not so much dealt with acceptance of certain writings into the Canon, but rather with their right to remain there' (A. Bentzen, *Introduction to the Old Testament*, I [Copenhagen, 1948], p.31).

[19] See the Mishnah tractate *Yadayim* ('Hands'), 3.2–5.

[20] M. Douglas, *Purity and Danger: An Analysis of Concepts of Pollution and Taboo* (Harmondsworth, 1970).

[21] See R. T. Beckwith, *The Old Testament Canon of the New Testament Church* (London, 1985), pp.278–281.

did or did not 'defile the hands' in this sense. Did Jeshua ben Sira's wisdom book (Ecclesiasticus) defile them or not? It was a work which inculcated true religion; objectively it was not easy to distinguish it in point of sacredness from Proverbs or Ecclesiastes. The conclusion, however was that it did not defile the hands. But what of Proverbs and Ecclesiastes? Proverbs seems to contradict itself in two adjacent verses: 'Answer not a fool according to his folly, . . . Answer a fool according to his folly . . .' (Prov. 26:4f.). (It was easily explained that in some circumstances the one precept, and in some circumstances the other precept, should be followed.) Ecclesiastes, on the face of it, was a much less orthodox book than Ben Sira's work: is it really fitting to believe that 'there is nothing better for a man than that he should eat and drink, and find enjoyment in his toil' (Eccles. 2:24)? (It was pointed out that this could be read as a question expecting the answer 'No'—'Is there nothing better for a man . . . ?')

Neither Esther nor the Song of Songs contains the name of God—unless indeed his name be concealed in Cant 8:6, where 'a most vehement flame' might be literally 'a flame of Yah'.[22] Both works might appear to be non-religious in character, but Esther provided the libretto for the popular festival of Purim, and if the Song could be allegorized so as to become a celebration of Yahweh's love for Israel, it could continue to be recognized as an inspired scripture. As for Ezekiel, the prescriptions in its closing chapters for the new temple and its services could with difficulty be made to agree with those in the Pentateuch, and the chariot vision of chapter 1 gave rise to mystical speculations and exercises which some rabbis believed to be spiritually dangerous. The opinion was expressed that Ezekiel ought to be 'withdrawn' (withdrawn, probably, from the synagogue calendar of public readings). Other pious souls were content to wait until Elijah came at the end of the age: the problems of Ezekiel would be among those which he was expected to solve. Happily, it was not necessary to wait so long: one Hananiah the son of Hezekiah sat up night after night burning the midnight oil to the tune of 300 measures until he had worked out a reconciliation between Ezekiel and Moses.[23] But this simply means that the rabbis of Jamnia, like religious disputants of other ages, enjoyed a really tough subject for theological debate; it

---

[22] Hebrew *šalhebetyāh* may be divided into the two words *šalhebet Yāh*. *Yāh* (AV 'Jah') is a short form of *Yahweh* (AV/KJV 'Jehovah').

[23] TB *Shabbāt* 13b; *Hᵃgîgāh* 13a; *Mᵉnāḥôt* 45a.

does not mean that at this late date the status of Ezekiel was in serious jeopardy.

From the same period as Josephus and the Jamnia debates comes an independent reference to twenty-four as the number of books of holy scripture. The Apocalypse of Ezra (otherwise called 4 Ezra and 2 Esdras)[24] was written after the destruction of the temple in AD 70, but purports to record revelations made to Ezra after the destruction of Solomon's temple centuries before. Ezra tells how, by divine illumination, he was enabled to dictate to five men over a period of forty days the contents of ninety-four books. 'And when the forty days were ended, the Most High spoke to me, saying, "Make public the twenty-four books that you wrote first and let the worthy and the unworthy read them; but keep the seventy that were written last, in order to give them to the wise among your people"' (4 Ezra 14:45f). The twenty-four books accessible to the public appear to be the twenty-four books of the Hebrew Bible; the other seventy were esoteric or apocalyptic works which yielded their secret meaning to an inner circle (such as, for example, the Qumran community).

A THREE-STAGE CANON?

A common, and not unreasonable, account of the formation of the Old Testament canon is that it took shape in three stages, corresponding to the three divisions of the Hebrew Bible. The Law was first canonized (early in the period after the return from the Babylonian exile), the Prophets next (late in the third century BC). When these two collections were closed, everything else that was recognized as holy scripture had to go into the third division, the Writings, which remained open until the end of the first century AD, when it was 'closed' at Jamnia.[25] But it must be pointed out that, for all its attractiveness, this account is completely hypothetical: there is no evidence for it, either in the Old Testament itself or elsewhere.

We have evidence in the Old Testament of the public recognition of scripture as conveying the word of God, but that is not the same thing as canonization.

When, on the occasion already referred to, Moses read 'the book of

---

[24] See p. 47, n. 11, 85, n. 11.
[25] This account has largely held the field since it was popularized by H. E. Ryle, *The Canon of the Old Testament* (London, 1892, ²1909).

the covenant' to the Israelites at the foot of Mount Sinai, they responded with an undertaking to keep the divine commandments: to them what Moses read was the word of God (Exod. 24:3–7). When, at a later date, the law-code of Deuteronomy was put 'beside the ark of the covenant of Yahweh' (Deut. 31:26), this was to be a token of its sanctity and a reminder to the people of the solemnity of their obligation to continue in the way which God had commanded them. When the same law-code, probably ('the book of the law'), was found in the temple in the reign of Josiah, it was read by the king's decree to a great concourse of the people of Judah and Jerusalem; the king entered into a solemn undertaking 'to perform the words of the covenant that were written in this book; and all the people joined in the covenant' (2 Kings 23:1–3). Again, after the return from the Babylonian exile, Ezra and his associates read publicly from 'the book of the law of Moses' which he had brought from Babylon to Jerusalem, and the national leaders made a firm covenant to order their lives from then on in accordance with the commandments which it contained (Neh. 8:1—9:38).

On all these occasions the authority of the word of God was acknowledged in what was read; but there is no mention as yet of anything in the nature of a collection to which such a document might be added, or in which others might be added after it. Even in the ban on adding anything to the law-code of Deuteronomy or taking any-thing from it (Deut. 4:2) the law-code is envisaged as quite self-contained; there is no word of adding it to other codes, as has actually been done in the final arrangement of the Pentateuch.[26] ('Pentateuch' is a term of Greek origin denoting the five books of the Law.)

Later prophets recognize the divine authority underlying the ministry of earlier prophets (cf Jer. 7:25; Ezek. 38:17), but the idea of collecting the oracles of a succession of prophets did not occur at once. Zechariah the prophet refers to 'the former prophets' (Zech. 1:4; 7:7), meaning those who prophesied before the exile, but he does not imply that their words have been published as a collection. Such a collection did come into being in the following centuries, but by what agency must be a matter of speculation. The earliest reference to such a collection is probably in Daniel 9:2, where Daniel found Jeremiah's

---

[26] It has been held, however, that Deuteronomy served as the introduction to the 'deuteronomic history' (comprising Joshua, Judges, Samuel and Kings), and that this combined work was the first instalment of the Old Testament canon; see R. E. Clements, *Prophecy and Tradition* (Oxford, 1975), pp.47–57.

prophecy of the duration of Jerusalem's desolations (Jer. 25:11f.) among 'the books'.

In the persecution under Antiochus Epiphanes many copies of the scriptures were seized and destroyed; possession of a copy of 'the book of the covenant' was punished with death (1 Macc. 1:56f.). It was necessary therefore to replace the lost copies when religious liberty was regained. In a letter purporting to be addressed by the Jews of Jerusalem and Judaea to the Jews of Egypt it is recalled that Nehemiah in his day 'founded a library and collected the books about the kings and prophets, and the writings of David, and letters of kings about votive offerings'.[27] Following his precedent, the letter goes on, Judas Maccabaeus also (between 164 and 160 BC) 'collected all the books that had been lost on account of the war which had come upon us, and they are in our possession' (2 Macc. 2:13f.).

Where these collected scriptures were housed is not stated, but it may well have been in the temple. The holy place was a fitting repository for the holy books. Josephus tells how a copy of the law formed part of the temple spoils carried in Vespasian's triumphal procession in AD 71; it was subsequently kept in the imperial palace.[28] It may have been from the temple, too, that the 'sacred books' came which Josephus received as a gift from Titus after the capture and destruction of the holy place.[29]

THE SIGNIFICANCE OF THE QUMRAN TEXTS

The discoveries made at Qumran, north-west of the Dead Sea, in the years following 1947 have greatly increased our knowledge of the history of the Hebrew scriptures during the two centuries or more preceding AD 70.[30] The texts discovered and studied appear to represent about five hundred separate documents, about one hundred of them being copies of books of the Hebrew Bible (some books in particular being represented by several copies). A few of these copies are substantially complete, but most are very fragmentary. All the books of

[27] The 'letters of kings about votive offerings' may be those reproduced in Ezra 6:3—7:26.

[28] *Jewish War*, 7.150, 162. This may be 'the Scroll of the Temple Court' mentioned in the Mishnah, *Mo'ed Qaṭan*, 3.4; *Kelim* 15.6.

[29] *Life*, 418.

[30] See F. M. Cross, *The Ancient Library of Qumran and Modern Biblical Studies* (Grand Rapids, ³1980).

the Hebrew Bible are represented among them, with the exception of Esther. This exception may be accidental (it is conceivable that a copy of Esther once included in the Qumran library has perished completely), or it may be significant: there is evidence of some doubt among Jews, as later among Christians, about the status of Esther.[31] Esther may have been felt to have too close an affinity to the ideals of Judas Maccabaeus and his kinsfolk in the Hasmonaean family, of whom the Qumran community utterly disapproved.[32]

But the men of Qumran have left no statement indicating precisely which of the books represented in their library ranked as holy scripture in their estimation, and which did not. A book setting forth the community's rule of life or liturgical practice was no doubt regarded as authoritative, just as the Book of Common Prayer is (or was) in the Church of England, but that did not give it scriptural status.

Among their books are several commentaries on books of the Hebrew Bible, explaining them according to the community's distinctive principles of interpretation.[33] The books thus commented on were certainly acknowledged as holy scripture: their words were the words of God spoken through his prophets or spokesmen, foretelling events of the commentators' own days, when the end of the current age was believed to be impending. We may confidently say, therefore, that the 'canon' of the Qumran community included the Pentateuch, the Prophets, the Psalms (possibly with a few supplementary psalms). It also included the book of Daniel, who is called 'Daniel the prophet'[34] (as in Matt. 24:15), and probably Job (an Aramaic targum or paraphrase of Job was found in Cave 11 at Qumran).[35]

But what of Tobit, Jubilees and Enoch,[36] fragments of which were also found at Qumran? These were in due course to be reckoned canonical by certain religious groups; were they reckoned canonical by the Qumran community? There is no evidence which would justify

---

[31] See pp.71, 79, 80.

[32] See the discussion in R. T. Beckwith, *The Old Testament Canon of the New Testament Church*, pp.283, 288–297; he points out that Esther conflicts with the Essenes' calender, which they believed to be divinely ordained.

[33] See p.58 with n.5.   [34] 4Q florilegium 2.3.

[35] The discovery of this work (edited by J. P. M. van der Ploeg, A. S. van der Woude and B. Jongeling, *Le Targum de Job* [Leiden, 1971]) reminds one of the notes appended to the Septuagint version of Job, said to have been 'translated out of the Syriac book', and of the Job Targum which Gamaliel ordered to be built into the temple walls (TB *Shabbāt* 115a).

[36] See pp.84–86, 182.

the answer 'Yes'; on the other hand, we do not know enough to return the answer 'No'. One of the community documents—the *Zadokite Work* (or the *Book of the Covenant of Damascus*)—attaches some degree of authority to *Jubilees*: 'As for the exact statement of all their epochs to which Israel turns a blind eye, it can be learned from the *Book of the Divisions of the Times into their Jubilees and Weeks.*'[37] The 'Temple Scroll' from Cave 11 (which should perhaps be more accurately called the 'Torah Scroll') is a repromulgation of the law of Moses, set in a deuteronomic framework, which was to be put into effect when national life was restored in accordance with Qumran ideals. The first editor of this document, the late Yigael Yadin, argued that it had canonical status in the community;[38] he thought that it too was referred to in the *Zadokite Work* as 'the sealed book of the law'[39] (but this is more probably a reference to the book found in the temple in the reign of Josiah).

From time to time the community documents indicate more explicitly which books were reckoned 'canonical' by quoting from them with introductory formulae which indicate their quality as divine revelation. When the *Zadokite Work* bases a ban on bigamy from the juxtaposition of the texts 'male and female he created them' (Gen. 1:27), 'they went into the ark two and two' (Gen. 7:9, 15), and 'he shall not multiply wives for himself' (Deut. 17:17),[40] it is evident that the documents from which the three texts are quoted are authoritative scripture.

It is probable, indeed, that by the beginning of the Christian era the Essenes (including the Qumran community) were in substantial agreement with the Pharisees and the Sadducees about the limits of Hebrew scripture. There may have been some differences of opinion and practice with regard to one or two of the 'Writings', but the inter-party disagreements remembered in Jewish tradition have very little to do with the limits of the canon. The idea that the Sadducees (like the Samaritans) acknowledged the Pentateuch only as holy scripture is based on a misunderstanding: when Josephus, for example, says that the Sadducees 'admit no observance at all apart from the laws',[41] he means not the Pentateuch to the exclusion of the Prophets

[37] CD 16.4.

[38] Y. Yadin, *The Temple Scroll* (Jerusalem, 1983), I, pp.390–395.

[39] CD 5.2.   [40] CD 4.21–5.2.

[41] Josephus, *Antiquities,* 18.16; his meaning is made plain in *Antiquities,* 13.297, where the Sadducees are said to 'hold that only the written laws should be reckoned

and the Writings but the written law (of the Pentateuch) to the exclusion of the oral law (the Pharisaic interpretation and application of the written law, which, like the written law itself, was held in theory to have been received and handed down by Moses).[42] It would be understandable if the Sadducees did not accept Daniel which contains the most explicit statement of the resurrection hope in the whole of the Old Testament.[43]

As for the Samaritans, their Bible was restricted to the Pentateuch. They had their own edition of the book of Joshua and a number of other traditions, but these were not recognized as holy scripture. The Samaritan Bible was basically a popular Palestinian recension of the Hebrew Pentateuch, which was subjected to an editorial process to bring it into line with certain aspects of Samaritan tradition which conflicted with Jewish tradition.[44] The Samaritan Bible has customarily been treated as evidence for the view that the final Samaritan schism took place at a time when the Pentateuch but not the Prophets or Writings had been 'canonized', but this is not necessarily so.[45]

When we think of Jesus and his Palestinian apostles, then, we may be confident that they agreed with contemporary leaders in Israel about the contents of the canon. We cannot say confidently that they accepted Esther, Ecclesiastes or the Song of Songs as scripture, because evidence is not available. We can argue only from probability, and arguments from probability are weighed differently by different judges. But when in debate with Jewish theologians Jesus and the apostles appealed to 'the scriptures', they appealed to an authority which was equally acknowledged by their opponents. This near-unanimity might suggest that some widely acknowledged authority had

---

valid, but that those handed down by tradition from the fathers need not be observed'. It was probably misinterpretation of Josephus, directly or indirectly, that led Origen (*Against Celsus*, 1.49) and Jerome (*Commentary on Matthew*, on 22:31f.) to say that the Sadducees accept the books of Moses alone as scripture.

[42] This oral law is the 'tradition of the elders' mentioned in Mark 7:5.

[43] Daniel 12:2. When Jesus appealed to scripture in refutation of the Sadducees' denial of resurrection, he cited Exod. 3:6, basing his argument on the character of God (Mark 12:26f.).

[44] See P. Kahle, *The Cairo Geniza* (London, 1947), pp. 147f.; F. M. Cross, *The Ancient Library of Qumran and Modern Biblical* Studies, pp. 172f., 192f.

[45] A. C. Sundberg argues that the Samaritan restriction of the canon to the Pentateuch involved 'a conscious rejection of the collection of Prophets, since the Prophets were then regarded as canonical in Jerusalem' (*The Old Testament of the Early Church* [Cambridge, Mass., 1964], p. 111); *cf* J. Barton, *Oracles of God*, pp. 282f.

promulgated a decision on the matter. It is not easy, however, to identify an authority in the relevant period which would have commanded the assent of such diverse groups. But, as later with the New Testament,[46] so with the Old Testament it is probable that, when the canon was 'closed' in due course by competent authority, this simply meant that official recognition was given to the situation already obtaining in the practice of the worshipping community.

[46] See p. 262

CHAPTER THREE

THE GREEK OLD
TESTAMENT

THE ORIGIN OF THE SEPTUAGINT

Almost from the time that Alexander the Great founded Alexandria in
Egypt in 331 BC, there was a Jewish element in its Greek-speaking
population, and this element continued to increase in the generations
that followed. There were Jewish settlements in most of the other
Greek-speaking cities established throughout the area of Alexander's
conquests, but none was so important as that in Alexandria. The
process of Jewish settlement there was facilitated by the fact that,
until 198 BC, Judaea formed part of the kingdom of the Ptolemies,
who succeeded to Alexander's empire in Egypt and made Alexandria
their capital.

Before long the Jews of Alexandria gave up using the language their
ancestors had spoken in Palestine and spoke Greek only. This would
have involved their being cut off from the use of the Hebrew Bible and
the traditional prayers and thanksgivings, had the scriptures not been
translated into Greek. The Greek translation of the scriptures was
made available from time to time in the third and second centuries BC
(say during the century 250-150 BC). The law, comprising the five
books of Moses, was the first part of the scriptures to appear in a Greek
version; the reading of the law was essential to synagogue worship,
and it was important that what was read should be intelligible to the

43

congregation. At first, perhaps, the law was read in Hebrew, as it was back home in Palestine, and someone was appointed to give an oral translation in Greek.[1] But as time went on a written Greek version was provided, so that it could be read directly.

In the course of time a legend attached itself to this Greek version of the law, telling how it was the work of seventy or rather seventy-two elders of Israel who were brought to Alexandria for the purpose. It is because of this legend that the term Septuagint (from Latin *septuaginta*, 'seventy') came to be attached to the version. As time went on, the term came to be attached to the whole of the Old Testament in Greek, and the original legend of the seventy was further embellished. The legend is recorded originally in a document called the *Letter of Aristeas*, which tells how the elders completed the translation of the Pentateuch in seventy-two days, achieving an agreed version as the result of regular conference and comparison. Later embellishments not only extended their work to cover the whole Old Testament but told how they were isolated from one another in separate cells for the whole period and produced seventy-two identical versions — conclusive proof, it was urged, of the divine inspiration of the work! Philo, the Jewish philosopher of Alexandria, relates how the translators worked in isolation from one another but wrote the same text word for word, 'as though it were dictated to each by an invisible prompter';[2] but both he and Josephus confirm that it was only the books of the law that were translated by the elders.[3] It was Christian writers who extended their work to the rest of the Old Testament and, taking over Philo's belief in their inspiration, extended that also to cover the whole of the Greek Old Testament, including those books that never formed part of the Hebrew Bible.[4]

A WIDER CANON?

It has frequently been suggested that, while the canon of the Palestinian Jews was limited to the twenty-four books of the Law, Prophets and Writings, the canon of the Alexandrian Jews was more comprehensive. There is no evidence that this was so: indeed, there is

---

[1] There was a comparable practice in Hebrew-speaking synagogues in Palestine and farther east, where the reading of the law and the prophets in Hebrew was followed by an oral interpretation or *targum* in Aramaic. (See p.53).

[2] Philo, *Life of Moses*, 2.57.   [3] Josephus, *Antiquities*, proem, 3.

[4] See pp.89, 96.

no evidence that the Alexandrian Jews ever promulgated a canon of scripture. The reason for thinking that they did, and that it was a more comprehensive canon that that acknowledged in Palestine, is that Greek-speaking Christians, who naturally took over the Greek Old Testament which was already in existence, took over the Greek version of a number of other books and gave some measure of scriptural status to them also.

While it was at Alexandria that the Hebrew scriptures were first translated into Greek, the use of the Greek version quickly spread to other Jewish communities throughout the Greek-speaking world, not excluding Judaea itself, where (as the New Testament shows) there were 'Hellenists' (Greek-speaking Jews) as well as 'Hebrews' (Hebrew - or Aramaic-speaking Jews).[5]

With few and fragmentary exceptions, the Septuagint manuscripts now in existence were produced by Christians. (From now on, the term 'Septuagint' is used in this work of the pre-Christian Greek version of the whole Old Testament.) Jewish copies of the Septuagint known to have survived are: *(a)* a fragment of Deuteronomy from the second century BC in the John Rylands University Library, Manchester (*P. Ryl.* 458), *(b)* another fragment of Deuteronomy of about the same date preserved in Cairo (*P. Fouad* 266), *(c)* fragments from the Qumran caves of two scrolls of Leviticus (4QLXXLv[a] and 4QLXXLv[b]) and one of Numbers (4QLXXNum) from Cave 4, and of Exodus (7QLXXEx) and the 'Letter of Jeremiah' (7QLXXEpJer) from Cave 7, *(d)* a fragmentary scroll of the Minor Prophets in Greek from Wadi Hever (8 HevXII gr), hailed in 1953, shortly after it was discovered, as 'a missing link in the history of the Septuagint' (it turned out to be identical, or nearly so, with the Greek text of those books used by Justin Martyr in the middle of the second century AD).[6]

The grandson of Jeshua ben Sira evidently knew the Greek version of the Hebrew Bible: in the preface to the Greek translation of his grandfather's book he apologizes for any defects in his work, on the ground that 'what was originally expressed in Hebrew does not have exactly the same sense when translated into another language. Not only this work, but even the law itself, the prophecies, and the rest of

---

[5] See Acts 6:1, according to which both these groups were represented at an early date in the church of Jerusalem.

[6] See D. Barthélemy, 'Redécouverte d'un chaînon manquant de l'histoire de la Septante', *Revue Biblique* 60 (1953), pp.18-29; *Les devanciers d'Aquila,* VTSup 10 (Leiden, 1963).

the books differ not a little as originally expressed.'[7]

In 2 Maccabees 15:9 Judas Maccabaeus, encouraging his followers before their battle with the Greek commander Nicanor (161BC), is described as 'encouraging them from the law and the prophets'. Judas would have used the Hebrew scriptures, but it would probably be right to infer that 'the law and the prophets' were known in Greek to the compiler of 2 Maccabees (c 50 BC) and indeed to Jason of Cyrene, a Hellenistic Jewish writer whose five-volume work on the Maccabaean struggle is abridged in 2 Maccabees.

Philo of Alexandria (c 20 BC-AD 50) evidently knew the scriptures in the Greek version only. He was an illustrious representative of Alexandrian Judaism, and if Alexandrian Judaism did indeed recognize a more comprehensive canon than Palestinian Judaism, one might have expected to find some trace of this in Philo's voluminous writings. But in fact, while Philo has not given us a formal statement on the limits of the canon such as we have in Josephus, the books which he acknowledged as holy scripture were quite certainly books included in the traditional Hebrew Bible. He indicates that special veneration is paid to 'the laws, inspired oracles given through the prophets, hymns and the other books by which knowledge and piety may be increased and brought to perfection'.[8] These are the books, he says, which the Therapeutae (a body of Jewish ascetics in Egypt comparable to the Essenes in Palestine) keep in their private sanctuaries. The books 'by which knowledge and piety may be increased and brought to perfection' are presumably poetical and wisdom books: how many of them Philo knew he does not say. He shows no sign of accepting the authority of any of the books which we know as the Apocrypha. It cannot be said certainly that he accepted *all* the books found in the Hebrew Bible: there are some, especially in the Writings, of which he makes no mention.

Josephus in his *Antiquities* generally depends on the Septuagint. He used the services of translators, to ensure the literary quality of his Greek, but the dependence on the Septuagint which the work evinces is probably his own and not simply theirs. For his precise delimitation of the canon of scripture, however, he almost certainly relied on Palestinian sources—this was what he had been taught by his instructors in the years before the war against the Romans which broke out in AD 66 (he had little enough opportunity of contact with Palestinian teachers after the war).[9]

[7] See p.31.   [8] Philo, *On the Contemplative Life*, 25.   [9] See p.32–34.

SEPTUAGINTAL ORDER OF BOOKS

The order of books in copies of the Septuagint which have come down to us differs from the traditional order of the Hebrew Bible, and lies behind the conventional order of the Christian Old Testament. The law, comprising the five books of Moses, comes first in both traditions; it is followed by the historical books, poetical and wisdom books, and the books of the prophets. As with the Hebrew Bible, so with the Septuagint, the order of books is more fluid when they are copied on separate scrolls than when they are bound together in codices. But there is no reason to think that the Christian scribes who first copied the Septuagint into codices devised a new sequence for its contents; it is more likely that they took over the sequence along with the text itself. It has been held indeed that the Septuagint order represents an early Palestinian order of the books in the Hebrew Bible, contemporary with, and possibly even antedating, the Hebrew order which became traditional.[10] The evidence is too scanty for any certainty to be attainable on this matter.

After the Pentateuch, the second division of the Septuagint corresponds largely with the Former Prophets in the Hebrew Bible, but Ruth is inserted (in keeping with its dramatic date) between Judges and 1 Samuel, and the books of Samuel and Kings (called in the Septuagint the four books of Kingdoms or Reigns) are followed by the books of Chronicles (called *Paraleipomena*, 'things left over'), 1 Esdras (a variant Greek edition of the history from 2 Chron. 35:1 to Neh. 8:13), 2 Esdras (our Ezra-Nehemiah),[11] Esther, Judith and Tobit. Judith and Tobit are not included in the Hebrew Bible; Esther in the

---

[10] See P. Katz, 'The Old Testament Canon in Palestine and Alexandria', *ZNW* 47 (1956), pp. 191-217.

[11] Esdras is the Greek form of Ezra. The nomenclature of the Esdras books is quite confusing. The following table provides a guide to the variations:

English (AV/KJV, RSV, etc.) Bible and Apocrypha		Septuagint		Latin Vulgate, Douay Bible, etc.
Ezra	=	2 Esdras 1–10	=	1 Esdras
Nehemiah	=	2 Esdras 11–23	=	2 Esdras
1 Esdras	=	1 Esdras	=	3 Esdras
2 Esdras	=		=	4 Esdras

2 Esdras (4 Esdras or 4 Ezra), which is not in the Septuagint, is for the most part (chapters 3–14) a Jewish apocalypse of the period following AD 70 (see p. 36), supplied with a Christian prologue (chapters 1–2) and epilogue (chapters 15–16).

Septuagint is a considerably expanded edition of the Hebrew Esther.

The third division contains the poetical and wisdom books: Psalms, Proverbs, Ecclesiastes, Song of Songs, Job, Wisdom and Ecclesiasticus (the book of Jeshua ben Sira). Of these, Wisdom (originally written in Greek) and Ecclesiasticus (originally written in Hebrew) are not found in the Hebrew Bible. An additional psalm (Ps. 151, known in Hebrew at Qumran) is appended to the Psalter.

As for the fourth division (the prophetical books), the twelve minor prophets precede the others in the early uncial manuscripts (notably the Sinaitic, Vatican and Alexandrine codices). Jeremiah is followed not only by Lamentations but also by the book of Baruch and the *Letter of Jeremiah*,[12] neither of which is in the Hebrew Bible. Daniel is amplified by two stories not in the Hebrew text — the History of Susanna, which is put at the beginning,[13] and the story of Bel and the Dragon, which is added at the end — while a prayer of confession and a canticle of praise to God *Benedicite omnia opera*) are put in the mouths of Daniel's three friends in the fiery furnace, so that 68 verses are inserted between verses 23 and 24 of chapter 3.

The books of Maccabees — two, three or four in number[14] — form a sort of appendix to the Septuagint; they do not belong to any of its main divisions.

Those works which appear in the Septuagint but not in the Hebrew Bible are sometimes referred to as the 'Septuagintal plus'; together with two or three other compositions they are the books which, since Jerome's time, have commonly been called the Apocrypha.[15]

THE SEPTUAGINT IN THE CHURCH

The scriptures known to Jesus and his disciples were no doubt the scrolls of the Hebrew Bible — the Law, the Prophets and the Writings — kept in synagogues for use during regular services and

[12] In AV/KJV the *Letter of Jeremiah* is printed as chapter 6 of Baruch.

[13] In the earliest stage of the Greek version it was perhaps appended to the canonical book.

[14] 1 Maccabees relates the persecution of the Jews under Antiochus IV (175–164 BC) and the Maccabaean (Hasmonaean) resistance from a pro-Hasmonaean viewpoint; 2 Maccabees relates part of the same story from a Pharisaic viewpoint; 3 Maccabees describes a threat to the Jews of Alexandria under Ptolemy IV (221–203 BC); 4 Maccabees presents a moralizing meditation on the martyrdoms described in 2 Maccabees.

[15] See pp.90–93.

possibly at other times. When Jesus was about to read the second lesson[16] in the Nazareth synagogue on the first sabbath that he visited his home town after the beginning of his public ministry, and 'there was given to him the book of the prophet Isaiah' (Luke 4:17), it was most probably a Hebrew scroll that he received. But even in Palestine, and not least in Jerusalem itself, there were many Greek-speaking Jews, Hellenists, and there were synagogues where they might go to hear the scriptures read and the prayers recited in Greek. Such was the Synagogue of the Freedmen where Stephen held debate in Jerusalem (Acts 6:9).

However much the wording of Stephen's defence in Acts 7 may owe to the narrator, the consistency with which its biblical quotations and allusions are based on the Septuagint is true to life. Since Stephen was a Hellenist, the Septuagint was the edition of the scriptures which he would naturally use.

As soon as the gospel was carried into the Greek-speaking world, the Septuagint came into its own as the sacred text to which the preachers appealed. In was used in the Greek-speaking synagogues throughout the Roman Empire. When Paul at Thessalonica visited the synagogue on three successive sabbaths and 'argued with them from the scriptures, explaining and proving that it was necessary for the Christ to suffer and to rise from the dead' (Acts 17:2f.), it was on the Septuagint that he based his arguments. We see him doing this earlier in greater detail in the synagogue of Pisidian Antioch. There, after the reading of the two regular sabbath lessons from 'the law and the prophets', he outlined the history of Israel from the Exodus in Moses's day to the beginning of David's reign, and showed how this course of events led inevitably and ultimately to the coming of Jesus, 'great David's greater Son', in whose death and resurrection the promises made by God to David found their fulfilment (Acts 13:17–37). For Christians, the Old Testament pointed forward to Jesus; it was, in fact, meaningless without him.

The Septuagint played its part even when the gospel was presented to complete pagans, like the unsophisticated Lycaonians at Lystra, who mistook Paul and Barnabas for divine beings (Acts 14:8–18), or the sophisticated members of the Athenian court of the Areopagus, who had no such exaggerated estimate of Paul (Acts 17:16–32). To them the Septuagint was not specifically quoted, yet the preliminary

[16] There were two scripture lessons in the synagogue service: the first lesson from the Law, the second from the Prophets (cf Acts 13:15).

arguments from God's work in creation and providence were securely based on the Greek scriptures.

'Greek Judaism', it has been said, 'with the Septuagint had ploughed the furrows for the gospel seed in the Western world';[17] but it was the Christian preachers who sowed the seed. So thoroughly, indeed, did Christians appropriate the Septuagint as their version of the scriptures that the Jews became increasingly disenchanted with it. The time came when one rabbi compared 'the accursed day on which the seventy elders wrote the Law in Greek for the king' to the day on which Israel made the golden calf.[18] New Greek versions of the Old Testament were produced for Jewish use—in particular, the very literal rendering of Aquila and a more idiomatic rendering by Theodotion.[19] (Theodotion's version of Daniel was so far superior to the earlier Septuagint version that Christians preferred it: in almost all manuscripts of the Greek Bible it is Theodotion's Daniel, not the original Septuagint version, that appears.)[20]

THE NEW TESTAMENT EVIDENCE

While the New Testament writers all used the Septuagint, to a greater or lesser degree, none of them tells us precisely what the limits of its contents were. The 'scriptures' to which they appealed covered substantially the same range as the Hebrew Bible. We cannot say with absolute certainty, for example, if Paul treated Esther or the Song of Songs as scripture any more than we can say if those books belonged to the Bible which Jesus knew and used. Paul possibly alludes to Ecclesiastes when he says that creation was made subject to 'vanity' (Rom. 8:20), using the same word (Gk. *mataiotēs*) as is used in the Septuagint for the refrain of that book: 'Vanity of vanities, all is vanity' (Eccles. 1:2; 12:8).

On the other side of the frontier which divides the books of the

[17] A. Deissmann, *New Light on the New Testament,* E. T. (Edinburgh, 1907), p.95.

[18] Tractate *Sopherim* 1.8f. The 'king' is Ptolemy II of Egypt (285–246 BC) who, according to the legend in the *Letter of Aristeas,* lent his good offices in arranging for the seventy-two translators to come to Alexandria to carry out their work.

[19] Theodotion's version may have been in part a revision of an earlier one. Another Greek version, made by one Symmachus in the late second or early third century AD, was used by the Jewish Christian group known as Ebionites.

[20] Two exceptions are LXX codices 88 (the Chigi manuscript of the Septuagint) and 967 (one of the Chester Beatty biblical papyri); these exhibit the original Septuagint version.

Hebrew Bible from the 'Septuagintal plus', the book of Wisdom was possibly in Paul's mind as he dictated part of the first two chapters of Romans, but that would not give it scriptural status: if he does allude to it, he probably contradicts it here and there.[21] The writer to the Hebrews probably had the martyrologies of 2 Maccabees 6:18—7:41 or 4 Maccabees 5:3—18:24 in view when he spoke of the tortures and other hardships which some endured through faith (Heb. 11:35b–38);[22] and when he says in the same context that some were sawn in two he may allude to a document which described how the prophet Isaiah was so treated.[23]

The Nestle-Aland edition of the Greek New Testament (1979) has an index of Old Testament texts cited or alluded to in the New Testament, followed by an index of allusions not only to the 'Septuagintal plus' but also to several other works not included in the Septuagint. Many of these last are resemblances rather than conscious allusions; only one is a straight quotation explicitly ascribed to its source. That is the quotation from 'Enoch in the seventh generation from Adam' in Jude 14 f; this comes recognizably from the apocalyptic book of Enoch (1 Enoch 1:9).[24] Earlier in Jude's letter the account of Michael's dispute with the devil over the body of Moses may refer to a work called the *Assumption of Moses* or *Ascension of Moses,* but if so, the part of the work containing this incident has been lost (Jude 9).[25]

There are, however, several quotations in the New Testament which are introduced as though they were taken from holy scripture, but their source can no longer be identified. For instance, the words 'He shall be called a Nazarene', quoted in Matthew 2:23 as 'what was spoken by the prophets', stand in that form in no known prophetical

[21] The exposure of pagan immorality in Rome 1:18–32 echoes Wisdom 12–14; the attitude of righteous Jews criticized by Paul in Rom. 2:1–11 has affinities with passages in Wisdom 11–15 (on these see A. Nygren, *Commentary on Romans,* E. T. [London, 1952], pp.113–120).

[22] This is particularly clear in his mention of 'a better resurrection' (verse 35b)— i.e. better than the restoration to mortal life granted to the sons of the widow of Zarephath and the Shunammite woman (verse 35a)—for a resurrection to immortality was the expressed hope of the mother and her seven sons in 2 Maccabees 7.

[23] Perhaps the *Ascension of Isaiah,* a composite work of the 2nd century BC to the 4th century AD. The oldest part tells of Isaiah's martyrdom under Manasseh.

[24] See p.85.

[25] The extant part (also known as the *Testament of Moses*) is certainly incomplete, but the *Assumption of Moses* may have been a separate work from the *Testament*; if so, it has been entirely lost.

book. It has been suggested that there may be an allusion to Isaiah 11:1, where the expected son of David is described as a 'branch' to grow out of the roots of Jesse, as though Heb. *nēṣer* ('branch') were to be read as *noṣrî* ('Nazarene').[26]

Again, in John 7:38 'Out of his heart shall flow rivers of living water' is introduced by the words 'as the scripture has said'—but which scripture is referred to? An allusion to some such passage as Zechariah 14:8, 'living waters shall flow out from Jerusalem' (interpreted along the lines of the 'river of the water of life' in Rev. 22:1), has been suspected, but there can be no certainty.

Paul's words in 1 Corinthians 2:9, 'What no eye has seen, nor ear heard. . .', introduced by the clause 'as it is written', resemble Isaiah 64:4, but are not a direct quotation from it. Some church fathers say they come from a work called the *Secrets of Elijah* or *Apocalypse of Elijah*, but this work is not accessible to us and we do not know if it existed in Paul's time.[27] The triplet 'Awake, O sleeper, / and arise from the dead, / and Christ shall give you light' (Eph. 5:14), may be a primitive baptismal hymn, but it is introduced by the words 'it is said' (so RSV for the more literal 'he says' or 'it says'), exactly like the quotation from Psalm 68:18 (LXX 67:19) in Ephesians 4:8.[28] Any resemblance to Jonah 1:6 is quite fortuitous. The naming of Moses' opponents as Jannes and Jambres in 2 Timothy 3:8 may depend on some document no longer identifiable; the names, in varying forms, appear in a number of Jewish writings, mostly later than the date of the Pastoral Epistles.[29]

We have no idea what 'the scripture' is which says, according to James 4:5, 'He yearns jealously over the spirit which he has made to dwell in us'; we cannot even be sure of the sense, for it might mean, 'The spirit which he has made to dwell in us yearns jealously.'[30]

[26] This device, by which it is suggested that one word be replaced by another having the same consonants but a different pattern of vowels, is familiar in the rabbinical writings: 'Read not X but Y.'

[27] On 1 Cor. 2:9 see p. 162 with nn. 8 and 9.

[28] See F. F. Bruce, *Colossians, Philemon, Ephesians,* NICNT (Grand Rapids, 1984), pp. 376–378.

[29] The earliest occurrence, *c.* 100 BC (in the form 'Yahaneh and his brother'), is in the *Book of the Covenant of Damascus* (CD 5. 18). See H. Odeberg, 'Iannēs, Iambrēs', *TDNT* 3, pp. 192f.; A. T. Hanson, *Studies in the Pastoral Epistles* (London, 1968), pp. 26–28.

[30] See P. H. Davids, *The Epistle of James,* NIGTC (Exeter/Grand Rapids, 1982), pp. 162–165.

SEPTUAGINT AND
NON-SEPTUAGINTAL VERSIONS

There are several places in which the Septuagint translators used a form of words which (without their being able to foresee it, naturally) lent itself to the purposes of New Testament writers better than the Hebrew text would have done. Thus, Matthew can quote as a prophecy of the virginal conception of Christ the Septuagint version of Isaiah 7:14, 'Behold, a virgin shall conceive and bear a son. . .' (Matt. 1:23), where the Greek word *parthenos* means specifically 'virgin', as the Hebrew *'almāh* need not. (Aquila, who provided a new Greek version of the Old Testament for Jewish use to replace the Septuagint, took care to employ the less specific Greek word *neanis,* 'girl' or 'young woman', to blunt the point of a Christian 'argument from prophecy'.) Similarly, the Septuagint of Amos 9:11f. provided James the Just at the Council of Jerusalem with divine authority for the Gentile mission more directly than the Hebrew text could have done (Acts 15:15–18). (Here the Septuagint translators themselves had gone a long way towards spiritualizing and universalizing an oracle which originally spoke of national revival and expansion.)[31]

But there are some places in the New Testament where the Old Testament is quoted in a different form from the Septuagint as it has come down to us. For example, in Matthew 12:18–21 the announcement of the Servant of the Lord in Isaiah 42:1–4 is quoted in what appears to be a non-Septuagintal version.[32] The statement, 'Vengeance is mine, I will repay' (from Deut. 32:35), is quoted in Romans 12:19 and Hebrews 10:30 in a form corresponding neither to the Hebrew text nor to the Septuagint, but to the Aramaic Targums on the Pentateuch. That renderings or paraphrases known to us only from the Targums were found also in Greek versions of the Old Testament in the first century AD is suggested also by such expressions as 'lest they should . . . be forgiven' (Mark 4:12) in a quotation from Isaiah 6:10 where the Hebrew and Septuagint read 'lest they . . . be healed'; and 'he gave gifts to men' (Eph. 4:8) in a quotation from

---

[31] LXX 'that the remainder of mankind may seek [me]' certainly makes a different impression from 'that they [the dynasty of David] may take possession of the remainder of Edom' (MT).

[32] See P. Kahle, *The Cairo Geniza* (London, 1947), pp. 166f., 2nd edition (Oxford, 1959), pp. 250–252; R. H. Gundry, *The Use of the Old Testament in St Matthew's Gospel,* NovTSup 18 (Leiden, 1967), pp. 110–116.

Psalm 68:18 (LXX 67:19) where the Hebrew and Septuagint read '... *received* gifts among men'.[33]

There is also a little evidence for forms of the Greek version which approximated to distinctive features of the Samaritan Bible. For example, Stephen's speech in Acts 7 is based throughout on the Septuagint, but his statement in verse 4 that Abraham left Harran for Canaan 'after his father died' is supported neither by the Septuagint wording (as we have received it) nor by the Masoretic text of the Hebrew Bible; it is, however, consistent with the Samaritan text, which gives Terah's age at death as 145, not 205 (Gen. 11:32).[34]

---

[33] On Targums see pp.44, 285. In Deut. 32:35; Is. 6:10 and Ps. 68:18 the Peshitta (the Syriac version of the Old Testament) agrees with the targumic construction.

[34] The Masoretic text (MT) is the traditional Jewish text of the Hebrew Bible. If, as MT and LXX agree, Abraham was born when his father was 70 (Gen. 11:26) and left Harran for Canaan when he himself was 75 (Gen. 12:4), then Terah had still 60 years to live. In James Ussher's chronology the statement of Acts 7:4 is reconciled with the MT evidence by the supposition that Terah was 70 when his oldest son was born but was 130 when Abraham was born.

CHAPTER FOUR

THE OLD TESTAMENT BECOMES A NEW BOOK

WITNESS TO CHRIST

At the beginning of its existence, then, the Christian church found itself equipped with a book, a collection of sacred scriptures which it inherited. It was not based on the book: it was based on a person, Jesus Christ, crucified under Pontius Pilate, raised from the dead by God and acknowledged by his followers as Lord of all. But the book bore witness to him; in this role they found it indispensable. At the same time they found the record of his life and teaching, his suffering and triumph, indispensable to their understanding of the book.

In this they were but following a precedent established by Jesus himself. Throughout his ministry he appealed to the scriptures. The insistence that 'so it is written' is too deeply embedded in all the gospel strata to be reasonably regarded as only the product of the church's reflection on the events of his life and death in the light of Easter and its aftermath. If the main lines of Old Testament interpretation found in the various New Testament writers are traced back to their origin, that origin cannot be found elsewhere than in Jesus' own teaching.

From the inauguration of his Galilaean ministry with the announcement that the appointed time had come for the kingdom of God to draw near (Mark 1:15), the appeal to what is written recurs throughout Jesus' ministry until at the end he submits to his captors in Gethsemane with the words: 'Let the scriptures be fulfilled' (Mark 14:49).

According to the Acts of the Apostles, the early preaching of the gospel to Jews and God-fearing Gentiles was regularly marked by the appeal to the fulfilment of Old Testament scripture in the work of Jesus. It is to him, Peter assures Cornelius, that 'all the prophets bear witness' (Acts 10:43). When Philip is asked by the Ethiopian on his homeward journey from Jerusalem to whom the prophet is referring as he describes the suffering of the Isaianic Servant, Philip does not hesitate: 'beginning with this scripture he told him the good news of Jesus' (Acts 8:35). The impression given in Acts is confirmed by Paul: 'the gospel of God . . . concerning his Son', he says, was 'promised beforehand through his prophets in the holy scriptures' (Rom. 1:1−3), and throughout his exposition of the gospel in the letter to the Romans he shows in detail what he means by this. Thanks to the illumination thrown on them by their fulfilment in Christ, the ancient scriptures became a new and meaningful book to the early Christians. The prophets themselves, we are assured in 1 Pet 1:10−12, had to search hard to find out 'what person or time was indicated by the Spirit of Christ within them when predicting the sufferings of Christ and the subsequent glory'; they had to learn that their ministry was designed for the generation which witnessed the fulfilment of what they foretold.

Various figures of Old Testament expectation were now identified with Christ—the prophet like Moses (Deut. 18:15−19), the son of David (2 Sam. 7:12−16), the servant of Yahweh (Is. 42:1, etc.), the righteous sufferer (Ps. 22:1, etc.), the stricken shepherd (Zech. 13:7), and others. It is not simply that a number of texts out of context are given a Christian significance: the New Testament interpretation of a few Old Testament words or sentences actually quoted often implies the total context in which these words or sentences occur. Moreover, different New Testament writers will quote different words from the same context in a manner which suggests that the whole context had been given a Christian interpretation before those writers quoted from it. It has been pointed out, for example, that from Ps. 69:9 ('zeal for thy house has consumed me, and the insults of those who insult thee have fallen on me') the former part is applied to Jesus' cleansing of the temple in John 2:17 and the latter part to his patient endurance of verbal abuse in Romans 15:3. While no one is likely to maintain that the one writer has influenced the other, 'it would be too much of a coincidence if the two writers independently happened to cite the two halves of a single verse, unless they were both aware that at least this whole verse, if not any more of the Psalm, formed part of a scheme of scriptural passages generally held to be especially significant'.[1] This implies something more substantial in the way of primitive Christian exegesis than a chain of isolated proof-texts or 'testimonies'.

Alongside this contextual element goes another, which has analogies elsewhere in Judaism: the bringing together and giving a unified exegesis to widely separated scriptures which have a significant term in common. For example: at a very early date the reference in Psalm 118:22 to the stone rejected by the builders which has become the 'head of the corner' (or capstone of the pediment) was seen to be specially applicable to Jesus, rejected by men but exalted by God. As Peter said to the chief priests and their colleagues, 'this is the stone which was rejected by you builders, but which has become the head of the corner' (Acts 4:11)[2]. But other 'stone' passages from the Hebrew Bible were attracted to this one and an integrated Christian interpretation was provided for all together: Jesus is also the tested corner stone of sure foundation in Isaiah 28:16, the rock of refuge amid the flood waters in Isaiah 8:14 which causes the downfall of those who stumble against it, the stone in Nebuchadnezzar's dream which pulverizes the great image of pagan world-dominion (Dan. 2:34f.).[3] Similarly (and especially in the light of Jesus' preferred self-designation as the Son of Man) we find the 'one like a son of man' of Daniel 7:13 brought into close relation with the 'son of man' of Psalm 8:4 beneath whose feet all things have been placed and possibly also with the 'son of man' of Psalm 80:17 whom God makes strong for himself.[4]

Something of the same order appears in the biblical exegesis of the Qumran community, where the prophets are found to foretell the circumstances of the community's rise and progress, and especially the fortunes of its leader, the 'Rightful Teacher'. If in Habakkuk 1:4 'the wicked circumvent the righteous', or in Psalm 37:12 'the wicked plots

[1] C. H. Dodd, *The Old Testament in the New* (London, 1952), p.8; *cf* his *According to the Scriptures* (London, 1952), p.57 ('it is more probable that both writers were guided by a tradition in which this psalm was already referred to Christ').

[2] It is used as a 'testimony' already in the synoptic tradition (Mark 12:10f. and parallels).

[3] *Cf* Luke 20:17f.; Rom. 9:32f.; 1 Pet. 2:6–8. See J. R. Harris, *Testimonies*, I (Cambridge, 1916), pp.27–32.

[4] *Cf* 1 Cor. 15:24–28; Heb. 2:6–9.

against the righteous', this is understood without more ado by the Qumran commentators as a prediction of the attacks made on the Teacher by his enemies. To a great degree the Hebrew scriptures thus became a new book to the community. Other Jews read the same scriptures, but lacked the key to their interpretation. This key had been given to the Teacher, and by him to his followers: God had shown the prophets what was going to take place, but the knowledge of *when* it would take place was withheld from them and revealed in the fulness of time to the Teacher.[5]

If the early Christians recognized the righteous sufferer in the Psalms as Jesus, the persecutors of the righteous sufferer were readily identified with Jesus' enemies, and with none more readily than Judas Iscariot. Here again the cue seems to have been given by Jesus himself: there is no good reason to doubt that at the Last Supper he used the words of Psalm 41:9, 'he who ate of my bread has lifted his heel against me', to indicate to his companions that he knew there was a traitor in the camp.[6] It was no difficult matter to find other passages in the Psalter which could be similarly applied to Judas. Two such passages are applied to him by Peter in Acts 1:20 when he considers with his fellow-apostles who should be co-opted to fill the vacancy left by Judas's defection.[7]

With such dominical and apostolic precedent the church was able so to read the Old Testament writings that they yielded not only an increasing store of 'testimonies' regarding the person and work of Christ but even additional details about New Testament events. (At some levels this interpretative method is still practised: I have heard a preacher argue from the AV/KJV rendering of Isaiah 53:9, 'he made his grave with the wicked', that our Lord, before he was crucified, was compelled to dig his own grave.) This tendency we find in full vigour in Justin Martyr and in Cyprian's *Testimonies against the Jews* (second and third centuries AD); it was carried to excess in the Middle Ages, when the passion narrative (for example) was lavishly embellished

[5] See F. F. Bruce, *Biblical Exegesis in the Qumran Texts* (London, 1960); G. J. Brooke, *Exegesis at Qumran* (Sheffield, 1985).

[6] *Cf* John 13:18 (also 17:12, 'none of them is lost but the son of perdition, that the scripture might be fulfilled').

[7] Pss. 69:25 (LXX 68:25); 109:8 (LXX 108:8). For Ps. 69 *cf* n. 1 above. Compare also the application of Ps. 2:1f. in Acts 4:25—28 to 'Herod and Pontius Pilate with the Gentiles and the peoples of Israel' (a similar, but not identical, application of Ps. 2:1f. is found in Tertullian, *On the Resurrection of the Flesh*, 20).

with Old Testament *motifs* divorced from their context as well as with elements from other sources.[8]

THE MYSTERY DISCLOSED

That the Old Testament prophecies were 'mysteries' whose solution awaited their fulfilment in the New Testament age was axiomatic in the early church. Occasionally the word 'mystery' itself is used in this sense (as it was freely used in the Qumran commentaries). 'To you', says Jesus to his disciples, 'the mystery of the kingdom of God has been given, but to outsiders all these things come as riddles, so that they see without perceiving, and hear without understanding; otherwise they would turn back and receive forgiveness' (Mark 4:11f.).[9]

In the Pauline writings one aspect of the gospel — the manner and purpose of its communication to the Gentile world — is treated as a 'mystery . . . which was not made known to the sons of men in other generations as it has now been revealed to Christ's holy apostles and prophets in the Spirit' (Eph. 3:4f.). That the Gentiles would place their hope on the Son of David and rejoice in the God of Israel was affirmed in the Old Testament, as Paul emphasizes in a series of quotations in Romans 15:9–12, but how this prospect would be realized and what its implications would be could not be appreciated until the Gentile mission was launched in the apostolic age.

The individual New Testament writers have their distinctive interpretative methods. Matthew records how this or that incident in the life of Jesus took place 'in order that it might be fulfilled which was spoken through the prophet' (Matt. 1:23, etc.). Paul sees the partial and temporary setting aside of Israel as clearly stated in the Law, the Prophets and the Psalms as he finds the ingathering of the Gentiles adumbrated there.[10] The writer to the Hebrews sees the priestly and

[8] See the fourteenth-century German mystical treatise now called *Christi Leiden in einer Vision geschaut* ('Christ's Sufferings seen in a Vision'), ed F.P. Pickering (Manchester, 1952); also F. P. Pickering, 'Christi Kreuzigung: Das neutestamentliche Wort, das mittelalterliche Bild', in *Literatur und Darstellende Kunst im Mittelalter* (Berlin, 1966), pp.146–192, and 'The Gothic Image of Christ', in *Essays on Mediaeval German Literature and Iconography* (Cambridge, 1980), pp.3–30. Another example is the fifteenth-century English poem *Quia amore langueo*, where Cant. 1:5 (understood as 'I suffer pain for love's sake') serves as a text for the sufferings of Christ (*The New Oxford Book of English Verse*, ed. Helen Gardner [Oxford, 1972], No.11).

[9] An allusion to Is. 6:9f.

[10] *Cf* Rom. 9:6–11:27.

sacrificial order of Israel as an earthly 'copy' (ineffective in itself) of the heavenly reality which was perfected by the work of Christ. [11] John the evangelist portrays Jesus as giving substance to a number of Old Testament *motifs* — the word, the glory, the tabernacle;[12] the bread of life, the water of life, the light of life. [13] In the Apocalypse may be seen what has been called 'a rebirth of images' from the Old Testament and other ancient lore, some of which might have been thought unadaptable to a Christian purpose, yet all pressed into service to depict the triumph of Christ. [14] However differently the interpretative tradition is developed by those writers, the core of the tradition is common to all: Jesus is the central subject of the Old Testament revelation; it is to him that witness is borne throughout.

One important phase of this interpretative tradition is the tracing of a recurrent pattern in the story of God's dealing with his people. Something of this sort is already discernible in the Old Testament itself, where the bringing of the people of God back from the Babylonian exile is presented as a repetition of his delivering power manifested earlier in the exodus from Egypt. [15] New Testament writers in their turn appear to view the history of Israel from Egypt to Canaan as recapitulated either in the personal experience of the Messiah or in the corporate experience of the messianic people. [16]

Recapitulation in the Messiah's personal experience (perhaps by way of appying Isaiah 63:9, 'In all their affliction he was afflicted')[17] appears especially in the Old Testament quotations of Matthew's nativity narrative where, for example, the reference to the exodus in Hosea 11:1 ('out of Egypt I called my son') is said to have been fulfilled in the holy family's flight into Egypt and return thence to the land of Israel. [18] Something similar may be implicit in the parallel between Jesus' forty days in the wilderness and Israel's forty years of wilderness

[11] Heb. 9:1 — 10:18.

[12] These three representations of the divine presence are brought together in John 1:14, 'the *Word* became flesh and *tabernacled* among us, and we beheld his *glory*.'

[13] John 6:35; 4:10–14 and 7:37–39; 8:12.

[14] See A. M. Farrer, *A Rebirth of Images* (London, 1949).

[15] See Is. 43:2, 16, 19; 48:21; 52:12; 63:7–14.

[16] *Cf* Luke 9:30f, where Moses and Elijah talk with Jesus on the mount of transfiguration about his 'exodus' which was to be accomplished at Jerusalem.

[17] LXX renders differently: 'Not an ambassador, nor a messenger, but he himself saved them.'

[18] But see J. Barr, *Holy Scripture* (Oxford, 1983), p.98.

wandering, both periods of testing coming as the sequel to a 'baptismal' experience.[19]

As for the recapitulation of the Egypt-to-Canaan sequence in the life of the church, this pervades the New Testament epistles, Pauline and non-Pauline alike, and must reflect an extremely primitive Christian tradition.

Israel had the paschal lamb; 'Christ our passover has been sacrificed for us', says Paul (1 Cor. 5:7)—'a lamb without blemish and without spot', says Peter (1 Pet. 1:19).[20] Israel passed through the Red Sea, being thus 'baptized into Moses', says Paul (baptized without being immersed, as a Scots divine once pointed out, whereas the Egyptians were immersed without being baptized);[24] Christians for their part are 'baptized into Christ' (1 Cor. 10:2; Gal. 3:27). Israel had manna from heaven and water from the rock to sustain and refresh them in the wilderness; Christians too have their supernatural food and drink (1 Cor. 10:3f., 16). But for all these privileges, the generation that left Egypt died in the wilderness because of rebellion against the God who brought them out; Christians should take due warning lest disobedience on their part brings them into comparable disaster (1 Cor. 10:6–12). And here the writer to the Hebrews takes over: Israel in the wilderness had a promised 'rest' to look forward to, but failed to enter into it on account of unbelief; so Christians may miss the rest that remains for the people of God if they in their turn cherish 'an evil heart of unbelief, in falling away from the living God' (Heb. 3:12; 4:11).[22]

Then there is an interpretative principle which has been called the 'real presence' of Christ in the Old Testament.[23] In a Pauline passage already referred to, the rock which accompanied the Israelites in the wilderness is said to have been 'Christ' (1 Cor. 10:4)[24]—it was from Christ, that is to say, that they drew their spiritual refreshment then,

[19] Mark 1:13; cf Deut. 8:2 (it is noteworthy that Jesus' three citations of scripture in response to the tempter, reproduced in Matt. 4:4, 7, 10 par. Luke 4:4, 8, 12, are drawn from Deut. 6 and 8).

[20] Melito dwells on this motif in his *Paschal Homily*, 69, etc. (see p.68).

[21] Neil Macmichael, quoted by J. Macleod, *Scottish Theology* (Edinburgh, 1945), pp.253f.

[22] This warning comes in the course of an exposition and application of Ps. 95:7–11 (LXX 94:7–11).

[23] A. T. Hanson, *Jesus Christ in the Old Testament* (London, 1965), p.7, etc.

[24] A halfway stage towards Paul's statement that 'the rock was Christ' may be found in the identification of the rock with divine wisdom, attested in Philo, *The Worse attacks the Better*, 115 (cf Wisdom 11:4).

just as Christians do today. Another instance is found in what is probably the original reading of Jude 5, '*Jesus*, who delivered a people from the land of Egypt, later destroyed those who did not believe.' In place of 'Jesus' various authorities for the text have 'the Lord' or 'God' or the Greek definite article (to be translated 'he who delivered . . . '). But these various readings have arisen because of the difficulty felt to inhere in the reading 'Jesus'; no scribe would have substituted 'Jesus' for any one of them.[25] What could 'Jesus' mean in this context? The reference is not to Moses' servant and successor Joshua, as it is in Acts 7:45 and Hebrews 4:8. Joshua led Israel into the promised land (thus providing the material for a rich Joshua-Jesus typology),[26] but he did not deliver them from the land of Egypt. Jude's point seems to be that the one who led Israel out of Egypt was the Son of God before his incarnation (the Son of God who in incarnation was called Jesus). The fact that Yahweh, the personal name of the God of Israel, was commonly read as 'Lord' (Gk. *kyrios*) in the Septuagint, and that Jesus was called 'Lord' (Gk. *kyrios*) in the church,[27] made it the easier to identify Jesus with 'the Lord' who went before Israel in a pillar of cloud and fire, who rescued them from the power of the Egyptians, who healed them in the wilderness (Exod. 13:21; 14:30; 15:26). It was even easier to identify Jesus with the covenant-messenger, the angel of Yahweh's presence, who led them under Moses towards the land of rest (Exod. 14:19; 23:20–23; 32:34; 33:2, 14; Is. 63:9).[28]

The Hebrew scriptures, especially in their Greek dress, thus became for the early church a new book, a Christian book, a book primarily designed to bear witness to Jesus. Not only so, but others who were introduced to those writings through Christians were evidently predisposed to read them from a Christian perspective.

'One of the extraordinary features of the early Church', it has been said, 'is the number of men who were converted by reading the Old Testament'[29] — converted, that is to say, from paganism to Christianity. It does not appear that those men had any antecedent

---

[25] See B. M. Metzger, *A Textual Commentary on the Greek New Testament* (London/ New York, 1971), pp.725f.

[26] *Cf* Letter of Barnabas 6:8f.; Justin, *Dialogue with Trypho*, 113, 132; see J. R. Harris, *Testimonies*, II (Cambridge, 1920), pp.51–57.

[27] See especially Phil. 2:9–11.

[28] Compare Justin's interpretation of 'my name is in him' (Exod. 23:21) in *Dialogue with Trypho*, 75.

[29] W. Barclay, *The Making of the Bible* (London, 1961), p.41.

conviction of the authority of the Old Testament, but as they read it, it 'found' them (in Coleridge's sense of the word).[30] One wonders, however, if they were completely ignorant of an interpretative tradition which helped them to read the Christian gospel there.[31]

A good example is provided by Tatian in an autobiographical section of his *Address to the Greeks* (c AD 170). After unsatisfying experiences of Greek philosophical and legal literature and of mystery religions, he says:

> I withdrew myself and sought best how to discover the truth. While I was earnestly employed in this matter, I happened to light upon certain 'barbaric' [i.e. non-Greek] writings, too old to be compared with the opinions of the Greeks and too divine to be compared with their error. I found myself convinced by these writings, because of the unpretentious cast of the language, the unstudied character of the writers, the ready comprehension of the making of the universe, the foreknowledge of things to come, the excellence of the precepts and the placing of all things under the rule of one principle. My soul being thus taught by God, I understood that the pagan writings led to condemnation, whereas these put an end to the slavery that is in the world, rescuing us from many rulers (*archons*), yes, from ten thousand tyrants. These writings do not indeed give us something which we had not received before but rather something which we had indeed received but were prevented by error from making our own.[32]

These last words suggest that Tatian's reading of the Old Testament was preceded or accompanied by some awareness of the line of interpretation which enabled him to understand it in a Christian sense.

A SHARED HERITAGE

But this Christian book, as it was to the church, comprised the holy scriptures of the Jewish people. Even the Septuagint version, which the Gentile church took to its heart, was in origin a Jewish translation.

[30] S. T. Coleridge, *Confessions of an Inquiring Spirit* (London,[2] 1849), pp.11, 13.

[31] See E. Flesseman-van Leer, 'Prinzipien der Sammlung und Ausscheidung bei der Bildung des Kanons', *ZTK* 61 (1964), p.407 with n.14.

[32] Tatian, *Address to the Greeks*, 29 cf Justin, *Dialogue with Trypho*, 8.1; Theophilus, *To Autolycus*, 1.14.

When the law and the prophets were read week by week in the synagogue, whether in the Hebrew original or in the Greek translation, they were understood in a Jewish sense, according to the 'tradition of the elders'. Jews and Christians had the same sacred book, but that did not serve as a bond of unity between them.

As Jews heard the scriptures read, they learned that every male child had to be circumcised when he was eight days old if he was to be reckoned a member of the people of God. They learned that every seventh day was to be observed as a rest day, and that certain other days throughout the year were to be specially set aside for sacred purposes. They learned, moreover, that the flesh of certain animals was not to be eaten, because they were 'unclean', and that the flesh even of 'clean' animals might be eaten only under certain stringent conditions—for example, both their fat and their blood were forbidden for food. These restrictions were so binding that any infringement of them imperilled one's membership in the chosen people.

Christians—even, to an increasing degree, Christians who had been brought up to observe these regulations—soon came to adopt a relaxed attitude to them. In the new order inaugurated by Christ circumcision was irrelevant. The keeping of the sabbath and other sacred days was not obligatory but voluntary. As for food-restrictions, Jesus was recorded as having once given a ruling which meant, in effect, that all kinds of food were 'clean'.[33]

Yet the text of scripture had not changed: what had changed was the Christians' understanding of it in the light of their Master's teaching and achievement. It is easy to appreciate how Jews, who did not share the Christians' estimate of the person and work of Jesus, found this playing fast and loose with the divine commandments an incomprehensible and totally deplorable proceeding.

Christians, on the other hand, who found such luminous testimony to Christ and the gospel in the same scriptures, wondered how Jews could read them with such lack of comprehension. One explanation was that a 'judicial blinding' prevented Jews from seeing what was so plain to Christians. Paul uses the story of Moses' face, which shone with reflected glory after he had been in the presence of God, so that he had to put a veil or mask on it (Exod. 34:29–35); in Paul's application of the story, the veil is somehow transferred from Moses' face to the minds of the synagogue congregation 'whenever Moses is read', so that

[33] Mark 7:19.

they cannot see 'the glory of God in the face of Christ' (2 Cor. 3:7–4:6).

Justin Martyr in his *First Apology* criticizes the Jewish belief that the one who introduced himself to Moses in the burning bush as 'the God of Abraham and the God of Isaac and the God of Jacob' was 'the Father and Creator of the universe'. The Jews are wrong, says Justin (as the spirit of prophecy says, 'Israel does not know me, my people have not understood me');[34] it was the Son of God who spoke to Moses from the bush.[35] He bases his argument on the statement that 'the angel of the Lord appeared' to Moses in the bush (Exod. 3:2), and it is the Son of God, says Justin, 'who is called both angel and apostle'.[36] But Justin is wrong: he is contradicted by Jesus himself. When Jesus, in his dispute with some Sadducees, based the truth of the resurrection on the affirmation of Exodus 3:6, 'I am the God of Abraham and the God of Isaac and the God of Jacob', he certainly identified the speaker with 'the Father and Creator of the universe'.[37] But even the plain sense of Jesus' words (which were not unknown to Justin)[38] could not dislodge from his mind the force of the interpretative principle that, where 'the angel of the Lord' is mentioned in the Old Testament narrative (especially if the phrase alternates, as it does in the narrative of the burning bush, with 'God' or 'the Lord'), it is Christ before his incarnation that is meant.

The inability of Jews and Gentiles to comprehend one another, despite their common Bible, is well illustrated in Justin's *Dialogue with Trypho*. Trypho is a Jew who has escaped from the disaster which befell the Jews of Palestine with the suppression of the second Jewish revolt against Rome (AD 135); he and Justin meet in Ephesus and fall into conversation. Justin tells Trypho how he was converted to Christian faith from Greek philosophy; Trypho smilingly suggests that it would have been better to stick to Plato than to desert him for the opinons of men of no repute. This leads them to discuss the issues between Christianity and Judaism: the two men are unprejudiced, friendly and courteous in their language, but they achieve no meeting of minds. Both appeal to the Old Testament, but they cannot agree on its meaning, because they argue from incompatible principles of interpretation. Quite often, indeed, the modern Christian reader is

[34] Is. 1:3 LXX.   [35] Justin, *First Apology*, 63.11f.
[36] Justin, *First Apology*, 63.5.
[37] Mark 12:24–27 par. Matt. 22:29–32 and Luke 20:34–38.
[38] Justin quotes Luke 20:35f. in *Dialogue with Trypho*, 81.4.

bound to agree with Trypho's interpretation against Justin's.

For example, they discuss the incident of the burning bush, just mentioned. After listening to Justin's interpretation, Trypho says, 'This is not what we understand from the words quoted: we understand that, while it was an *angel* that appeared in a flame of fire, it was *God* who spoke to Moses.'[39] Here Trypho's understanding is sounder than Justin's.

On the same principle Justin argues that it was Christ who announced Isaac's birth to Abraham and Sarah (Gen. 18:10),[40] who overthrew the cities of the plain (Gen. 19:23),[41] who spoke to Jacob in his dreams at Bethel and Paddan-aram and wrestled with him at Peniel (Gen. 28:13–15; 31:11–13; 32:24–30),[42] who appeared to Joshua as captain of the Lord's host (Josh. 5:13–15),[43] and so forth. All this Trypho finds quite unacceptable. Even more unacceptable to him is Justin's claim that Jewish rabbis have deliberately altered the text of scripture so as to obscure clear references to Christ. For instance, Justin's Greek text of Psalm 96:10 (LXX 95:10) read 'the Lord reigned *from the tree*' — to him a clear prediction of the crucifixion. Trypho's Bible did not contain these additional words (and neither does ours). 'Whether the rulers of our people', said Trypho, 'have erased any portion of the scriptures, as you allege, God knows; but it seems incredible.'[44] Again, Trypho was right.

Trypho even comes to the point of agreeing that Justin is right in saying that, according to the scriptures, the Messiah must suffer;[45] but that, he insists, does not prove Jesus to be the Messiah. After two days' discussion the two men part as friends, but neither has begun to convince the other.

Justin's exploitation of the *motif* of the 'real presence' of Christ in the Old Testament has passed into much traditional Christian theology, but it goes far beyond the interpretative tradition of the New Testament and indeed goes beyond the limits of the rational use of language.

Quite apart from the differences between the Hebrew text and the Septuagint, Jews and Christians could no longer be said to read the same scriptures in any material sense, in view of the divergent traditions of interpretation which they followed. The accepted Christian

---

[39] *Dialogue*, 60.1.   [40] *Dialogue*, 56.6–8.   [41] *Dialogue*, 56.18–21.
[42] *Dialogue* 58.   [43] *Dialogue*, 62.4f.   [44] *Dialogue*, 73.
[45] *Dialogue*, 90.1.

tradition became more sharply anti-Judaic, and the Jewish tradition in turn became increasingly careful to exclude renderings or interpretations, previously quite acceptable, which now proved to lend themselves all too readily to a Christian purpose.[46] So, in spite of the shared heritage of the holy book, the two opposed traditions hardened. Only in more recent times, with the acceptance on both sides of the principles of grammatico-historical exegesis, have the hard outlines softened, so that today Jews and Christians of varying traditions can collaborate happily in the common task of biblical interpretation.[47]

[46] Rabbi Aqiba's colleagues were scandalized when he seemed to accept the identification of the 'one like a son of man' of Dan. 7:13 with the Davidic Messiah (TB *Ḥagigah* 14a; *Sanhedrin* 38b). See also p.295 with n.37.

[47] But this collaboration can scarcely be expected to extend to the 'plenary sense' of the Old Testament as developed in Christian tradition; see pp.316–334.

CHAPTER FIVE

THE CHRISTIAN CANON
OF THE OLD TESTAMENT

A. IN THE EAST

Apart from a few fragments from pre-Christian generations, our witnesses to the text of the Septuagint are exclusively Christian. At an early date the Christians used the codex form and not the older scroll form for their copies of the Septuagint.[1] The oldest surviving Christian copies of the Septuagint have the form of codices. These are seven of the Chester Beatty biblical papyri (a collection, now in the Chester Beatty Museum and Library, Dublin, whose acquisition was first announced in 1931). As listed in the catalogue of Septuagint codices, they are Codd. 961 (Genesis), 962 (another copy of Genesis), 963 (Numbers—Deuteronomy). 964 (Ecclesiasticus), 965 (Isaiah), 966 (Jeremiah), 967/8 (Ezekiel, Daniel, Esther). (Another codex in the same collection contained the Greek text of 1 Enoch and the *Paschal Homily* of Melito, Bishop of Sardis.[2]) With three New Testament codices,[3] these apparently made up the Bible of a Greek-speaking church somewhere in Egypt. They were copied between the mid-second and late fourth centuries AD; they are all sadly defective but some are in a better condition than others.

[1] See C. H. Roberts and T. C. Skeat, *The Birth of the Codex* (London, 1983).
[2] See p. 70
[3] P^{45}, P^{46}, P^{47} in the catalogue of New Testament manuscripts. See pp. 129, 130.

THREE EARLY UNCIALS

The great uncial codices of the complete Greek Bible from the fourth and fifth centuries AD tell us something of the books which were acknowledged as having the status of holy scripture or at least being not unworthy to be bound up along with books of holy scripture. Here, for example, are the contents of the codices *Sinaiticus* (Aleph). *Vaticanus* (B) and *Alexandrinus* (A)[4], so far as their Old Testament part is concerned:

Sinaiticus 4th century:

Genesis..., Numbers..., Judges..., 1 & 2 Chronicles,[5] 1 & 2 Esdras, Tobit, Judith, 1 & 4 Maccabees, Isaiah, Jeremiah, Lamentations, the Twelve, Psalms, Proverbs, Ecclesiastes, Song of Songs, Wisdom, Sirach, Job. (Exodus, Leviticus and Deuteronomy are missing, as also are most of Joshua—4 Kingdoms; the text of the Twelve Prophets is incomplete.)

Vaticanus 4th century:

Genesis, Exodus, Leviticus, Numbers, Deuteronomy, Joshua,[6] Judges, Ruth, 1–4 Kingdoms, 1 & 2 Chronicles, 1 & 2 Esdras, Psalms, Proverbs, Ecclesiastes, Song of Songs, Job, Wisdom, Sirach, Esther, Judith, Tobit, the Twelve, Isaiah, Jeremiah, Baruch, Lamentations, Letter of Jeremiah, Ezekiel, Daniel. (The books of Maccabees are not included.)

Alexandrinus 5th century:

Genesis, Exodus, Leviticus, Numbers, Deuteronomy, Joshua, Judges, Ruth, 1–4 Kingdoms, 1 & 2 Chronicles, the Twelve, Isaiah, Jeremiah, Baruch, Lamentations, Letter of Jeremiah, Ezekiel, Daniel, Esther, Tobit, Judith, 1 & 2 Esdras, 1–4

[4] The use of letters of the alphabet as short-hand labels for the chief uncial manuscripts (manuscripts written in capital letters) was inadvertently begun by Brian Walton, bishop of Chester, who in his *Biblia Sacra Polyglotta* (London, 1655–57) used A to designate *Codex Alexandrinus*. B was later used to designate *Codex Vaticanus*, and so on. When Tischendorf discovered *Codex Sinaiticus*, he did not wish to do it the indignity of labelling it with a letter lower down the alphabet than A and B, so he designated it by *Aleph*, the first letter of the Hebrew alphabet.

[5] In this and all following lists of the Greek Old Testament books, 'Chronicles' translates Gk. *Paraleipomena* (see p.90, n.39.

[6] In LXX the book of Joshua is regularly called *Iēsous Nauē* (Latin *Jesus Nave*), i.e. 'Joshua (the son of) Nun', *Nauē* being a form which *Nun* took through corruption in the course of transmission.

Maccabees, Psalms, Job, Proverbs, Ecclesiastes, Song of Songs, Wisdom, Sirach, [Psalms of Solomon]. (The Psalms of Solomon, a collection of eighteen poems from the middle of the first century BC, were probably never accepted as holy scripture. The work is listed, at the end of *all* the biblical books, in the catalogue of contents prefaced to *Codex Alexandrinus*, but its text is not reproduced.)

JUSTIN MARTYR

The story of the origin of the Septuagint, as told in the *Letter of Aristeas*, is summarized by Justin Martyr (*c* AD 160), who evidently regards the Septuagint version as the only reliable text of the Old Testament. Where it differs from the Hebrew text, as read and interpreted by the Jews, the Jews (he says) have corrupted the text so as to obscure the scriptures' plain prophetic testimony to Jesus as the Christ.[7] He tells how the compositions of the prophets were read in the weekly meetings of Christians along with the memoirs of the apostles;[8] the memoirs of the apostles indicated the lines along which the prophets' words were to be understood.

MELITO OF SARDIS

Few of the early Christian writers had occasion to give a precise list of the Old Testament books recognized and used in their own circles; therefore, for our present purpose, special interest attaches to those who do give such a list. One of these was Melito, bishop of Sardis about AD 170. Melito's use of the Old Testament is well illustrated by his *Paschal Homily*,[9] which is based on the reading of the Exodus narrative; following the precedent set by Paul in 1 Cor. 5:7f.; 10:1–4, he expounds the narrative typologically with reference to Christ, but takes it for granted that the gospel story itself is well enough known to his hearers without its being necessary for him to appeal to any writing of the Christian age.

His list of Old Testament books is given in the course of a letter to a friend of his named Onesimus. For its preservation we are indebted to Eusebius, who has included in his *Ecclesiastical History* quotations from so many writers of the first three centuries AD whose works are otherwise lost (in whole or in part). Melito ascertained the number and

[7] See p.66.   [8] *First Apology*, 67.3. See p.127.   [9] See p.68.

names of the books, he tells us, during a visit to the east in which he 'reached the place where these things were preached and enacted'. So, he says,

> having learned accurately the books of the old covenant, I set them down and have sent them to you. These are their names:
> Five books of Moses—Genesis, Exodus, Numbers, Leviticus, Deuteronomy.
> Joshua the son of Nun, Judges, Ruth, four books of Kingdoms, two books of Chronicles.
> The Psalms of David, the Proverbs of Solomon (also called Wisdom), Ecclesiastes, the Song of Songs, Job.
> The Prophets: Isaiah, Jeremiah, the Twelve in a single book, Daniel, Ezekiel, Esdras.[10]

Melito's list probably includes all the books of the Hebrew Bible except Esther. Esdras will be Ezra-Nehemiah, reckoned as one book in the Hebrew enumeration, as in the Septuagint (2 Esdras), and Lamentations may have been reckoned along with Jeremiah as a sort of appendix to it. The order Numbers-Leviticus is no doubt a slip; the order of the prophetical books was not fixed. It is uncertain if Esdras is reckoned to be a prophet; if so, there is nothing surprising in that: any inspired writer was *ipso facto* a prophet. None of the writings in the 'Septuagintal plus' is listed: the 'Wisdom' included is not the Greek book of Wisdom but an alternative name for Proverbs. According to Eusebius, Hegesippus and Irenaeus and many other writers of their day called the Proverbs of Solomon 'the all-virtuous Wisdom'.[11]

Since Melito says that he ascertained the number and names of the books in Palestine, it may be that he derived them from a Jewish source. He is the first extant writer to describe them comprehensively as 'the books of the old covenant' (or Old Testament).[12] This does not necessarily imply that he would have called the evangelic and apostolic writings 'the books of the new covenant' (or New Testament); this expression is first attested a decade or two later.

A BILINGUAL LIST

Of uncertain date, but perhaps not far removed in time from Melito's list, is a list contained in a Greek manuscript copied in AD 1056,

---

[10] In Eusebius, *Hist. Eccl.* 4.26.12–14.   [11] *Hist. Eccl.* 4.22.9.
[12] See p. 180.

belonging to the library of the Greek patriarchate in Jerusalem, discovered in 1875 and published in 1883.[13] In this list the names of Old Testament books are given both in Aramaic (transcribed into the Greek alphabet) and in Greek.[14] Twenty-seven books are listed:[15]

> Genesis, Exodus, Leviticus, Joshua, Deuteronomy, Numbers, Ruth, Job, Judges, Psalms, 1 Samuel (= 1 Kingdoms), 2 Samuel (= 2 Kingdoms), 1 Kings (= 3 Kingdoms), 2 Kings (= 4 Kingdoms), 1 Chronicles, 2 Chronicles, Proverbs, Ecclesiastes, Song of Songs, Jeremiah, the Twelve, Isaiah, Ezekiel, Daniel, 1 Esdras, 2 Esdras, Esther.

If 1 and 2 Esdras are Ezra and Nehemiah,[16] and Lamentations was included with Jeremiah as an appendix, then these twenty-seven books are identical with the twenty-four of the Hebrew Bible, as usually reckoned. It is difficult to account for the bizarre order in which the books are listed. The list reappears, in a revised and tidier form, in a treatise by Epiphanius, fourth-century bishop of Salamis in Cyprus.[17]

ORIGEN

The next surviving Christian list of Old Testament books was drawn up by Origen (AD 185–254), the greatest biblical scholar among the Greek fathers. He spent the greater part of his life in his native Alexandria, where from an early age he was head of the catechetical school in the church of that city; then, in AD 231, he moved to Caesarea in Palestine, where he discharged a similar teaching ministry. He was an indefatigable commentator on the books of the Bible: to

[13] MS 54, folio 76a, discovered and published by Ph. Bryennios. It was this manuscript that first gave to the modern world the text of the *Didachē* ('Teaching of the Twelve Apostles').

[14] See J.-P. Audet, 'A Hebrew-Aramaic List of Books of the Old Testament in Greek Transcription', *JTS* n.s. 1 (1950), pp.135–154.

[15] The number twenty-seven may be intended to correspond to the twenty-two letters of the Hebrew alphabet plus the special forms which five of these letters take at the end of a word. See pp.90, 213.

[16] As in Origen (see p.74) and in the Latin Vulgate and versions dependent on it (see pp.90, 107).

[17] Epiphanius, *On Weights and Measures*, 23 (*cf* p.81). See also R. T. Beckwith, *The Old Testament Canon of the New Testament Church* (London, 1985), pp.188–190, 224, n.15.

this work he devoted his mastery of the long-established techniques of Alexandrian scholarship. One feature of his work which makes it difficult for students today to appreciate him as he deserves is his proneness to allegorical interpretation, but this was part and parcel of the intellectual tradition which he inherited, and indeed allegorization was the only means of extracting from large areas of the text a meaning which he and his contemporaries would have found acceptable.[18]

Origen's chief contribution to Old Testament studies was the compilation called the Hexapla (Greek for 'sixfold'). This was an edition of the Old Testament which exhibited side by side in six vertical columns (1) the Hebrew text, (2) the Hebrew text transcribed into Greek letters, (3) Aquila's Greek version, (4) Symmachus's Greek version, (5) the Septuagint, (6) Theodotion's Greek version. For certain books two and even three other Greek versions were added in further columns.[19] Origen paid special attention to the Septuagint column; his aim was to present as accurate an edition of this version as was possible. By means of critical signs, for example, he indicated places where the Septuagint omitted something found in the Hebrew text or added something absent from the Hebrew text. The Hexapla in its entirety probably never existed but in its original manuscript, but this was preserved at Caesarea for the use of scholars until the Arab conquest of Palestine in the seventh century. Eusebius and Jerome were among the students who made use of it.

Origen's list of Old Testament books, like Melito's, was preserved by Eusebius.[20] It comes in the course of his commentary on the first Psalm. There he says:

> We should not be ignorant that there are twenty-two books of the [Old] Testament, according to the tradition of the Hebrews, corresponding to the number of letters in their alphabet.... These are the twenty-two books according to the Hebrew:
> That which among us is entitled Genesis, but among the Hebrews, from the beginning of the book, *Bereshith*, that is 'in

---

[18] See R. P. C. Hanson, *Allegory and Event: A Study of the Sources and Significance of Origen's Interpretation of Scripture* (London, 1959); M. F. Wiles, 'Origen as Biblical Scholar', *CHB* I, pp.454–489. See p.195 below.

[19] Eusebius *Hist. Eccl.* 6.16 1–17.1.

[20] In *Hist. Eccl.* 6.25.1, 2. On Origen's treatment of the Old Testament scriptures see R. P. C. Hanson, *Origen's Doctrine of Tradition* (London, 1954), pp.133–137.

the beginning'. Exodus, *We-elleh shemoth*, that is, 'these are the names'. Leviticus, *Wayyiqra*, 'and he called'. Numbers, *Homesh piqqudim*[21]. Deuteronomy, *Elleh hadde barim*, 'these are the words'. Joshua the son of Nun, *Yoshua'ben-Nun*. Judges, and Ruth therewith in one book, *Shophetim*. 1 and 2 Kingdoms, one book with them, *Samuel*, 'the called of God'.[22] 3 and 4 Kingdoms in one book, *Wehammelekh Dawid*, that is 'the kingdom of David'.[23] 1 and 2 Chronicles in one book, *Dibrē yamim*, that is 'words of days'. 1 and 2 Esdras[24] in one book, *Ezra*, that is 'helper'. The book of Psalms, *Sephar tehillim*. The Proverbs of Solomon, *Me[sha]loth*.[25] Ecclesiastes, *Qoheleth*. Song of Songs (not, as some suppose, Songs of Songs), *Shir hash-shirim*. Isaiah, *Yesha'iah*. Jeremiah with Lamentations and the Epistle in one book, *Yirmeyahu*. Daniel, *Daniyyēl*. Ezekiel, *Hezeqi'ēl*. Job, *Hiyyōb*. Esther, *Esthēr*. Outside these are the books of Maccabees, entitled *Sar bēth sha-beñe'ēl*.[26]

Origen lists the books according to their Greek and Hebrew names. He excludes from his total of twenty-two the books of Maccabees (how many they are, he does not say). But (apart from Maccabees) he has listed only twenty-one books: one, namely the book of the Twelve Prophets, has accidentally dropped out in the course of transmission. His twenty-two books (when the book of the Twelve is restored to the

[21] Lit. 'the fifth of the musters (censuses)'. The five books of the Pentateuch were sometimes called 'the five fifths of the law'; each of them therefore was a 'fifth'. This name was given to Numbers (as was the LXX name *arithmoi*, 'numbers') because of the censuses of chapters 2 and 26. In the Hebrew Bible Numbers is designated $B^e midbar$, 'in the wilderness', from its first distinctive phrase, like the other Hebrew names of Pentateuchal books here reproduced by Origen.

[22] A reference perhaps to the etymology of ($s^e mû'ēl$), 'name of God'. In another place Origen explains the name as meaning 'There is God himself' ($sam hû'$ '$ēl$); see Hanson, *Allegory and Event*, p.170, n.6 (quoting *Homily* on 1 Sam. 1:5).

[23] These are the opening words of 1 Kings, but they mean 'and King David', not (as Origen mistranslates them) 'and the kingdom of David'.

[24] That is, Ezra-Nehemiah (as in Jerome's Vulgate).

[25] Eusebius's text reads *melōth*, from which something seems to have dropped out in transmission. The form $m^e \check{s}\bar{a}l\hat{o}t$ is an unusual plural of *māšal*, 'proverb' (the usual plural being $m^e \check{s}\bar{a}l\hat{i}m$).

[26] This was presumably the title of 1 Maccabees, which (unlike the other books of Maccabees) was originally written in Hebrew. It seems to mean 'prince of the house of the heroes' (lit. 'sons of God'), which may have been a designation of Judas Maccabaeus, the hero of the book. Another, but unnecessary, suggestion is that *sar* ('prince') has been corrupted from *sēfer* ('book').

list) correspond to the twenty-four of the Hebrew Bible, except that he includes the *Letter of Jeremiah* (an item in the 'Septuagintal plus') along with Lamentations as part of Jeremiah.

In this same commentary on Psalm 1 Origen enlarges on the appropriateness of the number twenty-two. 'For', he says, 'as the twenty-two letters appear to form an introduction to the wisdom and the divine teachings which are written down for men and women in these characters, so the twenty-two divinely-inspired books form an ABC into the wisdom of God and an introduction to the knowledge of all that is.'[27]

Origen's care to confine the books listed to those found in the Hebrew Bible (apart from his inclusion, perhaps by an oversight, of the 'Letter of Jeremiah') is the more noteworthy because the evidence suggests that the church of Alexandria, in which he was brought up, did not draw the boundaries of holy scripture very sharply. Clement of Alexandria, for example, quotes not only from the 'Septuagintal plus' but also from 4 Ezra, 1 Enoch and even from such an out-of-the-way work as the *Apocalypse of Zephaniah*.[28] But when Origen moved to Caesarea he not only found himself among Christians with a different tradition from that of Alexandria but also had opportunity of contact and discussion with Palestinian Jews.[29] From them he acquired some knowledge of the Hebrew language and Hebrew scriptures—enough to enable him to complete his *Hexapla* project—and it was plain to him that, when dealing with Jews, he could appeal to no authoritative scriptures but those which they acknowledged as canonical.

Even so, Origen made free use of the 'Septuagintal plus' and did not hesitate to refer to other works not even included in the Septuagint, without implying that they were among the books which are indisputably recognized as divinely inspired. His attitude to some books changed over the years. At one time, like Clement, he was happy to quote 1 Enoch as the work of the antediluvian patriarch, but later he doubted its authority.[30]

---

[27] This comes from a portion of his commentary on Psalm 1 preserved in *Philocalia* 3.

[28] What remains of this pseudepigraphic work (to be dated in the 1st century BC or 1st century AD) is edited and translated by O. S. Wintermute in *The Old Testament Pseudepigrapha*, ed. J. H. Charlesworth, I (Garden City, N.Y., 1983), pp. 497–515.

[29] He had already profited by the instruction of Jewish teachers in Alexandria; see N. R. M. de Lange, *Origen and the Jews* (Cambridge 1976), pp.25, 40.

[30] He quotes it as if it were holy scripture in *On First Principles* 1.3.3; 4.1.35 (from

His attitude to the 'Septuagintal plus' is interestingly illustrated by his letter to Julius Africanus.[31] Julius Africanus, born in Jerusalem, was a contemporary and friend of Origen. About AD 238 he read a controversial work by Origen in which appeal was made to the *History of Susanna*, one of the Septuagintal additions to Daniel, as though it were an integral part of Daniel. He spent some time considering this matter and preparing relevant arguments; then he sent a respectful letter to Origen in which he questioned the propriety of using the *History of Susanna* as though it belonged to the authentic book of Daniel. It was evident, he pointed out, that the *History of Susanna* was originally written in Greek, because the crux of the story turned on a double pun which was possible only in Greek. In the story Daniel conducts a separate examination of each of the two false witnesses against Susanna and asks under what kind of tree her alleged offence was committed; he receives inconsistent answers and pronounces an appropriate doom against each. To the one who specifies a mastic tree (Gk *schinos*) he says, 'God will cut you in two' (*schizō̄);*[32] to the one who specifies a holm-oak (Gk. *prinos*) he says, 'God will saw you asunder' (Gk. *priō̄*).[33] At one time Origen himself had acknowledged the force of this argument: according to Jerome, he expressed agreement with those in whose judgment this section was composed in Greek. But in replying to Julius Africanus he points out that there are many things in the Greek Bible which are not found in the Hebrew text, and the church cannot be expected to give them all up.[34] As for the double pun, Origen had consulted several Jews but none of them could give him the Hebrew names of the trees in question: he does not rule out the possibility that there might be two Hebrew names of trees which did lend themselves to such a play on words. He implies, too, that the *History of Susanna* is an excellent theme for rich allegorical

---

his Alexandrian period); later, in *Against Celsus* 5.54, he says, 'the books superscribed with Enoch's name are by no means recognized in the churches as divine' (similar reservations are expressed in his *Commentary on John* 6:42; *Homily* on Num. 8:2). See Hanson, *Origen's Doctrine of Tradition*, p.136; A. C. Sundberg, *The Old Testament in the Early Church* (Cambridge, Mass., 1964), pp.165f.; R. M. Grant, *The Formation of the New Testament* (London, 1965), p.170.

[31] Translated, with Africanus's letter to which it is a reply, in ANF IV, pp.385–392.

[32] Susanna 54f.

[33] Susanna 58f. The verb is that used in Heb. 11:37 ('they were sawn in two'), where Origen (*Letter to Africanus*, 9) sees a reference to the martyrdom of Isaiah.

[34] Cf Jerome, *Commentary on Daniel*, prologue; also on Dan. 13:54–59.

interpretation.[35] One might get the impression that, where the relation of the Hebrew Bible to the Septuagint is concerned, Origen is anxious to eat his cake and have it. He is certainly unwilling to deviate from the regular practice of the church.[36]

ATHANASIUS

Unfortunately, for the bulk of Origen's work we are dependent on Latin translations, especially the translation of Rufinus of Aquileia (c 345–410), carried out well over a century after Origen's death. Rufinus thought it proper to conform Origen's language to the orthodoxy and usage of a later age. For example, he represents Origen as using the word 'canon' in the sense of 'canon of scripture', as we understand the term.[37] But it is a near-certainty that Origen never used the Greek word *kanōn* in this sense. The first writer known to have used it thus is Athanasius, bishop of Alexandria. In one of his works[38] Athanasius mentions the *Shepherd* of Hermas (a work which elsewhere he calls 'a most profitable book')[39] as 'not belonging to the canon'.[40] More often he uses the verb *kanonizō* ('canonize') in the sense 'include in the canon'. This is so in his most important treatment of the subject.

One of the minor decisions of the Council of Nicaea (AD 325) was that, to guard against any disagreement about fixing the date of Easter, the bishop of Alexandria should have the privilege, year by year, of informing his brother bishops (well in advance) of the date of the following Easter. Throughout his long tenure of that see (328–373) Athanasius issued forty-five such 'festal letters'. In each he took the opportunity of dealing with some other matter of current importance. In the thirty-ninth letter, announcing the date of Easter in 367, he dealt with the canon of the Old and New Testaments.[41] He

[35] *Letter to Africanus*, 15.

[36] In his *Commentary on Matthew* (part 2, 61), he says that he quotes from the *History of Susanna*, although he knows that it is not in the Hebrew Bible, 'because it is received in the churches'. See Hanson, *Origen's Doctrine of Tradition*, p.134.

[37] In the Latin translation of his *Homily* on Joshua 2:1 there is a reference to the *Assumption of Moses*, 'although it is not received in the canon', but the words (*licet in canone non habeatur*) are those of Rufinus.

[38] *On the Decrees* (= *Defence of the Nicene Definition*), 18.

[39] *On the Incarnation of the Divine Word*, 3.

[40] Gk. *mē on ek tou kanonos*.

[41] An English translation of this letter is provided in NPCF, series 2, IV, pp.551f.

was concerned about the introduction by some people of heretical or spurious works (which he calls 'apocryphal') among the books of holy scripture, and goes on, echoing the prologue to Luke's gospel:

> Inasmuch as some have taken in hand to draw up for themselves an arrangement of the so-called apocryphal books and to intersperse them with the divinely inspired scripture, concerning which we have been fully persuaded, even as those who from the beginning were eyewitnesses and ministers of the word delivered it to the fathers: it has seemed good to me also, having been stimulated thereto by true brethren, to set forth in order the books which are included in the canon and have been delivered to us with accreditation that they are divine. My purpose is that each one who has been led astray may condemn those who have led him astray and that those who have remained untarnished may rejoice at having these things brought to remembrance again.
>
> The books of the Old Testament, then, are twenty-two in number, for (as I have heard) this is the traditional number of letters among the Hebrews.

He then lists them by name in order, after the following pattern:

1. Genesis
2. Exodus
3. Leviticus
4. Numbers
5. Deuteronomy
6. Joshua the son of Nun
7. Judges
8. Ruth
9. 1 and 2 Kingdoms
10. 3 and 4 Kingdoms
11. 1 and 2 Chronicles
12. 1 and 2 Esdras[42]
13. Psalms
14. Proverbs
15. Ecclesiastes
16. Song of Songs
17. Job

---

[42] Ezra-Nehemiah.

18. The Twelve Prophets
19. Isaiah
20. Jeremiah, with Baruch, Lamentations and the Epistle
21. Ezekiel
22. Daniel

Athanasius's total is the same as Origen's, but he lists Ruth separately from Judges and omits Esther.

Athanasius then lists the New Testament books.[43] He follows with some general comments on the unique value of holy scripture (including the admonition: 'Let no one add to these nor take anything from them'),[44] and continues:

> But for the sake of greater accuracy I must needs, as I write, add this: there are other books outside these, which are not indeed included in the canon, but have been appointed from the time of the fathers to be read to those who are recent converts to our company and wish to be instructed in the word of true religion. These are the Wisdom of Solomon, the Wisdom of Sirach, Esther, Judith and Tobit[45] . . . But while the former are included in the canon and the latter are read [in church], no mention is to be made of the apocryphal works. They are the invention of heretics, who write according to their own will, and gratuitously assign and add to them dates so that, offering them as ancient writings, they may have an excuse for leading the simple astray.

As Athanasius includes Baruch and the 'Letter of Jeremiah' in one book with Jeremiah and Lamentations, so he probably includes the Greek additions to Daniel in the canonical book of that name, and the additions to Esther in the book of that name which he recommends for reading in church. He makes no mention of the books of Maccabees.

Evidently Athanasius makes a distinction between those books which are 'included in the canon' and others which are recommended for their inspirational and edifying quality. Only those works which

---

[43] See p.208.

[44] See p.23. Compare Novatian, *On the Trinity*, 16: 'But woe is pronounced on those who add, as also on those who take away.'

[45] He adds the *Didachē* and the *Shepherd* here; these bear the same relation to the canonical books of the New Testament as the five just listed bear to those of the Old Testament.

belong to the Hebrew Bible (apart from Esther)[46] are worthy of inclusion in the canon (the additions to Jeremiah and Daniel make no appreciable difference to this principle); other works belonging to the 'Septuagintal plus', however great their value, are relegated to a second grade. The 'apocryphal' writings are not those which have been called so since Jerome's time (i.e., for the most part, the 'Septuagintal plus'), but heretical works: they are subversive and ought to be utterly rejected.

In practice Athanasius appears to have paid little attention to the formal distinction between those books which he listed in the canon and those which were suitable for the instruction of new Christians. He was familiar with the text of all, and quoted from them freely, often with the same introductory formulae— 'as it is written', 'as the scripture says', etc.

CANONS OF LAODICEA

Shortly before Athanasius issued his thirty-ninth festal letter, a church council was held at Laodicea in the Lycus valley (c AD 363). The 'canons' or rules promulgated by this council were acknowledged by later church councils as a basis of canon law.[47] Canon 59 lays it down that 'no psalms composed by private individuals or any uncanonical (akanonista) books may be read in church, but only the canonical books (kanonika) of the New and Old Testament'. Canon 60 (the last of the series) then enumerates those canonical books. But the genuineness of Canon 60 is open to doubt; it is probably indebted to the canon of Athanasius and other lists. It follows Athanasius closely, except that Ruth is attached to Judges as part of No. 7 and Esther follows immediately as No. 8.

LATER GREEK FATHERS

In the last two decades of the fourth century other Greek fathers drew up lists of the canonical books, to much the same effect as their predecessors. Cyril, bishop of Jerusalem from 348 to 386, gives a list

[46] He does not say in so many words why Esther is not included in the canon: he may have inherited a tradition, going back possibly to a Jewish source, which denied it canonical status; cf what is said below of Gregory Nazianzen and Amphilochius. See further J. Ruwet, 'Le canon alexandrin des écritures: Saint Athanase', Biblica 33 (1952), pp. 1–29.

[47] See NPNF, series 2, XIV, pp. 125–160; a translation of Canons 59 and 60 appears on pp. 158f.

which follows Origen's, except that Baruch is included in one book with Jeremiah, as well as Lamentations and the 'Letter of Jeremiah'.[48] Gregory of Nazianzus (c 330–390) may have been the first of many down the ages to produce a list of books of the Bible in verse, for easier memorization. In order to accommodate the names of the books he had to employ a variety of metres. Like Athanasius, he gives the total of Old Testament books as twenty-two and omits Esther.[49] Another metrical canon was drawn up by Amphilochius, bishop of Iconium, who died some time after 394. After listing the same Old Testament books as Gregory, he adds a line: 'Along with these some include Esther.'[50] We have mentioned already that Epiphanius (c 315–403) adapts an earlier bilingual list which yields a total of twenty-seven Old Testament books.[51] In another place Epiphanius appends the Wisdom of Solomon and Ben Sira to a list of *New* Testament books.[52]

THEODORE OF MOPSUESTIA AND OTHERS

Theodore, bishop of Mopsuestia (modern Misis) in S. E. Cilicia from 392 to 428, is best known as the most illustrious exponent of the exegetical school of Antioch. Some of his views on the canonicity of Old Testament books were regarded as dangerously radical. In his commentary on Job he denies the 'higher inspiration' of Proverbs and Ecclesiastes.[53] Of the Song of Songs he had no great opinion at all.[54] He rejected the traditional titles to the Psalms and was suspected of rejecting Job and Chronicles.[55]

---

[48] See NPNF, series 2, VII, p.27 (*Catechetical Lecture*, 4.35).

[49] Gregory, Hymn 1.1.12.31, lines 11–29.

[50] Amphilochius, *Iambics to Seleucus*, lines 251–288. He goes on to list the New Testament books (see.p.212), and concludes with the words: 'This would be the most unerring canon of the divinely inspired books.' He is the next writer after Athanasius to use 'canon' (GK. *kanōn*) in this sense.

[51] See p.72 with n.17.

[52] Epiphanius, *Panarion* 76.5. Compare the mention of Wisdom in the Muratorian list.

[53] The expression is H. B. Swete's (*DCB*, IV, *sv* 'Theodorus of Mopsuestia', p.940). See also M. F. Wiles, 'Theodore of Mopsuestia as Representative of the Antiochene School', *CHB* I, pp.489–510.

[54] See Swete, *ibid.*

[55] Leontius of Byzantium, *Against the Nestorians and Eutychians*, 3.12–16. See A. C. Sundberg, *The Old Testament of the Early Church*, pp.144f.; R. T. Beckwith, *The Old Testament Canon of the New Testament Church*, pp.190f., 225, n.22, 307–310, 333, n.138.

The earliest form of the Syriac Old Testament appears to have lacked Esther, Ezra-Nehemiah and Chronicles. This might be because their canonicity was doubted, or it might be a fortuitous consequence of the fact that these books are the last in the traditional sequence of the Hebrw scriptures.[56]

The further history of the canon among eastern Christians will not be surveyed here: suffice it to say that in 1642 and 1672 respectively Orthodox synods at Jassy (Iasi) and Jerusalem confirmed as 'genuine parts of scripture' the contents of the 'Septuagintal plus' (the canonicity of which had been taken for granted), specifically: 1 Esdras (= Vulgate 3 Esdras), Tobit, Judith, 1, 2 and 3 Maccabees, Wisdom, Ben Sira (Ecclesiasticus), Baruch and the *Letter of Jeremiah*. The Septuagint remains the 'authorized version' of the Old Testament in Greek Orthodoxy, its deviations from the traditional Hebrew text being ascribed to divine inspiration. Most Orthodox scholars today, however, follow Athanasius and others in placing the books of the 'Septuagintal plus' on a lower level of authority than the 'proto-canonical' writings.[57]

---

[56] In view of the fact that Theodore was Nestorius's teacher, it is noteworthy that the Nestorians also omitted Ecclesiastes and the Song of Songs; see F. P. W. Buhl, *Canon and Text of the Old Testament*, E. T. (Edinburgh, 1892), p.53; L. Rost, 'Zur Geschichte des Kanons bei den Nestorianern', *ZNW* 27 (1928), pp.103–106; R. T. Beckwith, *The Old Testament Canon of the New Testament Church*, pp.191f., 195–197.

[57] See T. [Kallistos] Ware, *The Orthodox Church* (Harmondsworth, 1963), pp.208f.; also M. Jugie, *Histoire du canon d l'Ancien Testament dans l'église grecque et l'église russe* (Paris, 1909).

CHAPTER SIX

THE CHRISTIAN CANON
OF THE OLD TESTAMENT

B. IN THE LATIN WEST

The Bible began to be translated into Latin, so far as can be ascertained, in the latter half of the second century AD, in the Roman province of Africa. The province of Africa was Latin-speaking, so far as official usage is concerned; this was pre-eminently true of Roman Carthage, refounded as a colony in 46 BC. The need for a Latin version of the scriptures was realized here decades before a similar need was felt in Rome itself. The Jewish community in Rome was largely Greek-speaking, and so was the church, from the first beginnings of Roman Christianity in the 40s of the first century until the end of the second century.[1]

Until Jerome produced a new translation of the Old Testament from the Hebrew text at the end of the fourth century, the Latin Old Testament was a rendering of the Septuagint, including the 'Septua-gintal plus'. There was little if anything to indicate to readers of the

---

[1] Victor, bishop of Rome towards the end of the second century, is said to have been the first Roman bishop to write in Latin (Jerome, *On Illustrious Men, 34*). The first Christian treatise in Latin to have survived is Novatian, *On the Trinity* (written shortly before AD 250). In this treatise all the christological proof-texts are drawn from the Old Testament.

Old Latin version that the 'Septuagintal plus' stood on a different footing from the rest of the Old Testament.[2]

TERTULLIAN

Tertullian of Carthage is the first writer to be considered among the Latin fathers: he flourished at the end of the second century and the beginning of the third. He calls the two Testaments 'instruments' (Latin *instrumenta*), using the word in its legal sense. The Old Testament is 'the whole instrument of Jewish literature';[3] he gives the impression that he knows exactly what it contains, although he nowhere gives a list of its contents. His Old Testament was evidently co-extensive with the Septuagint (including the 'Septuagint plus'); indeed, in one place he implies that it might justifiably be extended beyond the limits of the Septuagint.[4]

It is not enough to locate and list quotations from various 'fringe' books, or allusions to them. A Christian writer may quote works to which he would not dream of ascribing divine authority (as Paul, for example, quotes Menander in 1 Cor. 15:33).[5] The quotation or allusion must be accompanied by words which show that the writer did regard it as holy scripture. Thus, when Tertullian (*Against Marcion*, 4.11) quotes 'Come, my bride, from Lebanon' (Cant. 4:8), it is plain that he acknowledges the Song of Songs as divinely inspired, for he takes the words to be addressed by Christ to the church.

He regards Wisdom as a genuine work of Solomon,[6] and the 'Letter of Jeremiah' as authentically Jeremiah's.[7] The Song of the Three Habrews[8] and the story of Bel and the Dragon[9] are to him integral parts of Daniel. On the other hand, we cannot prove that he regarded Judith as canonical because he cites Judith (who remained unmarried after her husband's death) as an example of monogamy, or 1 Maccabees

[2] The 'books' in the possession of the Scillitan martyrs (*c.* AD 180) along with the letters of Paul may have been parts of the Old Testament; see pp.183f.

[3] *On Women's Dress*, 1.3.   [4] See below, p.85 (on 1 Enoch).

[5] The line 'Evil communications corrupt good manners' (AV/KJV) comes from Menander's comedy *Thais*; it had probably passed into general circulation as a proverbial saying (like so many lines from Shakespeare).

[6] Wisdom 1:1 is ascribed to Solomon in *Prescription*, 7, and in *Against the Valentinians*, 2.

[7] *Letter of Jeremiah* 3 (Baruch 6:3) is ascribed to Jeremiah in *Scorpion Antidote*, 8.5.

[8] See references to Dan. 3:49f. (LXX) in *On Prayer*, 29.1, to Dan. 3:58–79 in *Against Hermogenes*, 44.4, to Dan. 3:52–68 in *Against Marcion*, 5.11.1.

[9] See references in *On Idolatry*, 17f., in *On Fasting*, 7.

because he refers to the freedom fighters' resolution to resist their assailants even on the sabbath, to show that the weekly sabbath was intended to be a temporary provision.[10] But the probability is that he did regard Judith and 1 Maccabees, with the rest of the 'Septuagintal plus', as part of the ancient 'instrument'.

The Apocalypse of Ezra (4 Ezra) was never included in the Septuagint (for this reason its Greek text has not survived).[11] But Tertullian knows and accepts its account of Ezra's restoring the sacred scriptures of Israel which had been destroyed at the time of the Babylonian conquest.[12] Another work which found no place in the Septuagint was the composite apocalyptic work called 1 Enoch[13] (only about one-third of its Greek text has survived). The Ethiopic church is the only part of Christendom to have canonized it (for this reason it is only in the Ethiopic version that it is extant in its entirety). A number of early Christian writers mention it with reservations,[14] but Tertullian approved of it, and would have been willing to see it included in the ancient *instrumentum*. (He knew that he was incompetent to include it on his own initiative; the canonization of religious writings is not an individual responsibility.) One reason for his approval of it was the fact that it was quoted, evidently as a genuine prophecy of the antediluvian patriarch Enoch, by Jude, who calls himself 'servant of Jesus Christ and brother of James' (Jude 1, 14f.).[15] But that in itself would not have been enough; others were disposed to exclude Jude from the New Testament because of its quoting a work of doubtful authenticity. There was the further, and quite potent reason that Tertullian's attitude to the subject of his treatise On Women's Dress was

[10] Judith 8:4, in *On Monogamy*, 17; 1 Macc. 2:41, in *Answer to the Jews*, 4.

[11] See p.47, n.11. Its Christian prologue (chapters 1, 2) and epilogue (chapters 15, 16) are sometimes designated 5 and 6 Esdras (Ezra) respectively. When God says in 4 Ezra 7:28 that 'my Son the Messiah' will be revealed and then, after 400 years, die, this is the expected Messiah of David's line (4 Ezra 12:32) but has nothing to do with the Christian Messiah (even if the Latin version calls him 'Jesus' in 7:28).

[12] See p.36.

[13] See p.51. Since Enoch (whose name in Hebrew may mean 'initiated') was translated from earth to heaven (Gen. 5:24; cf. Heb. 11:5), he was envisaged as a suitable recipient of special revelations. Two other collections of Enoch literature are 2 Enoch (the *Book of the Secrets of Enoch*), composed in Greek but extant only in a Slavonic version, and 3 Enoch (also called the 'Hebrew Enoch' or the *Book of the Palaces*), a work of Jewish mysticism. All three are translated, with introductions, in J. H. Charlesworth (ed.), *The Old Testament Pseudepigrapha*, I (Garden City, N.Y., 1983), pp.5–315.

[14] E.g. Clement of Alexandria and Origen (see pp.75, 191).   [15] See p.193.

reinforced by the statement in 1 Enoch 8:1 that it was Azaz'el, leader of the fallen angels,[16] who first introduced women to 'bracelets, decorations, antimony (for eye-shadow), ornamentation, the beautifying of the eyelids, all kinds of precious stones, and all colouring tinctures'.[17]

The second section of 1 Enoch, comprising chapters 37–71, is commonly called the 'Parables of Enoch'; it is of different authorship from chapters 1–36 and probably of later date. In it God is repeatedly called 'the Lord of spirits'. Tertullian gives this title to God in his work *Against Marcion* (5.11.8). Actually, he intends to quote 2 Corinthians 3:18, 'from the Lord who is the Spirit' (lit. 'from the Lord the Spirit'), but he quotes it from memory, and his memory has been influenced by this similar expression, which he may owe to acquaintance with the 'Parables of Enoch'.

Since 1 Enoch is not included in the Hebrew Bible, nor yet in the Septuagint (which was, of course, a Jewish translation), Tertullian hazards the unworthy suspicion (of a kind which he was not alone among early Christians in entertaining)[18] that it was rejected by Jews because it spoke of Christ. He may have had in mind the figure of 'the Son of Man' who appears here and there throughout the 'Parables of Enoch'; but that 'Son of Man' is not Jesus— he turns out, in fact, to be identified with Enoch himself.[19]

A compilation to which Tertullian and other early Christian writers assigned genuine prophetic authority was the *Sibylline Oracles*. The *Sibylline Oracles* which they knew were Jewish and Christian poems composed in an oracular idiom at various times between 200 BC and AD 250.[20] But those writers who quote them took them at face value as the genuine prophecies of an ancient pagan prophetess— 'the Sibyl', says Tertullian, 'who antedated all literature and was a true prophetess of truth.'[21] In an attack on idolatry he quotes from the third *Sibylline Oracle* (written by Jews in Egypt about the middle of the second century BC) to the effect that in the tenth generation after the flood

[16] Azaz'el appears in Lev. 16:8, 10, 26, as the being to whom the scapegoat was dedicated on the annual day of atonement.

[17] Tertullian, *On Women's Dress*, 1.3.

[18] Compare Justin Martyr's charge (p.66).

[19] At the end of the *Parables of Enoch* Enoch is transported to 'the heaven of heavens' and told by an angel, 'You are that Son of Man' (1 Enoch 71:14).

[20] They are edited and translated by J. J. Collins in *The Old Testament Pseudepigrapha*, ed. Charlesworth, I, pp.317–472.

[21] *To the Nations*, 2.12.

'there reigned Kronos, Titan and Iapetos, the mighty children of Gaia and Ouranos' (Tertullian gives the Latin equivalents of those names: 'Saturn, Titan and Iapetus, the mighty children of Terra and Caelum').[22] But it was not suggested that the *Sibylline Oracles* should be included in the Jewish or Christian holy scriptures: to those who took them at face value they constituted a parallel body of divine prophecy, communicated and transmitted through Gentiles. Hence the mediaeval hymn *Dies Irae* speaks of

> That day of wrath, that dreadful day,
> When heaven and earth shall pass away,
> As David and the Sibyl say.[23]

David, representing Old Testament prophecy, stands here alongside the Sibyl as foretelling the final dissolution of the created universe.

Tertullian may stand for all the Latin fathers before the time of Jerome: the Bible which they used provided them with no means of distinguishing those parts which belonged to the Hebrew canon from those which were found only in the Septuagint. It appears that in several of their copies Baruch was appended to Jeremiah rather than distinguished as a separate book: Cyprian, Hilary and Ambrose all quote from Baruch but ascribe the words quoted to Jeremiah.[24]

JEROME

Eusebius Sofronius Hieronymus, to give Jerome his formal Latin name, was born in AD 346 or 347 at Stridon in Dalmatia. His parents, who were Christians, were able to give him an excellent education. He came to Rome in his 'teens to perfect his classical studies in the school of Donatus, one of the most celebrated grammarians of his day.[25] In due course he became a master of Greek as well as Latin literature. As the result of a nearly fatal illness at Antioch in 374 he resolved

---

[22] *Sibylline Oracle,* 3.108−111.

[23] The David reference may be to Ps. 102:26 (cf. Heb. 1:11f.); the Sibyl reference is to *Oracle* 2.196−213, which describes the destruction of the universe in the final conflagration (cf. 2 Pet. 3:10−12).

[24] Cyprian in *Testimonies against the Jews,* 2.6 (quoting Baruch 3:35−37), Hilary, *On the Trinity,* 4.42: 5.39 (quoting the same passage); Ambrose, *On the Faith,* 1.3.28 (quoting the same passage), *On Penitence,* 1.9.43 (quoting Baruch 3:1f.).

[25] Jerome, *Apology against Rufinus,* 1.16, 30.

thenceforth to devote himself to biblical, no longer to secular, literature.[26] He spent the next four or five years leading the life of a hermit in the desert east of Antioch; he pursued sacred learning unremittingly and began to study Hebrew with the aid of a Jewish Christian. At the same time he familiarized himself with the Aramaic vernacular of the country regions around him. After this period of seclusion he returned to Antioch and was ordained to the presbyterate.

He was present in 381 at the Council of Constantinople and went from there to Rome, perhaps to attend the Council held there in 382 to review the acts of the Constantinopolitan Council.[27] In Rome he was invited to stay on and give secretarial and other help to Pope Damasus. Among the services which Damasus asked him to perform was the revision of the existing Latin Bible—a necessary service, because of the unsatisfactory condition of the text (according to Jerome himself, there were almost as many different forms of text as there were copies).[28] Between 382 and 384 he produced a new Latin version of the four gospels and a revision of the Latin Psalter (for which he had recourse not only to the best accessible manuscripts of the Septuagint but also to Aquila's Greek translation).[29] This revision of the Psalter, the 'Roman Psalter' (as it is called to distinguish it from his later 'Gallican Psalter' and 'Hebrew Psalter'), is held by many to be the version of the Psalter still used in St Peter's basilica in Rome.

Damasus died in 384. Jerome may have been encouraged to think of himself as a possible successor,[30] but mercifully (for the church's sake and for his own) he was not elected, and soon afterwards he left Rome for good. After two years' pilgrim journeys in the Near East, he settled in Bethlehem, where he established a monastery for himself and spent the rest of his life in biblical study and other literary activity.

To begin with, he planned to continue revising the Latin Old Testament by reference to the Septuagint. He produced a further revision of the Psalms, for which he availed himself of Origen's *Hexapla* at Caesarea (this 'Gallican Psalter', as it is called, is the version of the Psalter reproduced to this day in editions of the Latin Vulgate). But he soon became convinced that the only satisfactory way to translate the Old Testament was to cut loose from the Septuagint and

---

[26] It was at this time that he had his vision of the day of judgment in which he was charged with being a Ciceronian rather than a Christian (*Epistle* 22.30).

[27] See p.97.

[28] *Epistle Prefatory to the Gospels* (addressed to Damasus).

[29] *Epistle* 32.1; 36.12.   [30] *Epistle* 45.3.

work from the original Hebrew — the 'Hebrew verity', as he called it.[31] Accordingly, he gave himself to this task and completed the translation of the Hebrew Bible into Latin in 405. This work included a further version of the Psalter, the 'Hebrew Psalter', a rendering direct from the original; religious conservatism, however, preferred to go on using the more familiar wording based on the Septuagint.[32]

For this work Jerome needed to perfect his knowledge of Hebrew, and did not hesitate to rely on the help of Jewish teachers. Of these he mentions three: a Jew from Tiberias who helped him with the translation of Chronicles;[33] one from Lydda, 'reputed to be of the highest standing among the Hebrews', whom he hired to help him to understand the book of Job;[34] and Bar Anina, who came to him by night at Bethlehem 'like another Nicodemus' (fearing the disapproval of his fellow-Jews if he were known to give this kind of assistance to a Christian) to give him lessons in Hebrew.[35] Jerome's dependence on Jewish instructors increased the suspicion of some of his Christian critics who were put off in any case by such an innovation as a translation of the sacred writings from Hebrew (with its implied disparagement of the divinely-inspired Septuagint).[36]

Jerome's study of the Hebrew Bible quickly made him aware of the question of the 'Septuagintal plus'. The first books which he translated from Hebrew were Samuel and Kings, and in his prologue to their translation (the 'Helmeted Prologue', as he called it)[37] he set out the principles on which he proposed to work. He begins by enumerating the books of the Hebrew Bible. He knows the Jewish reckoning of the total as twenty-four (comparable, he says, with the twenty-four elders

---

[31] *Epistle* 106.9; *Apology against Rufinus*, 2.33.

[32] Similarly the Great Bible version of the Psalms (1539), naturally used in the Edwardian editions of the Book of Common Prayer (1549, 1552), was not replaced by the superior AV/KJV rendering when the Prayer Book was repromulgated in 1662, but remains in use to this day.

[33] *Prologue to Chronicles* (translation from the Septuagint).

[34] *Prologue to Job*.

[35] *Epistle* 84.3.

[36] For example, Rufinus, who had formerly been a friend of Jerome's but ceased to be so after Jerome's criticisms of his translation of Origen, accused him of hiring help from the 'synagogue of Satan'; the authority of the Seventy, he said, inspired by the Holy Spirit and confirmed by the apostles, cannot be overthrown by the authority of one man 'under the inspiration of Barabbas' (*Apology against Jerome*, 2.30, 33).

[37] *Prologus galeatus*, because it stood in front of his translation to defend the principles on which he carried it out.

of the Apocalypse),[38] but he prefers to reckon them as twenty-two (taking Ruth with Judges and Lamentations with Jeremiah), corresponding to the number of letters in the Hebrew alphabet.[39] Or, if allowance be made for the five letters which have special final forms, the total could be reckoned as twenty-seven (Samuel, Kings, Chronicles, Ezra-Nehemiah and Jeremiah-Lamentations being split into two books each).

Then he goes on:

> Whatever falls outside these must be set apart among the Apocrypha. Therefore Wisdom, which is commonly entitled Solomon's, with the book of Jesus the son of Sirach,[40] Judith, Tobias[41] and the *Shepherd* are not in the canon. I have found the first book of Maccabees in Hebrew;[42] the second is in Greek, as may be proved from the language itself.[43]

It is strange to find the *Shepherd* listed among the *Old* Testament Apocrypha.[44] But Jerome's use of the term 'Apocrypha' calls for comment. Athanasius had distinguished three categories of books: canonical, edifying (but not canonical) and apocryphal. The 'edifying' books (the Wisdom of Solomon and of Ben Sira, Esther, Judith and Tobit, with the *Didachē* and the *Shepherd* from the New Testament age) might be read in church; the 'apocryphal' books were to be avoided altogether. This threefold distinction was maintained, among the Latin fathers, by Rufinus of Aquileia (c. 345–410), who referred to the second category as 'ecclesiastical' books.[45] But those 'ecclesias-

---

[38] So also in the prologue to Daniel he says: 'I point out that, among the Hebrews, Daniel is not included among the Prophets but among those who composed the Hagiographa (sacred writings). By them all scripture is divided into three parts, the Law, the Prophets and the Hagiographa—that is, into five plus eight plus eleven books.'

[39] In this reckoning the third division comprises nine, not eleven books, which Jerome enumerates thus: Job, Psalms, Proverbs, Ecclesiastes, Song of Songs, Daniel, Chronicles (for which the Latin Bible took over the Greek title *Paraleipomena*), Ezra-Nehemiah (in the Latin Bible, 1 and 2 Esdras), Esther.

[40] Jerome follows the Greek spelling Sirach (see p.31).

[41] In the Greek Bible Tobit is the father (after whom the book is named), Tobias is the son. In the Latin Bible both father and son (and book) are commonly called Tobias.

[42] The Hebrew text has disappeared, but may occasionally be discerned behind the translation-Greek. For the title of the Hebrew book see p.74 with n.26.

[43] See p.46.   [44] See p.166.

[45] Rufinus, *On the Creed*, 38: 'our fathers', he says, 'called them "ecclesiastical".' A generation earlier, Hilary of Poitiers (c. 315–367) follows Origen's list when

tical' books are designated 'apocryphal' by Jerome. This term originally meant 'hidden'; it was applicable, for example, to the seventy books which Ezra is said to have copied along with the twenty-four 'public' books: the seventy were to be delivered in secret to the wise among the people (4 Ezra 14:26, 46f.).[46] But it is the usage of a word, not its etymology, that determines its meaning. Origen indeed suggests in his letter to Africanus that the story of Susanna had been 'hidden among the Hebrews at a remote date and preserved only by the more learned and honest'; but he intends in no way to under-value Susanna.[47] Indeed, he says, the Jewish authorities hid from the knowledge of the people any passages which contained any scandal against elders, rulers or judges, some of which have been preserved in 'apocryphal' writings.[48] Tobit and Judith, he was informed by Jews, were not to be found even among the Hebrew 'apocryphal' books, yet they were valued and used in the church.[49]

Jerome's precise view on the function of the works which he relegated as 'apocryphal' is made clear in his prologue to 'the three books of Solomon' (Proverbs, Ecclesiastes and the Song of Songs):

> There circulates also the 'all-virtuous'[50] Wisdom of Jesus the son of Sira, together with a similar work, the pseudepigraph entitled the Wisdom of Solomon.[51] The former of these I have also found in Hebrew, entitled not 'Ecclesiasticus', as among the Latins, but 'Parables'.[52] ... The latter is nowhere found among the Hebrews: its very style smacks of Greek eloquence, and several ancient writers affirm it to be the work of Philo the Jew.[53] Therefore as the church indeed reads Judith, Tobit and

---

enumerating the Old Testament books (*Tractates on the Psalms*, introduction, 15) but in his writings generally cites the 'Septuagintal plus' in much the same terms as the books found in the Hebrew Bible.

[46] See p.36.   [47] *Letter to Africanus*, 12 (see p.76).

[48] *Letter to Africanus*, 9.

[49] *Letter to Africanus*, 13. See R. T. Beckwith, *The Old Testament Canon of the New Testament Church*, p.325, n.30.

[50] This adjective (Gk. *panaretos*) was applied to the wisdom literature generally (see p.71 with n.11).

[51] One should beware of translating Jerome's words here as though they meant 'another pseudepigraph entitled the Wisdom of Solomon'. Jerome must not be suspected of supposing that Ben Sira's wisdom book was ascribed to another than its real author.

[52] A substantial part of the Hebrew text has survived.

[53] See p.166 with n.23.

the books of Maccabees, but does not receive them among the canonical books, so let it also read these two volumes for the edification of the people but not for establishing the authority of ecclesiastical dogmas.

In this prologue to Jeremiah Jerome points out that he has not included the book of Baruch in his version of the major prophet because it is neither read nor recognized among the Hebrews; he is prepared for the abuse which will be heaped on his failure to acknowledge it. In the prologue to his version of Daniel he points out that the current Greek form of that book is not the original work of the Seventy but Theodotion's version — 'I do not know why', he adds (but if he had studied the original Septuagint version carefully and compared it with the Hebrew and Aramaic text he would have discovered why).[54] 'Among the Hebrews', he says, the book of Daniel contains 'neither the history of Susanna nor the hymn of the three young men nor the fables of Bel and the dragon', but he has appended them to his translation of the book, he adds, 'lest among the uninstructed we should seem to have lopped off a considerable part of the volume'.[55] He knows the argument used by Africanus in his letter to Origen about the history of Susanna, that the play on the names of the two trees cannot have originated in Hebrew, and shows how an equally telling play on their names can be made in Latin.[56]

He translated the book of Esther from Hebrew, but was content to add the 'Septuagintal plus' of the book as it stood in the Old Latin. He says that he translated Tobit and Judith from Aramaic;[57] the other books of what he called the Apocrypha he left unrevised in their existing Latin version.

What Jerome calls the Apocrypha corresponds to Athanasius's

[54] The original Septuagint version of Daniel is a free and interpretative rendering; Theodotion's version follows the Hebrew and Aramaic text more closely (see p.000). About half of Daniel (2:4b—7:28) is in Aramaic; the rest is in Hebrew. Other parts of the Old Testament which have Aramaic, not Hebrew, as their original text are Ezra 4:8—6:18; 7:12–26; Jer. 10:11.

[55] He was charged with doing this very thing by Rufinus (*Apology against Jerome*, 2.33).

[56] Thus the reply 'under a holm-oak *(sub ilice)* could meet with the riposte 'you will perish forthwith' *(ilico)*; 'under a mastic tree' *(sub lentisco)* could be countered with 'may the angel crush you into seeds' *(in lentem)*.

[57] Portions of Tobit in both Aramaic and Hebrew have been identified among the fragments from Qumran Cave 4. The Semitic original of Judith is no longer extant.

second category of Old Testament books, called by Rufinus and others 'ecclesiastical books' (i.e. books for reading in church). It is, however, a little confusing to find that Jerome sometimes uses the word 'apocryphal' in the sense given to it by Athanasius—of those books in Athanasius's third category which have no place in the church. Thus he argues that in 1 Corinthians 2:9 ('What no eye has seen, nor ear heard . . .') Paul is giving a free paraphrase of Isaiah 64:4, and refuses to follow those writers who 'run after the ravings of the apocryphal books' and find the origin of the words in the *Apocalypse of Elijah*.[58] When, in prescribing a reading list for the young Paula, he says, 'Let her avoid all apocryphal writings',[59] it may be works of this category that he has in mind.

But it is in no pejorative sense that Jerome has bequeathed the designation 'Apocrypha' for the writings of the 'Septuagintal plus'. They are not in the canon properly speaking, he says, they may not be used for the establishment of doctrine, but they retain great ethical value which makes them suitable for reading in the course of Christian worship. What authority he had for saying that 'the church' received them for this purpose is not clear. But he was quite happy, not only in his earlier works but in some of the latest, to quote from them with the same introductory formulae as he used when quoting from the 'Hebrew verity' or the New Testament books. He is capable of such *obiter dicta* as: 'Ruth, Esther and Judith have been given the great honour of conferring their names on sacred volumes.'[60]

After completing his translation, Jerome continued his biblical studies with a series of commentaries on Old Testament books; he also (and less profitably) continued his activity as a bitter controversialist, when he found a foeman worthy of his steel. He died in 420. He and Origen stand alone among early church fathers for their expertise as biblical scholars; of the two, Jerome has exercised the greater and more long-lasting influence.[61]

---

[58] No doubt he has Origen in mind, though he does not name him; Origen gives this as the source of the quotation in his *Commentary on Matthew* (on 27:9). See also p. 162 with nn. 8, 9.

[59] *Epistle* 107.12.

[60] *Epistle* 65.1.

[61] On Jerome see P. W. Skehan, 'St Jerome and the Canon of the Holy Scriptures' in *A Monument of St Jerome*, ed. F. X. Murphy (New York, 1952); also E. F. Sutcliffe, 'St Jerome's Pronunciation of Hebrew', *Biblica* 29 (1948), pp. 112–125; 'St Jerome's Hebrew Manuscripts', *Biblica* 29 (1948), pp. 195–204; 'Jerome', *CHB* II (Cambridge,

AUGUSTINE

Jerome's younger contemporary Augustine (354–430), bishop of Hippo Regius in North Africa (modern Bona in Algeria) from 395 until his death, 'the greatest man that ever wrote Latin',[62] was strong where Jerome was weak (in his power as a theological thinker) and weak where Jerome was strong (in linguistic training). He appreciated many aspects of Jerome's work, but lacked his sensitivity for the 'Hebrew verity' (having no Hebrew himself). The two men maintained a friendly correspondence with each other. In one letter (sent in 403) Augustine expresses a strong desire that Jerome would provide a (new) Latin translation of the Septuagint rather than of the Hebrew text, for if his translation from the Hebrew is adopted by the Latin-speaking churches, discrepancies will arise between their usage and that of the Greek churches, in which the Septuagint will naturally continue to be read.[63] He adds that even in Latin-speaking churches too much innovation in rendering may cause disorder: a riot broke out in one North African church, he says, when the bishop, reading Jonah 4:6, called the plant which shaded Jonah from the sun an 'ivy' (Lat. *hedera*), in accordance with Jerome's new version, and not a 'gourd' *(cucurbita)*, the term to which they were accustomed. The bishop was forced to change the rendering so as not to lose his congregation. Jerome replied at length, defending his practice and his interpretation with regard to this and other scriptures.[64]

Nevertheless Augustine acknowledged that an acquaintance with both Hebrew and Greek was necessary in order to understand the scriptures properly, and especially (where the Old Testament was concerned) an acquaintance with Hebrew. Translations from Hebrew are few, but translations from Greek are two-a-penny. 'For, in the

---

1969), pp.80–101; W. H. Semple, 'St Jerome as a Biblical Translator', *BJRL* 48 (1965–66), pp.227–243; J. Barr, 'St Jerome's Appreciation of Hebrew', *BJRL* 49 (1966–67), pp.281–302; J. Barr, 'St Jerome and the Sounds of Hebrew', *Journal of Semitic Studies* 12 (1967), pp.1–36; H. F. D. Sparks, 'Jerome as Biblical Scholar', *CHB* I (Cambridge, 1970), pp.510–541; J. N. D. Kelly, *Jerome* (London, 1975).

[62] A. Souter, *The Earliest Latin Commentaries on the Epistles of St Paul* (Oxford, 1927), p.139; 'For me, at least', said Souter in the same sentence, 'he is the greatest Christian since New Testament times.'

[63] Augustine, *Epistle* 71 = Jerome, *Epistle* 104. Augustine had made the same request to Jerome eight or nine years previously (*Epistle* 28.2 = Jerome, *Epistle* 56.2). Cf. Augustine, *Epistle* 81.34f.

[64] Jerome, *Epistle* 112 = Augustine, *Epistle* 75.

earliest days of the faith, when a Greek manuscript came into anyone's hands and he thought he possessed a little facility in both languages [i.e. Greek and Latin], he ventured to make a translation.'[65]

Augustine himself has left an explicit statement on the limits of the canon of scripture. It is contained, he says, in the following books:

> Five books of Moses: Genesis, Exodus, Leviticus, Numbers, Deuteronomy.
>
> One book of Joshua the son of Nun, one of Judges, one short book called Ruth, which seems rather to belong to the beginning of Kings; next, four books of Kings and two of Chronicles— these last not following consecutively but running parallel, so to speak, and covering the same ground. . . .
>
> There are other books which appear to follow no regular order, being connected neither with the order of the preceding books nor with one another, such as Job, Tobias, Esther and Judith, the two books of Maccabees and the two of Esdras [i.e. Ezra and Nehemiah]: these last seem to be rather a sequel to the continuous regular history which ends with the books of Kings and Chronicles.
>
> Next come the prophets, in which there is one book of the Psalms of David; and three books of Solomon—Proverbs, Song of Songs and Ecclesiastes. Two books indeed, one called Wisdom and the other Ecclesiasticus, are ascribed to Solomon because of a certain resemblance of style, but the most probable opinion is that they were written by Jesus the son of Sirach.[66] Still, they are to be numbered among the prophetical books, since they have won recognition as being authoritative.
>
> The remainder are the books which are strictly called the Prophets. There are twelve separate books of the prophets which are joined to one another and, having never been disjoined, are reckoned as one book; the names of these prophets are Hosea, Joel, Amos, Obadiah, Jonah, Micah, Nahum, Habakkuk, Zephaniah, Haggai, Zechariah and Malachi. Then there are the four major prophets: Isaiah, Jeremiah, Daniel, Ezekiel. The authority of the Old Testament[67] is contained within the limits of these forty-four books.

[65] *On Christian Learning*, 2.16.

[66] In his *Retractations* 2.2 Augustine withdraws his mention of Jesus Ben Sira as author of Wisdom.

[67] In his *Retractations* 2.3 Augustine acknowledges that this customary use of 'Old Testament' has no apostolic authority; the one biblical instance of the expression (2 Cor. 3:14) refers to the covenant at Sinai.

Then he enumerates twenty-seven books of the New Testament as they had been enumerated by Athanasius.[68]

It may or may not be a coincidence that the total of forty-four Old Testament books is twice the traditional twenty-two. This larger total is reached by counting the twelve Minor Prophets separately (even if, as he says, they were traditionally 'reckoned as one book') and adding the 'apocryphal' books (as Jerome called them). The additions to Esther and Daniel are included in the books to which they are attached. Lamentations, Baruch and the *Letter of Jeremiah* (which in the Latin Bible is counted as the sixth chapter of Baruch) are included with Jeremiah.

Augustine's classification of the books is interesting; so are some of his comments on individual books, such as his remark that Ruth is rather a prologue to the four books of Kings (i.e. Samuel-Kings) than an appendix to Judges (this, no doubt, because it gives the ancestry of King David).

Augustine did not ignore completely the differences between the Hebrew text and the Septuagint. The latter, he had no doubt, was produced by seventy wise men, as the legend said, and as each of these was divinely inspired their united witness must be reckoned weightier than that of one man, even if that one man were so learned as Jerome. When there were differences between the two forms of text, whether additions, omissions or changes of wording, the student should consider their significance.[69] Thus, according to the Hebrew text, Jonah proclaimed in Nineveh, 'Yet forty days, and Nineveh shall be overthrown' (Jon. 3:4); according to the Septuagint, he said, 'Yet three days...'. Augustine supposed that Jonah actually said 'forty days' (which might make the reader think of the forty days' appearances of the risen Christ, according to Acts 1:3); the seventy translators, equally by the Spirit of God, said 'three days', in which the sensitive reader will recognize an allusion to Christ's resurrection on the third day. As, then, the apostles themselves drew their prophetic testimonies from the Hebrew and the Septuagint alike, so Augustine concludes that 'both sources should be employed as authoritative, since both are one, and both are inspired by God'.[70]

---

[68] *On Christian Learning*, 2.13.   [69] *City of God*, 18.42, 43.

[70] *City of God*, 18.44. A similar argument appears in his *Exposition* of Ps. 87:10 (RSV 88:11), where the Hebrew reads 'Do the shades (translated 'giants' in Jerome's Hebrew Psalter) rise up to praise thee?' but the Septuagint rendering (followed in Jerome's Gallican Psalter) is 'Will physicians raise them up and give thee thanks?'

CHURCH COUNCILS

Augustine's ruling supplied a powerful precedent for the western church from his own day to the Reformation and beyond.

In 393 a church council held in Augustine's see of Hippo laid down the limits of the canonical books along the lines approved by Augustine himself. The proceedings of this council have been lost but they were summarized in the proceedings of the Third Council of Carthage (397), a provincial council.[71] These appear to have been the first church councils to make a formal pronouncement on the canon. When they did so, they did not impose any innovation on the churches; they simply endorsed what had become the general consensus of the churches of the west and of the greater part of the east. In 405 Pope Innocent I embodied a list of canonical books in a letter addressed to Exsuperius, bishop of Toulouse; it too included the Apocrypha.[72] The Sixth Council of Carthage (419) re-enacted the ruling of the Third Council, again with the inclusion of the apocryphal books.

What is commonly called the Gelasian decree on books which are to be received and not received takes its name from Pope Gelasius (492–496). It gives a list of biblical books as they appeared in the Vulgate, with the Apocrypha interspersed among the others. In some manuscripts, indeed, it is attributed to Pope Damasus, as though it had been promulgated by him at the Council of Rome in 382. But actually it appears to have been a private compilation drawn up somewhere in Italy in the early sixth century.[73]

Augustine's exposition combines the 'giants' and the 'physicians'. On Augustine see further S. J. Schultz, 'Augustine and the Old Testament Canon', *EQ* 28 (1956), pp.93–100; A. –M. La Bonnardière (ed.), *Saint Augustin et la Bible* (Paris, 1986), and (more generally) P. R. L. Brown, *Augustine of Hippo: A Biography* (London, 1967), and *Religion and Society in the Age of Saint Augustine* (London, 1972).

[71] See NPNF, series 2, XIV, pp.453f.

[72] Innocent, *Epistle* 6.7. His order is unusual: after the four books of 'Kingdoms' he continues with Ruth, the Prophets (four major and twelve minor), five books of Solomon (including Wisdom and Ben Sira), Psalms, Job, Tobit, Esther, Judith, 1 and 2 Maccabees, 1 and 2 Esdras (= Ezra-Nehemiah), 1 and 2 Chronicles.

[73] A critical edition was issued by E. von Dobschütz, *Das Decretum Gelasianum...* = *TU* 38.4 (Leipzig, 1912). See also C. H. Turner, 'Latin Lists of the Canonical Books, I: The Roman Council under Damasus, AD 382', *JTS* 1 (1899–1900), pp.554–560; J. Chapman, 'On the *Decretum Gelasianum* "De Libris recipiendis et non recipiendis"', *Revue Bénédictine* 30 (1913), pp.187–207, 315–353; E. Schwartz, 'Zum Decretum Gelasianum', *ZNW* 29 (1930), pp.161–168.

CHAPTER SEVEN

BEFORE AND AFTER
THE REFORMATION

JEROME TO THE REFORMATION

Jerome's Latin Bible made its way slowly but surely in the western church, gradually ousting the Old Latin version. If even an enlightened reader like Augustine was a little disconcerted by what seemed to be Jerome's ruthless rejection of the Septuagint as a basis for the Old Testament translator, it may well be imagined what resistance was offered by the rank and file to Jerome's innovations. They were not at all impressed by the argument that the new translation was much more accurate than the old: then, as now, accuracy was a matter of concern only to a minority. Nevertheless, the sheer merit of Jerome's version won the day, until it came to be known as the 'Vulgate' or 'common' edition—a designation previously used of the version that Jerome's work superseded.

So far as the Old Testament canon was concerned, this too was a matter of interest only to a minority. For purposes of devotion or edification, why make any distinction between Esther and Judith, or between Proverbs and Wisdom?

It became customary to add to copies of the Latin Bible a few books which Jerome had not even included among those which were to be read 'for the edification of the people', notably 3 and 4 Esdras and the Prayer of Manasseh. Of these, 3 Esdras (or the 'Greek Ezra') is the 1 Esdras of the Septuagint (and of the common English Apocrypha); 4

Esdras (the 'Apocalypse of Ezra'), frequently referred to as 4 Ezra, is the 2 Esdras of the common English Apocrypha (it had never been included in the Septuagint)[1]; the Prayer of Manasseh, composed to give substance to the allusion to that king's prayer in 2 Chron. 33:12f., 18f., may belong to the first or second century BC but first appears in extant literature in a manual of church order called the *Doctrine of the Apostles* (early 4th century AD). It is a beautiful prayer of penitence (but, like 4 Esdras, had never belonged to the Septuagint).

Throughout the following centuries most users of the Bible made no distinction between the apocryphal books and the others: all alike were handed down as part of the Vulgate. But the vast majority of western European Christians, clerical as well as lay, in those centuries could not be described as 'users' of the Bible. They were familiar with certain parts of the Bible which were repeated in church services, and with the well-known Bible stories, but the idea of well defined limits to the sacred books was something that would not have occurred to them. Even among the most literate Christians a lack of concern on such matters sometimes manifests itself. Thus, of some of the Old English translators of the Bible it has been pointed out that, while 'Bede, Aldhelm, Aelfric all protest against the widespread popular use' of some completely uncanonical writings, 'all three themselves use others' of the same kind.[2]

With the revival of serious biblical study in the early Middle Ages, fresh attention was paid to questions of canonicity. Nowhere was this revival more marked than in the Abbey of St Victor at Paris in the twelfth century. In the school attached to the abbey Hebrew sources were explored and a new emphasis was placed on the literal sense of scripture. Hugh of St Victor, who was prior of the abbey and director of its school from 1133 until his death in 1141, enumerates the books of the Hebrew Bible in a chapter 'On the number of books in holy writ' and goes on to say: 'There are also in the Old Testament certain other books which are indeed read [in church] but are not inscribed in the body of the text or in the canon of authority: such are the books of Tobit, Judith and the Maccabees, the so-called Wisdom of Solomon and Ecclesiasticus.'[3] Here, of course, the influence of Jerome can be

---

[1] On the Esdras literature see also pp.47 with n.11, 85 with n.11.

[2] G. Shepherd, in 'English Versions of the Scriptures before Wyclif', *CHB* II, p.364.

[3] Hugh of St Victor, *On the Sacraments*, I, Prologue, 7 (*PL* 176, cols. 185–186D). 'A continuous succession of the more learned Fathers in the West maintained the

discerned: for mediaeval students of the Bible in the Latin church there was no master to be compared with him.

For those who were more concerned with the spiritual than with the literal sense the distinction between first and second grades of canonicity was unimportant: the apocryphal books could be allegorized as easily as those which were stamped with 'Hebrew verity' and could be made to yield the same meaning.

There is evidence of some reaction on the part of mediaeval Jewish scholars to the Christian treatment of the Old Testament canon. E. I. J. Rosenthal has shown how Isaac Abravanel (1437–1509) applied Aristotelian categories to prove that the Jewish division of the sacred books into Law, Prophets and Writings was superior to the fourfold Christian division into legal, historical, poetical with wisdom, and prophetical books.[4] On the other hand, it has been shown that more than two centuries earlier Moses Nachmanides (1194–c 1270) read the book of Wisdom in an Aramaic text.[5]

The two Wycliffite versions of the complete Bible in English (1384, 1395) included the apocryphal books as a matter of course; they were part of the Vulgate, on which those versions were based. The 'General Prologue' to the second version (John Purvey's) contains a strong commendation of 'the book of Tobias' (Tobit) because of the encouragement it provides to those who are persecuted for righteousness' sake, teaching them 'to be true to God in prosperity and adversity, and . . . to be patient in tribulation; and go never away from the dread and love of God'. There is a recognition of the distinction drawn by Jerome between those books which might be used for the confirmation of doctrine and those which were profitable for their ethical lessons: 'Though the book of Tobias is not of belief, it is a full devout story, and profitable to the simple people, to make them keep patience and God's hests' (i.e. behests).[6]

---

distinctive authority of the Hebrew Canon up to the period of the Reformation' (B. F. Westcott, 'Canon of Scripture, The', Smith's *DB* I, p.507; he gives a list from Primasius to Cardinal Cajetan). See more generally B. Smalley, *The Study of the Bible in the Middle Ages* (Oxford, ²1952).

[4] *CHB* II, p.273 ('The Study of the Bible in Medieval Judaism').

[5] A. Marx, 'An Aramaic Fragment of the Wisdom of Solomon', *JBL* 40 (1921), pp.57–69.

[6] M. Deanesly, *The Lollard Bible* (Cambridge, [1920] 1960), p.256.

THE REFORMERS AND THE
OLD TESTAMENT CANON

With the sixteenth-century Reformation the issue came more sharply to the fore. When Luther, in his controversy with Johann Maier von Eck, maintained the authority of scripture alone (*sola scriptura*) over against that of the church, this quickly raised the question of what precisely constituted 'scripture alone'. It was Luther's protest against the abuse of the indulgence system (especially in the hands of Johann Tetzel) that led him ultimately to break with Rome. But the indulgence system was bound up with belief in purgatory and the practice of prayers for the dead, and these too were given up by Luther. When Luther was challenged to abide by his principle of 'scripture alone' and concede that scriptural authority for praying for the dead was found in 2 Macc. 12:45f. (where praying for the dead, 'that they might be delivered from their sin', is said to be 'a holy and pious thought'), he found a ready reply in Jerome's ruling that 2 Maccabees did not belong to the books to be used 'for establishing the authority of ecclesiastical dogmas'.[7]

(It may have been for this reason that Luther manifested a special animus against 2 Maccabees: he is reported as saying, 'I hate Esther and 2 Maccabees so much that I wish they did not exist; they contain too much Judaism and no little heathen vice.'[8] It is noteworthy that he shows his exercise of private judgement here by including Esther under the same condemnation as 2 Maccabees: Esther is one of the books which Jerome acknowledged as acceptable for the establishing of doctrine—though to be sure it is difficult to imagine what doctrine of Jewish or Christian faith could be established by the book of Esther.)[9]

[7] Luther's Wittenberg colleague A. R. Bodenstein von Karlstadt defended Jerome's position in *De canonicis scripturis libellus* (1520), but within the Apocrypha he gave a higher status to Wisdom, Ben Sira, Judith, Tobit, and 1 and 2 Maccabees than to the other books.

[8] *Tischreden* (Weimar edition 1, p.208): too much weight should not be laid on many of the *obiter dicta* in Luther's collected *Table Talk*.

[9] It might be said that Esther bears witness to the operation of divine providence, but that is not a distinctively Jewish or Christian doctrine (it was a central feature of Stoic belief). A powerful imagination can see what is otherwise invisible, as when W. Vischer could see the cross of Christ in Haman's gallows ('The Book of Esther', *EQ* 11 [1939], pp.3–21, especially pp.11–17). One still comes across allegorizations of the story in which Esther corresponds to the church (the bride of Christ), Mordecai to the Holy Spirit, and King Ahasuerus (believe it or not) to Christ.

Luther showed his acceptance of Jerome's distinction between the two categories of Old Testament books by gathering the Apocrypha together in his German Bible as a sort of appendix to the Old Testament (1534), instead of leaving them as they stood in the Vulgate. They were largely translated by various helpers, while he himself composed the prefaces. The section containing them was entitled: 'The Apocrypha: Books which are not to be held equal to holy scripture, but are useful and good to read.' In Zwingli's Zürich Bible (1524–29) the apocryphal books had already been separated from the rest of the Old Testament and published as a volume by itself. Luther's friend George Spalatin had translated the Prayer of Manasseh into German in 1519; another translation was included in the complete German Bible of 1534. As for 3 and 4 Esdras and 3 Maccabees, they were not included in Luther's Bible; they were added to later editions from about 1570 onward.

Luther had little regard for the Apocrypha in general, but his guidance in matters of the canon was derived not from tradition but from the gospel. In both Testaments 'what preaches Christ' was for him the dominant principle; in the Old Testament Genesis, Psalms and Isaiah preached Christ with special clarity, he found.

Erasmus took a humanist rather than an evangelical attitude to such questions. In his treatise on *The Freedom of the Will*, for example, he based an argument on Ben Sira's wisdom book (Ecclesiasticus): 'I cannot see', he said, 'why the Hebrews left this book out when they included Solomon's Parables and the amatory Canticles'.[10] The Erasmian attitude was expressed also by Calvin's convert Sebastian Castellio (1515–63), translator of the Bible into both Latin and French, whom the Reformed authorities in Geneva refused to ordain because he would not spiritualize the Song of Songs but held it to be a poem in celebration of human love.[11]

Tyndale did not live to complete the translation of the Old Testament; had he done so, he would probably have followed Luther's precedent (as he did in other respects[12]) by segregating the apocryphal books in a section of their own. In an appendix to his 1534 revision of the New Testament he translated those Old Testament passages which were prescribed to be read in church as Epistles on certain days

[10] Erasmus, *The Freedom of the Will* (1524), quoted by R. H. Bainton, *CHB* III, p.6.
[11] See B. Hall, *CHB* III, pp.71f. ('Biblical Scholarship: Editions and Commentaries').   [12] See p.246.

according to the use of Sarum. A few of these are from the Apocrypha; they appear, naturally, in their liturgical aequence. [13]

Coverdale's English Bible of 1535 followed the example of its continental predecessors by separating the apocryphal books (and parts of books) from the rest of the Old Testament and placing them after Malachi, with a separate title-page: 'Apocripha: the bokes and treatises which amonge the fathers of old are not rekened to be of like authorite with the other bokes of the byble, nether are they founde in the Canon of Hebrue.' Then come their titles, beginning with 3 and 4 Esdras. But one apocryphal work was left *in situ*, as a note at the foot of the title-page explains: 'Vnto these also belongeth Baruc, whom we haue set amonge the prophetes next vnto Jeremy, because he was his scrybe, and in his tyme.' (In a 1537 edition of Coverdale, however, Baruch was removed from its position among the protocanonical books and placed after Tobit.) The next page has an introduction indicating the inferior authority of these books.

Thomas Matthew's Bible of 1537 (actually edited by John Rogers) reproduced Coverdale's Apocrypha, but added the Prayer of Manasseh. This was the first appearance of the Prayer of Manasseh in English; for Matthew's Bible it was translated from the French version in Olivétan's Bible (1535). Richard Taverner's Bible of 1539, a revision of Matthew's Bible, omits the introduction to the Apocrypha found in Coverdale and Matthew. Taverner's Bible was revised in turn by Edmund Becke (1549–51); Becke added a translation of 3 Maccabees, which now appeared for the first time in an English dress. He also provided a completely new translation of 1 Esdras, Tobit and Judith, and in an introduction of his own to the apocryphal books justified their separation from the protocanonical works but commended their reading 'for example of life'.

The Great Bible, first published in 1539, was edited by Coverdale but used Matthew's Bible as its basis (and that meant Tyndale's Bible, so far as Tyndale's work extended). [14] The first edition reproduced Coverdale's introduction to the Apocrypha but called the books Hagiographa, not Apocrypha. (*Hagiographa*, 'holy writings', was originally the Greek equivalent of Hebrew $K^e\underline{t}\hat{u}\underline{b}\hat{i}m$, the 'Writings',

[13] E.g. Sir. 15.1–6 for St John the Evangelist's Day (December 27), Wisdom 5:1–5 for St Philip and St James' Day (May 1).

[14] Of the Old Testament books in English Tyndale published only the Pentateuch and Jonah, but he left in manuscript the translation of the historical books from Joshua to 2 Chronicles; this was published in Matthew's Bible.

the third division of the Hebrew Bible.) The fifth edition of the Great Bible (1541) omitted the introduction and supplied a new title-page in which the list of apocryphal books was preceded by the words: 'The fourth part of the Bible, containing these bokes.' This form of words was plainly calculated to play down the distinction between the Apocrypha and the protocanonical books.

THE COUNCIL OF TRENT

Meanwhile the Counter-Reformation concerned itself with the canon of scripture as well as with many other issues which the Reformers had put in question. The Council of Trent, convened in 1545, had to consider the relation of scripture and unwritten tradition in the transmission of Christian doctrine; it made pronouncements, among other things, on the text, interpretation and canon of scripture. These subjects were dealt with during the fourth session (April, 1546): it was decreed that among various forms of the biblical text it was to the 'ancient and vulgate edition' that ultimate appeal should be made, and that this edition comprised what we call the protocanonical and deuterocanonical books without distinction. It was decided not to enter into the question of difference in status between one group of books and another. Thus Jerome's distinction between the books certified by the 'Hebrew verity' and the books which were to be read only 'for the edification of the people' was in effect set aside.

This was probably the first occasion on which a ruling on the canon of scripture was given by a general (or ecumenical) council of the church, as opposed to a local or provincial council. A similar list had indeed been promulgated by the Council of Florence over a hundred years before, but there was some doubt whether this particular Florentine decree carried full conciliar authority. The decree of Trent (like its companion decrees) was fortified by an anathema pronounced against all dissentients.[15]

The ruling that the 'ancient and vulgate edition' (the Latin Vulgate) be treated as the authoritative text of holy scripture required the provision of an accurate edition of this text. After the abortive attempt to make this provision in the Sixtine edition of 1590, the need was adequately met (for the next three centuries, at least) by the Clemen-

[15] Sessio IV: *Decretum de canonicis scripturis*. See F. J. Crehan, *CHB* III, pp. 199–202 ('The Bible in the Roman Catholic Church from Trent to the Present Day').

tine Vulgate of 1592. In this edition 3 and 4 Esdras and the Prayer of Manasseh were added as an appendix: they formed no part of the canon of Trent and were not included in the Sixtine Vulgate. It was the Clementine edition of the Old Testament that formed the basis of the English Douay version of 1609–10.

The decree of Trent was repromulgated by the first Vatican Council of 1869–70, which explained further that the biblical books were not acknowledged as canonical because they had first been produced by human intelligence and then canonized by the church's authority, but rather because they had God for their author, being inspired by the Holy Spirit and then entrusted to the church.[16] As for the status of the books which Jerome called apocryphal, there is general agreement among Roman Catholic scholars today (as among their colleagues of other Christian traditions) to call them 'deuterocanonical' (a term first used, it appears, in the sixteenth century);[17] Jerome's distinction is thus maintained in practice, even if it does not enjoy conciliar support.

THE ELIZABETHAN SETTLEMENT

The Thirty-Nine Articles of Religion, which have been (in theory at least) authoritative for the doctrine and discipline of the Church of England since 1562/63[18], were in essence a repromulgation of the Forty-Two Articles of 1553 (issued seven weeks before the death of Edward VI). The doctrine of scripture is dealt with in Article VI of the Thirty-Nine, which corresponds to Article V of the Forty-Two. Unlike the earlier Article, however, which simply affirmed the sufficiency of the scriptures for 'all things necessary to Salvation', Article VI includes a precise statement of the contents of the Old Testament scriptures. Headed 'Of the sufficiency of the holy Scriptures for salvation', it proceeds:

> Holy Scripture containeth all things necessary to salvation: so that whatsoever is not read therein, nor may be proved thereby,

---

[16] *Dogmatic Constitution on the Catholic Faith*, ch.2 ('Of Revelation').

[17] According to F. J. Crehan (*CHB* III, p.206), the word 'deuterocanonical' was first used in this way by a converted Jew, Sixtus of Siena (1520–1569).

[18] All thirty-nine were approved by Convocation at that time, but Article 29 ('Of the Wicked which eat not the Body of Christ in the use of the Lord's Supper') was held over (probably at Queen Elizabeth's instance) and did not receive legal ratification until 1571.

is not to be required of any man, that it should be believed as an article of the Faith, or be thought requisite or necessary to salvation. In the name of the holy Scripture we do understand those Canonical Books of the Old and New Testament, of whose authority was never any doubt in the Church.

Of the Names and Number of the Canonical Books

> Genesis; Exodus; Leviticus; Numbers; Deuteronomy; Joshua; Judges; Ruth; The First Book of Samuel; The Second Book of Samuel; the First Book of Kings; The Second Book of Kings; the First Book of Chronicles; The Second Book of Chronicles; The First Book of Esdras; The Second Book of Esdras; The Book of Esther; The Book of Job; The Psalms; The Proverbs; Ecclesiastes, or Preacher; Cantica, or Songs of Solomon; Four Prophets the greater; Twelve Prophets the less.

And the other Books (as *Hierome* saith) the Church doth read for example of life and instruction of manners; but yet doth it not apply them to establish any doctrine; such are these following:

> The Third Book of Esdras; The Fourth Book of Esdras; The Book of Tobias; The Book of Judith; The rest of the Book of Esther; The Book of Wisdom; Jesus the Son of Sirach; Baruch the Prophet; The Song of the Three Children; The Story of Susanna; Of Bel and the Dragon; The Prayer of Manasses; The First Book of Maccabees; The Second Book of Maccabees....'

A certain naïveté may be noted in the remark about books 'of whose authority was never any doubt in the Church'. The First and Second Books of Esdras, as in the Vulgate, are the books of Ezra and Nehemiah. The book of Lamentations has not been lost: it is tacitly included, as an appendix to Jeremiah, in 'Four Prophets the greater'.

The distinction made by 'Hierome' (Jerome) between the books belonging to the Hebrew Bible and the others is reaffirmed. The Third and Fourth Books of Esdras and the Prayer of Manasses (Manasseh) are placed on the same level of deuterocanonicity as the Apocrypha in general.

In accordance with the recognition of the apocryphal books as profitable 'for example of life and instruction of manners', readings from them are included in the Anglican lectionary, especially among the 'lessons proper for holy-days' (e.g. on All Saints' Day, Wisdom 3:1–10 is the Old Testament lesson for Mattins and Wisdom 5:1–17 for Evensong). In the *Book of Homilies*, the reading of which is commended in Article XXXV, the apocryphal books are frequently quoted, and are even referred to as the Word of God.[19]

Two distinct tendencies in English Protestantism in the Elizabethan age are represented by the two new versions of the English Bible published under Elizabeth—the Geneva Bible (1560) and the Bishops' Bible (1568). The Geneva Bible was produced by English Protestants who sought refuge at Geneva during the reign of Mary Tudor (1553–58); it was issued with a dedication to Elizabeth. It included the apocryphal books in a section following the Old Testament (except that the Prayer of Manasseh is printed as an appendix to 2 Chronicles); they are introduced by this 'argument':

> These bokes that follow in order after the Prophetes vnto the New testament, are called Apocrypha, that is bokes, which were not receiued by a commune consent to be red and expounded publikely in the Church, nether yet serued to proue any point of Christian religion, saue in asmuche as they had the consent of the other Scriptures called Canonical to confirme the same, or rather whereon they were grounded: but as bokes proceding from godlie men, were receiued to be red for the aduancement and furtherance of the knowledge of the historie, and for the instruction of godlie maners: which bokes declare that at all times God had an especial care of his Church and left them not vtterly destitute of teachers and meanes to confirme them in the hope of the promised Messiah, and also witnesse that those calamities that God sent to his Church, were according to his prouidence, who had bothe so threatened by his Prophetes, and so broght it to passe for the destruction of their enemies, and for the tryal of his children.'[20]

Coming from the Geneva of Calvin and Beza, this is a moderate and reasonable repetition and expansion of Jerome's position: the apocryphal books are not to be used for the confirmation of doctrine (except in so far as they are based on the teaching of the canonical

---

[19] In the *Second Book of Homilies* (1563), homily 10 ('Of the reverend estimation of God's Word'), the book of Wisdom is commended as the 'infallible and undeceivable word of God'.

[20] In the Geneva Bible list of apocryphal books 3 and 4 Esdras, as they are called in the Vulgate, appear as 1 and 2 Esdras and have so been called in the 'Protestant' Apocrypha ever since. (When the two canonical 'Esdras' books are called Ezra and Nehemiah, as in the Geneva Bible, the risk of confusion is avoided.)

books) but serve 'for the instruction of godly manners'. It is added that they provide valuable source-material for the history of the inter-testamental period, and illustrate the principles of God's providential dealings with his people, as he prepared them for the fulfilment of his promise in the coming of Christ. The heirs of the Geneva Reformers would have been well advised had they maintained this balanced attitude to the Apocrypha.

Some of the users of the Geneva Bible, however, had little time for the Apocrypha. To cater for them, some copies of this version printed in 1599, both on the Continent and in London, were bound up without the section containing the Apocrypha. The omission of the section is obvious because the page-numbering ran consecutively throughout the volume, and there is a hiatus in the numbering between the two Testaments; moreover, the apocryphal books are listed in the preliminary table of contents. An edition of the Geneva Bible published at Amsterdam in 1640 omitted the Apocrypha as a matter of policy: a defence of the omission was printed between the Testaments.[21]

The Bishops' Bible, first published at London in 1568, was the work of men committed to the Elizabethan settlement: in it the section containing the Apocrypha was equipped with a special title but nothing was said to indicate any distinction in status between its contents and the other books.

SEVENTEENTH AND EIGHTEENTH CENTURIES

The Authorized (King James) Version of 1611 was formally a revision of the last (1602) edition of the Bishops' Bible; it included a version of the Apocrypha as a matter of course. Four years later, the Archbishop of Canterbury, George Abbot, a firm Calvinist in theology, forbade the binding or selling of Bibles without the Apocrypha on penalty of a year's imprisonment.[22] This measure seemed to be necessary because of the increasingly vocal Puritan objection to the inclusion of the Apocrypha among the canonical books. In 1589 an attack on their

---

[21] But the Prayer of Manasseh, being appended to 2 Chronicles, was retained.

[22] In those days the authority of the Archbishop of Canterbury was reinforced by sanctions: in 1631 the King's Printers were fined £300 by Archbishop Laud for their negligence in omitting the vital word 'not' from the commandment 'Thou shalt not commit adultery' (a misprint which secured for that edition the sobriquet of 'The Wicked Bible').

inclusion by John Penry ('Martin Marprelate') had called forth a spirited reply from an earlier Archbishop, John Whitgift. Now, despite the penalty enacted by Archbishop Abbot, copies of the AV/KJV without the Apocrypha began to be produced in the years from 1626 onward.

The tide was running in the Puritan favour in those years: in 1644 the Long Parliament ordained that the Apocrypha should cease to be read in services of the Church of England. Three years later the Assembly of Divines at Westminster introduced their historic Confession of Faith with a chapter 'Of the Holy Scripture'. In order to make it plain precisely which books were comprised in the holy scripture, the second paragraph of this chapter ran:

> II. Under the name of the Holy Scripture, or the Word of God written, are now contained all the Books of the Old and New Testaments, which are these:

OF THE OLD TESTAMENT

Genesis	I. Kings	Ecclesiastes	Amos
Exodus	II. Kings	The Song of	Obadiah
Leviticus	I. Chronicles	Songs	Jonah
Numbers	II. Chronicles	Isaiah	Micah
Deuteronomy	Ezra	Jeremiah	Nahum
Joshua	Nehemiah	Lamentations	Habakkuk
Judges	Esther	Ezekiel	Zephaniah
Ruth	Job	Daniel	Haggai
I. Samuel	Psalms	Hosea	Zechariah
II. Samuel	Proverbs	Joel	Malachi

OF THE NEW TESTAMENT

The Gospels	to the Romans	To Timothy I	second Epistles of
according to	Corinthians I	To Timothy II	Peter
Matthew	Corinthians II	To Titus	The first, second
Mark	Galatians	To Philemon	and third Epistles
Luke	Ephesians	The Epistle to	of John
John	Philippians	the Hebrews	The Epistle of Jude
The Acts of	Colossians	The Epistle of	The Revelation
the Apostles	Thessalonians I	James	
Paul's Epistles	Thessalonians II	The first and	

> All of which are given by inspiration of God, to be the rule of faith and life.

The third paragraph follows with the uncompromising declaration:

> III. The Books commonly called Apocrypha, not being of divine inspiration, are no part of the canon of the scripture; and therefore are of no authority in the Church of God, nor to be any otherwise approved, or made use of, than other human writings.

This went considerably beyond the position approved by the translators of the Geneva Bible. Naturally churches which adopted the Westminster Confession as their chief subordinate standard — notably the Church of Scotland and other Presbyterian churches — preferred to use copies of the Bible which did not include the Apocrypha.

An interesting sidelight on the general Puritan attitude in England under the Commonwealth is provided by a piece of spiritual autobiography by John Bunyan in *Grace Abounding*. About 1652, he relates, during a time of deep depression, he found comfort in a text which came to his mind: 'Look at the generations of old, and see: did ever any trust in the Lord and was confounded?' He could not remember where it came from, could not find it in his Bible, and received no help from others whom he asked for guidance in his quest. Then, after the lapse of a year, he writes:

> casting my eye upon the Apocrypha books, I found it in Ecclesiasticus, chap. 2:10. This at first did somewhat daunt me, because it was not in those texts that we call holy and canonical; yet as this sentence was the sum and substance of many of the promises, it was my duty to take the comfort of it. And I bless God for that word, for it was of good to me. That word doth still oft-times shine before my face.'[23]

Bunyan shows his robust commonsense here: despite being initially somewhat 'daunted' by the realization that he had found divine comfort in an apocryphal text, he appropriated it as a genuine word of God because it summarized so many biblical promises of God's faithfulness to his people.

After the Restoration of 1660 the readings from the Apocrypha reappeared in the Anglican lectionary. The exclusion of these books,

---

[23] *Grace Abounding*, 62–65. It is implied that his Bible contained the 'Apocrypha books' but that he did not habitually read them as he read the rest of the volume, having been taught that they were not 'holy and canonical'.

however, became increasingly popular in English nonconformity. It may be indicative of the Puritan or nonconformist influence in American Christianity that the first edition of the English Bible to be printed in America (Philadelphia, 1782) lacked the Apocrypha.[24] (The first edition of the Bible in any European language to be printed in America was a German Bible of 1743; it did include the Apocrypha.)[25]

BIBLE SOCIETIES AND COMMON BIBLE

Early in the nineteenth century the canon of the Old Testament excited more widespread interest both in Britain and on the Continent than is usual for such a question. In 1804 the British and Foreign Bible Society was formed to promote the production and circulation of the scriptures, together with their translation into languages in which they were not available. Its committee consisted of laymen, drawn in equal numbers from the Church of England and the Free Churches. Later in the same year a German Bible Society was formed, followed in 1812 by the Russian Bible Society and in 1816 by the American Bible Society.

In view of the interdenominational character of the British Society, it was provided from the outset that editions of the Bible which it sponsored should have neither note nor comment. But before long it was realized that some editions handled by the Society contained something more objectionable in the eyes of many of its supporters than any note or comment could be — the apocryphal books, which (according to the Westminster Confession), 'not being of divine inspiration, are no part of the canon of the scripture'. To begin with, the Society had taken little thought for the Apocrypha, one way or the other: one of its most famous relics, the 'Mary Jones Bible', included the Welsh version of those books and actually shows Mary's signature at the end of Maccabees.[26]

The Free Churchmen on the committee, and most of the Anglicans (in view of their evangelical orientation), had no interest in circulating

[24] Before the Declaration of Independence American Christians were debarred by British copyright regulations from printing the *English* Bible. The first Bible printed in America was John Eliot's Algonquin version (NT 1661, OT 1663).

[25] It included the seventy verses 2 Esdras (4 Ezra) 7:36–105, which were missing from the AV/KJV Apocrypha.

[26] E. Fenn, *CHB* III, p.391 ('The Bible and the Missionary').

the Apocrypha. But the Society supported similar groups on the European Continent which did circulate editions containing the Apocrypha, especially for areas in which Bibles without the Apocrypha would not have been acceptable. In the 1820s objections were voiced to such support, and a dispute broke out which lasted for five years. The Society's Scottish Auxiliaries in particular opposed the use of the Society's money, however indirectly, for the distribution of Bibles containing the Apocrypha. The protagonist on the Scottish side was Robert Haldane, an able lay theologian (best known otherwise as the author of a distinguished commentary on Paul's letter to the Romans).[27] The Society in 1826 adopted the policy of neither circulating itself, nor aiding others in circulating, Bibles containing the Apocrypha—but not before the Scottish Auxiliaries had constituted themselves as the separate National Bible Society of Scotland. The formation of this new Society, however, expanded rather than hindered the work of Bible distribution (and the same can be said of the Trinitarian Bible Society, which began its separate existence on another issue in 1831).[28]

When the British and Foreign Bible Society began to distribute exclusively editions lacking the Apocrypha, the Bible-buying public seemed quite content with such editions. That being so, other Bible publishers saw no reason why they should continue producing Bibles with the Apocrypha. For a century and a half now it has been practically impossible to buy over the counter in any ordinary bookshop in Britain or America a copy of the Authorized (King James) Version containing the Apocrypha. Or, in the words of Principal John Macleod, a wholehearted subscriber to the Westminster Confession, 'the issue of the long and painful conflict was that the English-speaking world was furnished with the unadulterated Protestant Canon of Scripture as its everyday possession, a thing that was by no means universally the case before; and for over a century it is with such a Canon that it is familiar.'[29]

When the British and Foreign Bible Society undertook to provide

---

[27] The English edition of this commentary (Edinburgh, 1835–39), the expansion of an earlier French work, was reprinted by the Banner of Truth Trust (London, 1958). More germane to the Apocrypha controversy was his *The Books of the Old and New Testaments proved to be Canonical* (Edinburgh, 1845, [7]1877).

[28] More recently the British and Foreign Bible Society has been able to surmount the problem which it faced in the 1820s.

[29] J. Macleod, *Scottish Theology* (Edinburgh, 1943), pp.226f.

the copy of the Bible for presentation to King Edward VII at his coronation in 1902, the Archbishop of Canterbury (Frederick Temple) ruled that a 'mutilated Bible' (one lacking the Apocrypha) was unacceptable for the purpose, and as the Society was prevented by its constitution from providing an 'unmutilated' edition, a suitable copy had to be procured at short notice from another source.

A controversy broke out in Germany later in the nineteenth century over suggestions that the apocryphal books, because of their theological defects, should no longer be printed as part of the Bible. The case for retaining them was persuasively argued by some of the leading conservatives among Protestant theologians, and the controversy stimulated more intensive critical study of these books and of the arguments for excluding or retaining them.[30]

The British Revised Version of the Bible included a revision of the Apocrypha, published in 1895 (the New Testament had been issued in 1881, the complete Bible, apart from the Apocrypha, in 1885). The parallel American revision, the American Standard Version of 1901, never included the Apocrypha. The Apocrypha did, however, appear in the Revised Standard Version (in 1957, five years after the rest of the work). They also appeared as part of the New English Bible when the complete work was published together in 1970.

Roman Catholic versions of the Bible, like the Jerusalem Bible of 1966 (and the New Jerusalem Bible of 1985) and the New American Bible of 1970 included the Apocrypha as an integral part of the Old Testament. But an ecumenical milestone was reached in 1973 with the appearance of the Common Bible, an edition of the RSV with the Apocrypha/Deuterocanonical Books printed between the Testaments in a form which received the blessing not only of Catholic and Protestant church leaders but also of the Archbishop of Thyateira and Great Britain, the leader of the Greek Orthodox community in Britain.[31] This does not mean that there is now universal agreement on the Old Testament canon. There are some Protestants who still regard the Apocrypha as a perquisite of the Church of Rome, like a reviewer who greeted the New English Bible with the words: 'The Apocrypha part of the Bible! This is certainly a New Bible indeed. Rome can rightly rejoice that at last her view of the canon of Scripture

---

[30] See B. M. Metzger, *An Introduction to the Apocrypha* (Oxford, 1957), pp. 202f.

[31] The commendation of the Greek Orthodox Archbishop is the more telling because the OT part of the work is not based on the Septuagint, which is the authoritative text for the Orthodox Church (see p. 82).

has displaced that of the Apostolic Church.'[32] Again, we shall not see the New International Version of 1978 (a most praiseworthy enterprise) expanded by the inclusion of the Apocrypha.[33] But the greater availability of these books means that there is a better appreciation of their character, and of the issues involved in delimiting the canon of the Old Testament.

[32] I. R. K. Paisley, *The New English Bible: Version or Perversion?* (Belfast, 1961), p.3. The reviewer cannot have been unaware that the Apocrypha were included in every major Protestant version of the English Bible from Coverdale to the Revised Standard Version.

[33] The New International Version was sponsored by the New York International Bible Society, a more conservative body than the American Bible Society. On the other hand, while the Good News Bible of 1979, sponsored by the American Bible Society and the British and Foreign Bible Society, was first published without the Apocrypha, it is planned to complete it with a translation of these books into 'today's English'.

PART THREE

NEW TESTAMENT

CHAPTER EIGHT

WRITINGS OF THE
NEW ERA

If the church of early days found the Hebrew scriptures in their Greek
dress to be such an effective Bible, why (it may be asked) was it felt
necessary to augment them with what later came to be called the New
Testament writings?

THE LORD AND THE APOSTLES

Jesus wrote no book: he taught by word of mouth and personal
example. But some of his followers taught in writing as well as orally.
Often, indeed, their writing was a second-best substitute for the
spoken word. In Galatians 4:20, for example, Paul wishes that he
could be with his friends in Galatia and speak to them directly so that
they could catch his tone of voice as well as his actual words but, as he
could not visit them just then, a letter had to suffice. The letter to the
Hebrews has many of the features of a synagogue homily, based on
some of the scripture lessons prescribed for the season of Pentecost,[1]
and there are indications towards the end that the writer would have
preferred to deliver it face to face had he been free to visit the
recipients.[2] We in our day may be glad, for our own sakes, that

[1] And possibly on one of the 'proper psalms' for the day (Ps. 110); see A. E.
Guilding, *The Fourth Gospel and Jewish Worship* (Oxford, 1960), pp.72, 100.
[2] *Cf* Heb. 13:18–23.

Galatians and Hebrews had to be sent in writing; but their authors were not thinking of us.

On the other hand, there was an occasion when Paul cancelled a planned visit to Corinth and sent a letter to the church of that city instead, because he judged that, in the circumstances, a written communication would be more effective than anything he could say (2 Cor. 1:23 — 2:4). And no doubt his judgment was right: his critics in the Corinthian church conceded that, while his bodily presence was unimpressive and his speech of no account, his letters were 'weighty and powerful' (2 Cor. 10:10). Some New Testament documents were evidently designed from the outset to be written compositions, not substitutes for the spoken word. But in the lifetime of the apostles and their colleagues their spoken words and their written words were equally authoritative. For later generations (including our own) the spoken words are lost; the written words alone remain (and by no means all of these), so that we have to be content with fragments of their teaching.

If Jesus wrote no book, what he said was treasured and repeated by those who heard him, and by their hearers in turn. To those who confessed him as Lord his words were at least as authoritative as those of Moses and the prophets. They were transmitted as a most important element in the 'tradition' of early Christianity, together with the record of his works, his death and resurrection. These were 'delivered' by the original witnesses and 'received' in turn by others not simply as an outline of historical events but as the church's confession of faith and as the message which it was commissioned to spread abroad.[3] It was by means of this 'tradition' that the Christians of the first two centuries were able to understand the Old Testament documents as the scriptures which bore witness to Christ.

But the perpetuation of the words and deeds of Jesus could not be entrusted indefinitely to oral tradition of this kind. Oral tradition might serve to preserve for many generations a body of teaching in rabbinical schools which were trained to receive and deliver it 'without losing a drop'.[4] But the Christian tradition was not meant to be scholastic property: it was to be imparted to a wider public, and (from

---

[3] *Cf* the use of the verbs 'deliver' and 'receive' in 1 Cor. 11:23 and 15:3.

[4] Eliezer ben Hyrkanos, an eminent rabbi about the end of the first century AD, was commended by his teacher as 'a well-cemented cistern that never loses a drop' (*Pirqê Abôt* 2.8); but Eliezer was later so intransigent, so incapable of adapting his mind to changing conditions, that he had to be excommunicated (TB *Baba Meṣia*[c] 59a, b).

the rise of the Gentile mission) to a public whose culture was thoroughly literate. It was both desirable and inevitable that the oral tradition should be committed to writing if it was not to be lost. So long as some slender contact with the eyewitnesses and their hearers was maintained, there were those, like Papias, bishop of Hierapolis in Phrygia (c AD 125), who preferred oral tradition to written records. 'I did not suppose', said Papias, 'that what I could get from the books would help me so much as what I could get from a living and abiding voice.'[5]

In the absence of an adequate context for these words (quoted by Eusebius from a long-lost work of Papias),[6] it is uncertain what Papias meant by 'the books' *(ta biblia)*. He knew of at least two gospel writings, but when a Christian of his time spoke of 'the books', he usually meant the Old Testament. It is in any case a good thing that, by Papias's time, written accounts of the deeds and words of Jesus were available, for, if the surviving fragments of Papias's work give any guidance here, the oral tradition which he was able to gather amounted to little more than the last scrapings of the barrel.[7]

The authority of Jesus was invoked for their teaching by the apostles—a designation which in the New Testament is not always confined to the twelve. Paul asserts his title to recognition as an apostle on the strength both of his Damascus-road commission and of his subsequent energetic and fruitful activity in preaching the gospel and planting churches;[8] and he mentions other apostles over and above the twelve and himself.[9] Those whose apostleship was recognized by fellow-Christians were acknowledged to be Christ's agents, speaking by his authority. Their interpretation of the Old Testament writings

---

[5] Quoted by Eusebius, *Hist. Eccl.* 3.39.4. Writing perhaps in his later years (c. AD 125/130), Papias describes his procedure in earlier days thus: 'If ever any one came who had been a companion of the elders, I would inquire about the elders' words. "What", I would ask, "did Andrew or Peter say, or Philip or Thomas or James, or John or Matthew or any other of the Lord's disciples?" "And what do Aristion and John the elder, the Lord's disciples, say?"' The 'elders' appear to have been disciples of the apostles. Aristion and John the elder (the latter being specifically so called, perhaps, to distinguish him from the John mentioned previously) were 'elders' who were old enough to have heard the Lord himself and survived into Papias's lifetime.

[6] Papias's *Exegesis of the Dominical Oracles*.

[7] One can still study with profit the two chapters on Papias in J. B. Lightfoot's *Essays on the Work entitled 'Supernatural Religion'* (London, 1889), pp. 142–216.

[8] E.g. in 1 Cor. 9:1f.; 2 Cor. 3:1–3.

[9] E.g. in Rom. 16:7; 1 Cor. 15:7; Gal. 1:19.

was therefore, in practice, as binding as those writings themselves. Was their teaching as authoritative as that which came from the Lord's own lips? Probably a difference was felt, except possibly when a prophet gave voice to an utterance in the Lord's name. Paul can claim that Christ speaks in him (2 Cor. 13:3), but when answering the Corinthians' detailed questions about marriage and divorce he makes a careful distinction between a ruling given by the Lord in person, which is binding without question, and his own judgment, which his converts may accept or not as they choose—he thinks they will be wise if they accept it, but he cannot impose it (1 Cor. 7:10f., 12–40). A ruling from the Lord is even more binding than an Old Testament commandment. Paul quotes Deuteronomy 25:4 ('You shall not muzzle an ox when it is treading out the grain') to demonstrate that the preacher of the gospel is entitled to get his living by the gospel, but his final argument for this principle is that the Lord himself has so commanded (1 Cor. 9:8–14).

In a later letter in the Pauline collection this argument is repeated: the same Old Testament commandment is quoted and coupled this time with an express saying of Jesus: 'for the scripture says, "You shall not muzzle an ox when it is treading out the grain", and, "The labourer deserves his wages"' (1 Tim. 5:18). What is striking here is that a saying of Jesus known to us from Luke 10:7 is linked with an Old Testament text under the common rubric: 'the scripture says.' It has to be considered whether 'the scripture' refers strictly to the commandment from Deuteronomy, or also to a written collection of sayings of Jesus which may have served as a source for the Third Evangelist, or even to the Gospel of Luke itself. (Here the comparative dating of 1 Timothy and Luke would have to be taken into account.)

In what is usually regarded as the latest of the New Testament documents, reference is made to one of the writings of Paul, who is said to speak to the same effect 'in all his letters. There are some things in them hard to understand [the writer goes on], which the ignorant and unstable twist to their own destruction, as they do the other scriptures' (2 Pet. 3:15f.). Here Paul's letters seem to form a recognizable collection, and to be given the status of scripture, since they are associated with 'the other scriptures'. If the date of 2 Peter were more certainly known, it would provide an important landmark in the history of the canonization of the New Testament documents. On the other hand, if the Pauline letters are here reckoned along with 'the other scriptures', this might in itself imply their addition to the

Old Testament writings, perhaps in a kind of appendix, rather than the emergence of a new and distinct collection of 'scriptures'.

Clement of Rome, in his letter to the Corinthian church (c AD 96), quotes the words of Jesus as being at least on a level of authority with those of the prophets. 'The Holy Spirit says', he states, introducing a conflated quotation from Jeremiah 9:23f. and 1 Samuel 2:10 ('Let not the wise man boast in his wisdom nor the strong man in his strength nor the rich man in his riches, but let him who boasts boast in the Lord, to seek him out and to practise judgment and righteousness'), and then he goes on: 'especially remembering the words of the Lord Jesus, "Be merciful, so that you may obtain mercy..."' (with further quotations from the Sermon on the Mount).[10]

Ignatius, bishop of Antioch (c 110), refers to some people who refuse to believe anything that is not recorded 'in the archives' (or 'in the charters', meaning presumably the Old Testament scriptures), even if it is affirmed 'in the gospel'. When Ignatius replies 'It is written' or 'scripture says' (presumably meaning a gospel writing), they retort, 'That is the question'—in other words, 'Is the gospel scripture?' Ignatius responds with a rhetorical outburst, in which he affirms that his ultimate authority is Jesus Christ: whatever authority the 'archives' (or 'charters') have is summed up and brought to perfection in his passion and resurrection—in short, in the Christian faith.[11]

Further references to the gospel writings as 'scripture' are made in the second-century homily conventionally called the Second Epistle of Clement. In one place Isaiah 54:1 ('Rejoice, O barren one...') is quoted and the author goes on: 'And another scripture says, "I came not to call the righteous, but sinners"' (cf Mt. 9:13).[12] Later the

---

[10] 1 Clem. 13:1f. In 1 Clem. 46:7f. a plea for unity, fortified by various quotations, is concluded with 'Remember the words of the Lord Jesus', followed by a warning against leading Christ's elect ones into sin, resembling such sayings as those of Mt. 26:24 and Luke 17:2 (perhaps quoted from oral tradition rather than from a written text). Cf. Acts 20:35.

[11] Ignatius, *To the Philadelphians* 8.2. Another possibility is that Ignatius's 'It is written' refers to Old Testament texts which were invoked as 'testimonies' to Christ; his opponents' retort 'That is the question' (Gk. *prokeitai*) would then mean: 'Do these Old Testament texts in fact refer to Christ?' See B. M. Metzger, *The Canon of the New Testament* (Oxford, 1987), p.48.

[12] 2 Clem. 2:1–4. This homily has usually been dated in the mid-second century, but a case for dating it c AD 100 has been argued by K. P. Donfried, *The Setting of Second Clement in Early Christianity*, NovT Sup 38 (Leiden, 1974).

dominical saying, 'Whoever has confessed me before men, I will confess him before my Father' (cf. Mt. 10:32), is followed by 'And he says also in Isaiah, "This people honours me with their lips, but their heart is far from me"' (Is. 29:13),[13] while in yet another place it is declared that 'the books and the apostles say that the church is not of present-day origin but has existed from the beginning'.[14] The apostles' authority is evidently not less than that of 'the books' (the Old Testament writings); their Lord's authority is *a fortiori* on a par with that of the law and the prophets.

Rather earlier than this homily is the *Letter of Barnabas* (perhaps the work of an Alexandrian Christian), which uses the clause 'as it is written' to introduce the quotation 'Many are called, but few are chosen' — words found nowhere in the Bible apart from the gospel of Matthew (Mt 22:14).[15] Polycarp, bishop of Smyrna, writing to the church of Philippi between AD 110 and 120, reminds his readers, who (perhaps by their own testimony) were 'well versed in the sacred letters', that 'it is said in these scriptures, "Be angry and sin not" and "Do not let the sun go down on your anger"'.[16] The former injunction comes from Psalm 4:4, but it is quoted in Ephesians 4:26, where it is followed by the second injunction. We cannot be completely sure of Polycarp's wording, as this part of his letter is extant only in a Latin version of the Greek original, but he appears definitely to ascribe scriptural status to a New Testament writing.

So does the gnostic leader Basilides, a younger contemporary of Polycarp; he was well acquainted with several of the documents which came to be included in the New Testament. For example, he introduces a quotation from Romans 8:19, 22 with the phrase 'as it is written'[17] and says that the events of our Lord's life took place 'as it is written in the gospels'.[18] He quotes 1 Corinthians 2:13 as an expression used in 'the scripture'.[19]

Dionysius, bishop of Corinth about 170, complains that letters he has written have been falsified by omissions and interpolations; of those responsible for this misdemeanour he says, 'the woe is laid up in store for them' (having in mind perhaps the warning pronounced in Rev. 22:18f. against any one who alters the words of the Apocalypse

[13] 2 Clem. 3:2–5. (Is. 29:13 is quoted in Mk. 7:6.)   [14] 2 Clem. 14:2.
[15] Barnabas 4:14.   [16] Polycarp, *To the Philippians* 12:1.
[17] Quoted by Hippolytus, *Refutation of All Heresies*, 7.25.2.
[18] Quoted by Hippolytus, *Refutation*, 7.27.8.
[19] Quoted by Hippolytus, *Refutation*, 7.26.3.

by addition or subtraction). 'Therefore it is not surprising', he goes on, 'that some have dared to falsify even the dominical scriptures, when they have plotted against writings so inferior to these.'[20] The 'dominical scriptures' could be gospels or other New Testament writings, but they might conceivably be the Old Testament writings, especially those passages which were used as 'testimonies' concerning Christ.

About the same time the Palestinian Christian Hegesippus could report after his journeys among the Mediterranean churches that 'in every [episcopal] succession and in every city the preaching of the law and the prophets and of the Lord is faithfully followed'.[21]

These quotations do not amount to evidence for a New Testament canon; they do show that the authority of the Lord and his apostles was reckoned to be not inferior to that of the law and the prophets. Authority precedes canonicity; had the words of the Lord and his apostles not been accorded supreme authority, the written record of their words would never have been canonized.

It has at times been suggested that the replacement of oral tradition in the church by a written collection is in some ways regrettable. The author of a volume entitled *Is 'Holy Scripture' Christian?* (a title which he concedes is 'perhaps foolish') quotes G. Widengren, a Swedish scholar, to the effect that 'the reduction to writing of an oral tradition is always a sign of loss of nerve' and mentions a remark ascribed by Oxford oral tradition to R. H. Lightfoot 'that the writing of the gospels was an early manifestation of the operation of original sin in the church'.[22] But, in a society like the Graeco-Roman world of the early Christian centuries, where writing was the regular means of preserving and transmitting material deemed worthy of remembrance, the idea of relying on oral tradition for the recording of the deeds and words of Jesus and the apostles would not have generally commended itself (whatever Papias and some others might think).

In the first half of the second century, then, collections of Christian

[20] Quoted by Eusebius, *Hist. Eccl.* 4.23.12.

[21] Quoted by Eusebius, *Hist. Eccl.* 4.22.3.

[22] C. F. Evans, *Is 'Holy Scripture' Christian?* (London, 1971), pp.6f. The Widengren quotation (not specifically referring to the New Testament) comes from 'Literary and Psychological Aspects of the Hebrew Prophets', *Uppsala Universitets Årsskrift*, 1948, No. 10, p.9; Widengren speaks of a 'crisis of credit' and acknowledges indebtedness to H. S. Nyberg. This title of Evans's book is borrowed from the title of one of his essays reproduced as a chapter in it; it is at the end of this essay that he speaks of 'the chapter's perhaps foolish title' (p.36).

writings which were due one day to be given canonical status were already taking shape—notably the fourfold gospel and the corpus of Pauline letters.

THE FOURFOLD GOSPEL

Before the term 'gospel' (Gk. *euangelion*) came to be given to any single one of the four gospels (or to one of the many other works of the same literary *genre*), it meant (1) the good news of the kingdom of God preached by Jesus, (2) the good news about Jesus preached by his followers after the first Easter and Pentecost, (3) the written record of the good news current in a particular locality, (4) the fourfold gospel.

When Ignatius used the term 'gospel', in which sense did he use it? In his letter to the church of Smyrna, he speaks of heretics who have thus far been persuaded 'neither by the prophecies nor by the law of Moses nor by the gospel',[23] and says that the best defence against false teaching is 'to pay heed to the prophets and especially to the gospel, in which the passion has been revealed to us and the resurrection has been accomplished'.[24] If he was referring to one written gospel, it was most probably Matthew's. Roughly contemporary with Ignatius's letters (or perhaps a decade or so earlier) is the manual of church order called the *Didachē* (superscribed 'The Lord's teaching to the Gentiles through the twelve apostles'), proceeding possibly from the neighbourhood of Antioch, where 'the gospel' is clearly the gospel of Matthew (the form of the Lord's Prayer found in Mt. 6:9–13 is prescribed for regular use 'as the Lord commanded in his gospel').[25]

Evidence of another kind comes from Papias. How many gospel writings Papias knew is uncertain: Eusebius preserves comments which he made on two, thinking that they contained information that was worth quoting. One of the comments Papias claims to have derived from someone whom he calls 'the elder': it relates to Mark's record:

> Mark became Peter's interpreter and wrote down accurately all that he remembered, whether the sayings or the doings of the Lord, but not in order—for he had neither heard the Lord nor followed him, but followed Peter later on, as I said. Peter was

[23] *To the Smyrnaeans* 5:1.   [24] *To the Smyrnaeans* 7:2.
[25] *Didachē* 8.2. So too the baptismal formula prescribed ('into the name of the Father and of the Son and of the Holy Spirit') is that of Mt. 28:19 (*Didachē* 7.1).

accustomed to teach as occasion required, but not as though he were making a compilation of the dominical oracles. So Mark made no mistake in writing down certain things as he called them to mind; for he paid attention to one thing: to omit none of the things he had heard and to make no false statements in any of them. [26]

Eusebius then quotes a sentence from Papias on Matthew:

Matthew compiled the oracles in the Hebrew speech, and each one interpreted them as best he could. [27]

Papias says nothing (so far as is known) of a gospel collection; it is not even certain that the two pieces of information just quoted came from the same context in his work; their juxtaposition may be due to Eusebius.

On Mark's record Papias speaks somewhat defensively, as though he knew of criticisms that had been voiced against it, especially on the ground that its order was defective. To this Papias replies that Mark did not set out to write an orderly account: his aim was to record in writing whatever Peter had to tell of the works and words of Jesus; and Peter simply mentioned from time to time those things which the circumstances of the moment required. In what he wrote down Mark made no mistake: in order, as in matter, he adhered to what Peter said. (In fact, Papias does less than justice to the literary unity of Mark's gospel: whatever Mark's sources were, he wove them into the fabric of his work with the skill of an independent author.)[28]

But if Mark was criticized for his defective order, it is implied that the critics had in mind some other record which served as a standard from which Mark deviated. This record might have been Matthew's: when Papias says that Mark did not make a compilation of the dominical oracles, he indicates that Mark was not concerned to do what Matthew (according to his account) actually did. Certainly in the earlier part of Mark's record his order differs from Matthew's. But another possibility is that the standard from which Mark allegedly deviated was the gospel of John, which was produced in Papias's own province of Asia. Certainly the differences in order between John's

---

[26] Eusebius, *Hist. Eccl.* 3.39.15.,   [27] Eusebius, *Hist. Eccl.*, 3.39.16.
[28] See F. F. Bruce, 'The date and character of Mark', in *Jesus and the Politics of his Day*, ed. E. Bammel and C. F. D. Moule (Cambridge, 1984), pp.69–89.

gospel and the three synoptic accounts taken together are plain enough. Although no express evidence survives of Papias's acquaintance with John's gospel, Eusebius's statement that he used 'testimonies' from John's first epistle suggests that he must have known his gospel too.[29] But so far as references to John in Papias's surviving fragments go, we should gather that he was more interested in ascertaining what John said than in reading what he wrote.

Papias's account of Mark was derived from someone whom he calls 'the elder' or 'the presbyter'—presumably someone who in his earlier life had known one or more of the apostles. It is not clear that his account of Matthew was derived from such an authority.[30] The 'oracles' which Matthew compiled are doubtless the oracles of the Lord, on which Papias himself wrote his *Exegesis* or explanation in five volumes (scrolls). His statement that Matthew compiled them 'in the Hebrew speech'[31] has been taken to show that the reference is not to our Gospel of Matthew, which bears all the signs of being an original Greek composition. But Papias, or any informant on whom he relied here, may not have been able to recognize translation-Greek or distinguish it from untranslated Greek.

A generation after Papias, Justin Martyr, a native of Palestine who had become a Christian while resident in the province of Asia but was now living in Rome, shows his knowledge of a gospel collection. If Justin's work *Against Marcion* (known to Irenaeus and Eusebius)[32] had survived, it would probably have told us more about the status of the New Testament documents in Justin's circle than his works which do survive—his *Dialogue with Trypho* and his two *Apologies*, defences of

[29] Eusebius, *Hist. Eccl.*, 3.39.17. See J. B. Lightfoot, *Essays on 'Supernatural Religion'*, pp.186–207; R. M. Grant, *The Formation of the New Testament* (London, 1965), pp.69–72.

[30] In view of Eusebius's poor estimate of Papias's intelligence (*Hist. Eccl.*, 3.39.13), T. W. Manson argued that he would not have troubled to record Papias's private opinion on a matter of this importance: 'we are justified in supposing that Eusebius regarded this fragment as a piece of earlier tradition preserved by Papias' (*Studies in the Gospels and Epistles* [Manchester, 1962], p.70. Manson went on to argue that the 'oracles' said to have been compiled by Matthew were utterances of Jesus, no less authoritative in the eyes of the church than the oracles of the Hebrew prophets.

[31] 'Hebrew' might mean 'Aramaic', as sometimes in the New Testament (e.g. Jn. 19:13, 17).

[32] *Cf* Irenaeus, *Against Heresies*, 4.6.2, where an extract from this work of Justin shows the latter's knowledge of, and dependence on, the Gospel of John; also Eusebius, *Hist. Eccl.* 4.11.8f.

Christianity addressed respectively to the Emperor Antoninus Pius (138–161) and to the Roman senate (between 144 and 160). In his *Dialogue* Justin speaks of the 'memoirs' *(memorabilia)* of Peter (possibly the gospel of Mark)[33] and in his *First Apology* he refers to the 'memoirs of the apostles'. These memoirs, he says, are called gospels, and they are read in church along with the 'compositions of the prophets'.[34]

We are on firmer ground when we come to Justin's disciple Tatian. After Justin's martyrdom (AD 165), Tatian went back to his native Assyria, and there introduced what was to be for centuries a very influential edition of the gospels, his *Diatessaron*. This word is a musical term, meaning 'harmony of four'; it indicates clearly what this edition was. It was a continuous gospel narrative, produced by unstitching the units of the four individual gospels and restitching them together in what was taken to be their chronological order. The gospel of John provided the framework into which material from the gospels of Matthew, Mark and Luke was fitted. The *Diatessaron* began with John 1:1–5, after which, instead of John 1:6 ('There was a man sent from God, whose name was John'), it reproduced Luke's account of the birth of John (Luke 1:5–80). But John's order was not followed slavishly: the cleansing of the temple, for example, was located in Holy Week, where the synoptic account places it (Mark 11:15–17 and parallels), and not at the beginning of Jesus' ministry, where it appears in John 2:13–22.[35]

Tatian was an Encratite,[36] member of an ascetic group which believed that vegetarianism was an essential element in the gospel: it was perhaps on this account that the *Diatessaron* changed John the Baptist's diet from 'locusts and wild honey' (Mark 1:6 and parallels) to 'milk and honey'. It is possible that here and there he amplified his

---

[33] *Dialogue*, 106.3; *cf* 100.4, etc., for the 'memoirs of the apostles'. Justin uses the Greek word *apomnē moneumata*, familiar in classical literature, as in Xenophon's *Memorabilia of Socrates*.

[34] *First Apology*, 66.3; 67.3. R. G. Heard suggests that Justin took over Papias's phraseology ('The *apomnē moneumata* in Papias, Justin and Irenaeus', NTS 1 [1954–55], pp.122–129).

[35] On Tatian and the *Diatessaron* see R. M. Grant, *The Earliest Lives of Jesus* (London, 1961), pp.22–28; B. M. Metzger, *The Early Versions of the New Testament* (Oxford, 1977), pp.10–36.

[36] From Gk. *enkratēs*. 'continent'; the Encratites may have taken their designation from the one occurrence of this adjective in the New Testament: Tit. 1:8 (AV/KJV 'temperate', RSV 'self-controlled'). Tatian is said to have rejected some Pauline epistles, but to have accepted Titus (Jerome, *Commentary on Titus*, preface).

narrative with information from a fifth 'gospel'; his reference to a light which shone around at Jesus' baptism, for example, may have been taken from the *Gospel according to the Hebrews*.[37] But this does not affect the fact that the *Diatessaron* is essentially an integrated edition of the four gospels which we know as canonical. These four evidently shared a status on their own, not only in Tatian's idiosyncratic mind but in the circles to which he belonged, both in Rome and in Northern Mesopotamia.

The *Diatessaron* circulated at an early date not only in Syriac (the language of Tatian's native territory) but also in Greek: our earliest surviving relic of it is a vellum fragment in Greek from the third century, found among the ruins of a Roman fort at Dura-Europos on the Euphrates.[38] It was in its Syriac form that it really took root: it was the preferred edition of the gospels in many Syriac-speaking churches for over two hundred years, and they were most reluctant to give it up in the early fifth century, under episcopal pressure, for a new version of the 'separated' gospels (part of the *Peshiṭta*). Ephrem, one of the greatest of the Syriac fathers (*c* 306–373), wrote a commentary on the *Diatessaron,* which is still extant.[39]

Of the four gospels, John's took longer to win universal acceptance among catholic Christians than the others because (almost from its first publication) some gnostic schools treated it as though it supported their positions.[40] The earliest known quotation from John comes in the gnostic writer Basilides (*c* 130);[41] the earliest known commentary on John was written by the gnostic Heracleon (*c* 180).[42] But those,

---

[37] See G. Quispel, *Tatian and the Gospel of Thomas* (Leiden, 1975).

[38] First edited by C. H. Kraeling, *A Greek Fragment of Tatian's Diatessaron from Dura = Studies and Documents,* 3 (London, 1935). The fragment combines Mt. 27:56f. with the parallel passages in the other three gospels (Mk. 15:40f.; Lk. 23:49–51; Jn. 19:38).

[39] Ephrem's commentary is extant in its entirety in an Armenian translation, published in 1836 by the Mechitarists in Venice; a Latin version of the Armenian, completed in 1841 by J. –B. Aucher, was published at Venice in 1876. But in 1957 a considerable portion (about two-thirds) of Ephrem's Syriac original was identified in a parchment manuscript of the Chester Beatty collection: this was edited and translated into Latin by L. Leloir, O.S.B., in the series *Chester Beatty Monographs,* 8 (Dublin, 1963).

[40] It may be, indeed, that 1 Jn. took issue with people who were perverting the teaching of the Fourth Gospel in this way.

[41] According to Hippolytus, Basilides quoted Jn. 1:9 (*Refutation,* 7.22) and Jn. 2:4, 'my hour has not yet come' (*Refutation,* 7.27).

[42] Heracleon's work is copiously quoted in Origen's *Commentary on John.*

like Justin Martyr,[43] who read it more carefully found that it supplied more effective anti-gnostic ammunition than any other New Testament book.[44]

The popularization of the codex form of book among Christians of the period covered in this chapter made it practicable to bind all four gospel writings together. The nearly simultaneous popularization of the codex and publication of the fourfold gospel may have been purely coincidental: on the other hand, one of the two processes may have had some influence on the other.[45] The fragment of John 18 in the Rylands collection, Manchester (P^{52}), dated c AD 130, came from a codex, but it is naturally impossible to say whether it was a codex of John's gospel only or of the fourfold gospel. The manuscript P^{75} in the Bodmer collection, from the late second or early third century, was probably, when complete, a codex of the fourfold gospel rather than a codex of Luke and John only. The earliest surviving codex which still contains portions of all four gospels is P^{45} in the Chester Beatty collection, from the early third century. It contains Acts as well as the fourfold gospel—an exceptional collocation, for in the early textual history of the New Testament Acts was more often included in a codex with the catholic epistles.

THE PAULINE CORPUS

We do not know by whom or in what place the first edition of Paul's collected letters was produced. C. F. D. Moule has suggested that it was Luke's doing: 'it is entirely in keeping with his historian's temperament to collect them.'[46] As for the place, Ephesus, Corinth

---

[43] Justin's identification of Christ with the *logos* ('Word') is probably dependent on Jn. 1:1–14, although Justin develops it along lines of his own (*First Apology*, 46.1–6); again, the words, 'Christ also said, "Unless you are born again, you will not enter into the kingdom of heaven"' (*First Apology*, 61.4), can scarcely be anything other than a quotation from memory of John 3:3, 5. See also p.175, n.32.

[44] Justin says nothing about the authorship of the Fourth Gospel. He names the apostle John as author of the Apocalypse (*Dialogue*, 81.4). The first known writer to call the evangelist John is Theophilus, bishop of Antioch c AD 180 (*To Autolycus*, 2.22). See more generally M. F. Wiles, *The Spiritual Gospel* (Cambridge, 1960).

[45] See the negative conclusions on such influence drawn by C. H. Roberts and T. C. Skeat, *The Birth of the Codex* (London, 1983), pp.62–66.

[46] C. F. D. Moule, *The Birth of the New Testament* (London, ³1981), p.264.

and Alexandria have been suggested.[47] The suggestion of Alexandria has been supported by the consideration that the editorial care devoted to the forming and publishing of the collection is entirely in line with the traditions of Alexandrian scholarship; on the other hand, Alexandria lay right outside the sphere of Pauline Christianity.

What is important is this: from the early second century onward Paul's letters circulated not singly, but as a collection.[48] It was as a collection that Christians of the second century and later knew them, both orthodox and heterodox. The codex into which the letters were copied by their first editor constituted a master-copy on which all subsequent copies of the letters were based. There are relatively few variant readings in the textual tradition of Paul's letters which may go back to a time earlier than the formation of the Pauline corpus—the time when the letters still circulated singly.[49]

The oldest surviving copy of the Pauline corpus is the Chester Beatty manuscript P^{46}, written about AD 200. Of this codex 86 folios are extant out of an original 104. It evidently did not include the three Pastoral Epistles (1 and 2 Timothy and Titus); on the other hand, it did include Hebrews, which comes second in its sequence of letters, between Romans and 1 Corinthians. The sequence was probably based on descending order of length (like the present sequence of the Pauline letters):[50] although 1 Corinthians is longer than Hebrews, it may have been placed after it to avoid its separation from 2 Corinthians.[51]

The Chester Beatty codex of Paul's letters, with P^{45} and the other biblical papyri in the same collection, seems to have formed part of the Bible of a Greek-speaking country church in Egypt. A Pauline codex

---

[47] Ephesus by E. J. Goodspeed, *The Meaning of Ephesians* (Chicago, 1933); J. Knox, *Marcion and the New Testament* (Chicago, 1942), pp.174f.; C. L. Mitton, *The Formation of the Pauline Corpus of Letters* (London, 1955), pp.45–49; Corinth by A. Harnack, *Die Briefsammlung des Apostels Paulus* (Leipzig, 1926), pp.8f.; W. Schmithals, *Paul and the Gnostics*, E.T. (Nashville/New York, 1972), p.263; Alexandria by G. Zuntz, *The Text of the Epistles* (London, 1954), p.278.

[48] The earliest reference to a collection of his letters is in 2 Pet. 3:15f. See p.120.

[49] See G. Zuntz, *The Text of the Epistles*, pp.14–17, 269–283; also, more generally, L. Mowry, 'The Early Circulation of Paul's Letters', *JBL* 63 (1944), pp.73–86.

[50] In most present-day editions of the New Testament Paul's letters to churches appear in descending order of length (except that Galatians is actually rather shorter than Ephesians); his letters to individuals follow, also in descending order of length.

[51] See W. H. P. Hatch, 'The Position of Hebrews in the Canon of the New Testament', *HTR* 29 (1936). pp.133–135; C. P. Anderson, 'The Epistle to the Hebrews and the Pauline Letter Collection', *HTR* 59 (1966), pp.429–438.

of the same date emanating from Rome would not have included Hebrews (the Roman church did not recognize Hebrews as Pauline until the fourth century).[52] Marcion's edition of Paul's letters (his *Apostle*), published about 144, was most probably based on a Pauline codex known to him, which (like Marcion's own edition) included neither Hebrews nor the Pastoral Epistles.[53] The most natural inference from such evidence as we have suggests that the original edition of the Pauline corpus contained ten letters only.

Before the production of this collected edition, a beginning had already been made with gathering some of Paul's letters together. He himself encouraged the churches of Colossae and Laodicea, two neighbouring cities in the Lycus valley of Phrygia, to exchange letters which they had received from him (Col. 4:16). His letter to the churches of Galatia was evidently sent in one copy, with the final paragraph written in his own hand (Gal. 6:11); this copy would have been taken from one church to another, but some churches may have made a transcript of it before passing it on (others may have been eager to get rid of it and forget its contents as soon as possible). There are indications that the letter to the Romans circulated in a shorter form among other churches than Rome, for which it was primarily written; this could even have been done on Paul's own initiative.[54] The letter to the Ephesians bears some marks which indicate that it was designed as an encyclical, not directed to one particular church (one ingenious, but not very convincing, theory is that it was composed as an introduction to the first collected edition of Paul's letters).[55]

It might be expected that local collections of letters would be made

---

[52] Under the influence of Athanasius; see p.221.   [53] See p.138.

[54] See T. W. Manson, 'St. Paul's Letter to the Romans—and Others', *BJRL* 31 (1948), pp.224–240, reprinted in his *Studies in the Gospels and Epistles* (Manchester, 1962), pp.225–241, and in *The Romans Debate*, ed. K. P. Donfried (Minneapolis, 1977), pp.1–16; also H. Gamble, *The Textual History of the Letter to the Romans* = *Studies and Documents*, 42 (Grand Rapids, 1977).

[55] See E. J. Goodspeed, *The Formation of the New Testament* (Chicago, 1926), p.28; *The Meaning of Ephesians* (Chicago, 1933); *The Key to Ephesians* (Chicago, 1956); J. Knox, *Philemon Among the Letters of Paul* (London, ²1960), pp.85–92 (Knox elaborates Goodspeed's thesis by supposing that the first collector of Paul's letters and the author of Ephesians was Paul's convert Onesimus, known to Ignatius as bishop of Ephesus). G. Zuntz shows good reason to conclude that 'whoever wrote Ephesians, it was not the editor of the *corpus*' (*The Text of the Epistles*, pp.276f.). In the original text of Ephesians, no destination is specified; the words 'at Ephesus' (Eph. 1:1) are a later editorial addition. (See p.139, n.15.)

at an early stage—the letters to the churches of Macedonia (Thessalonica and Philippi), for example, or those to Christians in the Lycus valley (Colossians, Philemon and Ephesians).

When Clement of Rome sent his 'godly admonition' to the church of Corinth about AD 96, he plainly had access to a copy of 1 Corinthians, and probably to copies of some other Pauline letters. He was able to remind the Corinthian Christians of Paul's warning against party-spirit, addressed to their church forty years back (1 Cor. 1:11; 11:18).[56] (He also had access to a copy of Hebrews, which is not surprising if that letter was originally sent to a house-church in Rome.)[57] It has even been surmised that Clement's letter, with its evident interest in Paul's correspondence, stimulated members of the Corinthian church to seek out and collect scattered pieces of that correspondence which were still to be found in their archives. Such informal copying, circulating and collecting of Paul's letters preceded the publication of a definitive collection.

At what time the Pastoral Epistles were first included in the Pauline corpus is uncertain. In the absence of specific evidence it may be thought that their inclusion was part of the catholic church's response to the promulgation of Marcion's 'canon' (which is the subject of the following chapters).[58] But, as P^{46} shows, in some places the Pauline collection continued to be copied without the Pastorals, even where (as in Egypt) it was amplified by the inclusion of Hebrews.

FROM TWO COLLECTIONS TO ONE

The gospel collection was authoritative because it preserved the words of Jesus, than whom the church knew no higher authority. The Pauline collection was authoritative because it preserved the teaching of one whose authority as the apostle of Jesus Christ to the Gentiles was acknowledged (except by those who refused to recognize his commission) as second only to the Lord's. The bringing together of these two collections into something approximating the New Testament as we know it was facilitated by another document which linked the one to the other. This document was the Acts of the

---

[56] 1 Clem. 47:1–4.

[57] 1 Clem. 17:1; 70:1–6, etc. Clement gives no title to the epistle nor does he drop any hint about its authorship (which he may very well have known).

[58] See p. 151.

Apostles, which had been severed from its natural companion, the Gospel of Luke, when that gospel was incorporated in the fourfold collection. Acts had thereafter to play a part of its own, and an important part it proved to be.[59] 'A canon which comprised only the four Gospels and the Pauline Epistles', said Harnack, 'would have been at best an edifice of two wings without the central structure, and therefore incomplete and uninhabitable.'[60]

[59] See pp.15 1f.
[60] A Harnack, *History of Dogma*, E.T., II (London, 1896), p.48, n.2.

CHAPTER NINE

MARCION

MARCION AND HIS TEACHING

Marcion is the first person known to us who published a fixed collection of what we should call New Testament books. Others may have done so before him; if so, we have no knowledge of them. He rejected the Old Testament, as having no relevance or authority for Christians; his collection was therefore designed to be a complete Bible.

Marcion was born about AD 100 at Sinope, a seaport on the Black Sea coast of Asia Minor. His father was a leader in the church of that city, and Marcion was brought up in the apostolic faith. Of all the apostles, the one who appealed to him most strongly was Paul, to whom he became passionately devoted, concluding ultimately that he was the only apostle who preserved the teaching of Jesus in its purity. He embraced with intelligence and ardour Paul's gospel of justification by divine grace, apart from legal works. Adolf von Harnack did not really exaggerate when he called Marcion 'the only man in the early church who understood Paul', although he had to add, 'and even in his understanding he misunderstood him.'[1] Paul's refusal to allow any element of law-keeping in the message of salvation was taken by

---

[1] A. von Harnack, *History of Dogma*, E. T., (London, 1894), p.89 (where the translation is slightly different from that given above).

Marcion to imply that not only the Old Testament law, but the Old Testament itself, had been superseded by the gospel. The gospel, he believed, was an entirely new teaching brought to earth by Christ. The law and the prophets made no sort of preparation for it, and if some passages in Paul's correspondence suggested that they did, those passages must have been interpolated by others—by the kind of judaizers against whom Paul polemicized in Galatians and other letters.[2]

Marcion appears to have remained in communion with the catholic church so long as he lived in Asia Minor. There is some reason to think that he shared his radical thoughts with leading churchmen of the region, such as Polycarp of Smyrna and Papias of Hierapolis, but found them unresponsive.[3]

Perhaps it was in the hope of finding a more positive response from the more enlightened churchmen of Rome that he made his way to the imperial capital early in the principate of Antoninus Pius (who became emperor in AD 138). On his arrival in Rome he made a handsome donation of money to the church (he is said to have been a shipowner and was probably quite well off).[4] His understanding of the gospel and its implications was so self-evidently right to his own way of thinking that he could not believe that it would fail to be equally self-evident to any unprejudiced mind. But the Roman churchmen were so disturbed by his doctrine that they not only rejected it but even returned the money he had presented to the church.

Not only did Marcion regard Paul as the only faithful apostle of Christ; he maintained that the original apostles had corrupted their Master's teaching with an admixture of legalism. Not only did he reject the Old Testament; he distinguished the God of the Old Testament from the God of the New. This distinction of two deities, each with his independent existence, betrays the influence of gnos-

---

[2] On Marcion and teaching see above all A. von Harnack, *Marcion: Das Evangelium vom fremden Gott* (Leipzig, 1921, [2]1924), with its supplement *Neue Studien zu Marcion* (Leipzig, 1923); also R. S. Wilson, *Marcion: A Study of a Second-Century Heretic* (London, 1932); J. Knox, *Marcion and the New Testament* (Chicago, 1942); E. C. Blackman, *Marcion and his Influence* (London, 1948).

[3] Some contact with Polycarp may be implied in the story of Marcion's seeking an interview with him (perhaps in Rome, when Polycarp visited the city in AD 154) and asking him if he recognized him, only to receive the discouraging reply: 'I recognize —the firstborn of Satan!' (Irenaeus, *Against Heresies* 3.3.4). For a contact with Papias see p. 157.

[4] Tertullian, *Against Marcion*, 4.4, 9; *Prescription*, 30.

ticism on Marcion's thought. The God who created the material universe, the God of Israel, was (he held) a totally different being from the Father of whom Jesus spoke. The Father was the good and merciful God of whom none had ever heard until Jesus came to reveal him. As in the teaching of most gnostic schools, the God who made the material world was an inferior deity—inferior in status and morality alike—to the supreme God who was pure spirit. The gnostic depreciation of the material order finds an echo in Marcion's refusal to believe that Jesus entered human life by being 'born of a woman' (Gal. 4:4).

Enlightened and unprejudiced the church leaders in Rome might be, yet they understandably found this teaching unacceptable. So Marcion, despairing of being able to convince the catholic church anywhere of the truth of his message, withdrew from the catholic fellowship and established a church of his own. This church survived for several generations—surprisingly, when it is considered that its membership was maintained solely through conversion. It could not keep its numbers up by incorporating the children of existing members, for celibacy was obligatory on all its membership. At the same time, Marcion was a faithful enough Paulinist to allow no discrimination against female members of his church in matters of privilege or function: for him, as for Paul, there was 'neither male nor female' (Gal. 3:28).

ANTITHESES, GOSPEL AND APOSTLE

He provided his followers with an edition of the holy scriptures, to which he prefaced a series of *Antitheses*, setting out the incompatability of law and gospel, of the Creator-Judge of the Old Testament and the merciful Father of the New Testament (who had nothing to do with either creation or judgment). The *Antitheses* opened up with a lyrical celebration of divine grace, which should arouse a sympathetic echo in every evangelical heart: 'O wealth of riches! Ecstasy, power and astonishment! Nothing can be said about it, nor yet imagined about it; neither can it be compared to anything!'[5]

The holy scriptures to which the *Antitheses* served as an introduction inevitably included no part of the Old Testament; they consisted of an

[5] See F. C. Burkitt, 'The Exordium of Marcion's Antitheses', *JTS* 30 (1929), pp.279f.

edition of the Greek New Testament. Marcion did not call it the New Testament, so far as we know; indeed, he may not have given any one title to the edition as a whole. He referred to it by the titles which he gave to its two component parts: *Gospel* and *Apostle*.[6] Our main source of information about it is Tertullian's treatise *Against Marcion*, written over half a century later, when Marcion had been dead for some decades. Hostile and vituperative as Tertullian's treatment is, his factual data appear to be reliable.

Marcion's *Gospel* was an edition of the Gospel of Luke. Why he should have chosen Luke's gospel is a matter of speculation: perhaps in his native environment it had already come to be associated in a special way with Paul.[7] He nowhere mentioned Luke's name in connexion with it; it was presented simply as the gospel of Christ. Its text was purged of those elements which were inconsistent with Marcion's understanding of the truth and which therefore, on his principles, must have been interpolated by judaizing scribes. The birth of John the Baptist was omitted; it implied a connexion between Jesus and something that went before. The birth of Jesus himself was omitted: Jesus entered the world not by birth but by a descent as supernatural as was his later ascension. (Marcion found the whole idea of conception and childbirth disgusting.)

It is possible that the text of Luke which Marcion used as the basis for his *Gospel* was not identical with the text that has come down to us; it may have been an earlier edition, lacking the first two chapters—a sort of 'Proto-Luke'.[8] Even so, Marcion's *Gospel* cannot be equated with any 'Proto-Luke' recovered by modern methods of source criticism.[9] But even if the text which lay before Marcion did lack the first two chapters, it began at latest with Luke 3:1, 'In the fifteenth year of Tiberius Caesar', and those are the words with which Marcion's *Gospel* began. But the material which follows immediately on that

---

[6] In Greek: *Euangelion* and *Apostolikon*.   [7] See pp. 161, 174.

[8] P. L. Couchoud argued that the canonical Luke was an expansion of Marcion's gospel, and indeed that all the synoptic gospels were later than Marcion's canon ('Is Marcion's Gospel one of the Synoptics? *Hibbert Journal* 34 [1935–36], pp. 265–277; see also A. Loisy's rebuttal, 'Marcion's Gospel: A Reply', in the same volume, pp. 378–387). J. Knox leant to a modification of this theory, envisaging the canonical Luke-Acts as a reaction to Marcion's Gospel-Apostle compilation (*Marcion and the New Testament*, pp. 106–167; 'Acts and the Pauline Letter Corpus', in *Studies in Luke-Acts*, ed. L. E. Keck and J. L. Martyn [Nashville/New York, 1966], pp. 279–287).

[9] See B. H. Streeter, *The Four Gospels* (London, 1924), pp. 199–222; V. Taylor, *Behind the Third Gospel* (Oxford, 1926).

time-note was unacceptable to him. The account of John the Baptist's ministry and his baptism of Jesus implies some continuity between Jesus and the old order. So does the genealogy of Luke 3:23–38, tracing Jesus' ancestry back to Adam through David and Abraham. The temptation narrative (Luke 4:1–13) represents Jesus quoting from Deuteronomy three times, as though it had authority in his eyes—an impossibility, according to Marcion's principles. Equally impossible, for Marcion, was the idea that Jesus, preaching in the synagogue at Nazareth (Luke 4:16–30), should have claimed that his ministry was the fulfilment of Old Testament prophecy. So, having begun his edition of the *Gospel* with the time-note of Luke 3:1, 'In the fifteenth year of Tiberius', Marcion went straight on to Luke 4:31 and continued: 'Jesus came down to Capernaum'—as though he came down there and then from heaven, fully grown.[10]

In place of 'Thy kingdom come' in his version of the Lord's Prayer (Luke 11:2), Marcion's *Gospel* had the interesting variant: 'Let thy Holy Spirit come on us and cleanse us.' He may have found this in the copy of Luke which served as the basis for his edition, or it may have been his own emendation; in the latter case, it is interesting that it should have found its way into the textual tradition of 'orthodox' Christians: it is cited by the church fathers Gregory of Nyssa[11] and Maximus of Turin,[12] and is the reading of one or two Greek manuscripts of the gospels.[13]

'The old is good' (Luke 5:39) is omitted because it might be taken to imply approval of the Old Testament order. The reference to Jesus' mother and brothers could not be retained in Luke 8:19 (Jesus belonged to no human family) and the description of Zacchaeus as a son of Abraham in Luke 19:9 had to go. There are other peculiarities of Marcion's *Gospel* which can be explained with equal ease, but there are some which do not appear to have arisen from his presuppositions and which probably bear witness to the second-century text which he used.

Marcion's *Apostle* was an edition of ten letters of Paul. The three Pastoral Epistles (1 and 2 Timothy and Titus) are not included: this could be the result of his deliberately leaving them out, but more probably the copy of the Pauline corpus which he used as the basis of

[10] Tertullian, *Against Marcion*, 4.7.1.   [11] Bishop of Nyssa, AD 371–394.
[12] Early 5th century AD.
[13] See I. H. Marshall, *The Gospel of Luke*, NIGTC (Exeter/Grand Rapids, 1978), p.458.

his edition lacked them, as the Chester Beatty codex of Paul's letters (P^{46}) evidently did.[14]

At the head of his *Apostle* Marcion placed the letter to the Galatians. We do not know if it occupied this position in any other copy of Paul's letters, but there was a special appropriateness in this position to Marcion's way of thinking, for here the antithesis between Paul and the Jerusalem apostles (as he read the letter) was expressed most sharply. To Marcion the letter mounted a direct attack on the Jerusalem apostles, for it was at their instance, or at least by their agents, that the attempt was being made to win Paul's Gentile converts in Galatia over to a judaistic perversion of Christianity. The Jerusalem leaders might have reached an agreement with Paul at the conference described in Galatians 2:1–10, but they had broken that agreement by their effort to subvert the pure faith of the Galatian churches.

The remaining letters were arranged in descending order of length, the two letters to the Corinthians being reckoned together as one composite letter and the two letters to the Thessalonians being treated in the same way. The Marcionite order of Paul's letters was accordingly: Galatians, Corinthians (1 and 2), Romans, Thessalonians (1 and 2), 'Laodiceans' (which was the name Marcion gave to Ephesians), Colossians, Philippians, Philemon. The letter to the Ephesians appears in some ancient copies without the words 'in Ephesus' in Ephesians 1:1, and the copy which lay before Marcion probably lacked them.[15] What was he to call the letter, then? He found a clue in Colossians 4:16, where Paul gives directions for the exchange of his letter to the Colossians with one from Laodicea. This Laodicean letter could not be otherwise identified: why should it not be this letter which lacked internal evidence of its addressees?[16]

Marcion dealt with the text of Paul's letters in the same way as with the text of Luke's gospel: anything which appeared inconsistent with what he believed to be authentic Pauline teaching was regarded as a corruption proceeding from an alien hand and was removed. Even Galatians had been subjected to such corruption here and there, he

[14] It is most unlikely, however, that the reference in 1 Tim. 6:20 to the 'contradictions (*antitheses*) of what is falsely called knowledge (*gnōsis*)' is a reference to Marcion's *Antitheses*, as has sometimes been supposed.

[15] The words are absent from the oldest known copy of Paul's letters (P^{46}), from the Sinaitic and Vatican codices (first hand), and from some other manuscripts.

[16] For a later attempt to supply the supposedly missing letter to the Laodiceans see pp. 238–240.

found. The mention of Abraham as the prototype of all who are justified by faith (Gal. 3:6–9) could not be left standing and the tracing of any kind of relationship between law and gospel (as in Gal. 3:15–25) was equally unacceptable.

Marcion's edition of Romans lacked Romans 1:19—2:1; 3:21—4:25; all of Romans 9–11 except 10:1–4 and 11:33–36, and everything after Romans 14:23. The idea of establishing the law through faith (Rom. 3:31), the application of the story of Abraham in chapter 4, the grappling with the mystery of Israel's unbelief in chapters 9–11 (with their concentration of proof-texts from the Old Testament), were all incompatible with Paul's gospel as Marcion understood it. As for chapter 15, its opening section includes a general endorsement of the *Christian* value of the Old Testament scriptures (verse 4) and a string of quotations designed to show that the Gentile mission was foreseen and validated by Old Testament writers (verses 8–12), while its closing paragraph (verses 25–33) bears witness to a concern on Paul's part for the church of Jerusalem which Marcion must have found incredible, given his understanding of the relation between Paul and that church.

Marcion's edition of Romans seems to have affected the textual history of that epistle far beyond the frontiers of his own community. There is a whole group of manuscripts and versions of the Pauline letters in which Romans 14:23 is followed immediately by the doxology which appears in our editions as Romans 16:25–27; this bears witness to a state of the text in which the epistle ended with chapter 14. Marcion does not appear to have known the doxology.[17] Moreover, the edition of Romans which he used may have lacked the whole of chapter 16, with its long series of personal greetings. If, because of its general interest and importance, this epistle was circulated at an early stage among other churches than that to which it was primarily sent (whether on Paul's own initiative or on someone else's), the greetings might well have been omitted from the circular form, since they were manifestly intended for one group of recipients only.[18]

---

[17] Harnack thought that the doxology, in its original form, was composed by disciples of Marcion. See F. F. Bruce, *The Letter of Paul to the Romans*, TNTC (Leicester, ²1985), pp.267–269.
[18] P⁴⁶, which places the doxology at the end of chapter 15 (the only known manuscript to do so), bears witness to a text of the letter which lacked chapter 16. See p.131, n.54.

An example of a change reflecting Marcion's doctrine of God comes in Ephesians 3:9. The gospel is there described as 'the mystery hidden for ages in God who created all things' (hidden, that is to say, in the divine mind and not revealed until the fulness of the time had come). But to Marcion the 'God who created all things' had nothing to do with the gospel; he was a different being from the God and Father of our Lord Jesus Christ. So, by a very small change, Marcion made this text refer to 'the mystery hidden for ages *from* the God who created all things'.[19]

THE SO-CALLED MARCIONITE PROLOGUES

The Pauline letters in Marcion's *Apostle* were later supplied with prologues sufficiently objective in character to have been subsequently taken over and reproduced in 'orthodox' copies of the Latin New Testament, although they were originally composed by followers of Marcion. It has indeed been asserted more recently that, despite their traditional designation as 'Marcionite' prologues, there is nothing specifically Marcionite about them.[20] Before this can be discussed, it is best to reproduce them. Here they are, in Marcion's sequence of the letters:

Galatians

The Galatians are Greeks. They first received the word of truth from the apostle, but after his departure were tempted by false apostles to turn to law and circumcision. The apostle calls them back to belief in the truth, writing to them from Ephesus.

Corinthians (1 and 2)

The Corinthians are Achaeans. They likewise had heard the word of truth from apostles but had been subverted in various ways by false apostles—some led away by the wordy rhetoric of philosophy, others by the party of the Jewish law. The apostles call them back to the true wisdom of the gospel, writing to them from Ephesus.

---

[19] In the Greek text Marcion removed the preposition *en*, leaving the simple dative case of 'God' (*tō theō*).

[20] See J. Regul, *Die antimarcionitischen Evangelienprologe* (Freiburg, 1969), pp.13, 85, 88–94.

Romans

The Romans are in a region of Italy. They had been overtaken by false apostles, under pretext of the name of our Lord Jesus Christ, and led on into an acceptance of the law and the prophets. The apostle calls them back to the true evangelical faith, writing to them from Athens.

Thessalonians (1 and 2)

The Thessalonians are Macedonians in Christ Jesus. Having received the word of truth they persevered in the faith, even under persecution by their fellow-citizens; moreover, they did not accept what was said by false apostles. The apostle commends them, writing to them from Athens.

'Laodiceans' (= Ephesians)

The Laodiceans are Asians. Having received the word of truth, they persevered in the faith. The apostle commends them, writing to them from prison in Rome.

Colossians

The Colossians also are, like the Laodiceans, Asians. They also had been overtaken by false apostles. The apostle did not visit them himself, but puts them right by means of a letter. They had heard the word from Archippus, who indeed received a commission to minister to them. Therefore the apostle, now in chains, writes to them from Ephesus.

Philippians

The Philippians are Macedonians. Having received the word of truth they persevered in the faith, and did not accept false apostles. The apostle commends them, writing to them from prison in Rome.

Philemon

To Philemon he composes a personal letter on behalf of his slave Onesimus. He writes to him from prison in Rome.

These prologues are most fully intelligible when they are read in the same order as the epistles, as arranged in Marcion's *Apostle*. This in itself does not conclusively prove their Marcionite origin, for Marcion's order was conceivably derived by him from an earlier edition, although we have no knowledge of it at an earlier time.[21] But 'they emphasize, to the exclusion of any mention of the really important contents of the epistles, the relation of Paul to the recipients of the letter, and whether he had to vindicate himself against false apostles in it, and use such phrases as "the true evangelical faith", "the word of truth".'[22] Moreover, they detect anti-judaizing polemic in letters where it can scarcely be traced. Romans, for example, is one of the least polemical of Paul's letters; yet the prologue says that it was sent to the Roman Christians because they had been hoodwinked by false apostles claiming the authority of Christ and persuaded to submit to 'the law and the prophets'. The addition of 'the prophets' to 'the law' seems designed to exclude the Old Testament writings from any part in the gospel economy. Paul denies that any one can be justified by 'works of law' (Rom. 3:20) but when he uses 'the law' in the sense of the Old Testament writings, in whole or in part, he speaks of it with the highest respect; and as for 'the law and the prophets' taken together, he affirms that they bear witness to God's way of righteousness through faith in Christ, 'apart from law' (Rom. 3:21, a text omitted from Marcion's edition). No one but a Marcionite could have misrepresented the message of Romans as this prologue does. When we consider this set of prologues as a whole, it is difficult not to agree with F. C. Burkitt's conclusion: 'They are the work of one who was as much obsessed by the opposition of Paulinism to Judaizing Christianity as was Baur himself.'[23] The Muratorian list, at which we shall look shortly,[24] appears to be acquainted with these prologues, 'and it is certainly possible that its intention was to counter them directly with

[21] See N. A. Dahl, 'The Origin of the Earliest Prologues to the Pauline Letters', *Semeia* 12 (1978), pp.233–277; H. Y. Gamble, *The New Testament Canon* (Philadelphia, 1985), pp.41f.

[22] R. P. C. Hanson, *Tradition in the Early Church* (London, 1962), p.188.

[23] F. C. Burkitt, *The Gospel History and its Transmission* (London, [2]1907), p.354. Ferdinand Christian Baur (1792–1860), Professor in the University of Tübingen, in a series of publications from 'Die Christuspartei in der korinthischen Gemeinde', *Tübinger Zeitschrift für Theologie* 5 (1831), Heft 4, pp.61–206 (reprinted in *Ausgewählte Werke in Einzelausgaben*, ed. K. Scholder, I [Stuttgart, 1963], pp.1–76) to his *Church History of the First Three Centuries* (1853), E. T., I (London, 1878), pp.44–98, propounded the view that the first generation of church history was dominated by a conflict between Paul and his law-free gospel on the one side and the Jerusalem leaders, with their law-related gospel, on the other.

[24] See pp.158–169.

its own sound catholic observations'.[25]

It was probably when the Marcionite origin of the prologues was forgotten that they were taken over into catholic copies of the Pauline epistles. In due course they were supplemented by catholic additions, including a new prologue to Ephesians and prologues to 2 Corinthians and 2 Thessalonians (which did not appear as separate letters in Marcion's edition) and to each of the three Pastoral Epistles.[26]

The widespread view that Marcion provided the church with its precedent for establishing a canon of New Testament books has been expressed, among others, by Hans von Campenhausen: 'the idea and the reality of a Christian Bible were the work of Marcion, and the Church which rejected his work, so far from being ahead of him in this field, from a formal point of view simply followed his example.'[27] But this view is probably wrong. Theodor von Zahn, in an earlier generation, was prone to overstate his case, but on this point his judgement stands: 'Marcion formed his Bible in declared opposition to the holy scriptures of the church from which he had separated; it was in opposition to his criticism that the church in its turn first became rightly conscious of its heritage of apostolic writings.'[28]

[25] H. von Campenhausen, *The Formation of the Christian Bible*, E. T. (London, 1972), p.246. A similar judgment, but in exaggerated terms, had been expressed by A. von Harnack, 'Die Marcionitischen Prologe zu den Paulusbriefen, eine Quelle des Muratorischen Fragments', *ZNW* 25 (1926), pp.160–163.

[26] On the Marcionite prologues see also D. de Bruyne, 'Prologues bibliques d'origine marcionite', *Revue Bénédictine* 24 (1907), pp.1–16; P. Corssen, 'Zur Überlieferungsgeschichte des Römerbriefes', *ZNW* 10 (1909), pp.1–45, 97–102 (especially pp.37–39); A. von Harnack, 'Der Marcionitische Ursprung der ältesten Vulgata-Prologe der Paulusbriefen,' *ZNW* 24 (1925), pp.204–218; K. T. Schäfer, 'Marius Victorinus und die Marcionitischen Prologe zu den Paulusbriefen', *Revue Bénédictine* 80 (1970), pp.7–16.

[27] *The Formation of the Christian Bible*, p.148. The same view had already been expressed by Harnack, *Die Briefsammlung des Apostels Paulus* (Leipzig, 1926), p.21.

[28] T. von Zahn, *Geschichte des neutestamentlichen Kanons*, I (Erlangen/Leipzig, 1888), p.586.

CHAPTER TEN

VALENTINUS AND HIS
SCHOOL

While Marcion is the first person known to us who published a well
defined collection of what later came to be called New Testament
books, the question remains open whether he was actually the first to
do so or something of the sort was already in existence.

VALENTINUS AND THE NEW TESTAMENT

Some light may be thrown on the question by a remark of Tertullian's.
There are two ways, he says, of nullifying the scriptures. One is
Marcion's way: he used the knife to excise from the scriptures whatever
did not conform with his own opinion. Valentinus, on the other hand,
'seems to use the entire *instrumentum*' (which here means the New
Testament), but perverts its meaning by misinterpreting it.[1]

Valentinus was contemporary with Marcion: he came from
Alexandria in Egypt and lived in Rome from about AD 135 to 160.
Like Marcion, he was in communion with the church of Rome when
first he came to the city—indeed, if Tertullian is to be believed, he
had at one time reason to expect that he would become bishop of Rome
(this would have been at the time when Pius was actually elected).[2] He

[1] Tertullian, *Prescription*, 38.
[2] Tertullian, *Against Valentinians*, 4. Since before the episcopate of Pius the Roman
church appears to have been administered by a college of presbyters or bishops,
Valentinus may possibly have aspired to be admitted to this college.

probably owed to his Alexandrian training a love for allegorical interpretation, but his thinking developed along mystical and gnostic lines to a point where he broke with the church and became the founder of a gnostic school whose members were called, after him, Valentinians.

When Tertullian said that Valentinus 'seems to use the entire *instrumentum'*, Tertullian himself had quite a clear idea of the contents of the *instrumentum*.[3] But did Valentinus, sixty years before Tertullian wrote, have a clear idea? He would not have spoken of an *instrumentum*, for his language was Greek, not Latin. But would he have envisaged such a collection at all?

VALENTINIAN LITERATURE

Since 1945 we have been in a better position to say something positive about Valentinus's use of scripture than had been possible for over a thousand years. In that year the discovery was made in Upper Egypt of what are now called the Nag Hammadi documents, from the name of the town near which they were found. These documents, fifty-two in all, were collected together in thirteen leather-bound papyrus codices.[4] They were written in Coptic, but most of them were translations from a Greek original; they probably belonged to the library of a gnostic monastery, which was put into safe hiding in the fourth century AD. They include some Valentinian treatises; one or two of these (in the Greek original) may even have been the work of Valentinus himself.

This is particularly so with one of the most famous of them, called *The Gospel of Truth.*[5] This title does not imply that the treatise is a rival

[3] See p.181. There is a good discussion of the force of the juristic term *instrumentum* in Tertullian in Harnack's *Origin of the New Testament,* pp.209–217; Tertullian, he says, calls the two Testaments *instrumenta* 'because they are for the Church the decisive documents for the exposition and the proof of her doctrine' (p.212).

[4] Most of them are now available in an English translation in *The Nag Hammadi Library,* ed. J. M. Robinson (Leiden, 1977). A facsimile edition, in twelve volumes, is being published at Leiden (1972–) under the auspices of the Department of Antiquities of the Arab Republic of Egypt, in conjunction with UNESCO; another series in eleven volumes, *The Coptic Gnostic Library* (Leiden, 1975–), contains transcriptions, translations, introductions, notes and indices.

[5] First published in *Evangelium Veritatis,* ed. M. Malinine, H.–C. Puech, G. Quispel (Zurich, 1956), with facsimile, transcription, French, German and English translations, notes and vocabularies. A good annotated translation was produced by K. Grobel, *The Gospel of Truth* (Nashville/London, 1960). Another translation, by G. W. MacRae, appears in *The Nag Hammadi Library,* pp.37–49.

gospel; it indicates rather that the treatise presents a meditation on the true gospel of Christ. Some of the Christian fathers refer to the *Gospel of Truth* as a manifesto of the Valentinian school.[6] Now that it is available for study, its character can be clearly recognized. What concerns us here is the witness that it bears to the New Testament writings. This witness may not entitle us to say, with W. C. van Unnik, that 'round about AD 140–150 a collection of writings was known at Rome and accepted as authoritative which was virtually identical with our New Testament'.[7] But the treatise alludes to Matthew and Luke (possibly with Acts), the gospel and first letter of John, the Pauline letters (except the Pastorals), Hebrews and Revelation—and not only alludes to them but cites them in terms which presuppose that they are authoritative. Allegorical interpretation such as is found in the *Gospel of Truth* implies not only authority but some degree of inspiration in the texts so interpreted, whether the lessons derived by such allegorization are acceptable to later readers or not.[8]

Another Valentinian treatise in the Nag Hammadi collection is the *Epistle to Rheginus on Resurrection* which, like the *Gospel of Truth,* antedates the developed system of Valentinianism and may also be the work of Valentinus himself.[9] It presents an interpretation of Paul's teaching on resurrection and immortality in 1 Corinthians 15 (although scarcely an interpretation of which Paul would have approved).[10] To

[6] E.g. Irenaeus, *Against Heresies* 3.11.9.

[7] W. C. van Unnik, 'The "Gospel of Truth" and the New Testament', in *The Jung Codex,* ed. F. L. Cross (London, 1955), p. 124; *cf* his *Newly Discovered Gnostic Writings,* E.T. (London, 1960), pp. 58–68. But if van Unnik exaggerates somewhat, H. von Campenhausen goes to the other extreme in criticizing him in *The Formation of the Christian Bible,* E.T. (London, 1972), p. 140, n. 171.

[8] There is a famous allegorical interpretation of the parable of the lost sheep (Mt. 18:12f. par. Luke 15:4–6) in *The Gospel of Truth,* 31.35–32.17, known to Irenaeus (*Against Heresies,* 2.24.6), where the sheep symbolizes humanity's wandering in ignorance of the true knowledge and even the number ninety-nine receives unsuspected significance. In *The Gospel of Truth, 3* .40–34.20, there is an interesting discussion of the divine *aroma* ('the sons of the Father are his *aroma*') which seem to develops Paul's thought in 2 Cor. 2:14–16.

[9] First published in *De Resurrectione,* ed. M. Malinine, H.–C. Puech, G. Quispel, W. Till (Zürich, 1963), with facsimile, transcription, French, German and English translations, notes and vocabularies. A translation with introduction, analysis and exposition was produced by M. L. Peel, *The Epistle to Rheginos* (London, 1969). Dr Peel has also translated it ('The Treatise on Resurrection') for *The Nag Hammadi Library,* pp. 50–53.

[10] It bears a close resemblance to the view of Hymenaeus and Philetus, denounced in 2 Tim. 2:17f.

its author Paul is 'the apostle'; his words carry authority. Echoes are discernible in the treatise of other Pauline letters — Romans, 2 Corinthians, Ephesians, Philippians and Colossians — and the author shows acquaintance with synoptic and Johannine gospel traditions.

Neither in the *Gospel of Truth* nor in the *Epistle to Rheginus* is there any mention of a recognizable collection of New Testament writings. There is indeed in the *Gospel of Truth* a fascinating account of what is called 'the living book of the living', the 'testament' (*diathēkē*)[11] of Jesus which he appears to have both received from his Father (*cf* Rev. 5:7) and fastened to his cross (*cf* Col. 2:14).[12] But this is a spiritual book, written in the Father's heart before the world's foundation and now revealed in the hearts of those who accept the divine knowledge. Kendrick Grobel indeed thought that the writer's language might mark 'the transition from thinking of the pre-existent, unearthly Book to thinking (also) of an earthly embodiment of it: one of the Gospels, all the Gospels, or the NT as a whole';[13] but this possibility is too slender for any weight to be laid on it. It is not improbable, however, that the two treatises presuppose some conception of a category of early Christian writings produced by special inspiration and vested with special authority — the fourfold gospel, perhaps, with the Pauline *corpus* — but this cannot be proved in the absence of express evidence.

But let this be said: in the light of such treatises from Nag Hammadi it can be argued with some show of reason that Marcion's 'canon' was his revision of an existing collection of New Testament writings — in particular, that his *Apostle* was his revision of an existing copy of the Pauline letters.

PTOLEMY

Ptolemy, the principal disciple of Valentinus and probably his successor as recognized leader of the Valentinian school, acknowledged the supreme authority of the New Testament writings (in effect, those which were acknowledged in the *Gospel of Truth* and the *Epistle to Rheginus*), when they were properly interpreted — interpreted, that is

[11] The Greek word *diathēkē* appears untranslated in the Coptic text. See pp. 19, 181.

[12] *The Gospel of Truth*, 19.35–20.30; 21.3–7; 22.35–23.30.

[13] K. Grobel, *The Gospel of Truth*, p. 89.

to say, in accordance with the presuppositions of Valentinianism.[14] Those writings were 'supremely authoritative because they contained the apostolic tradition which came from the Saviour Jesus'.[15] The most orthodox churchman could hardly state the essence of the case more aptly. Indeed, Ptolemy is the first person known to us by name who criticized Marcionism.[16] This he did in his *Letter to Flora*[17] in which, over against Marcion's rejection of the Old Testament, he showed how the Mosaic law, when rightly understood (i.e. understood according to Valentinian principles) retained its value in the Christian order.[18]

[14] This insistence on proper interpretation is found equally in those who argue that the New Testament (and indeed the whole Bible) is authoritative when interpreted in accordance with the teaching preserved in its purity by the apostolic churches. See pp. 151, 269.

[15] R. M. Grant, *The Formation of the New Testament* (London, 1965), p. 127.

[16] See H. von Campenhausen, *The Formation of the Christian Bible*, pp. 165f.

[17] This letter is preserved in Epiphanius, *Panarion*, 33.3–7; an English translation is conveniently accessible in R. M. Grant (ed.), *Gnosticism: An Anthology* (London, 1961), pp. 184–190. 'Flora', like 'the elect lady' of 2 John, is conceivably the personification of some church (the church of Rome ?).

[18] More or less contemporary with the earlier Valentinian treatises is the anti-gnostic document called the *Epistle of the Apostles*, allegedly sent by the eleven to acquaint their fellow-believers throughout the world with a dialogue between them and the Lord after his resurrection: it makes free use of the Gospels of Matthew, Luke and John as well as of some apocryphal writings, like the *Infancy Gospel of Thomas*. See Hennecke-Schneemelcher-Wilson, *New Testament Apocrypha* I, pp. 189–227.

CHAPTER ELEVEN

THE CATHOLIC RESPONSE

A CATHOLIC COLLECTION

Both Marcion and Valentinus presented a challenge to the catholic church—that is, to those Christians who adhered to what they believed to be the apostolic teaching. The communities to which many of those Christians belonged claimed to have been founded by apostles, and there had been no ascertainable shift in their teaching since the time of their foundation. The distinctive features of Marcionitism and Valentinianism had this at least in common—they were recognized as innovations. This, the leaders of the catholic church knew, was not what they had heard from the beginning.[1] But their followers had to be shown where those new movements were wrong: if the teachings of Marcion and Valentinus were unsound, what was the sound teaching, and how could it be defended?

In the catholic response to this twofold challenge, what came to be called 'the rule of faith' played a crucial part. The 'rule of faith' was a summary of the tenets held in common by the churches of apostolic foundation: it is closely related to what is called 'apostolic tradition'. R. P. C. Hanson describes it as 'a graph of the interpretation of the Bible by the Church of the second and third centuries'.[2] In the

[1] Cf 1 John 2:24, 'Let what you heard from the beginning abide in you.'
[2] Tradition in the Early Church (London, 1962), p.127.

150

establishment and defence of the rule of faith the appeal to the Bible was basic. In debate with the Valentinians and others of similar outlook, the interpretation of the Bible was the point at issue; in debate with the Marcionites, the identity of the Bible had to be defined. Where the interpretation of the Bible was at issue, there was a tendency to maintain that only the catholic church had the right to interpret it, because the Bible was the church's book;[3] but in the Marcionite controversy an answer had to be given to the more fundamental question: What is the Bible?

Marcion had answered that fundamental question quite unambiguously. The Bible consisted of the *Gospel* and the *Apostle* which he promulgated. Was his answer right, or was it wrong? The leaders of the Roman church (and other churches that shared the same faith) had no doubt that his answer was wrong. What, then, was the right answer? If they had not given much thought to the limits of holy writ previously, they had to pay serious attention to the question now. And sooner rather than later they declared their mind on the matter.

We do not reject the Old Testament scriptures, as Marcion does, they said; we accept them, as did Jesus and the apostles (both the original apostles and Paul). As for the scriptures of the new order, we accept not one gospel writing only, but four (including the complete text of Marcion's mutilated *Gospel*). We accept not only ten letters of Paul, but thirteen (that is, including the three addressed to Timothy and Titus). We accept not the letters of Paul only, but letters of other apostles too. And we accept the Acts of the Apostles, a work which links the gospels and the apostolic letters, providing the sequel to the former and the background to the latter.[4] Tertullian argues that it was quite illogical for those who maintained the exclusive apostleship of Paul (like the Marcionites) to reject the one book which presented independent testimony to the genuineness of the apostolic claim which Paul repeatedly makes for himself.[5] (The trouble was, especially for the Marcionites, that Acts presents independent testimony also to

[3] This is the thesis of Tertullian's work *On the Prescription of Heretics* (in which *praescriptio* is a legal term meaning an 'objection' by the opposing party to the use of scripture by heretics).

[4] Nowadays this assessment of the importance of Acts in the New Testament would be contested by those who see it as departing from the perspective of Paul and the gospels alike and as providing a foundation for catholicism (not merely for catholicity). See also pp. 132f.

[5] *Prescription,* 22f.

the genuine apostleship of those whom Marcion condemned as apostates.)

The scriptures acknowledged by the catholic church formed, appropriately, a *catholic* collection. They represented a variety of perspectives in the early church. Marcion's list, on the other hand, was a sectarian one: it represented one viewpoint only—not so much Paul's as Marcion's own. As Marcion maintained the exclusive apostleship of Paul, there were other sectarians, at the opposite end of the spectrum, who regarded James of Jerusalem as the apostle *par excellence,* and deplored Paul as the 'enemy' of Jesus' parable who sowed the tares of error among the good wheat of the gospel (Mt. 13:25, 28).[6] But the catholic church, and the catholic scriptures, made room for both Paul and James and for other varieties as well. Ernst Käsemann can write of the New Testament canon as bearing witness to the *disunity,* not to the unity, of the first-century church;[7] more properly, it bears witness to the more comprehensive unity which transcends all the diversities and proclaims the one who is simultaneously the Jesus of history and the exalted Lord. There was farseeing wisdom in the decision 'to accept all that was thought to be truly apostolic, and to see it as mediating through human diversity, the one divine event'.[8]

In this regard Acts played a crucial part: it is indeed the hinge of the New Testament collection, giving it its 'organic structure'.[9] It is a truly catholic work, the keystone of a truly catholic canon. Peter, Paul and James are all honoured in it, together with such leaders of the Hellenistic advance as Stephen and Philip. Such a work could not have been countenanced by those who rejected all strands of apostolic Christianity but one, but it was admirably suited to the purpose of catholic churchmen.

The same catholic spirit is evident in the fourfold gospel. To begin with, each gospel was doubtless *the* gospel in the communities in which it circulated, but they were all greatly enriched when to the

---

[6] *Clementine Recognitions,* 1.70; *Epistle of Peter to James,* 2. Those who took this line were Ebionites and other representatives of that Jewish-Christian tradition which finds expression in the third-century *Clementine Recognitions* and *Homilies.*

[7] 'The Canon of the New Testament and the Unity of the Church', E.T. in *Essays on New Testament Themes* (London, 1964), pp.95–107; see p.272 below.

[8] C. F. D. Moule, *The Birth of the New Testament* (London, ³1981), p.255.

[9] A. von Harnack, *The Origin of the New Testament,* E.T. (London, 1925), p.67. See pp.132f. above.

witness of their own gospel there was added the witness of the others. Some scrupulous readers might feel that the inconcinnities of the four called for harmonizing activity, but others rejoiced in the plurality of testimony that was now available, recognizing with the compiler of the Muratorian list (an outstanding document of the catholic response) that the variation among the four writings 'makes no difference to the faith of believers, since in all of them everything has been declared by one primary Spirit'.[10] If only one of the four had received canonical status, if Marcion's precedent (for example) had been generally followed, the path of the gospel critic might have been smoother, but we should all have been gravely impoverished. The four were not originally composed in order that readers might have a fourfold perspective on the ministry of Jesus, but in the event their collocation has provided just that.

It is noteworthy too that Matthew's contribution, which became pre-eminently the church's gospel and stood at the head of the fourfold collection, is self-evidently a catholic work. Even if the other synoptic gospels were not available for comparison with it, it would be possible to discern a variety of strands in its record of Jesus' teaching—the particularist strand, 'Go nowhere among the Gentiles' (Mt. 10:5), and the more comprehensive strand, 'many will come from east and west. . .' (Mt. 8:11), transcended in the post-resurrection commission to 'make disciples of all the nations' (Mt. 28:19). The fact that this catholic work stands at the head of the New Testament points to the catholicity of the canon as a whole and not only of the gospel collection.[11]

In the apostolic generation separate spheres of public ministry were carefully demarcated, as is amply attested from Paul's letters (see Gal. 2:7–9; Rom. 15:20). But in the post-apostolic age the necessity of recognizing such separate spheres disappeared. While sectarian tendencies manifested themselves, the church as a whole paid heed to Paul's exhortation to recognize that all the apostles and teachers whom the Lord had sent, 'whether Paul or Apollos or Cephas' (1 Cor. 3:22), belonged to them all. It would be difficult to envisage, in the apostolic age, one and the same church claiming Peter and Paul together as joint-founders. It was *historically* ludicrous for Dionysius, bishop of

[10] See pp. 159, 160.
[11] *Cf* Harnack, *The Date of the Acts and of the Synoptic Gospels,* E.T. (London, 1911), pp. 133–135.

Corinth about AD 170, to make this claim for his own church[12] — Paul might have turned in his grave at the thought of Peter's sharing in what was so totally his own foundation (1 Cor. 3:10–15) — but there was a certain *theological* fitness in the claim, in so far as it expressed a resolve to appropriate the entire apostolic heritage. It is this resolve that is expressed in the New Testament canon, where every document that could reasonably be claimed as apostolic in origin and teaching found its place in due course.

THE SO-CALLED
ANTI-MARCIONITE PROLOGUES

One expression of the catholic response to Marcion's *Gospel* has been recognized in some gospel prologues which appear in certain Latin codices. At one time it was maintained by leading scholars that these belonged to a set of four gospel prologues drawn up in opposition to Marcionism shortly before Irenaeus began his literary career (c AD 180).[13] The tide has more recently turned against this opinion,[14] but two of the prologues, those to Luke and John, whether they originally belonged together or not, reflect an anti-Marcionite reaction.

The prologue to Luke (which is also extant in its Greek original in two codices of the tenth and eleventh centuries respectively) ends with a note on the authorship of Acts and of the Johannine apocalypse and gospel:

> Luke was a native of Syrian Antioch, a physician by profession, a disciple of the apostles. Later he accompanied Paul until the latter's martyrdom, serving the Lord without distraction, for he had neither wife nor children. He died in Boeotia[15] at the age of

[12] In Eusebius, *Hist. Eccl.* 2.25.8. Dionysius also treats the church of Rome as the joint foundation of Peter and Paul—an honour which Paul would have firmly declined.

[13] E.g. D. de Bruyne, 'Les plus anciens prologues latins des Évangiles', *Revue Bénédictine* 40 (1928), pp.193–214; A. von Harnack, *Die ältesten Evangelien-Prologe und die Bildung des Neuen Testaments* (Berlin, 1928). On their hypothesis of a set of four such prologues, that to Matthew was lost, as also was that to Mark apart from the closing words: '...was asserted by Mark, who was named "stump-fingered" (*colobodactylus*) because his fingers were shorter in relation to the rest of his bodily proportions. He was Peter's interpreter. After Peter's departure he wrote down this gospel in the parts of Italy.'

[14] Especially in J. Regul, *Die antimarcionitischen Evangelienprologe* (Freiburg, 1969).

[15] The region of Greece around Thebes.

eighty-four, full of the Holy Spirit. So then, after two gospels had already been written—Matthew's in Judaea and Mark's in Italy—Luke wrote this gospel in the region of Achaia, by inspiration of the Holy Spirit. At its outset, he indicated that other gospels had been written before his own, but that the obligation lay on him to set forth for the believers among the Gentiles a complete account in the course of his narrative, and to do so as accurately as possible. The object of this was that they might not be captivated on the one hand by a love for Jewish fables, nor on the other hand be deceived by heretical and vain imaginations and thus wander from the truth. So, right at the beginning, Luke has delivered to us the story of the birth of John [the Baptist], as most essential [to the gospel]; for John marks the beginning of the gospel, since he was our Lord's forerunner and associate both in the preparation for the gospel and in the administration of baptism and communication of the Spirit.[16] This ministry [of John's] was foretold by one of the twelve prophets.[17] Later on, the same Luke wrote the Acts of the Apostles. Later still, the apostle John, one of the twelve, wrote the Apocalypse on the island of Patmos, and then the gospel in Asia.

The anti-Marcionite tendency of this prologue appears in the emphasis with which it affirms the integrity of the first chapters of Luke with the gospel as a whole and the essential character of John the Baptist's ministry in preparing the way for the ministry of Jesus. Marcion's *Gospel* lacked the first two chapters of Luke and the account of John's ministry in Luke 3:2–22; it refused to recognize any link between Jesus and what went before him, whether the ministry of John or the predictions of Old Testament prophets.

When the author of the prologue says that Luke's gospel was written in Achaia, he may have wished to associate one gospel with the churches of the Greek mainland, as Matthew allegedly originated in Judaea, Mark in Italy and John in the province of Asia.

More intriguing is the so-called anti-Marcionite prologue to John, which survives in Latin only, although its original language was plainly Greek. It suffered some textual corruption in the transmission both of the Greek text and of the Latin translation, but the necessary

[16] Gk. *pneumatos koinōnia*. The Latin text reads *passionis socius*, 'a sharer in his suffering', which presupposes a Greek reading *pathēmatos* instead of *pneumatos*.
[17] Mal. 3:1; 4:5 (*cf* Mark 1:2; 9:11–13).

emendations are fairly obvious. As the Latin wording stands, it may be rendered thus:

> The gospel of John was published and given to the churches by John while he was still in the body, as Papias of Hierapolis, John's dear disciple, has related in his five exoteric, that is his last, books. He wrote down the gospel accurately at John's dictation. But the heretic Marcion was rejected by John, having been condemned by him for his contrary views. Marcion had carried writings or letters to him from the brothers in Pontus.

The most evident emendation here is the reference to Papias's 'five exoteric, that is his last, books'. This should be corrected to his 'five exegetical books'[18]—that is, the five books of Papias's *Exegesis of the Dominical Oracles*. In this work, it appears, Papias had given some account of the origin of John's gospel. Did he claim that he himself 'wrote down the gospel accurately at John's dictation'? Perhaps he did: chronologically, at least, it is not impossible. Papias was contemporary with Polycarp, who was born not later than AD 70. Irenaeus confirms that Papias was indeed one of John's disciples;[19] even Eusebius, who disapproved of Papias's views on eschatology, admits this reluctantly.[20] But more probably Papias said that '*they* wrote down the gospel'— 'they' being 'the churches', or possibly John's associates who added the words 'we know that his testimony is true' in John 21:24—and Papias's '*they* wrote down' was misread as '*I* wrote down' (a mistake quite easily made in Greek).[21]

But was Marcion condemned and rejected by John? This is wholly improbable, unless the meaning is that John's gospel provides a refutation of Marcion's teaching[22] (which is not a natural interpretation

---

[18] The Greek adjective *exēgētikois* was evidently corrupted to *exōterikois* ('external'), which was taken over into the Latin version *(exotericis)* and explained by the Latin adjective *externis; externis* was then corrupted in the Latin transmission to *extremis* ('last').

[19] In Eusebius, *Hist. Eccl.* 3.39.1.   [20] *Hist. Eccl.* 3.39.7.

[21] If Papias wrote *apegraphon* (imperfect tense), this could be either first person singular or third person plural. If he wrote *apegrapsan* (third person plural, aorist tense), this, in certain positions, could have been written *apegrapsā,* which then, by the obscuring of the stroke above the final letter, was misread *apegrapsa* (first person singular). See J. B. Lightfoot, *Essays on the Work entitled 'Supernatural Religion'* (London, 1889), pp.210–214.

[22] *Cf* Tertullian, *On the Flesh of Christ,* 3, apostrophizing Marcion: 'If you had not deliberately rejected or corrupted the scriptures which disagree with your opinion, the Gospel of John would have confounded you.'

of what the prologue says). The probability is that it was Papias himself who rejected Marcion. If Marcion (whose father is said to have been a church leader at Sinope in Pontus), served as a messenger from the Christians in Pontus to the church of Hierapolis, he may have shared his unconventional thoughts with Papias and met with a negative response. Perhaps on the same tour he approached Polycarp in Smyrna, and found him equally unforthcoming.[23]

This expressly anti-Marcionite prologue to John is clearly dependent on Papias's account; it is unfortunate that corruption in the course of transmission and ambiguity in the language make it so difficult to deduce from it what Papias actually said.

Happily, we can turn to a more substantial document of the catholic response to Marcionism and other 'Christian deviations'[24] of the second century.

---

[23] See p. 135.

[24] The expression is borrowed from the title of Horton Davies, *Christian Deviations* (London, 1953).

CHAPTER TWELVE

THE MURATORIAN
FRAGMENT

THE MANUSCRIPT AND ITS CONTENTS

In 1740 a Latin list of New Testament books was published by
Lodovico Antonio Muratori, a distinguished antiquarian and theologian in his day, from a codex copied in the seventh or eighth century
at the monastery of Bobbio, in Lombardy, but later lodged in the
Ambrosian Library, Milan (of which Muratori had at one time been
keeper); there it still is (catalogued J 101 sup., folios 10a–11a). [1]

The date at which the list was originally drawn up is disputed; it
belongs most probably to the end of the second century. [2] The Latin
text has suffered from being copied by one or more barely literate

[1] Some fragments of the list have been identified in four codices of the eleventh and
twelfth centuries at Monte Cassino. A facsimile and transcription of the list were
published by S. P. Tregelles, *Canon Muratorianus: The Earliest Catalogue of the Books of
the New Testament* (Oxford, 1867). A convenient edition of the text was published by
Hans Lietzmann as No. 1 in the series *Kleine Texte* (Berlin, [2]1933); it includes the text
of the Cassino fragments.

[2] A. C. Sundberg, Jr., presents a strong case for a fourth-century date in 'Canon
Muratori: A Fourth-Century List', *Harvard Theological Review* 66 (1973), pp. 1–41; he
finds the closest affinities of the list to be with fourth-century lists of eastern origin.
Quite apart from the question of dating, this article is one of the best recent studies of
the Muratorian list. On the point of dating, Sundberg has been ably answered by E.
Ferguson, 'Canon Muratori: Date and Provenance', *Studia Patristica* 18.2 (Kalamazoo,
MI, 1982), pp. 677–683.

scribes; there are several errors which cry out for emendation. Many scholars have held that behind the Latin wording lies an original Greek text, which has been completely lost;[3] on the whole, however, it seems more likely that Latin was its original language, and that the list dates from the time when the Roman church (which had been Greek-speaking since its foundation in the first century) was beginning to be bilingual.[4]

The document is best regarded as a list of New Testament books recognized as authoritative in the Roman church at that time. In addition to naming the books, it makes a number of observations on them, reflecting the contemporary opinion of some churchmen.

The manuscript is mutilated at the beginning. Since its first complete sentence mentions Luke as 'the third book of the gospel', it had presumably mentioned two others, and it is not excessively speculative to suppose that these were Matthew and Mark. If so, the first words to be preserved on the manuscript are the last words of a sentence about Mark: '. . . at these, however, he was present and so he set them down.' Then the document continues:

> The third book of the gospel: according to Luke.
>
> After the ascension of Christ, Luke the physician, whom Paul had taken along with him as a legal expert, wrote [the record] down in his own name in accordance with [Paul's] opinion. He himself, however, never saw the Lord in the flesh and therefore, as far as he could follow [the course of events], began to tell it from the nativity of John.
>
> The fourth gospel is by John, one of the disciples.
>
> When his fellow-disciples and bishops encouraged him, John said, 'Fast along with me three days from today, and whatever may be revealed to each, let us relate it one to another'. The same night it was revealed to Andrew, one of the apostles, that John in his own name should write down everything and that they should all revise it. Therefore, although different beginn-

---

[3] E.g. S. P. Tregelles, *Canon Muratorianus*, p.4 (following Muratori himself, who supposed it to be work of the Roman presbyter Gaius; see p.168 below); J. B. Lightfoot, *The Apostolic Fathers*, I: *S. Clement of Rome*, II (London, [2]1890), pp.405f.

[4] See p.83, n.1, with Jerome, *On Illustrious Men*, 53. Arguments for holding the Latin to be the original text have been presented by A. von Harnack, 'Über den Verfasser und den literarischen Charakter des Muratorischen Fragments', *ZNW* 24 (1925), pp.1–16; A. A. T. Ehrhardt, 'The Gospels in the Muratorian Fragment', *The Framework of the New Testament Stories* (Manchester, 1964), pp.11–36, especially pp.16–18.

ings are taught for the various books of the gospel, it makes no difference to the faith of believers, since in all of them everything has been declared by one primary Spirit, concerning his nativity, passion and resurrection, his association with his disciples and his twofold advent—his first in humility, when he was despised, which is past; his second resplendent in royal power, his coming again. It is no wonder, then, that John should so constantly present the separate details in his letters also, saying of himself: 'What we have seen with our eyes and heard with our ears and our hands have handled, these things have we written.' For in this way he claims to be not only a spectator but a hearer, and also a writer in order of the wonderful facts about our Lord.

The Acts of all the apostles have been written in one book. Addressing the most excellent Theophilus, Luke includes one by one the things which were done in his own presence, as he shows plainly by omitting the passion of Peter and also Paul's departure when he was setting out from the City for Spain.

As for the letters of Paul, they themselves show those who wish to understand from which place and for which cause they were directed. First of all [he wrote] to the Corinthians forbidding schisms and heresies; then to the Galatians [forbidding] circumcision; to the Romans he wrote at greater length about the order of the scriptures and also insisting that Christ was their primary theme. It is necessary for us to give an argued account of all these, since the blessed apostle Paul himself, following the order of his predecessor John, but not naming him, writes to seven churches in the following order: first to the Corinthians, second to the Ephesians, third to the Philippians, fourth to the Colossians, fifth to the Galatians, sixth to the Thessalonians, seventh to the Romans. But although [the message] is repeated to the Corinthians and Thessalonians by way of reproof, yet one church is recognized as diffused throughout the whole world. For John also, while he writes to seven churches in the Apocalypse, yet speaks to all. Moreover [Paul writes] one [letter] to Philemon, one to Titus and two to Timothy in love and affection; but they have been hallowed for the honour of the catholic church in the regulation of ecclesiastical discipline.

There is said to be another letter in Paul's name to the Laodiceans, and another to the Alexandrines, [both] forged in accordance with Marcion's heresy, and many others which cannot be received into the catholic church, since it is not fitting that poison should be mixed with honey.

But the letter of Jude and the two superscribed with the name of John are accepted in the catholic [church]; Wisdom also, written by Solomon's friends in his honour. The Apocalypse of John we also receive, and that of Peter, which some of our people will not have to be read in church. But the *Shepherd* was written by Hermas in the city of Rome quite recently, in our own times, when his brother Pius occupied the bishop's chair in the church of the city of Rome; and therefore it may be read indeed, but cannot be given out to the people in church either among the prophets, since their number is complete, or among the apostles at the end of the times.

But none of the writings of Arsinous or Valentinus or Miltiades do we receive at all. They have also composed a new book of psalms for Marcion; [these we reject] together with Basilides [and] the Asian founder of the Cataphrygians...'

COMMENTS ON THE LIST

Twenty-one of the books which we have received in our New Testament are listed here as acceptable.

Luke, says the compiler, was not an eyewitness or hearer of Christ. What then was the nature of his authority? It derived from his association with Paul. He accompanied Paul, it is said, as a legal expert. This choice of words is a powerful argument in favour of regarding Latin as the original language of the document: it reflects a feature of Roman provincial administration. A Roman provincial governor had a legal expert (*iuris studiosus*, the phrase used here) on his staff. This expert drafted legal documents 'in the name' or 'in accordance with the opinion' of his superior; so Luke (it is implied), having been attached to Paul's staff, issued his writings in his own name but in accordance with Paul's opinion. Luke's writings, that is to say, are endowed with apostolic authority although they do not appear under the apostle's name.[5]

Three points of interest arise in the account of the gospel of John.

---

[5] The argument from *iuris studiosus* is set forth by A. Ehrhardt, 'The Gospels in the Muratorian Fragment', pp. 16–18. Ehrhardt had the advantage of having been a Professor of Roman Law before he turned to the study of ecclesiastical history. Even so good a Latinist as Alexander Souter missed the point here: he tentatively adopted E. S. Buchanan's emendation of *quasi ut iuris studiosum*, 'as a legal expert', to *quasi adiutorem studiosum*, 'as a devoted helper' (*The Text and Canon of the New Testament* [London, ²1954], pp. 191, 193).

First, the tale about John's fellow-disciples preserves a tradition that others apart from John himself were involved in the production or at least in the publication of his work: we may recall the anonymous endorsement at the end of the work by those who say of the evangelist, 'we know that his testimony is true' (John 21:24)[6]. Next, the insistence that all the gospels received in the church bear witness to one and the same faith is a corollary of the claim that John's fellow-disciples shared responsibility for his gospel. This faith is summarized in a sequence paralleled in the old Roman creed.[7] Thirdly, the emphasis on the eyewitness character of John's record is linked with the opening words of his first epistle, affirming that the matters to be dealt with are those with which the writer has been in direct and personal touch. A contrast has been seen between those words of 1 John 1:1–3 ('that . . . which we have heard, which we have seen with our eyes . . . ') and the gnostic use of the quotation in 1 Corinthians 2:9 ('what no eye has seen, nor ear heard . . . . '). The words of this last quotation, derived by Paul from an unknown source, are ascribed to Jesus in the *Gospel of Thomas* and the *Acts of Peter*;[8] they appear to have been pressed into service as an initiation formula in some gnostic schools (the initiate was promised experiences in which the rank and file could not share).[9] The compiler of the Muratorian list was firmly anti-gnostic.

The list goes on to refer to Acts as 'the Acts of all the apostles'. This title embodies a patent exaggeration of the subject-matter of the book. Even the traditional designation 'the Acts of the Apostles' is an exaggeration. The book records some acts of some apostles, and nothing more than this is claimed in the Greek title (*praxeis apostolōn*, 'acts of apostles'). What the author originally called it is uncertain— perhaps 'Luke to Theophilus, Volume 2'. Two apostles in particular, Peter and Paul, have their acts recorded here. What was the reason for the Muratorian exaggeration? Possibly it marks a reaction against Marcion: Marcion claimed that Paul was the only faithful apostle of

---

[6] The tale about John's fellow-disciples was probably derived from Papias (*cf* Harnack, 'Über den Verfasser . . .', p.9; Ehrhardt, 'The Gospels in the Muratorian Fragment', pp.19–25).

[7] See Ehrhardt, 'The Gospels in the Muratorian Fragment', pp.25f.

[8] *Gospel of Thomas*, 17; *Acts of Peter*, 39.

[9] *Cf.* Hippolytus, *Refutation*, 5.24.1; Clement of Alexandria, *Stromateis*, 4.18. Ehrhardt ('The Gospels in the Muratorian Fragment', p.30) cites their use in this sense in *Pistis Sophia*, 114; in *Acts of Thomas*, 36, and even in a Manichaean fragment from Turfan (M 789).

Jesus, but the compiler of our list implies, in accordance with the judgment of the catholic church, 'We acknowledge *all* the apostles, and not Paul only; here is an authoritative document which records their acts and not only Paul's.' An alternative possibility is that in saying, 'The Acts of all the apostles have been written in one book', the compiler wishes to emphasize that Luke's Acts is the only genuine book of apostolic acts. From about AD 160 onwards there began to appear in various parts of the Christian world a number of compositions claiming to record the acts of this or that apostolic figure: the *Acts of Peter*, the *Acts of Paul*, the *Acts of John*, the *Acts of Andrew*, the *Acts of Thomas*.[10] The compiler may mean: none of these is authentic; all that can be known of any of the apostles is exclusively recorded in this 'one book'.

Yet the compiler shows acquaintance with at least one of these volumes of apocryphal Acts—the *Acts of Peter*. He tries to explain the omission from Luke's Acts of some events in the careers of the apostles by saying that Luke recorded only such things as took place in his own presence—an inept explanation, for the things that took place in Luke's presence are confined to those sections of Acts where the story is told in the first person plural (the so-called 'we' sections).[11] Luke, he says, omits all mention of Peter's martyrdom or Paul's embarkation for Spain because he was not there to witness them. Now these two events, unrecorded by Luke, are narrated in the *Acts of Peter*, which the Muratorian compiler evidently knew. The *Acts of Peter* opens with Paul's setting out for Spain from Ostia, at the mouth of the Tiber,[12] and ends with an account of Peter's crucifixion (head downwards, at his own request).[13] (Neither the writer of the *Acts of Peter* nor the compiler of the Muratorian list probably had any basis for Paul's voyage to Spain apart from his own statement of his travel plans in Rom. 15:24, 28.)

As for the letters of Paul, thirteen are listed, including the three Pastorals.[14] But special attention is paid to those addressed to churches,

---

[10] See pp.202f. [11] Acts 16:10–17; 20:5—21:18; 27:1—28:16.
[12] *Acts of Peter*, 1–3. [13] *Acts of Peter*, 36–41.
[14] The curious order of Paul's letters suggests that the basis was a list of the letters following more or less their order in Marcion's New Testament (with Galatians removed from its leading place). If this list were written in two columns, so that Corinthians came at the top of the first column and Romans at the top of the second, then someone copying the titles down the first column and up the second would produce an order not unlike that in the Muratorian fragment. See also N. A. Dahl, 'Welche Ordnung der Paulusbriefe wird vom Muratorischen Kanon vorausgesetzt?'

seven churches in all — so the compiler insists, but he is mistaken, for
Galatians was addressed to several churches (all the churches of Galatia,
in fact). In writing to seven churches, the reader is told, Paul followed
the precedent of John who, 'in his Apocalypse, while writing to seven
churches, yet speaks to all'.[15] The seven churches, that is to say, stand
for the whole worldwide church. Even the Pastoral Epistles, while
addressed to individuals, are credited with a catholic dimension.

This making Paul follow the precedent of John is chronologically
preposterous; it probably indicates, however, that for the compiler the
primary criterion of inclusion in the list was prophetic inspiration. In
the early church as a whole the predominant criterion appears to have
been apostolic authority, if not apostolic authorship; for this writer,
however, even apostolic authorship evidently takes second place to
prophetic inspiration.[16]

John's Apocalypse, being self-evidently the work of a prophet, was
naturally included in the list.[17] So also (but not so naturally) was the
Apocalypse of Peter — no doubt in the belief that it was a genuine work
by the prince of the apostles.[18] It is acknowledged, however, that it
did not find universal acceptance. But it was felt to be edifying — it
contained lurid pictures of the torments of the damned, which in due
course exercised some influence on Dante's *Inferno* — and it was undoubtedly orthodox (by the standards of the Roman church) and
therefore acceptable as the *Gospel of Peter*[19] was not.

The letter of Jude is listed, and two letters of John — probably 1
John and 2 John. It has sometimes been suggested that, since 1 John

ZNW 52 (1961), pp.39–53; 'The particularity of the Pauline Epistles as a problem in
the Ancient Church', in *Neotestamentica et Patristica* (= NovT Sup 6), ed. W. C. van
Unnik (Leiden, 1962), pp.261–271.

[15] K. Stendahl, 'The Apocalypse of John and the Epistles of Paul in the Muratorian
Fragment', in *Current Issues in New Testament Interpretation*, ed. W. Klassen and G. F.
Snyder (New York, 1962), goes so far as to suggest that, for the compiler of our list,
the canonicity of Paul's letters depended on that of John's Apocalypse. The analogy
between Paul's seven churches and John's is pointed out by Cyprian (*Exhortation for
Martyrdom*, 11) and Victorinus of Pettau (*On the Apocalypse*, 1.7, on Rev. 1:20). Quite
apart from the number of churches addressed by Paul, Tertullian emphasizes the
universal relevance of Paul's letters: 'when the apostle wrote to some, he wrote to all'
(*Against Marcion*, 5.17).

[16] On these criteria of canonicity see below, pp.255–269.

[17] Its position between Wisdom and the *Shepherd* does not mean that it is accorded
only marginal canonicity; its earlier mention in the discussion of Paul's letters is proof
enough of that.

[18] See p.261.   [19] See pp.200f.

has already been quoted, in the comment on the Fourth Gospel, the two letters mentioned here are 2 John and 3 John, but this is a less natural way to understand the reference. There is evidence elsewhere that 2 John and 3 John were 'canonized' separately.[20]

The letter to the Hebrews is not mentioned, which is only to be expected in a Roman canon of the second or third century. As the letter of Clement shows, Hebrews was known at an early date in the Roman church, but was not accorded the authority enjoyed by the letters of Paul. What is indeed surprising in a Roman list is to find no mention of 1 Peter. One eminent scholar thought that both 1 and 2 Peter were originally listed after the mention of John's Apocalypse, but were accidentally lost in the process of copying, through the omission of a line. When the existing text speaks of 'John's Apocalypse and Peter's', Theodor von Zahn thought that the list originally continued with the words: '. . . epistle. There is also another epistle of Peter'—followed by the clause 'which some of our people will not have to be read in church.'[21] But this was a purely conjectural emendation, not required by the text.

If it is surprising to find the Wisdom of Solomon (known to us as a book of the Old Testament Apocrypha) listed here among New Testament books, let it be reflected that, so far as its date goes, it may be closer to the New Testament age than to that of the Old Testament. (Some students have dated it as late as AD 40.)[22] As for the statement that it was 'written by Solomon's friends in his honour', this may reflect the tradition that Wisdom is much too late to be the work of Solomon himself. Those who hold that a Greek original lies behind

[20] There is evidence that 3 John was translated into Latin by a different hand from 1 and 2 John. See A. Harnack, *Zur Revision der Prinzipien der neutestamentlichen Textkritik* (Leipzig, 1916), pp.61f.; T. W. Manson, 'The Johannine Epistles and the Canon of the New Testament', *JTS* 48 (1947), pp.32f.; J. Lieu, *The Second and Third Epistles of John* (Edinburgh, 1986), pp.5–36. Behind the statement (in Latin) that two epistles of John 'are accepted in the catholic [church]', P. Katz, 'The Johannine Epistles in the Muratorian Canon', *JTS* n.s. 8 (1957), pp.273f., discerns a Greek form of words which means 'two . . . in addition to the catholic [epistle]'; cf C. F. D. Moule, *The Birth of the New Testament* (London, ³1981), p.266, n.2.

[21] Zahn, *Geschichte des neutestamentlichen Kanons*, II (Erlangen/Leipzig, 1890), p.142. B. H. Streeter concluded that, since 1 Peter was absent from the Syriac canon as late as the mid-fourth century AD, it was not among the books which Tatian took from Rome to Edessa c AD 172 (*The Primitive Church* [London, 1929], p.119).

[22] E.g. W. O. E. Oesterley, *An Introduction to the Books of the Apocrypha* (London, 1935), pp.207–209.

the Latin list have often suggested that 'friends' (*philoi* in Greek) was a wrong reading for 'Philo' (the Jewish philosopher of Alexandria, who lived *c* 20 BC – *c* AD 50); what the compiler allegedly wrote was 'written by Philo in Solomon's honour' or something like that. But this is an unnecessary supposition.[23]

The allegorical work known as the *Shepherd* of Hermas was read with appreciation in the Roman church and elsewhere,[24] but the compiler of our list excludes it from the New Testament scriptures. Its quality of inspiration might have entitled it to a place among the prophets, but the list of Old Testament prophets had been closed for a long time before the *Shepherd* was written;[25] it was too recent a work to be included in the New Testament list along with such a prophetic work as the Apocalypse of John. The *Shepherd*, says the compiler, was written 'quite recently, in our own times', when Pius, the brother of Hermas, was bishop of Rome. Pius was bishop of Rome some time during the period when Antoninus Pius was Roman emperor (AD 138–161), but the *Shepherd*, to judge by internal evidence, may have been written even earlier than that, about the beginning of the second century. It has indeed been argued that the words 'quite recently, in our own times', mean little more than 'in the post-apostolic age' and are not incompatible with a fourth-century date for the Muratorian list,[26] but this is not a natural way to understand them: the two terms 'quite recently' and 'in our own times',[27] taken together, seem to emphasize the recency of the work. Its recency is the main argument against acknowledging it as a biblical document, on a par with those of an earlier generation. In itself, the *Shepherd* might have been unexceptionable, but if the door had been opened for the admission of second-century prophecies, there would be many strange claimants for inclusion.

The Muratorian list mentions other works which are rejected out of hand. At the end of the section on Paul's epistles, two alleged letters of his are said to be Marcionite forgeries. One was addressed to the

---

[23] In any case, the stylistic objections to ascribing Wisdom to Philo's authorship, even if it was written in his lifetime, are almost insuperable.

[24] See pp. 183, 209f.

[25] Even so, there is evidence for 'the inclusion of the Shepherd of Hermas in many (Western) exemplars of the Old Testament, *even in the Middle Ages*' (A. Harnack, *The Origin of the New Testament*, E.T. [London, 1925], p. 171).

[26] See A. C. Sundberg, 'Canon Muratori: A Fourth-Century List', pp. 8–11.

[27] Latin *nuperrime, temporibus nostris*.

Laodiceans. We know that Marcion himself entitled the letter to the Ephesians 'To the Laodiceans'; possibly the Muratorian compiler knew of this title and, not realizing that it was identical with Ephesians, concluded that it must have been forged in Paul's name. Otherwise he may have known of an attempt to supply the missing Laodicean letter of Colossians 4:16—an attempt otherwise unknown to us. (We know a later 'Epistle to the Laodiceans', extant only in Latin; it is a perfectly innocuous and unimaginative cento of pieces from Paul's genuine letters, but is of interest in the history of the English Bible because a translation of it was included in fifteenth-century copies of the Wycliffite version.)[28]

Of the letter to the Alexandrines we know nothing. It cannot be identified with the letter to the Hebrews, which has no flavour of Marcion's teaching about it. The rejected letters may have much of the truth in them, but it is vitiated by the admixture of error, as if poison were to be mixed with honey. The Latin words for poison (fel) and honey (mel) rhyme with each other, so that we may have here a proverbial Latin tag. This has been used as a further argument for the Latin origin of the list, since the assonance could not be reproduced with the corresponding Greek words.

At the end of the list reference is made to other works which are utterly repudiated. Arsinous we do not know. Valentinus we have met already. Miltiades appears to have been a Montanist leader.[29] The 'book of psalms' compiled for Marcion may have taken the place among his followers that the Old Testament Psalter took in the catholic church, since the latter was naturally unacceptable to the Marcionites. Basilides, a gnostic teacher in Alexandria between AD 120 and 145, is said to have written a gospel and a commentary on it in twenty-four volumes.[30] The Latin text of the list would imply that Basilides was 'the Asian founder of the Cataphrygians', but the conjunction 'or' or 'and' must have dropped out before this last phrase.[31] Basilides is associated with Alexandria, not with the province of Asia, and he was not a Montanist, which is what the word

---

[28] See pp. 237–240.

[29] He is mentioned in Eusebius, *Hist. Eccl.* 5.16.3, where his name appears as that of a Montanist leader in a letter addressed to Avircius Marcellinus (see p. 281 below). (The name appears in the Muratorian fragment as Mitiades, but this is usually taken to be one of the many scribal mis-spellings).

[30] See Eusebius, *Hist. Eccl.* 4.7.4–7. See p. 128 above for his quotation of John 1:9.

[31] One of the Cassino fragments supplies the conjunction *siue* ('or').

'Cataphrygian' means.[32] (He lived a generation before the rise of Montanism.)

The 'Asian founder of the Cataphrygians' was Montanus, who launched a new charismatic movement in Upper Phrygia abut AD 156.[33] He claimed that the age of the Paraclete, foretold by Jesus, had now arrived, and that he was the mouthpiece of the Paraclete. The gift of prophecy was accordingly exercised in greater vigour than ever by him and his followers, and their utterances presented a challenge to the catholic view of the faith as something 'once for all delivered' (Jude 3). If Paul and John insisted in the first century that it was necessary to 'test the prophets' and make sure that their utterances were consistent with the authentic witness to Christ,[34] such testing was no less necessary a century later. The Montanist challenge from one direction, like the Marcionite and gnostic challenges from other directions, made it the more important that the limits of holy scripture should be clearly defined. Holy scripture, properly defined, would provide a check on uncontrolled prophecy as it did on undisciplined speculation.[35] Montanism extended its influence far beyond its native Phrygia; its menace was felt in Rome itself.[36]

One doughty opponent of the Montanists was a learned presbyter of the Roman church named Gaius, who flourished towards the end of the second century. He conducted a controversial correspondence with a Montanist leader in Asia named Proclus.[37] Gaius apparently tried to cut the ground from under the Montanists' feet by denying the authenticity of the document on which they relied for their teaching about the Paraclete, the Gospel of John.[38] This was an excessive price to pay for the maintenance of catholic orthodoxy, and a quite unneces-

[32] This is the earliest extant occurrence of the designation 'Cataphrygian'; it appears later in Eusebius, Epiphanius of Salamis (Cyprus) and John of Damascus.

[33] Eusebius, *Hist. Eccl.* 5.14.1–18.14.   [34] 1 Cor. 12:3; 1 John 4:1–3.

[35] See Harnack, *The Origin of the New Testament*, p.35.

[36] And in Carthage (see p.180).

[37] Eusebius, *Hist. Eccl.* 2.25.5–7; 3.31.4; 6.20.3.

[38] Eusebius, *Hist. Eccl.* 3.28.1f., implies that Gaius ascribed the Apocalypse to the heresiarch Cerinthus—a view mentioned but rejected by Dionysius of Alexandria (Eusebius, *Hist. Eccl.* 7.25.2–4). His rejection of the Fourth Gospel is implied in the title of Hippolytus's *Chapters against Gaius* or *A Defence of the Gospel and Apocalypse according to John*. According to Bar-Ṣalibi, twelfth-century Syriac commentator on the Apocalypse, 'Hippolytus of Rome states that a man named Gaius appeared, who said that neither the Gospel nor the Apocalypse was John's, but that they were the work of Cerinthus the heretic.' See T. H. Robinson, 'The Authorship of the Muratorian Canon', *Expositor* 7, 1 (1906), p.487. See p.178 below.

sary price. Those who agreed with Gaius on this point came to be called *Alogoi,* a word of double meaning: it meant primarily 'those who refuse the Logos' (the divine Word of John 1:1–14) but also, in its common usage, 'irrational people'.[39] But their negative attitude to the Fourth Gospel had no influence on catholic thought, in Rome or elsewhere. The Muratorian list reflects the Roman church's policy at this time to rebut the Montanist and other challenges to catholic truth by identifying the sure written sources of apostolic teaching or, as these sources came to be called later, the canon of the New Testament.

[39] Epiphanius, *Panarion* 50–52. See J. Chapman, *John the Presbyter and the Fourth Gospel* (Oxford, 1911), pp. 53–55.

CHAPTER THIRTEEN

IRENAEUS, HIPPOLYTUS, NOVATIAN

IRENAEUS

The Greek-speaking settlements in south-eastern Gaul were evangelized from the province of Asia—the area, indeed, from which those settlements had been founded many centuries before. Their evangelization took place probably early in the second century, if not earlier (it has been suggested by some that the 'Galatia' to which Crescens is said to have gone in 2 Timothy 4:10 was not the Anatolian Galatia but European Gaul). Our first definite knowledge of Christianity in south-eastern Gaul comes from a letter sent by two churches of the Rhône valley, those of Lyon and Vienne, to tell their friends in proconsular Asia of a fierce persecution which they had to endure in AD 177, in the principate of Marcus Aurelius.[1] For our present purpose this letter has an incidental interest in the use that it makes of scripture, one of the most striking instances being the occurrence of the formula 'that the scripture might be fulfilled' (common in the gospels to introduce Old Testament quotations) to introduce a quotation of Revelation 22:11.[2]

At the same time as this letter was sent to Asia, another letter was sent to Eleutherus, the bishop of Rome, to acquaint him and his

[1] The letter is reproduced in Eusebius, *Hist. Eccl.* 5.1.3–2.7.
[2] In Eusebius, *Hist. Eccl.* 5.1.58.

followers with the sufferings of the Gaulish churches. The letter for Rome was entrusted to Irenaeus, a presbyter in the church of Lyon, described by the senders as 'zealous for the covenant of Christ'.[3]

Irenaeus was born and brought up in the province of Asia. In his youth he came under the influence of Polycarp, bishop of Smyrna, and ever remembered with gratitude the instruction which he (with others) had received from him, including his reminiscences of contacts 'with John and with the others who had seen the Lord'.[4] Later he emigrated to the Rhône valley. One of the martyrs who died in the persecution of 177 was Pothinus, the nonagenarian bishop of Lyon. When the church of Lyon had time to recover somewhat after the persecution, Irenaeus was elected as bishop in place of Pothinus.

Of Irenaeus's literary works two have survived. The major one is usually called *Against Heresies,* comprising five books; his own title for it was *An Exposure and Refutation of the Knowledge (gnosis) that is Falsely So Called.*[5] The original Greek has been lost for the most part: the work has been preserved in a Latin translation of the fourth century and, so far as the fourth and fifth books are concerned, in an Armenian translation. His other surviving work, The *Demonstration of the Apostolic Preaching,* is shorter; it has been described as a manual of Christian evidences or an outline of the plan of salvation. It has been preserved in an Armenian translation.[6]

Irenaeus is the principal spokesman of the catholic response to Gnosticism and other second-century deviations. He was well placed to fill this rôle because of his links with widely separated areas of the Christian world. The gnostic schools maintained that it was they who best preserved the original teaching of the apostles; some of them claimed that the apostles' more esoteric teaching had been delivered privately to selected disciples who were worthy or gifted enough to receive it.[7] Irenaeus set himself to examine such claims and to establish the content of the genuine apostolic tradition. This tradition was maintained in living power, he argued, in those churches which were

---

[3] Eusebius, *Hist. Eccl.* 5.4.

[4] Irenaeus, 'Letter to Florinus', in Eusebius, *Hist. Eccl.* 5.20.4–8.

[5] The best edition of this work is by W. W. Harvey, *Sancti Irenaei Libros Quinque adversus Haereses,* 2 vols. (Cambridge, 1857, reprinted Ridgewood, N. J., 1965). There is an English translation in *ANF* I (Grand Rapids, 1956), pp.309–567. (The *ANF* divisions, going back to Massuet, 1712, are followed in the references below.)

[6] There is a good English edition by J. A. Robinson (London, 1920).

[7] Irenaeus, *Against Heresies,* 3.3.1.

founded by apostles and in which there had been a regular succession of bishops or elders since their foundation;[8] it was summed up in those churches' rule of faith or baptismal creed.[9] The doctrine maintained in such a church in Irenaeus's day might be assumed to be that which was first taught by the apostolic founder or founders, and transmitted through an unbroken succession of bishops. The burden of proof lay on those who argued that the doctrine had been changed in the course of transmission between the date of foundation and the time at which Irenaeus wrote. Moreover, the faith confessed in the churches founded by apostles was confessed in other churches of later foundation throughout the world: 'the churches planted in Germany have not believed or handed down anything different, nor yet the churches among the Iberians or the Celts, nor those in the east, nor yet in Egypt and Libya, nor those established in the centre of the world.'[10]

This account of the matter depended on certain presuppositions, some of which Irenaeus declared, while he was perhaps not wholly conscious of others. The Holy Spirit, he declared, gave the apostles perfect knowledge; they received no secret knowledge and delivered no secret tradition. With the churches which they founded they deposited everything that pertains to saving truth, and from these churches it must be learned—the more securely because of the complete and continuous succession of bishops in these churches.[11] He assumed that all the apostles were unanimous in their teaching. It is plain, however, from the New Testament that while (say) Paul, Peter and James were agreed on the basic facts of the gospel (1 Cor. 15:11), there were differences among them on the practical implications of those facts. But whatever differences there were, they were resolved in a second-century synthesis, and to Irenaeus this synthesis was the apostolic tradition.

---

[8] Heretics might appeal to the text of scripture, but their interpretation was vitiated because it did not accord with the rule of faith—the summary of Christian teaching handed down in the apostolic tradition (*Against Heresies*, 1.3.6).

[9] The baptismal creed, based on the confessional response of candidates for baptism, was different in origin from the rule of faith, but 'they came in time to interpenetrate each other, until from the fourth century onward the ecumenical creed supersedes the appeal to the rule of faith' (F. F. Bruce, *Tradition Old and New* [Exeter, 1970], p. 116).

[10] *Against Heresies*, 1.10.2. Elsewhere Irenaeus points out that, even when the tradition is unwritten, 'many barbarian nations which believe in Christ' assent to it, 'having [the way of] salvation written in their hearts through the Spirit' (3.4.2). Compare the testimony of Hegesippus quoted on p. 123 above.

[11] *Against Heresies*, 3.1–4.

In all Irenaeus's argument, moreover, scripture plays a dominant part. It is the abiding witness to the one living and true God, 'whom the law announces, whom the prophets proclaim, whom Christ reveals, whom the apostles teach, whom the church believes'.[12] Irenaeus is well able to distinguish 'the writings of truth' from 'the multitude of apocryphal and spurious writings'.[13] The Old Testament writings are indispensable witnesses to the history of salvation; the Septuagint version was divinely inspired,[14] the writings which we call the Apocrypha being evidently invested with the same authority as those translated from the Hebrew Bible.[15] As for the New Testament, Hans von Campenhausen describes 'the critical period between Marcion and Irenaeus' as 'the period in which the "New Testament" as such emerged'.[16] Irenaeus nowhere in his extant writings sets down a list of New Testament books, but it is evident that he had a clear notion of their identity. He makes free use of the phraseology about 'old covenant' and 'new covenant',[17] but does not yet use the latter expression to denote the collection of authoritative writings thrown up by the new covenant, as Clement of Alexandria and Tertullian of Carthage were soon to do.[18] The collection itself, however, was a reality to him. In using the scriptures to expose and refute subversive teaching, it was important to know which scriptures might effectively be so used,[19] and he knew them, and used them.

There is one place where Eusebius undertakes to reproduce Irenaeus's testimony to the traditions which he had received about the scriptures.[20] First he quotes his account of the origins of the four gospels; then he quotes his discussion of the number of the beast in Revelation 13:18,[21] and his remark that John saw his revelation 'not a long time ago, but almost in our own generation towards the end of Domitian's rule'.[22] Eusebius adds that Irenaeus makes many quotations from 1 John, and also from 1 Peter. Then he points out that Irenaeus

---

[12] *Against Heresies*, 2.30.9.   [13] *Against Heresies*, 1.20.1.

[14] *Against Heresies*, 3.21.2.

[15] As in the use made of the story of Susanna and the elders (*Against Heresies* 4.26.3) and the quotation from 1 Baruch 4:36—5:9 (5.35.1).

[16] *The Formation of the Christian Bible* E.T. (London, 1972), p.37.

[17] Cf *Against Heresies*, 4.32.1.   [18] See pp.180, 188.

[19] *Against Heresies*, 3, preface.   [20] Eusebius, *Hist. Eccl.* 5.8.1–8.

[21] *Against Heresies*, 5.30.1.

[22] *Against Heresies*, 5.30.3, quoted also in *Hist. Eccl.* 3.18.2f. If Irenaeus was born c AD 130, 'almost in our own generation' means 'in the generation before mine'.

cited the *Shepherd* of Hermas as 'scripture'[23] and quoted the book of Wisdom, and also that he referred to Justin Martyr,[24] Ignatius[25] and a certain unnamed 'apostolic presbyter'.[26] It is not suggested that the three last writers were accorded scriptural status.

. If none of Irenaeus's writings had survived, one could imagine some readers of this passage in Eusebius arguing from it that Irenaeus did not receive as scripture either the Acts of the Apostles or the letters of Paul. Such an argument would overlook what Bishop Lightfoot, in another connexion, called 'the silence of Eusebius'. To those who argued in his day that Papias said nothing about the gospels apart from what is said in the few extracts from his work that Eusebius reproduces, Lightfoot pointed out that Eusebius is concerned to quote the testimony borne by earlier writers to the 'disputed' books; as for the acknowledged books, he takes them for granted, pausing only to mention any anecdotes or other points of interest occurring in those writers' treatment of them.[27] So here, Eusebius says nothing of Irenaeus's well attested use of Acts and the Pauline letters, but thinks his remarks on the origins of the four gospels sufficiently interesting to quote:

> Matthew published among the Hebrews a gospel in writing also [i.e. in addition to the oral preaching] in their own speech, while Peter and Paul were preaching the gospel and founding the church in Rome. After their death Mark in his turn, Peter's disciple and interpreter, delivered to us in writing the contents of Peter's preaching. Luke also, the follower of Paul, set down in a book the gospel preached by him {i.e. by Paul}. Then John, the disciple of the Lord, the one who leaned back on his bosom, gave forth his gospel while he was living at Ephesus in Asia.[28]

[23] *Against Heresies*, 4.20.2 (quoting Mandate 1). In introducing Hermas's words as 'the scripture', Irenaeus does not imply apostolic scripture.

[24] He quotes from Justin's treatise *Against Marcion* in *Against Heresies*, 4.6.2.

[25] He quotes Ignatius, *To the Romans* 4.1, in *Against Heresies*, 5.28.4.

[26] Perhaps the 'apostolic presbyter' was Clement of Rome (believed to be a disciple of apostles), to whose letter (called *scriptura* in the sense of 'writing') various allusions are made in *Against Heresies*, 3.3.3.

[27] See J. B. Lightfoot, 'The Silence of Eusebius', *Essays on the Work Entitled 'Supernatural Religion'* (London, 1889), pp.32–58.

[28] *Against Heresies*, 3.1.1, quoted by Eusebius, *Hist. Eccl.* 5.8.2–4. See J. Chapman, 'St Irenaeus on the Date of the Gospels', *JTS* 6 (1904–5), pp.563–569.

There is another passage where Irenaeus expresses himself in often repeated words on the fourfold structure of the gospel record:

> As there are four quarters of the world in which we live, and four universal winds, and as the church is dispersed over all the earth, and the gospel is the pillar and base of the church, and the breath of life, so it is natural that it should have four pillars, breathing immortality from every quarter and kindling human life anew. Whence it is manifest that the Word, the architect of all things, who sits upon the cherubim[29] and holds all things together, having been manifested to mankind, has given us the gospel in fourfold form, but held together by one Spirit. ...Therefore they are guilty of vanity and ignorance, and of audacity also, who reject the form of the gospel and introduce either more or fewer faces of the gospels—in the former case, so that they should have the reputation of having discovered more than the truth, in the latter case, so that they should reject the dispensations of God.[30]

In his warning against either increasing or reducing the number of gospels Irenaeus may have in mind those who gave some degreee of credence to the more recent gnostic gospels or, on the other hand, people like Gaius of Rome and the *Alogoi* who at that very time were repudiating the Gospel of John.[31] But the general impression given by his words is that the fourfold pattern of the gospel was by this time no innovation but so widely accepted that he can stress its cosmic appropriateness as though it were one of the facts of nature.[32]

Irenaeus uses both the singular 'gospel' and the plural 'gospels' to designate the fourfold record, but his preference seems to be for the singular.[33] It is the mark of heresy, he says, to concentrate on one of the four to the virtual exclusion of the others, as the Valentinians, according to him, concentrated on the Gospel of John.[34] All four were inspired by the same Spirit as spoke through the prophets. This

---

[29] *Cf* Ps. 80:1 (LXX 79:2). Irenaeus goes on to relate the four gospels to the faces of the four living creatures of Ezek. 1:10 and Rev. 4:7—a lion (John), a calf (Luke), a man (Matthew), an eagle (Mark).

[30] *Against Heresies*, 3.11.8.

[31] It is their repudiation of John that is probably referred to in *Against Heresies*, 3.11.9. See pp. 168f.

[32] See F. S. Gutjahr, *Die Glaubenswürdigkeit des Irenäischen Zeugnisses über die Abfassung des vierten kanonischen Evangeliums* (Graz, 1904), pp. 8–10.

[33] *Cf Against Heresies*, 3.5.1; 3.11.8.   [34] *Against Heresies*, 3.11.7.

inspiration extended to the choice of one word rather than another: if Matthew 1:18 says 'the birth of *Christ* took place in this way' (as Irenaeus evidently found it in his copy) and not 'the birth of *Jesus* took place in this way', that is because the Spirit, foreseeing (as the evangelist himself did not) the rise of heretics who would admit that *Jesus* was born of Mary but maintain that *Christ* descended on him from heaven at his baptism, refuted them in advance by affirming that *Christ* was born of Mary.[35]

As for the Acts of the Apostles, it stands or falls with the Gospel of Luke; that is to say, it stands. Irenaeus appeals to Acts in refutation of the Ebionites who refuse to recognize the apostleship of Paul;[36] he appeals to it equally in refutation of the Marcionites who refuse to recognize any apostle other than Paul.[37] He does not list the letters of Paul, but he evidently accepted the whole corpus of thirteen letters (the Pastorals included); the only letter he does not mention is the short letter to Philemon, which he had no occasion to cite. There is a probable quotation from Hebrews 1:3 in the third book *Against Heresies,* where God is said to have created all things 'by the word of his power'.[38] Eusebius speaks of a 'book of various discourses' by Irenaeus in which he mentions Hebrews and quotes some passages from it,[39] but there is no suggestion that he regarded it as Pauline; indeed, a sixth-century writer named Stephen Gobarus says that (like Hippolytus shortly afterwards) he denied its Pauline authorship.[40]

By contrast with the Pauline corpus, Irenaeus makes little appeal to the catholic epistles. He knows 1 Peter as the work of the apostle Peter; twice he quotes 1 Peter 1:8 ('without having seen him, you love him. . .').[41] He quotes 1 and 2 John as the work of John the evangelist, 'the disciple of the Lord'.[42] There is one fairly clear quotation of James 2:23 ('he [Abraham] believed God, and it was reckoned to him as righteousness; and he was called the friend of God'),[43] but its source is

[35] *Against Heresies,* 3.16.2.   [36] *Against Heresies,* 3.15.1.
[37] *Against Heresies,* 3.13.1–14.4.   [38] *Against Heresies,* 2.30.9.
[39] *Hist. Eccl.* 5.26. In the same work Wisdom was also cited (see p. 174).
[40] Quoted by Photius, *Bibliotheca,* 232.
[41] *Against Heresies,* 4.9.2; 5.7.2. In 4.16.5, 1 Pet. 2:16 is quoted and ascribed to Peter. Elsewhere there are unascribed quotations from the same letters: Irenaeus seems to be specially fond of quoting 1 Pet. 1:12, 'things into which angels long to look' (*Against Heresies,* 2.17.9; 4.34.1; 5.36.2).
[42] 1 John 2:18–22 is quoted in part in *Against Heresies,* 3.16.4; 1 John 4:1–3 in 3.16.7; 1 John 5:1 in 3.16.8; 2 John 7 f in 3.16.7; 2 John 11 in 1.16.3.
[43] *Against Heresies,* 4.16.2.

not given, nor is any reference made to James. The Apocalypse is quoted frequently towards the end of the treatise *Against Heresies* as the basis of the eschatology held by Irenaeus and many of his predecessors and contemporaries;[44] it is ascribed to 'John the disciple of the Lord', and treated as a genuine prophecy, in keeping with its own claim (Rev. 1:3; 22:7, 10, 18, 19).[45] But when, in a discussion of John's eschatological teaching, 'the apostle' is quoted, the reference is to Paul, 'the apostle' *par excellence*.[46]

Irenaeus, in fact, recognized and appealed to the same collection of Christian writings as is listed in the Muratorian fragment, except that he included 1 Peter, which is not mentioned there. If the Muratorian list is of Roman origin, it may have been during one of his earlier visits to Rome that Irenaeus became acquainted with the contents of the 'New Testament' scriptures acknowledged in the church of the capital.[47] Perhaps we should be warned against calling it a 'closed' canon by the very fact that it was later added to;[48] but it was envisaged as a coherent *corpus,* comprising twenty-two books—all the books of the final New Testament, indeed, except Hebrews, James, 2 Peter, 3 John and Jude.

The Old and New Testaments together provided Irenaeus with a broad and secure foundation not only for the negative purpose of refuting heresy but even more for the positive exposition of what has been called 'the biblical theology of St Irenaeus'.[49] From his time on, the whole church in east and west has acknowledged the New Testament collection as making up, together with the Old Testament, the Christian Bible.

HIPPOLYTUS

Hippolytus of Rome (*c* 170–235), the last significant figure in the Roman church to write in Greek, was the greatest scholar of his age in

---

[44] *Against Heresies,* 5.26–36.   [45] *Against Heresies,* 4.20.11; 5.26.1.
[46] *Against Heresies,* 5.30.2; 5.36.2, 3.
[47] For the part of the Roman church in the fixing of the collection see A. von Harnack, *The Origin of the New Testament,* E.T. (London, 1925), pp.104–106; E. J. Goodspeed, *The Formation of the New Testament* (Chicago, 1926), pp.67–77.
[48] H. von Campenhausen says that to ascribe to Irenaeus the idea of a closed canon, 'to which nothing may be added and from which nothing is to be deleted', is to extend to the whole New Testament what he says about the fourfold gospel (*The Formation of the Christian Bible,* p.209, n.207).
[49] *Cf* J. Lawson, *The Biblical Theology of Saint Irenaeus* (London, 1948).

the west (though neither in scholarly depth nor in intellectual power could he match his younger contemporary Origen in the east).[50] He was for a short time bishop of a dissident group in the Roman church (the first antipope, one might say), but died in communion with the bishop of Rome in Sardinia, to which both of them were exiled; he has been venerated as a saint and martyr. His works include a *Refutation of all heresies* in ten books, a manual of the church order (the *Apostolic Tradition*), a commentary on Daniel in four books (the earliest orthodox commentary on any biblical book)[51] and other exegetical works. An incomplete list of his writings preserved on the back of his statue in Rome (rediscovered in 1551 and now in the Vatican Library) mentions one *On the Gospel of John and the Apocalypse,* possibly identical with his *Chapters against Gaius* (referred to by the Syrian writer Ebedjesu, *c* 1300), of which some Syriac fragments survive; this work evidently defended the apostolic authorship of the Gospel and Apocalypse of John against the anti-Montanist Gaius of Rome and the *Alogoi*.[52] Had the eccentric views of Gaius and the *Alogoi* been more influential than in fact they were, this work of Hippolytus might have played an important part in the history of the New Testament canon.

As it is, Hippolytus no more than Irenaeus has left us a list of New Testament books. But he evidently placed most of them on the same level of authority as the books of the Old Testament: he refers to 'all scripture' as comprising 'the prophets, the Lord, and the apostles'.[53] He knows Hebrews and quotes it, but not as scripture; he also appears to know (if only slightly) James, 2 Peter and Jude. He quotes on occasion some other early Christian works which in the event did not gain canonical status, such as the *Shepherd* of Hermas, the *Didachē* and the *Letter of Barnabas,* but he does not treat them as scripture.

---

[50] Origen heard Hippolytus preach in Rome about 212; in the course of his sermon Hippolytus referred to Origen's presence in the congregation (Jerome, *On Illustrious Men,* 61).

[51] Written apparently about 204.

[52] In his Commentary on the Apocalypse Dionysius bar Salibi (died 1171) refers repeatedly to Gaius and to Hippolytus's refutation of him. Bar Salibi (on Rev. 8:18, etc.) calls Gaius a heretic because of his rejection of the Apocalypse and the Fourth Gospel. But Gaius and the *Alogoi* appear to have been orthodox in all other respects. See p. 168.

[53] *Commentary on Daniel,* 4.49.

NOVATIAN

The first substantial work in Latin to come from a Roman Christian is the treatise *On the Trinity* by Novatian, written about 250, or a little earlier.[54] Like Hippolytus, he was an antipope: the puritan fellowship which followed him became known, after his own name, as the Novatians.

Novatian appeals to what he calls the 'rule of truth' (*regula veritatis*), which is the summary of scriptural teaching. He quotes freely from the Gospels (especially John) and the letters of Paul in support of his arguments, manifestly assigning to them the same authority as the Old Testament writings which he similarly quotes. However, we learn nothing from him about the history of the canon which we do not know from other sources.

[54] Translated in ANF V, pp.611–644.

CHAPTER FOURTEEN

TERTULLIAN, CYPRIAN AND OTHERS

TERTULLIAN

Tertullian of Carthage takes his place at the head of a distinguished series of Christian theologians who wrote in Latin.[1] His writings belong to the period AD 196–212; around the year 206 he became a Montanist. It is in his writings that we first find the designation 'New Testament' for the second part of the Christian Bible.

When Melito of Sardis spoke of 'the books of the old covenant',[2] the expression might be taken to imply the existence of books of the *new* covenant, but not necessarily so. The 'old covenant' certainly implies a 'new covenant', and *vice versa* (*cf* Heb. 8:13), but the existence of *books* of the old covenant does not demand the existence of books of the new covenant. Paul, in 2 Corinthians 3:14, speaks of 'the reading of the old covenant', meaning the reading of the law in the synagogue services, but while he speaks in the same context of the new covenant which supersedes the old, there can be at that stage no 'reading of the *new* covenant', except in so far as the law and the prophets can be read in the light of their fulfilment in the gospel. Paul indeed contrasts the written text of the old covenant with the *unwritten* form of the new

---

[1] See T. D. Barnes, *Tertullian: A Historical and Literary Study* (Oxford, 1971).
[2] See p. 71.

covenant: 'the letter kills; the Spirit gives life' (2 Cor. 3:6).[3]

But before long, as Harnack pointed out, in place of the divinely cancelled 'handwriting which was against us with its legal demands' (Col. 2:14),[4] 'there must be a new handwriting which is for us'.[5] It was inevitable, as the eyewitnesses and their hearers passed away, that the terms of the new covenant should be set down in writing. Occasional as his letters might be, Paul himself took the lead in this activity even in the lifetime of eyewitnesses.

The Greek word *diathēkē*, 'covenant', can denote a settlement of various kinds. Occasionally (as in Gal. 3:15 and Heb. 9:16f.) it means a last will and testament, a document which does not come into effect until its signatory has died. When the word was translated into Latin, it had to be decided which Latin word best represented the meaning of the Greek. The Latin vocabulary is not deficient in legal terminology. Tertullian uses two Latin words to represent Gk. *diathēkē*— *instrumentum*, a 'deed' or other properly drafted legal document, and *testamentum*, a 'testament' or 'will'.[6] He uses these words to denote not only the old and new covenants, but also the two bodies of literature associated with them. He himself may have preferred the term *instrumentum* (he is commonly thought to have been a jurist by profession),[7] but he implies that the term *testamentum* was more commonly in use among Latin-speaking Christians. Thus, when speaking of Marcion's *Antitheses,* he says that it set up two separate Gods, 'one belonging to one *instrumentum* (or, as it is more usual to say, *testamentum*) and one to the other'.[8] It is mainly because of Tertullian's use of *testamentum* in this sense that we speak in English of the Old Testament and the New Testament, although neither of these bodies of literature is in any real sense a will.

Since Tertullian recognized the New Testament as a collection of

---

[3] The 'letter' is the Mosaic law, which sentences the law-breaker to death (Num. 15:30f.; Deut. 17:1–6; 27:26); the 'Spirit' in the gospel promises forgiveness and life to the sinner.

[4] The 'handwriting' (RSV 'bond') of Col. 2:14 may be the law-breaker's signed acknowledgment of indebtedness, cancelled by the redemptive work of Christ on the cross.

[5] A. Harnack, *The Origin of the New Testament,* E.T. (London, 1925), p.13.

[6] He also uses, with regard to the Old or New Testament collection, *armarium* ('bookcase') and *paratura* ('equipment').

[7] T. D. Barnes casts doubt on this (*Tertullian,* pp.22–29).

[8] *Against Marcion* 4.1. In *Against Praxeas* 15 he uses both terms in one phrase: 'the whole *instrumentum* of both *testamenta*'.

books, he may be expected to have had a fairly clear idea which books it contained. He did not use the word 'canon', but approved of the idea which 'canon' later came to express. When he charged Valentinus with misinterpreting the *instrumentum* (i.e. the New Testament) and Marcion with mutilating it,[9] he knew exactly what he meant by the *instrumentum*. Although he nowhere formally enumerates its contents, it certainly comprised the four gospels and Acts, the thirteen epistles which bear Paul's name, 1 Peter, 1 John and Revelation (which he ascribes to John the apostle).[10] It also included the epistle of Jude, which he ascribes to the apostle of that name.[11]

The reason for his very positive evaluation of Jude is interesting. In his treatise *On Women's Dress* he approves the notion that female finery was first introduced on earth by the fallen angels (the 'sons of God') as a device for the seduction of the 'daughters of men' (Gen. 6:2–4).[12] This notion was given expression in the first part of the pseudepigraphic book of Enoch (a composite work of the last century BC and first century AD).[13] In Tertullian's eyes, a book containing such wholesome doctrine should not have been left out of the arsenal of sacred (Old Testament) books. (Perhaps, he suggests, it was rejected because people did not believe that an antediluvian book could have survived the deluge, or because its clear proclamation of Christ was resented.)[14] Tertullian found his good opinion of the book of Enoch confirmed by Jude's treatment of it as a genuine prophecy of 'Enoch, the seventh from Adam' (Jude 14f.).[15]

Of the remaining catholic epistles (James, 2 Peter, 2 and 3 John) Tertullian has nothing to say; we cannot tell whether he knew them or not. But of Hebrews he has something quite interesting to say. It had

[9] See p. 145.

[10] E.g. in *Against Marcion* 3.14: 'the apostle John in the Apocalypse describes a two-edged sword proceeding from the mouth of God.'

[11] *On Women's Dress*, 1.3. See p. 85 above.

[12] *On Women's Dress*, 1.2.

[13] What is commonly called 1 Enoch (extant in its entirety only in Ethiopic) comprises five main compositions. Perhaps only the first of these (1 Enoch 1–36) was known to Tertullian (most of it survives in Greek; the original language was evidently Aramaic). But see p. 86.

[14] Its clear proclamation of Christ is probably its announcement of the coming of the Lord with his holy myriads (1 Enoch 1:9), as quoted and interpreted in Jude 14f. See p. 51 above.

[15] On the other hand, Jerome says that Jude was widely rejected because of its quoting from 1 Enoch (*On Illustrious Men*, 4).

not come down to him as one of the New Testament books, and he himself had no authority to add it to the list; but in his judgment it was worthy to be ranked with the apostolic writings. He regarded it as the work of Barnabas, a man who 'learned his doctrine from apostles and taught it with apostles'.[16] He compared it, to its great advantage, with the *Shepherd* of Hermas, a work highly esteemed by many readers in the church of those days and treated by some as inspired scripture.[17] But Tertullian had no time for the *Shepherd*. He was an ethical rigorist, especially in his later years after he had joined the Montanists, and he deplored the laxity of the *Shepherd's* moral teaching.

Hermas tells, at the beginning of the *Shepherd*, how he committed, or thought himself to have committed, the sin of 'adultery in the heart' against which Jesus uttered a warning in the Sermon on the Mount (Mt. 5:28).[18] His conscience was burdened about this: he wondered if there was any forgiveness for a sin committed after baptism. It was revealed to him that for post-baptismal sin there was indeed forgiveness, but for one such sin only — no more.[19] Tertullian repudiated entirely this concession to human weakness and stigmatized the book as 'the *Shepherd* of the adulterers'; he recommended rather the teaching of Hebrews 6:4–6, according to which it was impossible for those once enlightened to be 'renewed again to repentance' if they fell by the way. (It is most probable that the writer to the Hebrews had the sin of apostasy in mind,[20] but Tertullian thought primarily of sexual sin.)

THE SCILLITAN MARTYRS

By Tertullian's time a good part of the New Testament (and probably of the Old Testament too) circulated among the churches of North Africa in a Latin translation (one of the Old Latin versions, to use the term applied to all Latin biblical translations before Jerome's Vulgate gained the ascendancy). On July 17, AD 180, a group of Christians from the North African town of Scillium were brought before the provincial governor and charged with being Christians. The governor reasoned with them and tried to make them see and acknowledge the error of their ways, but they proved obstinate and were accordingly led off to execution. In the course of the enquiry a box, the property of the

[16] *On Modesty*, 20.   [17] See p. 166.
[18] Hermas, *Shepherd*, Vision 1.1.   [19] Hermas, *Shepherd*, Vision 2.2.
[20] As RSV says explicitly, 'if they then commit apostasy' (Heb. 6:6).

church, was brought into court. On being asked what the box contained, the defendants replied, 'Books, and the writings of Paul, a just man.'[21] From this we gather that among the portions of scripture and other literature in the library of a small provincial church was a collection of Paul's letters, presumably in a Latin version. (The Roman province of Africa was the first area in which a Latin version of the New Testament was required; the church in Rome itself was Greek-speaking until the end of the second century, and indeed later.)

CYPRIAN

Thascius Caecilius Cyprianus was born to pagan parents early in the third century. He was educated in rhetoric at Carthage, and was converted to Christianity about 246. Such were his qualities that, two years later, he was elected bishop of Carthage, and occupied the see with distinction until his martyrdom in 258. He was a fluent writer, and shows a ready acquaintance with the Latin Bible and with the writings of Tertullian, to whom he refers as 'the teacher' (magister).[22]

It is plain that by Cyprian's day there existed a fairly complete Bible in the Old Latin version for him to memorize and cite as occasion required. His New Testament comprised four gospels,[23] Acts, Paul's letters to seven churches[24] and to Timothy and Titus,[25] 1 Peter, 1 John and the Apocalypse. These writings, like the prophetic scriptures of the Old Testament, were the product of divine inspiration.[26] He nowhere cites Philemon (probably because he had no occasion to refer to such a short book) nor the five disputed catholic epistles (James, 2

[21] 'Acts of the Scillitan Martyrs', appended to The Passion of St Perpetua, ed. J. A. Robinson, TS 1.2 (Cambridge, 1891).

[22] See M. A. Fahey, Cyprian and the Bible: A Study in Third-Century Exegesis, BGBH 9 (Tübingen, 1971).

[23] In Epistle 73.10 he compares the four gospels to the four rivers of Paradise (Gen. 2:10).

[24] Testimonies, 1.20, where he links Paul's letters to seven churches (overlooking the fact that Galatians was sent to several churches) with John's letters to seven churches (cf the Muratorian list, p. 164); To Fortunatus, 11, where Paul's letters and John's find their place in a more elaborate array of sevens.

[25] In quoting Tit. 3:10, where a heretic is to be admonished 'once or twice', Cyprian (Epistle 59.20; Testimonies 3.78) omits 'or twice' (as also do Ambrosiaster and Augustine).

[26] E.g. On the Lapsed, 7: the prophets of old and the apostles subsequently 'preached, being full of the Holy Spirit.'

Peter, 2 and 3 John, Jude). Neither does he cite Hebrews, but he echoes its opening words at the beginning of his treatise *On the Lord's Prayer:* 'God willed many things to be said and heard through his servants the prophets, but how much greater are those spoken by the Son!'[27] Like other western Christians of his age, he probably knew Hebrews but did not regard it as scripture. As for the Apocalypse, he manifests a marked predilection for it, quoting it frequently as a source-book for Christology and for the blessings of martyrdom; he has no doubt that it is 'divine scripture'.[28]

AGAINST DICE-PLAYERS

Among the works of Cyprian there has been transmitted a Latin homily *Against Dice-Players*. It is not his; from the note of authority which is evident in it the author may have been, like Cyprian, a bishop in North Africa, but perhaps a generation or so later. He expresses himself eloquently and vigorously in his attack on gambling, which he thinks excites the wildest passions: gambling is sheer idolatry, and the gambler, even if he has been baptized, cannot be acknowledged as a Christian. For our purpose the interest of the little work lies in its free quotation of scripture, especially from the New Testament (the quotations are introduced by such words as 'the Lord says', 'the apostle says', 'scripture says'). Even the *Shepherd* of Hermas is cited as 'divine scripture',[29] and an allusion to one or two passages from the *Didachē* (cited not as scripture but as the *Teachings of the Apostles*) is introduced among apostolic quotations.[30] But a preacher may allow himself greater liberty in such matters than the author of a theological treatise: even today, a British preacher may quote Shakespeare or Burns as well as the Bible, but if he is careful he will not let his hearers go away with the idea that the non-biblical quotations carry canonical authority.

[27] *On the Lord's Prayer,* 1 (*cf* Heb. 1:1f.).   [28] *Epistle* 63.12.
[29] *Against Dice-Players,* 2 (where Similitude 9.31.5 is quoted).
[30] *Against Dice-Players,* 4 (probably a memory quotation from *Didachē* 4.14; 14.1–3).

CHAPTER FIFTEEN

THE ALEXANDRIAN FATHERS

CLEMENT

Clement of Alexandria was contemporary with Tertullian. He was not a native of Alexandria (he was probably an Athenian by birth)[1] but he spent most of the last quarter of the second century there; he is thought to have emigrated from Alexandria to Asia Minor when the church of Alexandria was hard hit by persecution in AD 202. We know nearly as little of the man himself, apart from his writings, as we know of Tertullian; but what we do know shows clearly that he differed widely from Tertullian in temperament and outlook. Tertullian was uncompromising in the antithesis which he maintained between Christianity and pagan culture: 'What has Athens to do with Jerusalem?' he asked.[2] But Clement finds much good in pagan culture, as Justin Martyr did before him,[3] and claims everything that is good for Christ. In his journeys before he settled in Alexandria he had sat at the feet of many teachers, but the teacher to whom he acknowledges his greatest debt was Pantaenus, a convert to Christianity from Stoicism, the founder of the catechetical school of Alexandria.[4] Pantaenus himself had been no mean traveller: he is said to have gone

---

[1] Epiphanius (*Panarion* 32.6) mentions the tradition that he was an Athenian.
[2] Tertullian, *Prescription,* 7.   [3] See p.129.
[4] *Stromateis,* 1.1, quoted and interpreted by Eusebius, *Hist. Eccl.* 5.11.1–5.

as far as India, where he found the Christian faith already planted, and he had some knowledge of Indian culture.[5]

Clement's surviving writings include the *Protrepticus* or *Exhortation* (a call to the Greeks to accept the Christian faith), the *Pedagogue* (a beginner's handbook of Christian ethics and manners), a treatise on Mark 10:17–31 entitled *The Salvation of a Rich Man*, a volume of *Extracts from the Prophetic Scriptures*, and eight volumes of *Stromateis* or *Miscellanies*, a wide-ranging and discursive work undertaking to show that Christian knowledge *(gnōsis)* is superior to any other. He wrote another work in eight volumes—his *Hypotypōseis* or *Outlines*, containing notes on various biblical books. This would have supplied information more relevant to our present purpose than any of his other works, but unfortunately it is lost, apart from the merest fragments.

Christianity was no doubt planted in Alexandria quite early, but we know very little of its history in that city before the time of Pantaenus. It has often been held that in its earlier days it was strongly influenced by gnosticism.[6] A corrective to this view is provided by the evidence of Christian papyri in Egypt in the first two centuries,[7] but it is true that 'in the second century the Gnostic movement found very fertile soil in Egypt and left a deep mark even on the Church Catholic of Alexandria'.[8] Clement himself had very much the gnostic cast of mind. According to him the true Christian tradition consisted of the 'knowledge' which the risen Christ delivered to James the Just, Peter and John; they in turn delivered it to the other apostles, and these again to the seventy disciples (*cf* Luke 10:1), of whom, says Clement, Barnabas was one.[9] There is a secret knowledge which is reserved for those able to take it in: 'the wise do not utter with their mouths what they debate in council.'[10] He speaks of 'the gnostic superstructure on the foundation of faith in Christ Jesus'.[11] But he differed from most of the gnostics of the second century in that his *gnōsis* was orthodox by the standard of his day (exemplified, preeminently, by Irenaeus). Pantaenus expounded

[5] Eusebius, *Hist. Eccl.* 5.10.3.

[6] So W. Bauer, *Orthodoxy and Heresy in Earliest Christianity* (1934), E.T. (Philadelphia, 1971), pp.44–60; A. A. T. Ehrhardt, 'Christianity before the Apostles' Creed', in *The Framework of the New Testament Stories* (Manchester, 1964), pp.174–179.

[7] See C. H. Roberts, *Manuscript, Society and Belief in Early Christian Egypt* (London, 1979).

[8] H. Lietzmann, *The Beginnings of the Christian Church*, E.T. (London, 1949), p.98.

[9] *Hypotyposeis*, 7, quoted by Eusebus, *Hist. Eccl.* 2.1.4.

[10] *Strom.* 1.12.   [11] *Strom.* 5.4. See pp.302f. below.

the scriptures according to what was held to be the true tradition received from the apostles, and Clement followed his teaching. Clement was a true Christian humanist: he displays a wide catholicity in the variety of authors whom he cites for his own purposes. If Paul—both the Paul of the epistles and the Paul of Acts—could quote pagan writers in this way,[12] why should not Clement follow his example? He is specially prone to quote the 'divinely-inspired', the 'truth-loving' Plato,[13] finding in his philosophy adumbrations of distinctively Christian teaching. Plato, he holds, was practically a prophet as he expounded the doctrine of the Trinity, salvation by the cross of Christ, the institution of the Lord's Day.[14] It is not that he treats Plato as an authority on the level of the prophets or apostles, but as he reads Plato through Christian spectacles he recognizes many things in his writings that seem to foreshadow Christian truth, and he concludes that Plato was in some measure enlightened by the Spirit of God, where he was not dependent on Moses and the prophets. He can even quote Plato alongside our Lord: 'Many are called, but few are chosen' (Mt. 22:14) is given as a companion saying Plato's 'Many are the wand-bearers but few are the initiates.'[15]

In his reference to Christian writings Clement's catholicity is equally evident. He speaks of the two parts of the Christian Bible as the Old Testament and the New Testament,[16] but has nothing to say about the limits of the New Testament. He would probably have felt the idea of 'limits' to the writings having apostolic authority to be too restrictive: he at least does not use language about 'neither adding nor taking away'.[17] When he speaks of 'scripture' or 'the scriptures' he usually means the Old Testament writings. When he uses the term of Christian writings, he usually means the gospels. Otherwise he is as likely as not to use it of writings which never found a secure place within the New Testament, such as the *Didachē*.[18]

[12] *Cf* 1 Cor. 15:33 (Menander quoted); Acts 17:28 (Aratus and possibly Epimenides quoted).

[13] *Strom.* 1.8 ('the truth-loving Plato, as if divinely inspired, says...').

[14] *Strom.* 5.14 (the Trinity adumbrated in *Timaeus* 41A, the cross of Christ in *Republic* 2.5.361E–362A, the Lord's Day in *Republic* 10.14.616B).

[15] Plato, *Phaedo* 69C, a saying relating to the Eleusinian mysteries. Two similar sayings, with a gnostic flavour, appear in the *Gospel of Thomas* 74, 75.

[16] *Strom.* 1.9 ('Testaments'); 3.11 ('New Testament'); 4.21 ('Old Testament'); 5.13 ('Old and New Testament'). He stresses the inspiration of the LXX version of the Old Testament (*Strom.* 1.22).

[17] See p.22.   [18] *Strom.* 1.20.

The Old Testament was understood by him in a thoroughly Christian sense: 'faith in Christ and the knowledge of the gospel are the exegesis and fulfilment of the law.'[19] The law, the prophets and the gospel form a united authority.[20] The authentic gospel is fourfold. According to Eusebius, Clement preserved in his *Outlines* 'a tradition of the primitive elders' regarding the order of the gospels:

> He said that those gospels were first written which contain the genealogies [i.e. Matthew and Luke], but that the Gospel according to Mark took shape as follows: Peter had publicly proclaimed the word at Rome and told forth the gospel by the Spirit. Then those present, who were many, besought Mark, as one who had accompanied Peter for a long time and remembered the things he had said, to make a written record of what he had said. Mark did this, and shared his gospel with those who made the request of him. When Peter came to know of it, he neither vigorously forbade it nor advocated it. But John last of all (said the tradition), aware that the 'bodily' facts had been set forth in the [other] gospels, yielded to the exhortation of his friends and, divinely carried along by the Spirit, composed a spiritual gospel.[21]

The fourfold gospel was part of the tradition that Clement had received, and its contents were specially authoritative for him, but he had no objection to citing other gospel writings if it suited his purpose. He knows, for example, that the *Gospel according to the Egyptians* is not one of 'the four gospels that have been handed down to us',[22] but he quotes it none the less, not once but four times.[23] It was a thoroughly gnostic composition, but Clement can take a gnostic saying which it ascribes to Jesus and give it an ethical reinterpretation which could give no offence to anybody. In the perfect state, according to this saying, there will no more distinction of sex, since male and female will be reunited in one androgynous person; but Clement allegorizes this to mean the surmounting of naturally male and naturally female impulses (he puts the same interpretation on Paul's 'neither male or female' in Galatians 3:28—which reveals the quality of his exegetical judgment.)[24]

[19] *Strom.* 4.21.   [20] *Strom.* 4.1, etc.
[21] *Hypotyposeis,* quoted by Eusebius, *Hist. Eccl.* 6.14.5–7.
[22] *Strom.* 3.13.   [23] *Strom.* 3.6.9 (twice), 13.
[24] See my *Jesus and Christian Origins outside the New Testament* (London, ²1984), pp. 157f. *Cf* p. 311 below.

The Acts of the Apostles, which Clement quotes repeatedly, he knows to have been the work of Luke.[25] He acknowledges the 'Apostle', that is the Pauline collection, including not only the Pastorals but also (in accordance with the tradition of the church of Alexandria) Hebrews. He quotes 'the blessed presbyter' (probably Pantaenus) to the effect that Paul did not attach his own name to Hebrews because he was apostle to the Gentiles only, whereas the Lord himself was apostle to the Hebrews (cf Heb. 3:1; Rom. 15:8).[26] Clement reckoned that Paul wrote the letter in the Hebrew speech and Luke published it in a Greek translation for the benefit of Greek-speaking readers.[27]

This information comes from Clement's lost *Outlines*, from one of several extracts preserved by Eusebius. In this work, says Eusebius, Clement gave concise accounts of all scripture contained in the Testaments, including such disputed writings as Jude and the other catholic epistles, with the letter of Barnabas and the Apocalypse of Peter.[28] According to Cassiodorus (6th century), the catholic epistles on which Clement commented in his *Outlines* were 1 Peter, 1 and 2 John and James (but James may be a corruption or a slip for Jude).[29] 1 John is distinguished as John's 'larger epistle'.[30]

The earliest extant occurrence of the phrase 'catholic epistle' comes in an anti-Montanist work by one Apollonius, in reference to a writer named Themiso, who 'dared, in imitation of the apostle, to compose a "catholic epistle" for the instruction of those whose faith was better than his own'.[31] The apostle thus imitated was perhaps Peter.[32] Clement himself refers to the apostolic letter of Acts 15:24–29 as a 'catholic epistle',[33] possibly because it was addressed to more churches than one (those in the united province of Syria-Cilicia, as well as the metropolitan church of Antioch).

---

[25] E.g. *Strom.* 5.12 ('as Luke in the Acts of the Apostles relates that Paul said...').

[26] *Hypotyposeis,* quoted by Eusebius, *Hist. Eccl.* 6.14.4.

[27] *Hypotyposeis,* quoted by Eusebius, *Hist. Eccl.* 6.14.2f.

[28] *Hist. Eccl.* 6.14.1. Eusebius describes what were later called the 'canonical' writings as the 'intestamented *(endiathēkos)* scripture', following the example of Origen (in *Hist. Eccl.* 6.25.1).

[29] Cassiodorus, *Introduction to the Reading of Holy Scripture*, 8.

[30] *Strom.* 2.15.

[31] Eusebius, *Hist. Eccl.* 5.18.5.

[32] This could be the earliest known allusion to 2 Peter, if the reference to 'those whose faith was better than his own' echoes 'those who have obtained a faith of equal standing with ours' (2 Pet. 1:1).

[33] *Strom.* 4.15 (*cf Pedagogue,* 7).

Clement seems to have had no hesitation about the Apocalypse of John.[34] He probably had a clear enough idea of what he meant by 'the truly sacred writings'[35] in which believers are instructed by the Son of God, but he refers with the utmost freedom to many documents which he would perhaps not have included among these. A brief list of works which he cites will illustrate his hospitality in this regard: they include, in addition to some already mentioned (the *Gospel according to the Egyptians*, the letter of 'the apostle Barnabas',[36] the *Apocalypse of Peter*),[37] the *Gospel according to the Hebrews*,[38] the letter of Clement of Rome (who is actually called 'the apostle Clement'),[39] the *Didachē* (cited as 'scripture'[40]), the *Shepherd* of Hermas,[41] the *Preaching of Peter*,[42] the *Traditions of Matthias*,[43] the *Sibylline Oracles*.[44] He quotes some *agrapha*[45] or uncanonical sayings of Jesus,[46] and relates a few apocryphal anecdotes of the apostles and their colleagues.[47]

Although he is not mentioned by name in any of the surviving works of Origen, Clement was almost certainly a teacher of Origen and exercised no little influence over him. Some time after Clement's departure, Origen was appointed to lead the catechetical school in Alexandria. Clement accepted the tradition he had received with regard to the contents of the two Testaments, but the question of

[34] E.g. *Strom.* 6.13, 'as John says in the Apocalypse' (quoting Rev. 4:4).

[35] *Strom.* 1.20, probably in reference to the 'sacred writings' (*hiera grammata*) of 2 Tim. 3:15.

[36] He is called 'the apostle Barnabas' in *Strom.* 2.6.7 (*cf* 2.20, where he is called 'the apostolic Barnabas'). The letter of Barnabas is quoted also in 2.16, 18; 5.10. See p.122.

[37] Clement, *Extracts from the Prophetic Scriptures*, 41, 48, 49. See pp.161, 261.

[38] *Strom.* 2.9; 5.14 (practically the same saying appears in the *Gospel of Thomas*, 2). See p.311.

[39] *Strom.* 4.17; also 1.7; 6.8, etc. See pp.121, 268.   [40] See p.194.

[41] *Strom.* 1.17, 29; 2.9; 4.9. See pp.166, 194.

[42] *Strom.* 2.15; 6.5, 6, 7, 15. See p.194.

[44] *Exhortation*, 8; *Strom.* 3.3; 5.14. Old Testament pseudepigrapha quoted by Clement include 1 Enoch (*Extracts*, 53; see p.85) and the *Apocalypse of Zephaniah* (*Strom.* 5.11.77). See p.75.
(*Strom.* 5.11.77). See p.000.

[45] The term *agrapha* in this sense means not 'unwritten' but 'uninscripturated'— i.e. 'not in (canonical) scripture'.

[46] E.g. 'Seek what is great, and the little things shall be added to you' (*Strom.* 1.24).

[47] E.g. the story of the apostle John and the reclaimed robber (*Salvation of a Rich Man*, 42, quoted by Eusebius, *Hist. Eccl.* 3.23.5–19). See J. Ruwet, 'Clément d'Alexandrie: Canon des Ecritures et Apocryphes', *Biblica* 29 (1948), pp.240–271.

'canonicity' does not appear to be one in which he was greatly interested. Origen, however, a more disciplined thinker and more thorough-going biblicist, who discharged his teaching duties with a keen sense of responsibility, gave the question of 'canonicity' more careful attention.[48]

ORIGEN

Origen (AD 185–254) has not left in any one place a list of New Testament books comparable to his list of Old Testament books quoted above.[49] Eusebius gathered from several of Origen's works an account of his position on the books of the New Testament—on the gospels, from his commentary on Matthew; on the Pauline and catholic epistles and the Apocalypse, from his exposition of John; on Hebrews, from his homilies on that epistle.[50] That Origen did recognize a New Testament collection alongside the Old Testament is certain, although he expresses himself as if the use of the word 'Testament' (Gk. *diathēkē*) in this sense were fairly new in his circle: he speaks of 'what we believe to be the divine scriptures both of the Old Testament, as people say, and of the the New [Testament], as it is called'.[51]

Origen distinguished the undisputed (or acknowledged) books of the New Testament from those which were disputed (or doubtful). The undisputed books were the four gospels and Acts, the Pauline epistles, 1 Peter, 1 John and the Apocalypse. He does not appear to mention the number of Pauline epistles, but shows by his references to them throughout his works that he knew all thirteen—fourteen if Hebrews be included. As a matter of form he followed the Alexandrian tradition in regarding Hebrews as Pauline; but he recognized that the writer had a better Greek style than Paul. The thoughts of the epistle he found admirable, not inferior to those of Paul's acknowledged

---

[48] See B. F. Westcott, 'Origenes', *DCB* IV, pp.96–142; R. P. C. Hanson, *Origen's Doctrine of Tradition* (London, 1954); *Allegory and Event* (London, 1959); J. W. Trigg, *Origen* (London, 1985).

[49] See p.72.

[50] Eusebius, *Hist. Eccl.* 6.25.3–14. On the works of Origen from which Eusebius compiled his data see R. P. C. Hanson, *Origen's Doctrine of Tradition* (London, 1954), pp.133–145.

[51] *On First Principles* 4.1.1 = *Philocalia* 1. By 'divine scriptures' he means 'divinely inspired scriptures'.

letters: perhaps the thoughts were Paul's, while the language was due to one of his disciples (Clement of Rome, say, or Luke[52])—but 'who really wrote the epistle God only knows.'[53] Since, however, Origen knew that some churches did not accept Hebrews, he classed it as disputed.

Also disputed, according to Origen, were 2 Peter, 2 and 3 John, James and Jude. Origen is the earliest Christian writer to mention 2 Peter; it does not appear to have been known much before his day.[54] (The earliest manuscript to contain its text, along with the text of 1 Peter and Jude, is P^{72}, which was probably copied in Origen's lifetime.) The uncertainty which he mentions with regard to 2 and 3 John was probably due to their brevity, which led to their being easily overlooked.[55] (Their internal evidence makes it clear that they come from the same circle, if not from the same individual author, as the Fourth Gospel and 1 John.) There are several quotations from 'the reputed epistle of James'[56] in Origen's works. In some of his works which survive only in a Latin translation the author of the epistle is called 'the apostle' and 'the Lord's brother'; but Origen's Latin translator (Rufinus) tended to conform his wording to the orthodoxy of his own time (c AD 400). As for the epistle of Jude, Origen says in his commentary on Matthew that it was the work of the Lord's brother of that name (mentioned in Mt. 13:55): it 'has but few lines, but is filled with the words of heavenly grace'.[57] This probably turned the balance in its

[52] Whatever may be thought of Luke's claims to be regarded as the writer to the Hebrews, Clement of Rome cannot be seriously considered. Clement knows the epistle, it is true, but he misunderstands it: worse than that, he 'turns his back on its central argument in order to buttress his own arguments about the Church's Ministry by an appeal to the ceremonial laws of the Old Testament', thus making 'a retrogression of the worst kind' (T. W. Manson, *The Church's Ministry* [London, 1948], pp. 13f.). 1948], pp. 13f.).

[53] Eusebius, *Hist. Eccl.* 6.25.14.

[54] 'Peter . . . has left one acknowledged epistle, perhaps a second also, for it is doubtful' (in Eusebius, *Hist. Eccl.* 6.25.8).

[55] John 'has left also an epistle of very few lines, perhaps also a second and a third, for not all agree that these are genuine. Only, both of them together are not a hundred lines long' (in Eusebius, *Hist. Eccl.* 6.25.10). Alongside his distinction between 'undisputed' and 'disputed' books Origen uses the threefold classification 'genuine', 'false' and 'mixed', i.e. doubtful or disputed (*Commentary on John,* 13.17).

[56] *Commentary on John,* 18.6.

[57] *Commentary on Matthew,* 10.17. In the same comment he identifies the James mentioned in Mt. 13:55 with 'James the Lord's brother' of Gal. 1:19, but says nothing about the epistle of James.

favour in Origen's eyes; elsewhere in the same commentary, however, he indicates that it was not universally acknowledged.[58]

Origen thus mentions all twenty-seven books of our New Testament; twenty-one, he says, are acknowledged, and six are doubtful. But among doubtful books he also reckons some which in the end did not secure a place in the canon. Like Clement of Alexandria before him he treats the *Didachē* as scripture, and he calls the *Letter of Barnabas* a 'catholic epistle'[59] — a term which he also applies to 1 Peter.[60] R. M. Grant suggests that while he lived at Alexandria he accepted the more comprehensive tradition of the church there and acknowledged the *Didachē* and the *Letter of Barnabas,* together with the *Shepherd* of Hermas, as scripture, but that after he moved to Caesarea and found that these books were not accepted there he manifested greater reserve towards them.[61] He knew 1 Clement but does not indicate if he regarded it as scripture. He had doubts about the *Preaching of Peter,* which Clement of Alexandria regarded highly.[62] He refers to the *Gospel according to the Hebrews*[63] and the *Acts of Paul*[64] without at first either admitting or disputing their status as scripture; later, however, he had doubts about the *Acts of Paul.*[65]

In a different category altogether from the acknowledged and doubtful books are those which he calls 'false' — not only because they falsely claimed apostolic authorship (as some of them did) but more especially because they taught false doctrine. Such are the *Gospel according to the Egyptians,* the *Gospel of the Twelve,* the *Gospel according to Basilides,* and other heretical Gospels and Acts.[66]

---

[58] *Commentary on Matthew,* 17.30: 'and if indeed one were to accept the epistle of Jude...'.

[59] *Against Celsus,* 1.63.   [60] In Eusebius, *Hist. Eccl.* 6.25.5.

[61] R. M. Grant, *The Formation of the New Testament* (London, 1965), pp.171f.

[62] E.g. *On First Principles* 1, preface, 8: this work 'is not reckoned among the ecclesiastical books, and . . . is neither by Peter nor by any one else who was inspired by the Spirit of God.'

[63] E.g. *Commentary on John,* 2.6, where he explains Jesus' reference in the *Gospel according to the Hebrews* (cf Jerome, *Commentary on Micah,* 7.6) to 'my mother, the Holy Spirit', not by the fact that 'Spirit' is a feminine noun in Jesus' native language but by Jesus' statement in Mt. 12:50 that every one who does the will of the Father in heaven is his mother.

[64] *On First Principles,* 1.2.3. See p.202.

[65] *Commentary on John,* 20.12: 'If any one cares to accept what is written in the *Acts of Paul...*'

[66] See J. Ruwet, 'Les apocryphes dans l'oeuvre d'Origène', *Biblica* 23 (1942), pp.18–42, 24 (1943), pp.18–58, 25 (1944), pp.143–166.

Origen's conviction that the contents of the Old and New Testaments were, word for word, the product of the Spirit of God gave him confidence in the validity of their allegorical interpretation: this was the appropriate method of penetrating beyond the letter to the mind of the Spirit. Even so, he believed he could distinguish levels of revelation within the scriptures. The gospels, which record the fulfilment of all that the prophets had spoken, naturally present a more complete record of revelation than was possible in the age before Christ came. Even within the New Testament, the epistles, for all the apostolic authority by which they were written, have a derivative status as compared with the evangelic witness to the life and teaching of him in whom 'the perfect Word blossomed'.[67] The Gospels are the firstfruit of all the scriptures, as the Gospel of John is the firstfruit of all the gospels.[68] Moreover, Origen's doctrine of inspiration and his allegorizing method do not inhibit his bringing the whole of his scholarly apparatus to bear on exegetical problems when occasion arises.[69]

DIONYSIUS

When Origen left Alexandria for Caesarea in AD 231, he was succeeded as head of the catechetical school in Alexandria first by his colleague Heraclas and then (after a year or two) by his former pupil Dionysius, who became bishop of Alexandria in AD 247/8 and remained in that office until his death in 265. In the course of a treatise *On Promises* Dionysius undertook to refute another Egyptian bishop, Nepos by name, who attacked the allegorizing method of biblical interpretation, especially with regard to the Apocalypse. Nepos himself understood the Apocalypse, and particularly the millennial reign of the resurrected saints in Revelation 20:4–6, in a literal and earthly sense.

Dionysius not only defended the allegorical method, which he believed could bring to light in the Apocalypse hidden and wonderful truths which were too high for his own comprehension; he added some observations on the authorship of the book which reveal his sure touch in the field of literary criticism. He saw that the stylistic and lexical

---

[67] *Commentary on John*, 1.4.

[68] *Commentary on John*, 1.6. See R. P. C. Hanson, *Allegory and Event* (London, 1959), pp.210f.

[69] See H. von Campenhausen, *The Formation of the Christian Bible*, E.T. (London, 1972), p.317.

features of the book were such as to render it unlikely that it came from the same author as the Fourth Gospel and 1 John; he agreed that it was the work of a man called John, as indeed it claims to be (whereas the Fourth Gospel and 1 John are anonymous), and agreed further that this John, while not the apostle, was a 'holy and inspired person'. It was, he held, no disparagement of the Apocalypse to hold that it was written by someone other than John the son of Zebedee; at the same time, if it was the work of another John, it could not (he implies) be accorded quite the same status as might be claimed by a work of direct apostolic authorship.[70] In principle, then, Dionysius recognized what, in the language of a later day, came to be called a 'canon within the canon'.[71]

[70] In Eusebius, *Hist. Eccl.* 7.25.1–27.
[71] See pp.244, 270–272.

CHAPTER SIXTEEN

EUSEBIUS OF CAESAREA

EUSEBIUS THE HISTORIAN

Eusebius, bishop of Caesarea in Palestine from about 314 to his death in 339, may properly be acknowledged as the second Christian historian, the first being Luke.[1] Eusebius's greatest work is his *Ecclesiastical History,* in which he traces the fortunes of the Christian movement from the time of Christ to the establishment of the peace of the church under Constantine in AD 313. When Constantine became ruler of the eastern empire as well as the western (AD 324), a good *rapport* was established between him and Eusebius, on whose advice in matters ecclesiastical the emperor came increasingly to rely.

Eusebius wrote his *History* in stages during the first quarter of the fourth century. He had all the material for research available to him in the great church library of Caesarea, which went back to Origen's day

---

[1] Luke's claim to be the first is sometimes unjustly challenged; but see A. A. T. Ehrhardt, 'The Construction and Purpose of the Acts of the Apostles' (1958), in *The Framework of the New Testament Stories* (Manchester, 1964), pp.64–102; he cites with approval Eduard Meyer's estimate that Luke 'figures as the one great historian who joins the last of the genuinely Greek historians, Polybius, to the first great Christian historian, perhaps the greatest of all, Eusebius of Caesarea' (p.64). See J. B. Lightfoot, 'Eusebius of Caesarea', *DCB* II, pp.308–348; D. S. Wallace-Hadrill, *Eusebius of Caesarea* (London, 1960).

and had been richly endowed by Eusebius's mentor Pamphilus (martyred in 309).[2] Eusebius was deficient in some of the critical qualities requisite in a first-class historian, but he knew the importance of consulting primary sources, and indeed he introduces frequent quotations from them. We have to thank him for preserving portions of ancient writings (such as Papias's) which would otherwise be quite lost to us. But where his sources have survived independently, a comparison of their wording with his quotations confirms the accuracy with which he quoted them, and this gives us confidence in the trustworthiness of his quotations from sources which can no longer be consulted.[3]

ACKNOWLEDGED, DISPUTED AND SPURIOUS BOOKS

We have already been indebted to Eusebius for information about statements by earlier writers on the Old and New Testament scriptures. In one place he gives an account of the New Testament writings current throughout the churches in his own time.[4] He distinguishes three categories: (1) universally acknowledged, (2) disputed, (3) spurious. Of the universally acknowledged writings he says:

> In the first place should be placed the holy tetrad of the gospels. These are followed by the writing of the Acts of the Apostles. After this should be reckoned the epistles of Paul. Next after them should be recognized the so-called first epistle of John and likewise that of Peter. In addition to these must be placed, should it seem right, John's Apocalypse.

(Hebrews must be included among 'the epistles of Paul', which Eusebius elsewhere enumerates as fourteen.[5]) Then he goes on:

---

[2] Eusebius, *Hist. Eccl.* 6.32.3; Jerome, *Epistle* 34.1; see p.73.

[3] One must recognize his habit of extracting from their contexts just so much of passages quoted from earlier writers as suited his immediate purpose. But J. B. Lightfoot's emphatic witness remains valid: *'In no instance which we can test does Eusebius give a doubtful testimony'* (*Essays on 'Supernatural Religion'*, p.49; his italics).

[4] *Hist. Eccl.* 3.25.1–7.

[5] *Hist. Eccl.* 3.3.4 f. where he adds that 'some have rejected the letter to the Hebrews, saying that is is disputed by the church of the Romans as not being by Paul' (*cf* 6.20). In *Hist. Eccl.* 6.41.6 he mentions the despoiled believers of Heb. 10:34 as 'those of whom Paul testified'; in *Mart. Pal.* 11.9 he couples 'the heavenly Jerusalem' of Heb. 12:22 with 'Jerusalem above' of Gal. 4:26 as the city 'of which Paul spoke'.

To the books which are disputed, but recognized by the majority, belong the so-called epistle of James and that of Jude, the second epistle of Peter and the so-called second and third epistles of John, whether these are by the evangelist or by someone else with the same name.

As for the third category:

Among the books which are spurious should be reckoned the *Acts of Paul*,[6] the so-called *Shepherd*,[7] the *Apocalypse of Peter*[8] and in addition to these the so-called epistle of Barnabas[9] and the so-called *Teachings of the Apostles*,[10] and moreover, as I said, the Apocalypse of John, should it seem right. For, as I said, some reject it, while others count it among the acknowledged books. Some have also included in the list the *Gospel according to the Hebrews*,[11] in which special pleasure is taken by those of the Hebrews who have accepted Christ.

It is evident that by 'spurious' Eusebius means little more than uncanonical. Usually the adjective, when used of literature, implies that a work is ascribed (by itself or by others) to an author who did not really compose it (like the gospel or apocalypse ascribed to Peter).[12] But when Eusebius includes the *Shepherd* among the 'spurious' books, he does not suggest that the *Shepherd* was not actually written by Hermas — after all, Hermas, the slave, was such an unimportant person that no one would try to gain undeserved credit for a work by ascribing it to him. It is surprising to find John's Apocalypse listed, not among the disputed books, but both among those universally acknowledged and among the 'spurious' books, both times with the qualifying clause 'should it seem right'. Had Eusebius listed it among the disputed books that would not have been surprising, for it continued to be disputed among some of the eastern churches well after Eusebius's day.[13] Eusebius's apparent inconsistency arises from the fact that the Apocalypse was acknowledged by those churches whose opinion he valued most, whereas he himself was unhappy about it — he could not reconcile himself to its millenarian teaching. But

---

[6] See pp. 202, 261.   [7] See pp. 166, 191.
[8] See pp. 161, 261.   [9] See pp. 122, 191.
[10] See pp. 191, 194.   [11] See pp. 191, 194.
[12] The adjective is *nothos*, literally 'illegitimate' or 'bastard', as in Heb. 12:8.
[13] See p. 213.

when he calls it potentially 'spurious', he is not questioning its claim to be the work of one John (cf Rev. 1:4, 9 etc.); he was disposed to accept the opinion of Dionysius of Alexandria that the author was not the apostle and evangelist John but another John, also associated with Ephesus.[14] He would simply prefer it not to be in the canon.

So far (apart from his ambiguous attitude to the Apocalypse) Eusebius's threefold classification is plain enough. But then he says that the 'spurious' books might be ranked with the 'disputed' books, and tries, not very clearly, to say why nevertheless he lists them separately. The reason appears to be that, while in his day the 'spurious' books were not generally included in the canon, yet they were known and esteemed by many churchmen. If not canonical, they were at least orthodox. This could not be said of some other writings known to Eusebius, which claimed falsely to be the work of apostles and their colleagues, but in fact promoted heterodoxy. Such works, he says:

> are brought forward by heretics under the name of the apostles; they include gospels such as those of Peter, Thomas and Matthias and some others as well, or Acts such as those of Andrew and John and other apostles. None of these has been deemed worthy of citation in the writings of any in the succession of churchmen. Indeed, the stamp of their phraseology differs widely from the apostolic style, and the opinion and policy of their contents are as dissonant as possible from true orthodoxy, showing clearly that these are the figments of heretics. Therefore they are not to be reckoned even among 'spurious' books but must be shunned as altogether wrong and impious.

REJECTED GOSPELS AND ACTS

Of the works denounced by Eusebius the *Gospel of Peter* has a special interest. In the second century it was read and appreciated by Christians who were disposed to take it at face value as composed by Peter. Even Justin Martyr appears to quote it in one place.[15] Serapion, bishop of

---

[14] See pp. 195f.

[15] In *First Apology* 36.6, speaking of the passion of Christ, Justin says, 'And indeed, as the prophet had said, they dragged him and made him sit on the judgment-seat, saying "Judge us".' Compare *Gospel of Peter* 3:6 f. where Jesus' enemies 'made him sit on a judgment-seat, saying "Judge righteously, O king of Israel!"' The prophet referred to by Justin is Isaiah (cf Is. 58:2). The idea that Jesus was made to sit on the

Antioch towards the end of that century, found that it was held in high esteem in the church of Rhossus, which lay within his jurisdiction. To begin with, he was not troubled by this, because he knew the church of Rhossus to be orthodox in its belief. But later reports moved him to examine the work more carefully, and he found that it presented a 'docetic' view of the person of Christ—that is, the view that his human nature was only apparent and not real. A substantial fragment of the *Gospel of Peter* in Greek was identified as part of the contents of a parchment codex discovered in Upper Egypt in 1886; from this the docetic tendency of the work is evident. Jesus, it is said, remained silent on the cross, 'as though he felt no pain'. He is not expressly said to have died; rather, 'he was taken up'. His cry of dereliction is reproduced in the form, 'My power, my power, you have left me!' suggesting that at that moment the divine power left the physical shell in which it had been temporarily resident.[16]

Having discovered the true nature of the work, Serapion exposed its defects in a treatise entitled *Concerning the So-Called Gospel of Peter*.[17]

As for the *Gospel of Thomas* mentioned by Eusebius, that seems to be a gnostic work quoted by Hippolytus[18] and stigmatized as heretical by Origen;[19] its relation to the *Gospel of Thomas* found among the Nag Hammadi documents in 1945 is uncertain, but they are certainly not identical.[20] The *Gospel of Matthias* is also listed as heretical by Origen;[21] its relation to the *Traditions of Matthias* quoted by Clement of Alexandria is doubtful.[22]

---

judgment-seat could have arisen from a mistranslation of John 19:13 (as though it meant not 'Pilate sat' but 'Pilate made him sit'). But, as L. W. Barnard points out (*Justin Martyr: his Life and Thought* [Cambridge, 1967], p.64), Justin's reliance on uncanonical material is remarkably scanty compared with his points of agreement with our canonical gospels.

[16] For the *Gospel of Peter* see E. Hennecke-W. Schneemelcher-R. McL. Wilson (ed.), *New Testament Apocrypha*, I (London, 1963), pp.179–187.

[17] Eusebius, *Hist. Eccl.* 6.12.2–6.   [18] Hippolytus, *Refutation*, 5.7.20.

[19] Origen, *Homilies on Luke*, 1.

[20] Hippolytus quotes an alleged saying of Jesus from the Naassene *Gospel of Thomas*: 'He who seeks me will find me in children from seven years old, for there concealed I shall be made manifest in the fourteenth age' (*Refutation* 5.7.20). The Nag Hammadi *Gospel of Thomas* (a collection of 114 sayings of Jesus) exhibits signs of Naassene influence (the Naassenes were a gnostic party) but it does not include this saying. See Hennecke-Schneemelcher-Wilson, *New Testament Apocrypha*, I, pp.278–307; F. F. Bruce, *Jesus and Christian Origins outside the New Testament* (London, ²1984), pp.110–158.

[21] Origen, *Homilies on Luke*, 1.   [22] See p.191.

There is a group of five books of Acts bearing the names of apostles, dating from the second half of the second century onward — the Acts of Paul, Peter, Andrew, John and Thomas. Of these the last two are definitely gnostic works; the first two belong rather to the category of early Christian fiction, and the *Acts of Andrew,* while it has been suspected of a gnosticizing tendency, may have been the work of an author who remained within the fellowship of the catholic church.[23] The author of the *Acts of Paul,* a presbyter in one of the churches of Asia, was deposed from his office for his incursion into fiction. The best-known section of the work, the *Acts of Paul and Thecla,* scandalized Tertullian because it represented Paul as encouraging Thecla, one of his female converts, to teach and even baptize.[24] The *Acts of Peter* is mainly concerned with the last phase of Peter's life, his closing ministry and martyrdom in Rome, and not least his controversy there with Simon Magus.[25]

The *Acts of John* is ascribed to an author names Leucius (after whom, indeed, all five sets of apocryphal *Acts* have been called the 'Leucian Acts').[26] It contains a number of curious anecdotes about the apostle John, who is presented as a gnostic teacher. It includes an interesting gnostic hymn in which Jesus accompanies his disciples, performing a solemn dance at the same time. The hymn has been set to music by Gustav Holst. One of its quatrains embodies familiar themes from the Fourth Gospel: Jesus says,

> I am a lamp to you who see me,
> I am a mirror to you who know me,
> I am a door to you who knock on me,
> I am a way to you the traveller.

At the end of each 'I am' statement the disciples make the response 'Amen'.[27]

In the *Acts of Thomas* the apostle Thomas is described as visiting

---

[23] See Hennecke-Schneemelcher-Wilson, *New Testament Apocrypha,* II (London, 1965), pp.392–395.

[24] See p.261; see also E. M. Howe, 'Interpretations of Paul in *The Acts of Paul and Thecla',* in *Pauline Studies,* ed. D. A. Hagner and M. J. Harris (Exeter/Grand Rapids, 1980), pp.33–49.

[25] See p.163.

[26] So Photius, *Bibliotheca,* 114. The five circulated among the Manichaeans as an Acts-corpus. The Gelasian decree (see pp.234f.), among its 'books not to be received', includes 'all the books which Leucius, the devil's disciple, has made' (5.4.4).

[27] See Hennecke-Schneemelcher-Wilson, *New Testament Apocrypha,* II, pp.188–259 (the hymn is translated on pp.228–232).

India.[28] It is extant in Syriac; it is full of legend but certainly indicates that Christianity had been carried to India by the time the work was composed (about the middle of the third century). As is well known, the Mar Thoma Christians, with their Syriac liturgy, maintain their vigorous life and witness in India to the present day. We have to thank the *Acts of Thomas* for preserving the *Hymn of the Pearl,* a poem by the gnostic teacher Bardaisan, the founder of Christian Syriac literature. This poem tells the allegorical story of the soul that went down to Egypt for the sake of the one pearl: it has been called, despite its gnostic orientation, 'the most noble poem of Christian Antiquity'. That was the judgment of F. C. Burkitt, who added, 'it is worth while to learn Syriac, so as to be able to read it in the original'.[29]

CONSTANTINE'S FIFTY BIBLES

Eusebius may have performed a special service towards the fixing of the Christian canon of scripture. Not long after Constantine inaugurated his new capital at Constantinople on the site of ancient Byzantium (AD 330), he wrote to Eusebius, asking him to have fifty copies of the Christian scriptures (both Testaments in Greek) prepared for the use of the churches in the city. The emperor's letter is preserved in Eusebius's *Life of Constantine,* a panegyric composed soon after Constantine's death in 337.[30] The fifty copies were to be made on good parchment by trained scribes: the emperor would defray the entire cost and authorize the use of two public carriages to transport the copies to Constantinople. Eusebius proceeded without delay to comply with the emperor's request: the scriptures were prepared as specified and sent in 'magnificent and elaborately bound volumes'.[31]

[28] See Hennecke-Schneemelcher-Wilson, *New Testament Apocrypha,* II, pp.425–531 (G. Bornkamm, who edits the *Acts of Thomas* for this compilation, is the leading world-authority on it).

[29] F. C.Burkitt, *Early Christianity outside the Roman Empire* (Cambridge, 1899), p.61. The hymn is translated in Hennecke-Schneemelcher-Wilson, II, pp.498–504.

[30] *Life of Constantine,* 4.36.

[31] *Life of Constantine,* 4.37. The volumes are further said to have been 'in threefold and fourfold form'. The meaning of these words is disputed: they may have been written with three columns to a page (like *Codex Vaticanus*) or four (like *Codex Sinaiticus*); or the point may be that they were sent to the emperor three or four at a time. For the former suggestion see K. Lake, 'The Sinaitic and Vatican Manuscripts and the Copies sent by Eusebius to Constantinople', *HTR* 11 (1918), pp.32–35; for the latter, see T. C. Skeat, 'The Use of Dictation in Ancient Book-Production', *Proceedings of the British Academy* 42 (1956), pp.179–208 (especially pp.195–197).

There are several unanswered questions about these sumptuous copies. (We may reflect, in passing, that only a quarter of a century earlier the Christian scriptures were being assiduously sought out and destroyed by imperial authority.)[32] What type of text was used in these copies? It has frequently been surmised that the Vatican and Sinaitic codices of the Greek scriptures (one of them, if not both) are survivors from this consignment. That is unlikely: apart from some indications that the Vatican codex may have been produced in Egypt, they are our two chief witnesses to what is called the Alexandrian text type, and there is no indication that his text type was current in Constantinople and its neighbourhood in the period following 330. (Nevertheless, these two codices may give one a good idea of the appearance of the copies which were made for Constantine.) If a guess may be hazarded, it is more likely that the fifty copies exhibited the text of the recent edition of Lucian of Antioch (martyred in 312), the ancestor of the Byzantine or 'majority' text.[33] If they did, this would help to explain the popularity of this form of text in Constantinople and the whole area of Christendom under its influence from the late fourth century on, a popularity which led to its becoming in fact the majority text and to its being called by many students nowadays the Byzantine text. (But the New Testament text used by Eusebius himself belongs neither to the Alexandrian nor to the Byzantine type.)[34]

A more important question for our present purpose is: which books—and, in particular, which New Testament books—were included in these copies? We are not told, but the answer is not seriously in doubt. The copies contained all the books which Eusebius lists as universally acknowledged (including Hebrews, of course, but also including Revelation) and the five catholic epistles which he lists as disputed by some—in short, the same twenty-seven books as appear in our copies of the New Testament today. The emperor might not be greatly concerned about the particular type of text used for the copies—variations between text types make little difference to the general wording—but he would discover rather quickly if a book which he believed to be part of the scriptures had been left out. As for Revelation, it is clear that Constantine attached high importance to it:

[32] See pp. 216f.

[33] See B. M. Metzger, 'The Lucianic Recension of the Greek Bible', *Chapters in the History of New Testament Textual Criticism*, NTTS 4 (Leiden, 1963), pp. 1–41.

[34] Eusebius, as might be expected, seems to use a form of the Caesarean text type.

he used its imagery for purposes of his own imperial propaganda.[35] Eusebius personally might have preferred to omit it, but it was the emperor's preference, not his own, that he had to consider on this occasion. If these copies did indeed contain the twenty-seven books, no more and no less, that would have provided a considerable impetus towards the acceptance of the now familiar New Testament canon.

A related, though less important, question concerns the order of the New Testament books in those copies. Most probably the order was that followed in Eusebius's own list of the books: the four gospels, Acts, the Pauline epistles with Hebrews, the catholic epistles, Revelation. This is the order which was to become standard in manuscripts of the Greek New Testament; it superseded the order exhibited in the great uncial codices, in which the catholic epistles come immediately after Acts.

It is difficult, then, to accept the conclusion of one scholar, that the New Testament canon was still 'in the process of formation' in Eusebius's mind.[36] Eusebius's canon deviated from the consensus of his ecclesiastical milieu only in respect of the Apocalypse, and he knew his mind very well on that.

THE EARLY UNCIALS

The mention of the great uncials makes this a convenient point to list their New Testament contents, as their Old Testament contents have been listed above:[37]

Sinaiticus (4th century):

> Matthew, Mark, Luke, John; Romans, 1 Corinthians, 2 Corinthians, Galatians, Ephesians, Philippians, Colossians, 1 Thessalonians, 2 Thessalonians, Hebrews, 1 Timothy, 2

[35] See C. Odahl, 'The Use of Apocalyptic Imagery in Constantine's Christian Propaganda', *Centerpoint—The Journal of Interdisciplinary Studies* 4, Spring 1982, City University of New York, cited by W. R. Farmer, *Jesus and the Gospel* (Philadelphia, 1982), pp.273–275, nn.139, 154. On pp.184–187 of Farmer's work there is a good discussion of Constantine's influence on the definitive form and status of the New Testament. See also K. L. Carroll, 'Toward a Commonly Received New Testament', *BJRL* 44 (1961–2), pp.327–349 (especially p.341).

[36] A. C. Sundberg, Jr., 'Canon Muratori—A Fourth-Century List', *HTR* 66 (1973), p.29.

[37] See pp.69f.

Timothy, Titus, Philemon; Acts; James, 1 Peter, 2 Peter, 1 John, 2 John, 3 John, Jude; Revelation; *Letter of Barnabas, Shepherd* of Hermas (Vision 1.1.1—Mandate 4.3.6).[38]

(This is the only one of the great uncials to preserve all the New Testament books in their entirety. The placing of Acts after the Pauline epistles and before the catholic epistles reflects the earlier practice of binding Acts and the catholic epistles together in one smaller codex.)

Vaticanus (4th century):

Matthew, Mark, Luke, John; Acts; James, 1 Peter, 2 Peter, 1 John, 2 John, 3 John, Jude; Romans, 1 Corinthians, 2 Corinthians, Galatians, Ephesians, Philippians, Colossians, 1 Thessalonians, 2 Thessalonians, Hebrews 1:1—9:14.

(The end of this codex is defective: the remainder of Hebrews, with Paul's letters to individuals and Revelation, has been lost.[39] As in *Codex Sinaiticus,* Hebrews was placed between Paul's letters to churches and those to individuals. Also as in *Sinaiticus,* Acts is followed immediately by the catholic epistles, but they precede and do not follow the Pauline epistles. The Pauline epistles are divided into numbered chapters, the numbers not starting afresh with each epistle but running continuously throughout the whole corpus. This reveals that *Vaticanus* was based on an earlier copy in which Hebrews came between Galatians and Ephesians.[40] In that earlier copy Galatians began with chapter 54 and ended with chapter 59, but Ephesians began with chapter 70. These chapter numberings were taken over unchanged by *Vaticanus,* in which Hebrews, although its position has been changed, begins with chapter 60 and presumably ended with chapter 69; it is now broken off in the course of chapter 64, halfway through the epistle.)

Alexandrinus (5th century):

Matthew 25:6—28:20, Mark, Luke, John (from which two leaves, comprising 6:50—8:52, are missing);[41] Acts; James, 1

---

[38] For the *Letter of Barnabas* and the *Shepherd* of Hermas see pp. 122, 166.

[39] The remainder of Hebrews and the Apocalypse were supplied by a fifteenth-century scribe; see T. C. Skeat, 'The Codex Vaticanus in the Fifteenth Century', *JTS* n.s. 35 (1984), pp. 454–465.

[40] Hebrews appears in this position in the Sahidic (Coptic) version of Athanasius's thirty-ninth festal letter (see pp. 208f.)

Peter, 2 Peter, 1 John, 2 John, 3 John, Jude; Romans, 1 Corinthians, 2 Corinthians (three leaves, comprising 4:13—12:6, are missing), Galatians, Ephesians, Philippians, Colossians, 1 Thessalonians, 2 Thessalonians, Hebrews, 1 Timothy, 2 Timothy, Titus, Philemon; Revelation; 1 Clement, 2 Clement 1:1—12:5.

(The first twenty-five leaves of the New Testament are missing; so are the final leaves of the codex, which at one time, according to its prefatory table of contents, included the *Psalms of Solomon*. In the table, however, this document is separated from the others by a note 'The books together', which was followed by a number no longer decipherable; the two epistles of Clement were evidently included among 'the books', but not the *Psalms of Solomon*.)[42]

---

[41] A comparative calculation of the lines in these missing leaves makes it plain that the section on the woman taken in adultery (John 7:53—8:11) was not included.

[42] See p.70 for the *Psalms of Solomon*, pp.121f. for 1 and 2 Clement.

CHAPTER SEVENTEEN

ATHANASIUS AND AFTER

ATHANASIUS ON THE NEW TESTAMENT

As we have seen, Athanasius, bishop of Alexandria, devoted most of his thirty-ninth festal letter, announcing the date of Easter in AD 367, to a statement about the canon of scripture and its limits. After his list of Old Testament books, which has been quoted above,[1] he continues:

> Again, we must not hesitate to name the books of the New Testament. They are as follows:
>
>> Four gospels—according to Matthew, according to Mark, according to Luke, according to John.
>> Then after these the Acts of the Apostles and the seven so-called catholic epistles of the apostles, as follows: one of James, two of Peter, three of John and, after these, one of Jude.
>> Next to these are fourteen epistles of the apostle Paul, written in order as follows: First, to the Romans; then two to the Corinthians, and after these to the Galatians and next that to the Ephesians; then to the Philippians and two to the Thessalonians and that to the Hebrews. Next are two to Timothy, one to Titus, and last the one to Philemon.
>> Moreover, John's Apocalypse.

[1] See pp. 78f.

These are the 'springs of salvation',[2] so that one who is thirsty may be satisfied with the oracles which are in them. In these alone is the teaching of true religion proclaimed as good news. Let no one add to these or take anything from them.[3] For concerning these our Lord confounded the Sadducees when he said, 'You are wrong because you do not know the scriptures.'[4] And he reproved the Jews, saying, 'You search the scriptures, because... it is they that bear witness to me.'[5]

But for the sake of greater accuracy I must needs, as I write, add this: there are other books outside these, which are not indeed included in the canon, but have been appointed from the time of the fathers to be read to those who are recent converts to our company and wish to be instructed in the word of true religion. These are[6]... the so-called *Teaching of the Apostles* and the *Shepherd*. But while the former are included in the canon and the latter are read [in church], no mention is to be made of the apocryphal works. They are the invention of heretics, who write according to their own will, and gratuitously assign and add to them dates so that, offering them as ancient writings, they may have an excuse for leading the simple astray.

Athanasius is the first writer known to us who listed exactly the twenty-seven books which traditionally make up the New Testament in catholic and orthodox Christianity, without making any distinction of status among them. His order of books, on the other hand, is not that which has become traditional: he follows the Alexandrian precedent of placing the Pauline epistles after Acts and the catholic epistles, and within the 'Pauline' epistles he places Hebrews between 2 Thessalonians and 1 Timothy, as the great uncials do.[7]

By the 'apocryphal' books, of which no mention is to be made, Athanasius means those which Origen stigmatizes as 'false'[8] and Eusebius rejects as heterodox.[9] The *Didachē* and the *Shepherd*, while not meeting the requirements for canonical recognition, were edifying works and might profitably be read as such. It was therefore not

[2] A quotation from Is. 12:3.   [3] See p.23 with n.20.
[4] Mt. 22:29.   [5] Jn 5:39.
[6] For the Old Testament 'apocrypha' listed here see p.79.
[7] But see p.206, n.40 for its changed position in the Sahidic version of this letter. Athanasius quotes Heb. 11:3 and expressly ascribes it to Paul more than once (*On the Incarnation of the Divine Word*, 3.2; *On the Decrees: Defence of the Nicene Definition*, 18).
[8] See p.194.   [9] See p.200.

improper to bind such works together with the canonical books in copies of scripture, as in the Sinaitic and Alexandrine codices.[10]

CANONS OF LAODICEA

The last of the sixty canons of the Council of Laodicea is probably an addition to the others, which were promulgated at the time of the Council itself (c 363);[11] it may indeed reflect the influence of Athanasius's list, except that it does not include the Apocalypse among the canonical books. After listing the books of the Old Testament, it continues thus:

> Of the New Testament: Four gospels—according to Matthew, Mark, Luke and John. The Acts of the Apostles; seven catholic epistles, as follows: one of James, two of Peter, three of John, one of Jude. Fourteen epistles of Paul, as follows: one to the Romans, two to the Corinthians, one to the Galatians, one to the Ephesians, one to the Philippians, one to the Colossians, two to the Thessalonians, one to the Hebrews, two to Timothy, one to Titus, one to Philemon.[12]

LATER GREEK FATHERS

Cyril of Jerusalem (died 386), in one of his catechetical lectures, deals with the 'divinely inspired scriptures' and admonishes his hearer (or reader):

> Learn diligently from the church what are the books of the Old Testament, and what are those of the New. But read none of the apocryphal writings, for if you do not know those which are universally acknowledged, why should you trouble yourself in vain about those which are disputed?[13]...
>
> Of the New Testament there are (only) four gospels: the

---

[10] Athanasius is specially given to quoting from the *Shepherd*, 'a most profitable book' (*On the Incarnation*, 3.1), the opening words of Mandate 1, 'First of all believe that God is one, who created all things and fitted them together, and made all things to be out of that which is not' (*cf* also *On the Decrees*, 18; *Festal Letter* 11 [Easter 339], 4).

[11] See p.80.

[12] English translation in NPNF, series 2, XIV, p.159.

[13] Here follow the Old Testament books; see pp.80f.

others are pseudepigraphical and harmful (the Manichaeans indeed have written a *Gospel according to Thomas,* which by the fragrance of its evangelical title corrupts the souls of the more simple sort).[14] Receive also the Acts of the twelve Apostles, and in addition to these the seven catholic epistles of James and Peter, John and Jude. Then as a seal on them all, the last work of the disciples, receive the fourteen epistles of Paul. Let all the rest be set apart on a secondary level. As for the books which may not be read in churches, do not even read them by yourself, as you have heard me say.[15]

The Manichaean *Gospel of Thomas* is apparently a different work from the Naassene *Gospel of Thomas,* denounced by Hippolytus.[16] The authentic letters of Paul were in fact the first books of the New Testament to be written: it is odd to see them here referred to as a final 'seal' on all the others.[17] The temptation to find theological significance in what was originally a fortuitous or mechanical arrangement of biblical books is one to which some readers yield even today. By 'all the rest' Cyril means edifying works like the *Didachē* or the *Shepherd* which were not admitted to the canon but permitted to be read in church. Those which were unfit for reading in church, and therefore unfit for a Christian's private reading, were presumably what Athanasius called 'the apocryphal works', inculcating heresy.

Gregory Nazianzen's metrical list of 'the genuine books of inspired scripture', after enumerating the Old Testament books,[18] went on:

> Now enumerate those of the new mystery:[19]
> Matthew wrote the wonderful works of Christ for the Hebrews,
> Mark in Italy, Luke in Achaia.
> John, who visited heaven,[20] was a great herald to all.
> Then come the Acts of the wise apostles,

[14] For other works with the same title see pp. 162, 311.

[15] *Catechetical Lecture* 4.36 (NPNF, series 2, VII, pp. 27 f.).

[16] See p. 201.

[17] Cyril's language is based on the arrangement by which Acts and the catholic epistles precede Paul's epistles.

[18] See p. 81.

[19] That is, 'of the new revelation'; when used in a Christian sense, 'mystery' in the New Testament is something hitherto concealed in the divine counsel but now revealed.

[20] Gk. *ouranophoitēs,* a reference to John's experience in his Patmos vision (Rev. 4:1 f.), although Gregory did not include the Apocalypse in his canon.

and Paul's fourteen epistles,
and seven catholic epistles, of which James's is one,
two by Peter, three by John again,
and Jude's is the seventh. There you have them all.
Any one outside of these is not among the genuine writings.[21]

About the same time as Cyril and Gregory produced their lists Amphilochius of Iconium produced his—a metrical one like Gregory's, but less concise:

But this especially for you to learn
is fitting: not every book is safe
which has acquired the holy name of scripture.
For there appear from time to time pseudonymous
books, some of which are intermediate or neighbours,
as one might say, to the words of truth,
while others are spurious and utterly unsafe,
like counterfeit and spurious coins,
which bear the king's inscription
but as regards their material are base forgeries.
For this reason I will state for you the divinely inspired
books one by one, so that you may learn them clearly.

He proceeds to enumerate the Old Testament books,[22] and then goes on:

It is time for me to state the books of the New Testament.
Receive only four evangelists:
Matthew, then Mark, to whom Luke as third
count in addition, and John, in time
the fourth, but first in the sublimity of his doctrines,
for rightly do I call him the son of thunder
who sounded forth most loudly with the word of God.
Receive also Luke's second book,
that of the Acts of the universal apostles.
Next add the 'chosen vessel',
the herald to the Gentiles, the apostle
Paul, who wrote in wisdom to the churches
twice seven books: to the Romans one,
to which must be added two to the Corinthians,

---

[21] Gregory, *Hymn* 1.1.12.31, lines 30–39.   [22] See p.81.

that to the Galatians, that to the Ephesians, after them
that in Philippi; then the one written
to the Colossians, two to the Thessalonians,
two to Timothy, and to Titus and Philemon
one each, and one to the Hebrews.
But some say the epistle to the Hebrews is spurious;
they say not well, for its grace is genuine.[23]
So be it. What remains? Of the catholic epistles
some say there are seven, others that three only
are to be received: one of James,
one of Peter and one of John.
Some receive the three of John and in addition to them the two
of Peter, with Jude's as the seventh.
The Revelation of John, again,
some include, but the majority
say it is spurious. This is the most unerring
canon of the divinely inspired scriptures.[24]

Evidently Athanasius's unquestioning inclusion of the Apocalypse among the canonical books carried little weight among many eastern churchmen. Cyril of Jerusalem and Gregory Nazianzen leave it out of the canon, and while Amphilochius mentions it, he says that the majority reject it.

EPIPHANIUS

Epiphanius of Salamis in Cyprus gives a summary of canonical books in his treatise against heresies:

> If you had been begotten by the Holy Spirit and instructed in the prophets and apostles, you must have gone through (the record) from the beginning of the genesis of the world until the times of Esther in twenty-seven books of the Old Testament, which are (also) numbered as twenty-two, also in the four holy gospels, and in fourteen epistles of the holy apostle Paul, and in the writings which come before these,[25] including the Acts of the Apostles in their times and the catholic epistles of James, Peter, John and Jude, and in the Revelation of John, and in the Wisdom books, I mean those of Solomon and of the son of

[23] Compare Origen's reason for accepting Jude (p. 193).

[24] Amphilochius, *Iambics to Seleucus*, lines 289–319.

[25] 'Before these' in the arrangement by which Acts and the catholic epistles precede the Pauline epistles.

Sirach—in short, all the divine writings. Having gone through all these, I say, you should have condemned yourself for bringing forward as not unfitting for God but actually pious towards God a name which is nowhere listed, the name of a spurious book, nowhere mentioned in holy scripture.[26]

Epiphanius's curious appending of the wisdom books of Solomon and Ben Sira to his New Testament list has been noted already.[27] He appears to include the Apocalypse without hesitation. He knows that some have doubts about it, but he himself does not share them: 'St John through his gospel and epistles and Apocalypse has inparted the same holy spiritual gift.'[28]

CHRYSOSTOM

'John of the golden mouth' (Chrysostom), bishop of Constantinople from 397 to 407, quotes copiously from the New Testament books apart from the four controverted catholic epistles (2 Peter, 2 and 3 John, Jude) and the Apocalypse. A *Synopsis of Sacred Scriptures*, sometimes (but on doubtful grounds) attributed to him, follows a list of the Old Testament books with the fourteen epistles of Paul, the four gospels, the book of the Acts (ascribed to Luke) and the *three* catholic epistles.[29] For the rest, it is noteworthy that Chrysostom appears to be the first writer to use the phrase 'the books' (Gk *ta biblia*) of the two Testaments together;[30] in Christian usage the phrase had previously been restricted to the Old Testament writings. Chrysostom's usage is the origin of our word 'Bible'; while *biblia* ('books') is a plural word in Greek, it was taken over into Latin as a singular, *Biblia*, 'the Bible'.

THEODORE OF MOPSUESTIA AND
THE SYRIAC CANON

It had been thought by a number of scholars[31] that Theodore of Mopsuestia (died 428)[32] rejected the Apocalypse and all the catholic

---

[26] Epiphanius, *Panarion*, 76.22.5. He apostrophises the extreme Arian Aëtius (died 367), founder of the Anomoeans, and undertakes to refute his published set of heretical propositions.

[27] See p.81. [28] *Panarion* 51.35.

[29] Migne, *PG* 56.317. [30] *Homilies on Matthew*, 47.3.

[31] E.g. by B. F. Westcott, *On the Canon of the New Testament* (London, [3]1870), p.411.

[32] See p.81.

epistles except 1 Peter and 1 John, but it is more likely that he rejected these also. This is the most natural sense of the statement of Leontius of Byzantium (6th century) that he rejected the epistle of James and the catholic epistles that followed next to it.[33] Of the three major catholic epistles (James, 1 Peter, 1 John), the Syriac writer Isho 'dad of Merv (9th century) says that 'Theodore, the Interpreter, does not even mention them in a single place, nor does he bring an illustration from them in any one of the writings he made'.[34]

The earliest New Testament in the Syriac churches comprised the four gospels (either the *Diatessaron* or the 'separated gospels'), Acts and the Pauline epistles (evidently including the Pastoral Epistles and Hebrews).[35] From the early part of the fifth century the common Syriac version, the Peshitta, included the three major catholic epistles as well. Not until 508 were 2 Peter, 2 and 3 John, Jude and Revelation included in a Syriac edition of the New Testament (the Philoxenian version).[36] Even then, this enlarged New Testament was accepted only by the Jacobite (Monophysite) branch of the Syriac church; the Nestorians to this day acknowledge a canon of only twenty-two books.[37]

EASTERN DIVERSITY

Eastern Christendom thus cannot match the unanimity with which the New Testament canon of twenty-seven books has been accepted in the west from the end of the fourth century onward. The Greek Orthodox Church accepts the twenty-seven books as listed by Athanasius, but there are no readings from the Apocalypse in its lectionary.

[33] Leontius, *Against the Nestorians and Eutychians,* 3.14.

[34] Isho 'dad, *Commentary on the Epistle of James,* ed. M. D. Gibson, *Horae Semiticae* X (Cambridge, 1913), p.49 (Syriac), p.36 (English).

[35] Ephrem (4th century) wrote commentaries on the *Diatessaron,* on Acts, and on the Pauline epistles (among the latter he included the spurious 3 Corinthians, part of the *Acts of Paul;* see p.239).

[36] See B. M. Metzger, *The Early Versions of the New Testament* (Oxford, 1977), pp.3–75 (the Philoxenian version is discussed on pp.63–68); J. S. Siker, 'The Canonical Status of the Catholic Epistles in the Syriac New Testament', *JTS* n.s. 38 (1987), pp.311–340.

[37] The Monophysites deviated from Chalcedonian orthodoxy by ascribing to our Lord one nature, not two (divine and human); the Nestorians, by ascribing to him two persons (divine and human), not one. In the language of the early creeds 'person' has a technical sense unlike its present usage.

CHAPTER EIGHTEEN

THE WEST IN THE FOURTH CENTURY TO JEROME

ATTACK ON THE CHRISTIAN SCRIPTURES

At the beginning of the fourth century the churches in the Roman Empire found themselves involved in a new situation in which the distinction between the writings which properly ranked as holy scripture and all others became a matter of concern to ordinary church officials and not only to theologians. On February 23, AD 303, an imperial edict was posted, for implementation everywhere in the empire, requiring all copies of the Christian scriptures to be surrendered to the authorities for destruction.[1] This was one of the measures which inaugurated the last period of imperial persecution to be suffered by the church. There had been outbreaks of imperial persecution before, but the order for the surrender and destruction of the scriptures was something new. It marked the recognition of the vital role of the scriptures in Christian life and worship.

Something similar had been attempted during the attempt by Antiochus Epiphanes to abolish the practice of Jewish religion about 167 BC: 'the books of the law were torn to pieces and destroyed by fire, and where the book of the covenant was found in any one's possession, . . . the king's decree condemned him to death' (1 Macc. 1:56f.). But now the Jewish scriptures were not threatened: it was the New Testament that was at risk, since the Hebrew Bible remained unscathed (although the Septuagint, which was by this time almost

---

[1] Lactantius, *On the Deaths of the Persecutors,* 11–13; Eusebius, *Hist. Eccl.* 8.2.4 f.

216

exclusively the property of the church, was placed in jeopardy by the imperial edict along with the New Testament writings).

Nowhere in the empire was the edict put into more vigorous effect than in North Africa. The record has been preserved of an inquisition conducted by the mayor of Cirta, capital of Numidia, and his assistants.[2] The bishop was ordered to produce the sacred books: he replied that they were in the custody of the readers, whose names he was reluctant to give (saying that the municipal clerks knew them already). The readers and sub-deacons were questioned; when one of them proved not to be at home, his wife handed over his books, and the house was searched to make sure there were no others.

To hand over the sacred books, even when death was the penalty for non-compliance, was regarded as a serious offence, practically equivalent to apostasy. Those who handed them over were called *traditores,* which literally means 'handers over', but it is the word from which 'traitors' is derived. When peace returned to the church, it had to be carefully considered whether *traditores* could be restored to communion and, if so, what forms of discipline they should be required to undergo.

But a church might have a variety of books in its possession, not all of them sacred books. The officials who called for the surrender of the scriptures would probably be unable to distinguish the sacred books from others. If they would go away satisfied with a copy of the *Shepherd* of Hermas or a manual of church order, would it be all right to hand over books like these? When the police went to a reader's house and found him away from home, would his wife know whether the books she gave them were holy scriptures or not? And when the police searched the house to make sure there were no other books, how could they know which were 'canonical' and which were not? They would probably take away all documents which had a Christian character about them. But for Christians who were ordered to hand over books it must have become important to know which books must on no account be surrendered and those which might reasonably be regarded as 'not worth dying for'.[3]

---

[2] An English translation (from *Gesta apud Zenophilum,* CSEL 26, pp. 186–188) is provided in J. Stevenson (ed.), *A New Eusebius* (London, 1957), No. 249, pp. 287–289.

[3] W. R. Farmer, *Jesus and the Gospel* (Philadelphia, 1982), p. 220. Farmer emphasizes more than most writers on the subject the importance of persecution and martyrdom as a factor in the formation of the New Testament canon.

THE CLERMONT LIST

Codex Claromontanus[4] is a bilingual manuscript (Graeco-Latin) of the Pauline letters and Hebrews, dating from the sixth century (its common notation is D^P). Between Philemon and Hebrews it contains a Latin list of biblical books, noting the number of lines in each. The Old Testament books follow the Septuagint reckoning (on which the Old Latin version was based).[5] The New Testament books are then listed:

Four Gospels
    Matthew (2600 lines)
    John (2000 lines)
    Mark (1600 lines)
    Luke (2900 lines)
Epistles of Paul
    To the Romans (1040 lines)
    To the Corinthians I (1060 lines)
    To the Corinthians II (70 [*sic*] lines)
    To the Galatians (350 lines)
    To the Ephesians (375 lines)
    To Timothy I (208 lines)
    To Timothy II (289 lines)
    To Titus (140 lines)
    To the Colossians (251 lines)
    To Philemon (50 lines)

    To Peter I (200 lines)
    To Peter II (140 lines)
    Of James (220 lines)
    Of John I (220 lines)
    Of John II (20 lines)
    Of John III (20 lines)
    Of Jude (60 lines)
    —Epistle of Barnabas (850 lines)
    Revelation of John (1200 lines)
    Acts of Apostles (2600 lines)
    —The Shepherd (4000 lines)
    —Acts of Paul (3560 lines)
    —Revelation of Peter (270 lines)

[4] *Claromontanus,* from the Latin form of Clermont, near Beauvais, where the codex was originally identified; it is now in Paris.

[5] The Old Testament list (which deviates somewhat in order from what is usual) includes 4 Maccabees as well as 1 and 2 Maccabees.

The omission of Philippians and 1 and 2 Thessalonians is evidently accidental; so too, probably, is the omission of Hebrews.[6] The order of Paul's letters is not the order in which they appear in *Codex Claromontanus;*[7] the scribe apparently copied this list into the codex from an independent source. The order of the gospels and the other books is also unusual. Carelessness must be the reason for the misnaming of 1 and 2 Peter as the epistles '*to* Peter'; this is a slip which is sometimes heard when the New Testament lesson is announced in church, but it is surprising to see it perpetrated in writing. The four 'uncanonical' books — the *Letter of Barnabas,*[8] the *Shepherd,*[9] the *Acts of Paul*[10] and the *Revelation of Peter*[11] — have a dash written before each of their titles, as though to indicate their inferior status (a similar dash appears before 1 Peter, but this is to mark this and the following books off from the epistles of Paul, which precede them).

The majority opinion seems to be that this list is based on one drawn up at or near Alexandria about AD 300; in its original form it appears to mark a stage in the canonizing process intermediate between Origen and Eusebius.[12]

THE CHELTENHAM LIST

Another fourth-century Latin list was identified by Theodor Mommsen in 1885 in a tenth-century manuscript in what was the Sir Thomas Phillipps collection at Cheltenham.[13] (It is sometimes referred to as the Mommsen list.) It too comprises the books of both

---

[6] If (as is most probable) the Latin list is translated from a Greek original, the omission of the four epistles could be explained by the wandering of a scribe's eye from 'Ephesians' to 'Hebrews': in Greek, 'Ephesians' and 'Hebrews' have the same number of letters (eight) and the first letter and last four letters are identical in the two words.

[7] In *Codex Claromontanus* the epistles appear in the same sequence as we find in most modern editions of the New Testament.

[8] See p. 122.   [9] See p. 166.   [10] See p. 202.   [11] See p. 161.

[12] See T. Zahn, *Geschichte des neutestamentlichen Kanons,* II (Erlangen/Leipzig, 1890), pp. 157–172; A. Harnack, *Chronologie der altchristlichen Literatur,* II (Leipzig, 1904), pp. 84–86.

[13] See T. Mommsen, 'Zur lateinischen Stichometrie', *Hermes* 21 (1886), pp. 142–156; W. Sanday, 'The Cheltenham List of the Canonical Books of the New Testament and of the Writings of Cyprian', *Studia Biblica et Ecclesiastica,* III (Oxford, 1891), pp. 217–303, with appendix by C. H. Turner, pp. 304–325. Later a copy of the same list was identified in a ninth-century codex at St Gall, Switzerland.

Testaments. Its place of origin seems to have been North Africa, and a reference to the consulships of Valentinian and Valens suggests that it was drawn up in AD 365. Here too the titles of the books are followed by a note of the number of lines contained in each. After the Old Testament list the document goes on:

> Similarly the catalogue of the New Testament:
> The Four Gospels
>> Matthew (2700 lines)
>> Mark (1700 lines)
>> John (1800 lines)
>> Luke (3300 lines)
>> In all: 10,000 lines[14]
> Epistles of Paul—in number 13
> Acts of Apostles (3600 lines)
> Apocalypse (1800 lines)
> Epistles of John, 3 (350 lines)
>> one only
> Epistles of Peter, 2 (300 lines)
>> one only

Again, there are some unusual features in the order of the books, but no 'outside' books are listed. The number of lines in Paul's epistles is not given. Since his epistles are said to be thirteen in number, Hebrews is omitted. By mid-century the church in Rome had been persuaded by Athanasius to acknowledge Hebrews as canonical, but evidently the North African churches had not yet come into line on this. James and Jude are also omitted.

The repeated note 'one only' appended to the mention of the epistles of John and Peter 'expresses a preference for First John and First Peter exclusively', according to A. Souter;[15] since the compiler had inherited a list in which the number of lines was given for John's epistles together and for Peter's epistles together, he reproduced what he found in his source but indicated his personal preference for 1 John and 1 Peter only. So B. M. Metzger very persuasively suggests.[16] The compiler rejected the five disputed catholic epistles.

---

[14] Something has gone wrong: the total number of lines in the four gospels, as given, is 9500, not 10,000.

[15] *The Text and Canon of the New Testament* (London, ²1954), p.196, n.1.

[16] *The Canon of the New Testament* (Oxford, 1987), pp.231f.

ATHANASIUS VISITS ROME

In 340 Athanasius, exiled (for the second time) from his see in Alexandria, made his way to Rome and spent a few years in the fellowship of the church there. He established good relations with the bishop of Rome (Julius I) and other church leaders, and the Roman church profited in various ways from the presence within it of such a distinguished theologian from the east. It is probable that he persuaded the Roman Christians to fall into line with their eastern brethren in admitting the canonicity, if not the Pauline authorship, of Hebrews. From that time on the right of Hebrews to be accepted as a New Testament book was not seriously questioned at Rome, or in those western churches which fell within Rome's sphere of influence.

HILARY OF POITIERS

Hilary, bishop of Poiters (died 367), was in any case a follower of Athanasius and a champion of Nicene orthodoxy; in his exegetical and dogmatic writings he introduced several ideas of eastern theology to the west. He accepted not only the canonicity of Hebrews but its Pauline authorship: he quotes Hebrews 1:4 and 3:1, for example, as 'what Paul writes to the Hebrews'.[17] He similarly quotes James 1:17 ('with whom there is no variation') and ascribes it to 'the apostle James';[18] he is in fact the first western writer known to us to accept the letter of James as apostolic.[19]

COMMENTATORS ON PAUL

To the fourth century belong several Latin writers of commentaries on the letters of Paul.[20] The first of these was Marius Victorinus, a native of the province of Africa who became a leading teacher of rhetoric in Rome and was converted to Christianity about 355. In the years following 360 he wrote expositions of Galatians, Ephesians and Philippians.[21] He was a stout defender of Nicene orthodoxy, in the

---

[17] *On the Trinity*, 4.11.   [18] *On the Trinity*, 4.8.

[19] For his list of Old Testament books see p.90, n.45. He has left no comparable list of New Testament books.

[20] See A. Souter, *The Earliest Latin Commentaries on the Epistles of St Paul* (Oxford, 1927).

[21] See W. Erdt, *Marius Victorinus Afer, . . . Pauluskommentator* (Frankfurt, 1980).

presentation of which he gives clear evidence of the Neoplatonic pattern of his thought.[22]

More important for our purpose is the scholar whom we must (following Erasmus) call Ambrosiaster because his real name has not been preserved. He is the author of commentaries on the thirteen epistles which bear Paul's name, written at Rome while Damasus was bishop (366–384), but in the manuscript tradition they have been assigned chiefly to Ambrose, bishop of Milan (339–397). They are certainly not by Ambrose, but this certainty does not help us with a positive attribution (Ambrosiaster means 'pseudo-Ambrose'). The same writer is held (with good reason) to be the author also of a work entitled *Questions of the Old and New Testament,* which has been transmitted among the works of Augustine.[23]

The fact that Ambrosiaster did not include Hebrews among the Pauline epistles which he expounded is evidence enough that he set it in a category apart: he refers to it occasionally, both in his Pauline commentaries and in the *Questions,* in terms which show that he accepted it as canonical but did not know who wrote it.[24]

Another commentator on Paul's thirteen epistles is Pelagius (*c* 350–430),[25] the first British or Irish author known to us—the evidence is best satisfied if he be regarded as an Irishman *(Scotus)* born or resident in Britain.[26] Unlike Ambrosiaster, Pelagius cites Hebrews as Pauline, but the fact that he did not write a commentary on it may suggest that he did not regard it as Pauline in the same sense as the thirteen.

Among those commentators Victorinus refers to James the Lord's brother in terms which indicate that he viewed him as technically in

---

[22] See G. Geiger, *C. Marius Victorinus Afer, ein neuplatonischer Philosoph* (Metten, 1888/9); P. Henry, *Plotin et l'Occident* (Louvain, 1934), pp.44–62.

[23] See A. Souter, *A Study of Ambrosiaster,* TS 7.4 (Cambridge, 1905); *Earliest Latin Commentaries,* pp.39–95.

[24] The commentary on Hebrews included in some manuscripts along with Ambrosiaster's Pauline commentaries is actually by Alcuin of York (E. Riggenbach, *Die ältesten lateinischen Kommentare zum Hebräerbrief,* FGNTK 8 [Leipzig, 1907], pp.18–40).

[25] Souter, *Earliest Latin Commentaries,* pp.205–230. Souter was the first editor of Pelagius's commentaries: see his *Pelagius's Expositions of Thirteen Epistles of St Paul,* I–III, TS 9.1–3 (Cambridge, 1922–31). See also J. Ferguson, *Pelagius: An Historical and Theological Study* (Cambridge, 1956).

[26] Augustine and others say he was British; Jerome (*Commentary on Jeremiah,* 1, preface) calls him an Irishman *(Scotus).*

heresy and that, while he knew the letter of James, he did not regard it as canonical.[27] Ambrosiaster, on the other hand, accepted it as canonical. He also ascribed 3 John to 'John the apostle'. In fact he cites every book of the New Testament, with the exception of Jude.[28] One can well believe that Athanasius had persuaded the Roman church not only to acknowledge the canonical status of Hebrews but also to give up any lingering doubts about the canonicity of the five disputed catholic epistles.

LUCIFER, FILASTER AND AMBROSE

Lucifer, bishop of Cagliari in Sardinia (died 370/1), was a vigorous anti-Arian polemicist. His works are linguistically interesting because they were written in vulgar Latin;[29] they are important for the history of the Latin Bible because he quoted extensively from a pre-Vulgate text. His quotations are drawn from most of the New Testament books, including Hebrews; in one of his treatises he incorporates almost the whole of the letter of Jude in an attack on heresy.[30]

Filaster (Philaster), bishop of Brescia (died *c* 397), wrote a work *On Heresies,* sadly deficient in literary organization. His confusion appears in a list of the New Testament scriptures from which Hebrews and the Apocalypse are missing, although it is perfectly plain from other references in his work that he accepted both books as canonical, ascribing the former to the apostle Paul and the latter to the apostle John. Such works as the apocryphal Acts he recommends to the spiritually mature for their ethical instruction.[31]

Ambrose, the illustrious bishop of Milan (339–397), quotes Hebrews as canonical but is reticent about its authorship. He was familiar with the tradition of the Greek fathers, but prudently refrained

---

[27] Victorinus, *Commentary on Galatians,* on Gal. 1:19.

[28] See Souter, *Study of Ambrosiaster,* pp.196f. Ambrosiaster (on Gal. 5:10) quotes Jas. 5:20 ('as James says in his letter'); he quotes 2 Peter more than once (e.g. on Phil. 1:3–5) as the work of 'Peter the apostle'; on Rom. 16:23 he (no doubt wrongly) identifies Paul's host Gaius with the Gaius 'to whom the apostle John wrote' (in 3 John).

[29] Vulgar Latin is the colloquial Latin from which the Romance languages of Europe developed.

[30] Lucifer, *On Heretics,* 15.

[31] Filaster, *On Heresies,* 88.

from committing himself to Pauline authorship, on which he knew western theologians had well-founded misgivings.[32]

RUFINUS

Rufinus of Aquileia (345–410), at first the friend and then the opponent of Jerome, is best known as the translator of Origen, but has left some writings of his own, including *An Exposition of the Creed*. When the creed confesses faith in 'the Holy Spirit' and 'the holy church', Rufinus takes the opportunity to mention the books of the Old and New Testaments which have been inspired by the Spirit and handed down in the church.[33] He then lists the Old Testament books according to the Hebrew Bible (the writings which appear in the Septuagint but not in the Hebrew Bible are called not 'canonical' but 'ecclesiastical').[34] After listing the Old Testament books he goes on to list the same twenty-seven New Testament books as Athanasius, but not in the same order:

> Of the New Testament there are the four gospels (Matthew, Mark, Luke, John); the Acts of the Apostles (written by Luke); fourteen epistles of the apostle Paul, two of the apostle Peter, one of James (brother of the Lord, and apostle), one of Jude, three of John; the Revelation of John. These are the books which the fathers have comprised within the canon; from these they would have us deduce the evidences of our faith.[35]

As the Old Testament has appended to it books which are 'ecclesiastical' but not 'canonical', so has the New Testament. These are:

> the little book which is called the book of the *Shepherd* of Hermas, and that which is called *The Two Ways* or the *Judgment of Peter*. They would have all of these read in the churches but

---

[32] He implies (or assumes) Pauline authorship when, e.g., he quotes Col. 1:15 as coming from the 'apostle' and goes on: 'In another place also the apostle has declared that God made the Son "heir of all things, by whom also he made the worlds..."', quoting Heb. 1:2 (*On the Faith*, 1.48).

[33] *On the Creed*, 36–38. The form of the creed which Rufinus expounds is called the creed of Aquileia, an earlier form of what is traditionally known as the Apostles' Creed.

[34] *On the Creed*, 37f See p.90.

[35] *On the Creed*, 37. By placing Jude before the epistle of John, he brings the latter into close association with John's Apocalypse.

not appealed to for the confirmation of doctrine. The other writings they have named 'apocrypha'; these they would not read in the churches.[36]

Rufinus uses 'apocrypha' of heretical works, as Athanasius does. *The Two Ways* ('the way of life and the way of death') is a little body of ethical teaching or catechesis incorporated both in the *Didache* and in the *Letter of Barnabas*.[37] Jerome mentions the *Judgment of Peter* among the apocryphal works ascribed to Peter;[38] nothing is now known of it.

Not only does Rufinus ascribe fourteen epistles to Paul; he occasionally cites him as author when he quotes Hebrews,[39] although he recognizes that 'some do not receive it as his'.[40]

JEROME

In response to Pope Damasus's direction, Jerome produced his revised Latin version of the four gospels about 383.[41] How far he is responsible for the rest of the Vulgate New Testament is a disputed question.[42] But the important point is that the Vulgate New Testament—more precisely, the New Testament part of the Latin Bible which came in due course to be called the common or 'vulgate' edition—comprised twenty-seven books, and with the general acceptance of the Vulgate by western Christians the dimensions of the New Testament canon were fixed.

Jerome expresses himself more than once on the canon of scripture. Writing to Paulinus, bishop of Nola, for example, in 394, he outlines the books of the Old Testament at some length and then undertakes to deal more briefly with the New Testament.

> Matthew, Mark, Luke and John are the Lord's team of four, the true cherubim (which means 'abundance of knowledge'), endowed with eyes throughout their whole body; they glitter like sparks, they flash to and fro like lightning, their legs are straight and directed upward, their backs are winged, to fly in

---

[36] *On the Creed*, 38. On the *Shepherd* of Hermas see pp. 166, 210.

[37] See pp. 23, 122.   [38] Jerome, *On Illustrious Men*, 1.

[39] E.g., *On the Creed*, 3, where a quotation of Heb. 11:6 is introduced by the words: 'as the apostle Paul, writing to the Hebrews, says'.

[40] *Apology*, 1.39.   [41] See p. 88.

[42] See B. M. Metzger, *The Early Versions of the New Testament* (Oxford, 1977), pp. 356–362.

all directions. They are interlocked and hold on to one another, they roll along like wheels within wheels, they go to whatever point the breath of the Holy Spirit guides them.[43]

The apostle Paul writes to seven churches (for the eighth such letter, that to the Hebrews, is placed outside the number by most); he instructs Timothy and Titus; he intercedes with Philemon for his runaway slave. Regarding Paul I prefer to remain silent than to write only a few things.

The Acts of the Apostles seem to relate a bare history and to describe the childhood of the infant church; but if we know that their writer was Luke the physician, 'whose praise is in the gospel',[44] we shall observe likewise that all their words are medicine for the sick soul. The apostles James, Peter, John and Jude produced seven epistles both mystical and concise, both short and long—that is, short in words but long in thought— so that there are few who are not deeply impressed by reading them.

The Apocalypse of John has as many mysteries as it has words. I have said too little in comparison with what the book deserves; all praise of it is inadequate, for in every one of its words manifold meanings lie hidden.[45]

In comparing the four gospels to Ezekiel's four chrerubim or 'living creatures',[46] Jerome reproduces the details of Ezekiel's description of the cherubim to a point where he himself might have been puzzled to say exactly how they applied to the gospels. For the rest, we note that he places Acts and the catholic epistles together after the Pauline epistles,[47] that he distinguishes Hebrews from Paul's letter 'to seven churches',[48] and that he assigns apostolic authorship to all seven catholic epistles.

Elsewhere, however, he expresses himself more critically. In writing to Dardanus, prefect of Gaul, in the year 414, he answers his correspondent's questions about the 'promised land' of scripture and quotes highly relevant texts from Hebrews 11:13–16, 39f.; 12:22f. On the authority of these texts he says:

> This must be said to our people, that the epistle which is entitled 'To the Hebrews' is accepted as the apostle Paul's not

---

[43] From Ezek. 1:7–21.   [44] 2 Cor. 8:18 (see p.174).
[45] *Epistle* 53.9.   [46] *Cf* Irenaeus (p.175, n.29).
[47] *Cf Codex Sinaiticus* (pp.205f.).
[48] *Cf* the Muratorian list, Cyprian and Victorinus of Pettau (p.164 with n.15).

only by the churches of the east but by all church writers in the Greek language of earlier times, although many judge it to be by Barnabas or by Clement. It is of no great moment who the author is, since it is the work of a churchman and receives recognition day by day in the churches' public reading. If the custom of the Latins does not receive it among the canonical scriptures, neither, by the same liberty, do the churches of the Greeks accept John's Apocalypse. Yet we accept them both, not following the custom of the present time but the precedent of early writers, who generally make free use of testimonies from both works. And this they do, not as they are wont on occasion to quote from apocryphal writings, as indeed they use examples from pagan literature, but treating them as canonical and ecclesiastical works.[49]

Jerome's insistence that canonicity is not dependent on particular authorship, not even on apostolic authorship, reveals an insight which has too often been ignored in discussions about the canon of scripture, in earlier and more recent times alike.[50]

As for the catholic epistles, Jerome receives all seven as canonical, but he recognizes the questions that were raised about their authorship and authority. James the Lord's brother, he says, 'wrote a single letter, which is reckoned among the seven catholic epistles. Even so, some claim that is was published by another person under James's name and gradually gained authority as time went on'.[51] Peter 'wrote two epistles which are called catholic, the second of which, on account of its stylistic difference from the first, is considered by many not to be by him.'[52] In a letter to Hedibia (406/7) he suggests that the stylistic difference between the two might be due to the employment of two different translators (on whom Peter presumably relied to turn his Galilean Aramaic into Greek and write it down).[53] He ascribes 1 John to John the apostle and evangelist, but thinks that 2 and 3 John were written by another John, 'John the elder (presbyter)'.[54] The author of both 2 and 3 John introduces himself as 'the elder', and Jerome links this self-designation with Papias's 'John the elder'.[55] When he adds that to the memory of this John 'another sepulchre is shown at Ephesus to the present day, though some think that there are two memorials of one and the same John, the evangelist', he echoes the testimony of

---

[49] *Epistle* 129.3.   [50] See Augustine's position (p. 232).
[51] *On Illustrious Men*, 2.   [52] *On Illustrious Men*, 1.   [53] *Epistle* 120.11.
[54] *On Illustrious Men*, 9.   [55] See p. 119, n. 5.

Dionysius of Alexandria, preserved by Eusebius.[56] But Dionysius, followed by Eusebius, was concerned to find another John than the evangelist as author of the Apocalypse. With regard to the one remaining catholic epistle, 'Jude, the brother of James', says Jerome, 'left a short epistle which is reckoned among the seven catholic epistles, but it is rejected by many because in it he quotes from the apocryphal book of Enoch. Nevertheless by age and use it has gained authority and is reckoned among the holy scriptures.'[57]

Jerome gives the impression that on one or two of the canonical books he has private reservations, but by this time the canon was something 'given' and not to be modified because of the personal opinion of this or that churchman, however eminent. Similarly he gives the impression that he thought one or two of the 'outside' books worthy of inclusion in the canon, but by this time they were decidedly outside, and it was not for him, or anyone else, to add them.

The writing called the *Letter of Barnabas,* for example, he regards as the authentic work of Barnabas, Paul's colleague.[58] Since Paul at times appears to recognize Barnabas's standing as comparable with his own,[59] and since Barnabas and Paul are twice called 'apostles' by Luke,[60] it might be concluded that a letter of Barnabas, 'valuable for the edification of the church' (as Jerome says), should have its place in the canon with other apostolic writings. But it was not in the canon which Jerome had received, and therefore it 'is reckoned among the apocryphal writings' (as in an Old Testament context, so here Jerome uses the adjective 'apocryphal' of those 'ecclesiastical' writings which are read 'for the edification of the people but not for establishing the authority of ecclesiastical dogmas').[61] As a matter of fact, the *Letter of Barnabas* cannot be the work of the Barnabas who figures in Acts and in the Pauline epistles; it belongs to the later part of the first century and is probably of Alexandrian origin.

[56] See pp. 195f. It is more probable that there were two rival memorials to John the evangelist; see F. F. Bruce, *Men and Movements in the Primitive Church* (Exeter, 1979), pp. 139f.

[57] *On Illustrious Men,* 4.

[58] *On Illustrious Men,* 6. B. M. Metzger points out that in his book *On Hebrew Names* (composed in 388) Jerome lists the proper names in both Testaments and adds at the end thirteen from the *Letter of Barnabas* (*The Canon of the New Testament,* p. 236).

[59] *Cf* Gal. 2:1–10; 1 Cor. 9:6.

[60] Acts 14:4, 14. The sense in which Luke uses the term here of Paul and Barnabas is arguable; normally he restricts it to the twelve.

[61] See p. 122.

Jerome ascribes the *Shepherd* of Hermas to that Hermas to whom Paul sends greetings in Romans 16:14 (an ascription mentioned also by Eusebius, who does not commit himself to it).[62] The *Shepherd*, he says, 'is read publicly in some churches of Greece; it is in fact a useful book and many of the ancient writers quote from it as authoritative, but among the Latins it is almost unknown'[63]—which is remarkable, since it originated in Rome. In any case, whatever be the date of the *Shepherd*, there is nothing to be said in favour of identifying the author with Paul's Hermas.

With Jerome, then, the canon is a datum to be received gratefully, preserved faithfully, and handed on intact.

[62] Eusebius, *Hist. Eccl.* 3.3.6.   [63] *On Illustrious Men*, 10.

CHAPTER NINETEEN

AUGUSTINE TO THE END
OF THE MIDDLE AGES

AUGUSTINE

Augustine, like Jerome, inherited the canon of scripture as something 'given'. It was part of the Christian faith which he embraced at his conversion in 386 and, as with so many other elements of the Christian faith, he set himself to understand, defend and expound it.

In the second book of his work *On Christian Learning,* after listing the books within which, as he says, 'the authority of the Old Testament is contained',[1] he continues:

> That of the New Testament, again, is contained within the following:
> Four books of the gospel—according to Matthew, according to Mark, according to Luke, according to John. Fourteen epistles of the apostle Paul—one to the Romans, two to the Corinthians, one to the Galatians, to the Ephesians, to the Philippians, two to the Thessalonians, one to the Colossians, two to Timothy, one to Titus, to Philemon, to the Hebrews. Two [epistles] of Peter, three of John, one of Jude, and one of James. One book of the Acts of the Apostles, and one of the Revelation of John.[2]

[1] See p.95.   [2] *On Christian Learning,* 2.13.

These are the same twenty-seven books as were listed by Athanasius, although they are not in the same order.[3] Those which form groups are placed first—the four gospels, the fourteen epistles of Paul, the seven catholic epistles (with Peter's being accorded the primacy)—and then the two which stand on their own: Acts and Revelation.

While he received the twenty-seven books as they had been delivered to him, Augustine, like other Christian thinkers, considered the question: Why these, and no others? He prefaces his list of canonical books with these observations:

> Among the canonical scriptures he [the interpreter of the sacred writings] will judge according to the following standard: to prefer those that are received by all the catholic churches to those which some do not receive. Again, among those which are not received by all, he will prefer such as are sanctioned by the greater number of churches and by those of greater authority to such as held by the smaller number and by those of less authority. If, however, he finds that some books are held by the greater number of churches, and others by the churches of greater authority (although this is not a very likely thing to happen), I think that in such a case the authority on the two sides is to be considered as equal.[4]

It is plain from this that, when Augustine wrote, no ecclesiastical council had made a pronouncement on the canon which could be recognized as the voice of the church. All twenty-seven books had been delivered to him and his contemporaries, but not all with the same authority: the practice of different churches varied, and greater respect would be paid to those of higher prestige (especially, no doubt, to those of apostolic foundation) or to the majority consensus (and these two criteria might conceivably conflict at times).[5] The prestige of Jerome and Augustine ensured that their canon prevailed in the west, but the distinction between those books which were received by all and those which were disputed by some (namely, Hebrews, James, 2 Peter, 2 and 3 John, Jude, Revelation) was not entirely forgotten, and surfaced again in the fifteenth and sixteenth centuries.[6]

[3] See p.208.   [4] *On Christian Learning,* 2.12.

[5] This passage is discussed by C. R. Gregory, *Canon and Text of the New Testament* (Edinburgh, 1907), pp.287f. 'The "important" churches in Augustine's eyes', he says, 'are those that have apostolical bishops' seats: Alexandria, Antioch, Rome, and those that received Epistles from apostles.'

[6] See pp.242, 248.

Augustine enjoyed critical freedom, according to the standards of his time, in expounding the books within the canon. He tackles discrepancies between different gospel accounts of the same incident: how, for example, could John the Baptist say of Jesus, 'I myself did not know him' (Jn 1:31, 33), when, according to another evangelist, he could say to him, 'I need to be baptized by you' (Mt. 3:14)?[7] If Joseph was afraid to settle in Judaea because Archelaus was ruler there (Mt. 2:22), how could he settle happily in Galilee, where another son of Herod (Antipas) was ruler (Lk 3:1; cf Mt. 14:1)?[8] Or, to take a problem peculiar to one of the evangelists, why does Matthew 27:9 ascribe to Jeremiah an oracle which actually appears in Zechariah 11:13? (Matthew perhaps experienced a slip of memory, thinking of the incident of Jer. 32:6–15, and then reflected that this slip of memory may have been divinely prompted: after all, the prophets spoke with one voice.)[9]

In saying that Paul's epistles are fourteen in number, Augustine does not intend to foreclose the question of the authorship of Hebrews. 'In his earliest writings (down to 406) he cites the Epistle as Paul's; in the middle period he wavers between Pauline authorship and anonymity; in his old age (409–30) he refers to it always as anonymous.'[10] But he never questions its canonicity: for him, as for Jerome, canonicity and authorship are separate issues. It is not so certain as has sometimes been thought that the inclusion of Hebrews in the New Testament is due to the 'happy fault' of its wrong ascription to Paul.[11]

COUNCILS OF HIPPO AND CARTHAGE

The Council of Hippo (393) was probably the first church council to lay down the limits of the canon of scripture: its enactments are not

[7] *On the Consensus of the Evangelists*, 2.15.

[8] *On the Consensus of the Evangelists*, 2.8.

[9] *On the Consensus of the Evangelists*, 3.28–31.

[10] A. Souter, *The Text and Canon of the New Testament* (London, [2]1954), p.174, summarizing O. Rottmanner, 'Saint Augustin sur l'auteur de l'épître aux Hébreux', *Revue Bénédictine* 18 (1901), pp.257–261, reprinted in his *Geistesfrüchte aus der Klosterzelle* (Munich, 1908), pp.84–90.

[11] *Cf* W. F. Howard, 'The Greek Bible', in *The Bible in its Ancient and English Versions*, ed. H. W. Robinson (Oxford, 1940), p.68: 'To the mistaken critical judgement of the ancient Church we owe the presence in the New Testament of not a few books. The most striking instance is Hebrews, which was certainly not written by Paul. *O felix culpa!*'

extant, but its statement on the canon was repeated as Canon 47 of the Third Council of Carthage (397). [12] The relevant words are these:

> And further it was resolved that nothing should be read in church under the name of the divine scriptures except the canonical writings. The canonical writings, then, are these: . . .
> Of the New Testament:
>> The four books of the gospels,
>> the one book of the Acts of the Apostles,
>> the thirteen epistles of the apostle Paul,
>> the one [epistle] to the Hebrews, by the same,
>> two of the apostle Peter,
>> three of John,
>> one of James,
>> one of Jude,
>> John's Apocalypse—one book.
> . . . Let it be permitted, however, that the passions of martyrs be read when their anniversaries are celebrated.

Here Hebrews is ascribed to Paul, but listed separately from the thirteen letters which bear his name. As in Augustine's list, Peter's letters come first among the catholic epistles (but Jude follows James instead of preceding it). The permission given to read the account of a martyrdom when its anniversary came round was reasonable: no one would think that such an account was part of holy scripture. What was important was that nothing should be read as holy scripture which was not listed in the canon. Augustine himself is said to have read extracts from Cyprian's works in church occasionally, but none of his flock was given reason to suppose that he regarded Cyprian as canonical. [13]

The Sixth Council of Carthage (419) repromulgated in Canon 24 the resolution of the Third Council regarding the canon of scripture, and added a note directing that the resolution be sent to the bishop of Rome (Boniface I) and other bishops:

> Let this be made known also to our brother and fellow-priest Boniface, or to other bishops of those parts, for the purpose of confirming that Canon [Canon 47 of the Third Council], because we have received from our fathers that these are the books which are to be read in church. [14]

[12] See p.97.
[13] *On the Proceedings of Pelagius,* 25. See C. J. Costello, *St Augustine's Doctrine on the Inspiration and Canonicity of Scripture* (Washington, D.C., 1930), p.48.
[14] See NPNF, series 2, XIV, p.454.

POPE INNOCENT'S LIST

In his list of canonical books addressed to Exsuperius, bishop of Toulouse, in 405, Pope Innocent I specifies the books of the New Testament (after those of the Old Testament) as follows:

> Of the gospels—four,
> epistles of the apostle Paul—thirteen,
> epistles of John—three,
> epistles of Peter—two,
> epistle of Jude,
> epistle of James,
> Acts of the Apostles,
> John's Apocalypse.
> But the rest of the books, which appear under the name of Matthias or of James the less, or under the name of Peter and John (which were written by a certain Leucius), or under the name of Andrew (which [were written] by the philosophers Xenocharides and Leonidas), or under the name of Thomas, and whatever others there may be, you should know are to be not only rejected but also condemned.[15]

The omission of Hebrews from the New Testament books is surprising. The manuscripts, in fact, are divergent in their testimony: the three best ones reckon Paul's epistles as thirteen (written XIII), but the rest reckon them as fourteen (written XIIII).

THE GELASIAN DECREE

The sixth-century compilation commonly called the 'Gelasian decree' continues as follows after its list of Old Testament books:

> The order of the scriptures of the New Testament, which the holy and catholic Roman church accepts and venerates:
> Of the gospels four books:
> according to Matthew—one book
> according to Mark—one book

[15] Innocent, *Epistle* 6.7. With regard to the apocryphal works which he mentions, on Matthias see pp. 191, 201; on James the less it may be observed that an *Apocryphon of James* is included in the Nag Hammadi documents; on the Leucian Acts see p. 202; on the *Acts of Andrew* see p. 202; on Thomas the reference may be to a *Gospel of Thomas* (see p. 300) or the *Acts of Thomas* (see pp. 202f.).

>according to Luke—one book
>according to John—one book
>Also: of the Acts of the Apostles—one book
>Epistles of the apostle Paul—in number fourteen:
>>to the Romans—one epistle
>>to the Corinthians—two epistles
>>to the Ephesians—one epistle
>>to the Thessalonians—two epistles
>>to the Galatians—one epistle
>>to the Philippians—one epistle
>>to the Colossians—one epistle
>>to Timothy—two epistles
>>to Titus—one epistle
>>to Philemon—one epistle
>>to the Hebrews—one epistle
>Also: John's Apocalypse—one book
>Also: canonical epistles—in number seven:
>>of the apostle Peter—two epistles
>>of the apostle James—one epistle
>>of the apostle John—one epistle
>>of the other John, the elder—two epistles
>>of the apostle Jude the Zealot—one epistle
>The Canon of the New Testament ends. [16]

In this list it is worthy of note that John's Apocalypse precedes the catholic epistles, that the latter are called the 'canonical epistles', that within this group 2 and 3 John are assigned (as by Jerome) to another John than the evangelist (who is identified with the author of 1 John), and that Jude is called 'the Zealot' (this designation having evidently been transferred to him from the apostle Simon, called the Zealot in Luke 6:15 and Acts 1:13). [17]

The Gelasian decree follows its lists of books which are to received with a long catalogue of books which are not to be received, comprising a variety of apocryphal, spurious and heretical writings. [18]

---

[16] See E. von Dobschütz, *Das Decretum Gelasianum* (Leipzig, 1912), pp.27f. (see p.97, n.74).

[17] The apostle Judas—'not Iscariot'—is called 'Judas the Zealot' in some Old Latin texts of Mt. 10:3 (where our other witnesses read 'Thaddaeus'); Judas the Zealot is also listed among the apostles in the second-century *Epistle of the Apostles*, 2.

[18] See M. R. James, *The Apocryphal New Testament* (Oxford, 1924), pp.21–23, for a translation of the catalogue.

THE DIATESSARON IN WESTERN EUROPE

Throughout the Middle Ages the shape of the New Testament canon in Western Europe remained unchanged, but there were some interesting, if local and temporary, developments within it.

The *Diatessaron*, which was displaced by the 'separated gospels' in its Syrian and Mesopotamian homeland in the course of the fifth century, had a fresh lease of life in some parts of the west during the following centuries. When a gospel harmony from this period is identified, it is necessary to make sure that it is really based on Tatian's *Diatessaron* and that it is not rather an independent production. There is little room for doubt on this score with the Dutch gospel harmony, composed in the middle of the thirteenth century and best preserved in a Liège manuscript of about 1270–1280. This was evidently based on a lost Old Latin original, which in turn was derived from a Syriac and not a Greek copy of the *Diatessaron*.[19]

The influence of the *Diatessaron* can be recognized much earlier in the Old Saxon versified form of the gospel story, commonly known nowadays as the *Heliand* ('Saviour'), dating from the first half of the ninth century. This is not a straight translation, but the *Diatessaron* is evidently its basis.[20] It is the basis also of an East Franconian version of the gospel story, extant in its entirety in a late ninth-century manuscript.[21]

Apart from versions or paraphrases which show the specific influence of Tatian's *Diatessaron,* there are others which follow Tatian's arrangement of gospel material without being dependent on his wording. *Codex Fuldensis,* for example, is an important witness to the text of the Latin Vulgate; the copyist completed his work for Victor, bishop of Capua, who corrected it and signed his name in it in 546. But in the gospels, while the text is that of the Vulgate, the arrangement is that of Tatian.[22] Various mediaeval gospel harmonies were based on this

---

[19] In the last phrase of Luke 2:42, the Dutch wording means not 'according to the custom of the feast' (as it should) but 'according to the custom of their habits'. This is best explained as a confusion between two Syriac words, meaning respectively 'feast' and 'habit', which have the same consonants (and in fact share the same root). See W. B. Lockwood, 'Vernacular Scriptures in Germany and the Low Countries before 1500', *CHB* II, p.430. On the *Diatessaron* see also p. 127 above.

[20] See Lockwood, 'Vernacular Scriptures...', pp.418–420.

[21] See Lockwood, 'Vernacular Scriptures...'. p.418.

[22] See B. M. Metzger, *The Text of the New Testament* (Oxford, 1964), p.89; *The Early Versions of the New Testament* (Oxford, 1977), pp.20f., 28f., 335.

form of the text: Magdalene College, Cambridge, for example, possesses a manuscript from about 1400 which once belonged to Samuel Pepys, containing a Middle English Harmony.[23] Of a similar character is a mediaeval gospel harmony in the Tuscan dialect of Italy.[24]

THE LETTER TO THE HEBREWS

While the ascription of Hebrews to Paul was generally accepted throughout the Middle Ages, the precedent of Augustine, who recognized it as canonical and anonymous, encouraged some students to think of another author than Paul. Those who did so tended to prefer Luke—'Luke, that excellent advocate, translated that work of art from Hebrew into Greek', said Thomas Aquinas.[25] Rabanus Maurus and Archbishop Lanfranc of Canterbury were also among those who ascribed the work to Luke.[26]

It is uncertain what significance to attach to the omission of Hebrews from *Codex Boernerianus* (G^P) a ninth-century Graeco-Latin manuscript of the Pauline epistles. It ends with the letter to Philemon, after which stands a note: 'Here begins the letter to the Laodiceans'— but the text of that document is not included.

THE LETTER TO THE LAODICEANS

This reference to 'the letter to the Laodiceans' provides an occasion to mention the extraordinary popularity in the Middle Ages of a spurious work bearing that title.

When Paul writes to the Colossians, 'when this letter has been read among you, have it read also in the church of the Laodiceans; and see that you read also the letter from Laodicea' (Col. 4:16), the status of this 'letter from Laodicea' is not quite clear to a reader today (although no doubt it was perfectly clear to the original readers). Was it a letter originating from Laodicea, or was it a letter sent by Paul to the Laodicean church, which the Colossians were to procure 'from Laodicea'? The latter is more probable. If the reference is to a letter composed by Paul, have we any other information about it? From time

---

[23] See Metzger, *Early Versions*, p.25.
[24] See K. Foster, 'Vernacular Scriptures in Italy', *CHB* II, p.464.
[25] *Preface to the Epistle to the Hebrews.*
[26] See C. Spicq, *L'Epître aux Hébreux*, I (Paris, 1952), p.198, n.1.

to time it has been identified with what we know as the epistle to the Ephesians (the oldest form of which seems to contain no indication of the addressees' whereabouts or identity).[27] Marcion evidently made this identification, and gave Ephesians the title 'To the Laodiceans'.[28] The compiler of the Muratorian list speaks of a 'letter in Paul's name to the Laodiceans' which, he says, was 'forged in accordance with Marcion's heresy'.[29] This may be an unintelligent reference to the letter which Marcion entitled 'To the Laodiceans', or the compiler may actually have known a spurious work so designated.

There is extant a spurious work so designated, but it betrays no trace of Marcion's heresy. This work has been well described as a 'worthless patching together of Pauline passages and phrases, mainly from the Epistle to the Philippians'[30] (although its opening words are taken from Galatians). The chapter-headings supplied for it in a twelfth-century manuscript of the Latin Bible in Trinity College, Cambridge, sum up its contents thus:

1. Paul the apostle gives thanks to the Lord for the Laodiceans and exhorts them not to be deceived by those who would lead them astray.

2. Concerning the apostle's 'manifest' bonds,[31] in which he rejoices and exults.

3. The apostle admonishes the Laodiceans that, as they heard him when he was present with them, so they should retain his teaching and practise it without drawing back.

4. The apostle exhorts the Laodiceans to be steadfast in the faith and do those things which are marked by integrity and truth and which bring pleasure to God. He greets the brothers.[32]

The *Letter to the Laodiceans* was probably written in the fourth century; it is mentioned by Filaster[33] and Jerome[34] and quoted in the fifth-

---

[27] See p. 131.   [28] See p. 139.   [29] See p. 167.

[30] R. Knopf and G. Krüger in *Neutestamentliche Apokryphen*, ed. E. Hennecke (Tübingen, ²1924), p. 150, quoted by W. Schneemelcher in Hennecke-Schneemelcher-Wilson, *New Testament Apocrypha*, II, p. 129.

[31] From Phil. 1:13.

[32] The Latin text of these chapter-headings is reproduced by J. B. Lightfoot, *Saint Paul's Epistles to the Colossians and to Philemon* (London, 1875), p. 284 (in the course of an informative and judicial account of this apocryphon, pp. 281–300).

[33] Filaster, *Heresies*, 89.   [34] Jerome, *On Illustrious Men*, 5.

century work called the *Speculum*,[35] a topical arrangement of Bible texts, traditionally but mistakenly ascribed to Augustine. Its original language was Greek, but the original Greek text has not survived.[36] Its circulation in the eastern church seems to have been checked after it was pronounced a forgery by the Second Council of Nicaea (787). Almost as soon as it was composed, however, it was translated into Latin, and the Latin version flourished for a thousand years and more. It was drawn into the textual tradition of the Old Latin Bible, and later, although Jerome gave it no countenance, it was absorbed into the Vulgate text and is found in many Vulgate manuscripts, including *Codex Fuldensis,* mentioned above.

Pope Gregory the Great (*c* 595) says that Paul wrote fifteen letters,[37] although only fourteen were reckoned canonical: although he does not expressly say so, it is probable that this Laodicean letter was the fifteenth. Aelfric, abbot of Cerne in Dorset (late tenth century), is more explicit: he not only says that Paul wrote fifteen epistles but lists them, and names that to the Laodiceans as the fifteenth.[38] John of Salisbury, another English writer about two centuries later, writes to the same effect although he knows that he is contradicting Jerome: 'Jerome says that it is rejected by all; nevertheless it was written by the apostle.'[39] Yet another writer of that period, possibly Herveus Burgidolensis,[49] speaks of Paul as the author of fifteen or sixteen letters (including not only the Laodicean letter but another apocryphon, *3 Corinthians*).[41]

From the Latin text the *Letter to the Laodiceans* was translated into several of the western European vernaculars and was included in Bible versions in those languages. Although it did not form part originally of either the earlier or the later Wycliffite Bibles, two independent

[35] It quotes verse 4 of the work: 'See that you are not robbed by certain people who tell you vain tales in order to turn you away from the truth of the gospel which is proclaimed by me'.

[36] Reasons for believing that the extant Latin text is based on a Greek original are given by Lightfoot, *Colossians-Philemon,* pp.291–294. He provides a Greek retroversion.

[37] Gregory, *Moral Exposition of Job,* 35.25.

[38] Aelfricus Abbas, *A Saxon Treatise concerning the Old and New Testament,* ed. W. L'Isle (London, 1623), p.28, cited by Lightfoot, p.296.

[39] John of Salisbury, *Epistle* 143.

[40] *On the Epistle to the Colossians, ad loc.* (PL 181, col. 1355). J. B. Lightfoot notes the possibility that the author might be Anselm of Laon.

[41] *3 Corinthians* is included in the *Acts of Paul:* see Hennecke-Schneemelcher-Wilson, *New Testament Apocrypha,* II, pp.374–378. See p.215 above.

Middle English versions of the work made their way into the manuscript tradition of the Wycliffite Bible, and were repeatedly reproduced from the first half of the fifteenth century onward.

With the invention of printing in the middle of the fifteenth century, the Laodicean letter was included in some of the earliest printed editions of the New Testament. This did not happen in England, where the printing of the Bible was inhibited by the anti-Lollard Constitutions of Oxford (1408): the first printed edition of the New Testament in English (Tyndale's) had to be produced on the Continent (1525/26) and, being based on the Greek text, did not include the *Letter to the Laodiceans*. But the earliest printed German New Testaments (from 1466 onward) and Czech New Testaments (from 1475 onward) included it: it was omitted, however, from the new versions which were based on the Greek text, such as Luther's (1522) and the Czech Kralice Bible (1593).[42]

In France, Jacques Lefèvre d'Étaples (Faber Stapulensis) wrote a commentary on the Latin text of the Pauline epistles in 1513; in this he not only included the Laodicean letter but also the spurious correspondence of the philosopher Seneca with Paul.[43] A more critical assessment was made by Andreas Bodenstein von Karlstadt, who in 1521 listed the work among the New Testament apocrypha, together with the last twelve verses of Mark's gospel.[44] Any claims by the work to be treated as a genuine Pauline letter were finally exploded by Erasmus[45] and Luther.[46]

[42] The New Testament part of the Kralice Bible (the 'authorised version' of the Czech Bible) was based on an earlier translation from the Greek by Jan Blahoslav (1564).

[43] This third-century compilation was regarded as authentic even by Jerome (*On Illustrious Men*, 12). For an English translation see Hennecke-Schneemelcher-Wilson, *New Testament Apocrypha*, II, pp. 133–141.

[44] In his *Welche Bücher heilig und biblisch sind* (Wittenberg, 1521), a popular version of *De canonicis libris libellus* (Wittenberg, 1520).

[45] Erasmus, on Col. 4:16: 'it is not for any Tom, Dick or Harry to copy the mind of Paul.'

[46] The mere fact of its omission from Luther's New Testament was its sufficient quietus in the lands of the Reformation. It had already been omitted from the list of New Testament books published by the Council of Florence about 1440 (see p. 104).

CHAPTER TWENTY

THE NEW TESTAMENT CANON IN THE AGE OF PRINTING

BEFORE LUTHER

The dimensions of the New Testament canon were not seriously affected by the fifteenth-century revival of learning and the sixteenth-century Reformation. This is the more noteworthy because one of the features of these movements in the field of literature was the detection and exposure of hallowed forgeries. The most notorious of these was Laurentius Valla's demonstration of the spurious character of the so-called 'Donation of Constantine', the alleged justification for the secular dominion of the Papacy. In addition to this demonstration (so convincingly done that it required no repetition), Valla (1406/7–57) disproved the authenticity of the traditional correspondence between Christ and King Abgar of Edessa,[1] of the *Letter of Lentulus* (a thirteenth-century work purporting to give a contemporary description of the person of Christ),[2] of the fifth/sixth-century corpus of Neoplatonic treatises ascribed to Dionysius the Areopagite (Acts 17:34); he also exploded the legend which told how each of the apostles had con-

[1] First recorded in Eusebius, *Hist. Eccl.* 1.13.1–22; 2.1.6–8. See W. Bauer, 'The Abgar Legend', in Hennecke-Schneemelcher-Wilson, *New Testament Apocrypha*, I, pp.437–443.
[2] Translated in M. R. James, *The Apocryphal New Testament* (Oxford, 1924). pp.477f.

tributed a clause to the Apostles' Creed.[3] These activities did not endear Valla to the upholders of tradition for tradition's sake, but Valla had a powerful protector in King Alfonso V of Aragon, whose secretary he was (later, however, he became apostolic secretary to Pope Nicholas V).

It was not for nothing that Cardinal Bellarmine later described Valla as a 'precursor of Luther'.[4] At his death Valla left in manuscript a series of annotations on the New Testament. When Erasmus came upon a copy of this manuscript nearly fifty years later, he found that Valla had anticipated much of his own thinking and published the work at Paris in 1505. Valla showed little patience with theologians who wrote on the New Testament without paying any attention to the Greek text. These were Erasmus's own sentiments, but it was expedient that the odium which their publication would inevitably incur should fall on the dead Valla and not on the living Erasmus.

The study of the New Testament in Greek, which now became more accessible in the west, was bound to make an impact on all phases of biblical study. The Greek text was printed as part of the New Testament volume of the *Complutensian Polyglot* in Spain in 1514, but it remained unpublished until the whole work, in six volumes, was published in (probably) 1522.[5] By that time Erasmus had published two printed editions of the Greek New Testament (1516, 1519), and in 1522 a third edition appeared. There was no problem about the contents of the New Testament in these new editions: the twenty-seven established books were reproduced in them all, no more and no less. But questions within the canon were reopened. Erasmus denied the Pauline authorship of Hebrews and questioned the traditional authorship of the five 'disputed' catholic epistles; he thought also that on grounds of style the Apocalypse could not be attributed to the author of the Fourth Gospel.

His contemporary Cardinal Cajetan (Jacob Thomas de Vio), an able

---

[3] On the origins of this legend (possibly going back to Ambrose of Milan) see A. A. T. Ehrhardt, 'Christianity before the Apostles' Creed', in *The Framework of the New Testament Stories* (Manchester, 1964), pp. 151f.

[4] Quoted by J. A. Wagenmann in P. Schaff (ed.), *Religious Encyclopaedia* (New York, 1894), p. 1286.

[5] The first four volumes contained the Hebrew, Latin (Vulgate) and Greek (Septuagint) texts of the Old Testament in parallel columns, with the Aramaic Targum of Onkelos to the Pentateuch printed at the foot of the appropriate pages, with a Latin translation. The sixth volume contained a Hebrew lexicon and grammar.

exegete, likewise denied the Pauline authorship of Hebrews and questioned the traditional authorship of James, 2 and 3 John, and Jude; he defended the apostolic authorship of 2 Peter. Like Valla, he insisted that the study of the Vulgate was no substitute for the study of the scriptures in their original languges; for this in particular he was censured by the University of Paris.[6]

LUTHER'S NEW TESTAMENT

It was Cajetan who, as papal legate, examined Martin Luther at Augsburg in 1518 and tried in vain to gain his submission to the authority of the Pope. Luther's own views on the New Testament canon gained wide currency with the publication of his German New Testament in 1522. (The Greek basis for his translation was Erasmus's second edition of 1519.) The table of contents suggested that he distinguished two levels of canonicity in the New Testament: the names of the first twenty-three books (Matthew — 3 John) are preceded by serial numbers 1–23; the remaining four books — Hebrews, James, Jude and Revelation — are separated from those by a space and are given no serial number. Luther did not exclude the last four books from the canon, but he did not recognize in them the high quality of 'the right certain capital books', and expressed his opinion forthrightly in his individual prefaces to these books. In his preface to Hebrews it is plain that he had given up the traditional Pauline authorship: it was written, he says, by 'an excellent man of learning, who had been a disciple of the apostles and had learned from them, and who was very well versed in scripture'. (By 1537 he was sure that this 'excellent man of learning' was Apollos.[7]) It is in his preface to James in his 1522 New Testament that he calls it 'an epistle of straw'. He finds that it contradicts Paul and the other scriptures on justification by faith, and, while it promotes law, it does not promote Christ. Jude is a superfluous document: it is an abstract of 2 Peter. (Nowadays it would be generally agreed that 2 Peter is based on Jude, not *vice versa*.) Moreover, Jude is suspect because it contains history and teaching nowhere found in scripture (this is a reference to the Enoch quotation and the dispute

[6] On Erasmus and Cajetan see B. Hall, 'Biblical Scholarship: Editions and Commentaries', *CHB* III, pp.38–93, *passim*.

[7] Luther ascribes the work to Apollos in a sermon of 1537 on 1 Cor. 3:4ff. (*Luthers Werke*, Weimar edition, 45, p.389) and again in his Commentary on Genesis, 1545 (Weimar edition, 44, p.709).

about the body of Moses). As for Revelation, it 'lacks everything that I hold as apostolic or prophetic'.[8]

Luther knew that those books had been disputed in earlier days: that, however, is not his main reason for relegating them to a secondary status. He appears to have had no difficulty with 2 Peter or 2 and 3 John, which had also been disputed. His main reason is that in the four relegated books he could not find that clear promotion of Christ which was the principal note of holy scripture.[9] If one asked for Luther's criterion of canonicity (or at least primary canonicity), it is here. 'That which does not teach Christ is still not apostolic, even if it were the teaching of Peter or Paul. On the other hand, that which preaches Christ, that would be apostolic even if Judas, Annas, Pilate or Herod did it.'[10]

'The conclusion', says Roland H. Bainton, 'was a hierarchy of values within the New Testament. First Luther would place the Gospel of John, then the Pauline epistles and First Peter, after them the three other Gospels, and in a subordinate place Hebrews, James, Jude and Revelation. He mistrusted Revelation because of its obscurity. "A revelation", said he, "should be revealing".'[11] (There are some omissions in Bainton's summary: probably Acts would go along with the Synoptic Gospels, the Johannine letters with the Fourth Gospel, and — more doubtfully — 2 Peter with 1 Peter.)

The recognition of an 'inner canon' within the wider canon has persisted in the Lutheran tradition to the present day: the 'inner canon' is a Pauline canon. As Bainton goes on to say, 'the New Testament was for Luther a Pauline book'.[12] So it was for Marcion, but Luther was no Marcionite: for him 'the Old Testament was a Christian book'.[13] It could not be otherwise: it was an Old Testament text that set him on the road to peace with God: 'in thy righteousness deliver me' (Ps 31:1).[14]

---

[8] These prefaces are printed in the Weimar edition, *Die deutsche Bibel*, 7, pp.344f. (Hebrews), 384f. (James), 387 (Jude), 404 (Revelation).

[9] His expression is *was Christum treibet*, 'what presses Christ home', 'what promotes Christ'.

[10] Preface to James.

[11] R. H. Bainton, *Here I Stand: A Life of Martin Luther* (New York/Nashville, 1950), p.332. Luther evidently did not find Revelation to be (as the title of a book by Vernard Eller puts it) *The Most Revealing Book of the Bible* (Grand Rapids, 1974).

[12] Bainton, *ibid*.   [13] Bainton, *ibid*.

[14] From the preface to the Wittenberg edition of his Latin works, translated in *Luther's Works*, American edition, 34 (Philadelphia, 1960), pp.336f.

Luther's contemporary Karlstadt wrote a little work on the canon of scripture in which he distinguished three grades in the New Testament: (1) the Gospels and Acts, (2) the Pauline letters with 1 Peter and 1 John, (3) Hebrews, James, 2 Peter, 2 and 3 John, Jude, Revelation. To him the authorship of Hebrews was unknown, the authorship of James was doubtful, while he followed Jerome in ascribing 2 and 3 John to the elder John, not to the evangelist.[15]

TYNDALE'S NEW TESTAMENT

In the later part of 1525 the printing of William Tyndale's English translation of the New Testament was begun in Cologne.[16] When ten sheets (80 quarto pages) had been printed, the printer (Peter Quentel) was forbidden by the city authorities to proceed with the work. It had to be printed again from the beginning—this time by a Worms printer, Peter Schoeffler, who was able to complete the work by the end of February 1526. Two copies of this Worms octavo survive, but the table of contents is missing from both.[17] But 64 pages of the Cologne quarto are extant in a copy in the British Museum,[18] and they include the table of contents, which is set out as follows:

The bokes conteyned in the
newe Testament

i	The gospell of saynct Mathew
ii	The gospell of S. Marke
iii	The gospell of S. Luke
iiii	The gospell of S. Jhon
v	The actes of the apostles written by S. Luke
vi	The epistle of S. Paul to the Romans

---

[15] Karlstadt, *De canonicis libris libellus* (Wittenberg, 1520); German edition, *Welche Bücher heilig und biblisch sind* (Wittenberg, 1521); see B. M. Metzger, *The Canon of the New Testament*, pp.241f.

[16] Its basis was the third edition of Erasmus's Greek New Testament (1522). This was the first edition in which Erasmus (under protest) included the spurious text about the three heavenly witnesses (1 John 5:7); accordingly, it appeared in Tyndale's version and in succeeding English versions throughout the following century, including AV/KJV.

[17] A facsimile edition, *William Tyndale's New Testament 1526*, was published by Paradine Reprints, London, in 1976, to mark its 450th anniversary.

[18] A facsimile of these 64 pages is included in *The First Printed English New Testament*, ed. E. Arber (London, 1871).

vii	The fyrst pistle of S. Paul to the Corrinthians
viii	The second pistle of S. Paul to the Corrinthians
ix	The pistle of S. Paul to the Galathians
x	The pistle of S. Paul to the Ephesians
xi	The pistle of S. Paul to the Philippians
xii	The pistle of S. Paul to the Collossians
xiii	The fyrst pistle of S. Paul vnto the Tessalonians
xiiii	The seconde pistle of S. Paul vnto the Tessalonians
xv	The fyrst pistle of S. Paul to Timothe
xvi	The seconde pistle of S. Paul to Timothe
xvii	The pistle of S. Paul to Titus
xviii	Te pistle of S. Paul vnto Philemon
xix	The fyrst pistle of S. Peter
xx	The seconde pistle of S. Peter
xxi	The fyrst pistle of S. Jhon
xxii	The seconde pistle of S. Jhon
xxiii	The thryd pistle of S. Jhon

The pistle vnto the Ebrues
The pistle of S. James
The pistle of Jude
The revelacion of Jhon

As in Luther's table of contents, the last four titles are marked off from the others by a space and by the omission of serial numbers in front of them. But we do not know if Tyndale shared Luther's opinion of the inferior status of Hebrews, James, Jude and Revelation. The adoption of Luther's arrangement and title-page layout may have been purely mechanical. The Luther-Tyndale sequence of books was followed by Coverdale's Bible (1535) and Matthew's Bible (1537) and other English editions for the next few years, but the Great Bible of 1539 reverted to the now traditional order with Hebrews and James coming between Philemon and 1 Peter, and this order has been followed by most editions of the English Bible since then.

JOHN CALVIN

Calvin accepted the New Testament canon as it had been handed down. For him the authority of the New Testament, like that of all scripture, rested not on any church decree but on the self-authenticating quality of what was written, attested in the receptive heart by the inward witness of the Holy Spirit.[19] But on questions of authorship he freely exercised his philological and historical judgment. Hebrews was undoubtedly canonical, but it was undoubtedly not by Paul:[20] Calvin thought of Luke or Clement of Rome as a possible author.[21] Unlike Luther, he had no difficulty in accepting James: 'it contains nothing unworthy of an apostle of Christ.' But he would not commit himself positively on the author's identity: he might be James the Just or James the son of Alphaeus, one of the twelve (whom he took to be the 'pillar' James of Gal. 2:9).[22] As for 2 Peter, if it is canonical and therefore trustworthy, it must be accepted as having come from Peter—'not that he wrote it himself, but that one of his disciples composed by his command what the necessity of the times demanded.'[23] 1 John was the work of the beloved disciple.[24] When Jude introduces himself at the beginning of his epistle as 'the brother of James', he refers to James the son of Alphaeus.[25] Calvin's views on the authorship of 2 and 3 John and of Revelation are unknown: he wrote no commentaries on these books, although he quotes occasionally from them.

COUNCIL OF TRENT

When the Council of Trent, at its fourth session (April 1546), dealt with the canon of scripture, it listed the twenty-seven 'received' books of the New Testament. Its position differed from that of the Reformers not with regard to the contents of the New Testament canon but with regard to the according of equal veneration with scripture to the 'unwritten traditions' received ultimately 'from the mouth of Christ himself by the apostles, or from the apostles themselves at the dictation of the Holy Spirit', and also in its specifying the 'ancient and vulgate

[19] Calvin, *Institutes of the Christian Religion*, 1.7.1–5.

[20] Calvin, *The Epistle... to the Hebrews and the First and Second Epistles of Peter*, E. T. (Edinburgh, 1963), p.1.

[21] *Ibid.*, p.216 (on Heb. 13.23).

[22] Calvin, *Commentaries on the Catholic Epistles*, E. T. (Edinburgh, 1855), pp.276f.

[23] *The Epistle... to the Hebrews and the First and Second Epistles of Peter*, p.325.

[24] *The Gospel according to St. John 11–21 and the First Epistle of John*, E. T. (Edinburgh, 1961), p.231.

[25] *Commentaries on the Catholic Epistles*, pp.428f.

edition' of the Latin Bible to be the one authentic text of scripture.[26] Some modern interpreters of this decree of Trent suggest that the Vulgate was here singled out as authoritative over against more recent Latin versions of the Bible and that it was not intended to affirm its primacy over the Hebrew and Greek texts. Some members of the Council, like Cardinal Reginald Pole, thought that the authority of the Hebrew and Greek originals should be explicitly acknowledged. 'The majority considered this to be unnecessary', says E. F. Sutcliffe; but since he mentions that some members of the Council misinterpreted the decree as giving the Vulgate superior authority to the originals, such an acknowledgment would have been by no means superfluous.[27] A century after the Council of Trent the Westminster Assembly of Divines found it expedient to state that 'the Old Testament in Hebrew . . . and the New Testament in Greek . . . , being immediately inspired by God, and by his singular care and providence kept pure in all ages, are therefore authentical; so as in all controversies of religion, the Church is finally to appeal unto them'.[28] If this affirmation was not unnecessary at Westminster, where there was no antecedent bias in favour of the Vulgate, it was certainly not unnecessary at Trent. In any case, issues of contemporary concern and tension affected both what was expressed and what was not expressed. 'Today, . . . Catholics like every one else go back to the original languages and base their translations on the same critical principles'.[29]

THE THIRTY-NINE ARTICLES

After the detailed listing of the books of the Old Testament and Apocrypha in Article VI of the Thirty-Nine Articles, there is a brief statement about the New Testament:[30]

'All the books of the New Testament, as they are commonly received, we do receive, and account them Canonical.'

[26] *Acta Concilii Tridentini*, Sessio 4: *Decretum de canonicis scripturis; Decretum de definitione et usu sacrorum librorum.*

[27] E. F. Sutcliffe, 'The Council of Trent on the *Authentia* of the Vulgate', *JTS* 49 (1948), pp.35–42.

[28] Westminster Confession of Faith, 1.8.

[29] *Revised Standard Version: New Testament*, Catholic Edition (London, 1965), introduction.

[30] See pp.105f.

There was no need to name them one by one: the same twenty-seven books appeared in all relevant editions of the New Testament, in Greek, Latin or English, and in the European vernaculars. When the original Forty-Two Articles were promulgated under Edward VI, the New Testament books were accessible in the Great Bible and exactly the same books remained accessible when the Great Bible was superseded under Elizabeth I by the Geneva Bible of 1560 and the Bishops' Bible of 1568. The churchmen who were responsible for the wording of this Article no doubt knew that at one time five or even seven of the twenty-seven books had been disputed; to that extent it was not quite accurate to say that the canonical books were those 'of whose authority was never any doubt in the Church'. They would know also of Luther's reservations about four of the New Testament books. But such details were irrelevant to the situation with which they had to deal: the recognition of the twenty-seven books went back to Jerome and Augustine, and indeed to Athanasius.

THE WESTMINSTER CONFESSION OF FAITH

Unlike Article VI, the Westminster Confession of Faith included in its first chapter ('Of the Holy Scripture') a precise list of New Testament as well as of Old Testament books. Its list of all the biblical books has been reproduced earlier in our pages.[31] One point which the careful reader of the list of New Testament books will observe is that the Westminster Divines did not commit themselves on the Pauline authorship of Hebrews. The Pauline letters are headed 'Paul's Epistles', followed by 'to the Romans, Corinthians I', and so forth, without the repetition of 'Epistle(s)'; but after Philemon the heading 'Epistle' appears again in 'The Epistle to the Hebrews', which is thus marked off from the thirteen which bear Paul's name.

In the tradition of Calvin, the Westminster Confession denies that the authority of scripture rests 'upon the testimony of any man or church'; rather, 'our full persuasion and assurance of the infallible truth, and divine authority thereof, is from the inward work of the Holy Spirit, bearing witness by and with the word in our hearts.' While due allowance is made for the place of reason in the study of scripture and for the acceptance of whatever may be deduced from it 'by good and necessary consequence', yet 'nothing at any time is to be

[31] See p. 109.

added' to it, 'whether by new revelations of the Spirit, or traditions of men'. The canon of scripture is a closed canon. 'Nevertheless, we acknowledge the inward illumination of the Spirit of God to be necessary for the saving understanding of such things as are revealed in the word', but practical matters like church administration and the conduct of worship 'are to be ordered by the light of nature and Christian prudence, according to the general rules of the word'.[32]

A FIXED CANON

That the New Testament consists of the twenty-seven books which have been recognized as belonging to it since the fourth century is not a value judgment; it is a statement of fact. Individuals or communities may consider that it is too restricted or too comprehensive; but their opinion does not affect the identity of the canon. The canon is not going to be diminished or increased because of what they think or say: it is a literary, historical and theological datum.

William Whiston (1667–1752), the eccentric polymath who succeeded Sir Isaac Newton as Professor of Mathematics in Cambridge and who is probably best known in the English-speaking world as translator of the works of Josephus, defended the canonical entitlement of a work called the *Apostolic Constitutions*. This is a fourth-century compilation in eight books, including instruction on church order and worship, which claims to be issued by 'the apostles and elders to all those who from among the Gentiles have believed in the Lord Jesus Christ'. It was first printed at Venice in 1563, and engaged the interest of several scholars in the west.[33] Its date and character were discerned by James Ussher, Archbishop of Armagh (1581–1656), a scholar of uncommon critical ability. Whiston showed his critical incompetence by taking the claims of the *Apostolic Constitutions* at face value: they merited, he said, 'that caution and awful regard to their contents which the Authority of the Apostles of Christ, nay of Christ himself, and of God his Father, so visibly appearing therein does demand from us'; he received them as 'Genuine, Sacred, and Apostolical'.[34]

[32] Westminster Confession of Faith, 1.4, 5, 6.
[33] There is an English translation in ANF, VII, pp.391–505.
[34] W. Whiston, *Primitive Christianity Reviv'd* (London, 1711–12), III, pp.11f., quoted in S. Neill, *The Interpretation of the New Testament 1861–1961* (Oxford, 1964), p.46, n.1.

But even if Whiston's belief in the authenticity of this work had been as well founded was it as ill founded, there was no way in which it could have been added to the accepted canon of the New Testament in the sixteenth or seventeenth century. The same may be said about other suggestions which have been made from time to time for the addition of this document or the removal of that. Theologians may operate with the concept of an 'inner canon', but one person's inner canon will differ from another's. The most disputed of all the disputed books of the New Testament is probably 2 Peter, but the New Testament would be poorer without it: there are those who have seen the high-water-mark of the Christian revelation in its statement that God's purpose is that his people should 'become partakers of the divine nature' (2 Pet. 1:4). [35]

Again, private enterprise will provide editions of the gospels which include one or more of the Nag Hammadi documents along with some or all of the canonical gospels; or compilers of gospel harmonies or synopses will produce handbooks in which passages, say, from the *Gospel of Thomas* are presented in parallel columns with comparable passages from the New Testament books. These works may be useful to the student; they are irrelevant to the question of the canon. The literary critic of early Christian writings will probably find little help in the distinction between those of them which are canonical and those which are not; but the distinction is important for the theologian and the church member. Indeed, if the voice of God is heard in the Bible as it is heard in no other book, the canon has a relevance for all to whom the word of God is addressed.

[35] See W. R. Inge, *Things New and Old* (London, 1933), p.36.

PART FOUR

CONCLUSION

CHAPTER TWENTY-ONE

CRITERIA OF CANONICITY

TESTS IN THE APOSTOLIC AGE

The earliest Christians did not trouble themselves about criteria of canonicity; they would not have readily understood the expression. They accepted the Old Testament scriptures as they had received them: the authority of those scriptures was sufficiently ratified by the teaching and example of the Lord and his apostles. The teaching and example of the Lord and his apostles, whether conveyed by word of mouth or in writing, had axiomatic authority for them.

Criteria of a kind, however, were found to be desirable quite early. When prophets, for example, claimed to speak in the Lord's name, it became necessary to 'discern the spirits' by which they spoke. Some members of the church were given 'the ability to distinguish between spirits' (1 Cor. 12:10). According to Paul, the decisive criterion to apply to prophets is their testimony to Christ: 'no one can say "Jesus is Lord" except by the Holy Spirit' (1 Cor. 12:3). Somewhat later, John suggests a more specific test: 'every spirit which confesses that Jesus Christ has come in the flesh is of God' (1 Jn. 4:2). Such tests anticipated the later insistence on orthodoxy as a criterion of canonicity.

Again, when Paul suspected that letters were circulating in his name which were none of his, he gave his friends a simple criterion by which his genuine letters could be recognized although he regularly dictated his letters to amanuenses, he took the pen himself to write the final greetings—sometimes, but not necessarily, accompanied by his actual signature (*cf* 1 Cor. 16:21; Gal. 6:11; Col. 4:18; 2 Thess. 3:17; also Philem. 19). Paul's handwriting was evidently so distinctive that it could not be easily forged. This was, of course, a temporary criterion of authenticity. No document containing Paul's handwriting has survived to our day, and even if one had survived, the handwriting would not be recognizable as his at this late date.

APOSTOLIC AUTHORITY

Since Jesus himself left nothing in writing, the most authoritative writings available to the church were those which came from his apostles. Among his apostles none was more active in writing (as well as otherwise) than Paul. There were some in Paul's own day, and a few in later generations, who questioned his right to be called an apostle, but throughout the churches of the Gentiles his apostleship was generally undoubted—inevitably so, because a number of those churches would not have existed except for his apostolic ministry.[1] The authority of his authentic letters continued to be acknowledged after his death, not only by the churches to which they were severally addressed but by the churches as a whole. It is not surprising that Paul's letters were among the first, if not absolutely the first, of our New Testament documents to be gathered together and to circulate as a collection.

Letters in antiquity normally began with the writer's name, and so did Paul's letters. But many of the New Testament documents do not contain the writers' names: they are strictly anonymous—to us, completely anonymous. The writer to Theophilus was well enough known to Theophilus,[2] but his name has not been preserved either in the Third Gospel or in Acts; to us, therefore, these two works are anonymous. Traditionally they are ascribed to Luke, but if we wish to examine the validity of this tradition, we have to consider which Luke is meant, and what the probability is of their being the work of that Luke.

Similarly, the recipients of the letter to the Hebrews no doubt were well acquainted with its author (in *that* sense they would not have

[1] See Paul's argument in 2 Cor. 3:1–3: the existence of the church of Corinth was the only letter of accreditation he needed—at Corinth.
[2] See Lk. 1:3; Acts 1:1.

regarded it as an anonymous communication), but since it does not bear his name, his identity was forgotten after a generation or two, and has never been certainly recovered.

From the second century onward, two of the four Gospels were ascribed to apostles—to Matthew and John. Whether Marcion knew of this ascription or not we cannot say, but if he did, that in itself would have deprived them of all Christian authority in his eyes: these two men belonged to the group which, he believed, had corrupted the pure message of Jesus. An eccentric churchman like Gaius of Rome might ascribe the Fourth Gospel to Cerinthus,[3] but the views of eccentric churchmen have never disturbed the general consensus.

It is remarkable, when one comes to think of it, that the four canonical Gospels are anonymous, whereas the 'Gospels' which proliferated in the late second century and afterwards claim to have been written by apostles and other eyewitnesses. Catholic churchmen found it necessary, therefore, to defend the apostolic authenticity of the Gospels which they accepted against the claims of those which they rejected. Hence come the accounts of the origin of the canonical four which appear in the Muratorian list, in the so-called anti-Marcionite prologues, and in Irenaeus. The apostolic authorship of Matthew and John was well established in tradition. But what of Mark and Luke? Their authorship was also well established in tradition, but it was felt desirable to buttress the authority of tradition with arguments which gave those two Gospels a measure of apostolic validation. As early as Papias, Mark is said to have set down in writing Peter's account of the sayings and doings of the Lord, and Peter's apostolic authority was not in doubt.[4] As for Luke's Gospel, its author was early identified with the man whom Paul calls 'Luke, the beloved physician' (Col. 4:14). This meant that he was one of Paul's associates, and something of Paul's apostolic authority rubbed off on him.[5] Some, identifying Luke with the unnamed 'brother' of 2 Corinthians 8:18 'whose praise is in the gospel', went so far as to see in these words of Paul a reference to the Gospel of Luke, if they did not indeed go farther still and see a reference to it in Paul's mention of 'my gospel' (Rom. 2:16; 16:25; 2 Tim. 2:8).[6] Fortunately, the value of Luke's Gospel can be vindicated with stronger arguments than these; but the fact that these were the

---

[3] See p. 168.   [4] See pp. 124f., 308–310.
[5] 'Not an apostle but apostolic', says Tertullian of Luke (*Against Marcion,* 4.2.4).
[6] See pp. 161, 226.

arguments used in its defence in the second and third centuries shows how important some degree of apostolic authorization seemed to be for the books which the church accepted as uniquely authoritative.

The fortunes of the letter to the Hebrews provide a further example of the importance attached to apostolic authority (if not authorship). Those who (like the church of Alexandria) accepted this letter as the work of Paul recognized it without more ado as canonical. If someone with a critical faculty like Origen's realized that, as it stood, this document was not Paul's work, a way round this offered itself: the Greek text indeed was not Paul's (perhaps it was Luke's), but a Hebrew work of Paul lay behind it.[7] (An even better developed critical faculty might have indicated that Hebrews was not written in translation-Greek.) Those who (like well-informed members of the Roman church) knew that the work was not Paul's, esteemed it highly as an edifying document handed down from the early age of the church, but did not accept it as apostolic. When at last, in the fourth century, the church of Rome was persuaded to fall into line with the other churches and recognize Hebrews as canonical, a natural tendency followed to treat it as Pauline also—but Pauline with a qualification. 'I am moved rather by the prestige of the eastern churches', said Augustine, 'to include this epistle too among the canonical writings';[8] but he had reservations about its authorship. Like his older contemporary Jerome, he distinguished between canonicity and apostolic authorship.[9]

Even at an earlier period, apostolic authorship in the direct sense was not insisted on, if some form of apostolic authority could be established. Membership of the holy family apparently carried with it near-apostolic status: Paul indeed seems to include James the Lord's brother among the apostles (Gal. 1:19)—but so far as James was concerned there was the further consideration that to him, as to Paul himself, the Lord had appeared in resurrection (1 Cor. 15:7). If therefore the James who names himself as author of the letter addressed 'to the twelve tribes in the Dispersion' was identified with the Lord's brother, that was good enough reason for accepting the letter among the apostolic writings. And if 'Jude, a servant of Jesus Christ and brother of James' was indicated in those words to be another member of the holy family, that was sufficient to tip the balance in favour of

[7] See pp. 192f.
[8] Augustine, *Epistle* 129.3; *cf On the Deserts and Remission of Sins,* 1.50.
[9] See pp. 226f., 232.

accepting the short letter so superscribed, especially in view of the 'words of heavenly grace' of which (as Origen said) it was full.[10]

The early church knew several works claiming the authority of Peter's name.[11] Among these no difficulty was felt about 1 Peter; its attestation goes back to the first half of the second century, and it was handed down as one of the undisputed books.[12] There was considerable hesitation about 2 Peter, but by the time of Athanasius it was no longer a disputed book in the Alexandrian church or in western Christendom. Its explicit claim to be the work of the apostle Peter was probably felt to be supported by the fact that it contained nothing unworthy of him.

Among the Johannine writings 1 John was always closely associated with the Fourth Gospel: if the Gospel was acknowledged to be apostolic and canonical, so was this epistle, although it was as anonymous as the Gospel. Those who doubted the apostolic authorship of 2 and 3 John[13] and the Apocalypse tended to doubt their canonical status also. The disinclination to accept the Apocalypse was due not mainly to doubts about the identity of the John who wrote it with John the apostle; it was due much more to the antipathy which was widely felt in the Greek world to its millenarianism.[14] Dionysius of Alexandria, who ascribed it on grounds of literary criticism to another John than the apostle and evangelist, acknowledged it to be a genuine work of prophecy.[15]

Two aspects of the apostolic criterion were themselves used as subsidiary criteria—antiquity and orthodoxy.

ANTIQUITY

If a writing was the work of an apostle or of someone closely associated with an apostle, it must belong to the apostolic age. Writings of later date, whatever their merit, could not be included among the apostolic or canonical books. The compiler of the Muratorian list had a high regard for the *Shepherd* of Hermas; he recognized it evidently as a

---

[10] See pp. 193f.

[11] In addition to the canonical epistles of Peter there are the *Gospel, Acts, Apocalypse, Judgment* and *Preaching of Peter*, the *Epistle of Peter to James* (in the pseudo-Clementine literature), and the *Epistle of Peter to Philip* (one of the Nag Hammadi treatises).

[12] This statement is not affected by its omission from the Muratorian list, which is a problem on any dating of the list.

[13] See pp. 193, 220.   [14] As with Eusebius (see p. 199).   [15] See pp. 195f.

genuine work of prophecy. However, it had appeared too late to be included among the canonical prophets; and equally it had appeared too late to be included among the apostolic writings, for it was written only the day before yesterday, so to speak.[16]

This argument could have been employed more freely than it was in settling problems of authenticity, at a time when so many works were appearing which claimed to have been written by apostles and their associates. But perhaps most of the churchmen who concerned themselves with this problem lacked the information or the expertise to appeal confidently to the evidence for dating such documents: they preferred to judge them by their theology.

ORTHODOXY

In other words, they had recourse to the criterion of orthodoxy. By 'orthodoxy' they meant the apostolic faith—the faith set forth in the undoubted apostolic writings and maintained in the churches which had been founded by apostles. This appeal to the testimony of the churches of apostolic foundation was developed specially by Irenaeus.[17] Whatever differences of emphasis may be discerned by modern students within the *corpus* of New Testament writings, these are irrelevant to the issues which confronted churchmen of the second and third centuries. They had to defend the apostolic teaching, summed up in the rule of faith,[18] against the docetic and gnostic presentations which were so attractive to many in the climate of opinion at that time. When previously unknown Gospels or Acts began to circulate under the authority of apostolic names, the most important question to ask about any one of them was: What does it teach about the person and work of Christ? Does it maintain the apostolic witness to him as the historical Jesus of Nazareth, crucified and raised from the dead, divinely exalted as Lord over all?

A good example of the application of this test is provided by the case of Bishop Serapion and the *Gospel of Peter*. When Serapion found that this document was being read in the church of Rhossus, he was not greatly disturbed; he certainly did not examine its style and vocabulary (as Dionysius of Alexandria might have done) to see if its claim to be the work of Peter or a product of the apostolic age was well founded or not. But when he discovered that its account of the Lord's death was

[16] See p. 166.   [17] See pp. 171f.   [18] See p. 150.

tinged with docetism (it implies that he did not really suffer), then he decided that he ought to pay the church of Rhossus a pastoral visit to make sure that it had not been led astray by this heterodox teaching.[19]

Other 'Petrine' literature circulating among the churches was equally unauthentic, but since it did not inculcate heresy, it caused no great concern. The Muratorian compiler, for example, seems to draw upon the *Acts of Peter* (which gave an account of the apostle's Roman ministry and execution)[20] and he expressly includes the *Apocalypse of Peter* in his list (although he concedes that some refused to let it be read in church).[21] But in due course the non-apostolic character of these works became sufficiently evident to ensure that they did not find a permanent place in the New Testament canon.

It is doubtful if any book would have found a place in the canon if it had been *known* to be pseudonymous. The *Acts of Paul,* one of the earliest exercises in Christian novel-writing, dating from shortly after the middle of the second century, was orthodox enough, and indeed quite edifying (especially to those who believed that celibacy was a superior state of life to matrimony). It was not pseudonymous, for its author was known; but it was fictitious, and unworthy of the great apostle for love of whom it was said to have been written; the author was therefore deposed from his office as presbyter in one of the churches of Asia.[22] Anyone who was known to have composed a work explicitly in the name of an apostle would have met with even greater disapproval.

CATHOLICITY

A work which enjoyed only local recognition was not likely to be acknowledged as part of the canon of the catholic church. On the other hand, a work which was acknowledged by the greater part of the catholic church would probably receive universal recognition sooner or later. We have seen how the Roman church ultimately consented to receive Hebrews as canonical so as not to be out of step with the rest of orthodox Christendom.[23]

It might have been argued that the letters of Paul were too local and

---

[19] Eusebius, *Hist. Eccl.* 6.12.3 (see pp.200f.)   [20] See p.163.

[21] See p.164. According to the church historian Sozomen (writing between 439 and 450), the *Apocalypse of Peter* was read in his day on Good Friday in some Palestinian churches (*Hist. Eccl.* 7.19).

[22] See p.163, 202.   [23] See p.221, 258.

occasional in character to be accepted as universally and permanently authoritative.[24] The issues to which he addressed himself in the letters to the Galatians and the Corinthians, for example, were of temporary urgency in the churches to which those letters were sent. How could their inclusion among the scriptures of the catholic church be justified? The earliest answer given to this question was one which was evidently found satisfactory at the time, although to us it seems curiously far-fetched. It was this: Paul wrote letters to seven churches, and in view of the symbolic significance of the number seven, that means that he wrote for the church universal.[25] The same conception of seven as the number of perfection was applied to the seven churches addressed in the Apocalypse. Indeed, the compiler of the Muratorian list preposterously regards John as setting the precedent in this regard which Paul followed: in both sets of letters, what was written to seven was spoken to all. Even Paul's letters to individuals have an ecumenical reference, says the Muratorian compiler: 'they have been hallowed for the honour of the catholic church in the regulation of ecclesiastical discipline.'[26]

Each individual document that was ultimately acknowledged as canonical started off with local acceptance — the various epistles in the places to which they were sent, the Apocalypse in the seven churches of Asia, even the Gospels and Acts in the constituencies for which they were first designed. But their attainment of canonical status was the result of their gaining more widespread recognition than they initially enjoyed.

TRADITIONAL USE

Catholicity has been classically defined in the fifth-century 'Vincentian canon' as 'what has been believed everywhere, always, by all'.[27] What has always been believed (or practised) is the most potent factor in the maintenance of tradition. Suggested innovations have regularly been resisted with the argument 'But this is what we have always been taught' or 'what we have always done'. It was so in the

---

[24] See N. A. Dahl, 'The Particularity of the Pauline Epistles as a Problem in the Ancient Church', in *Neotestamentica et Patristica,* ed. W. C. van Unnik = NovTSup 6 (Leiden, 1962), pp.261–271.

[25] See pp.164, 184.   [26] See pp.160, 164.

[27] Vincent of Lérins, *Commonitorium* ('Notebook'), 2.3: *quod ubique, quod semper, quod ab omnibus creditum est.*

early Christian centuries with the recognition of certain books as holy scripture, and it is still so (whether this is consciously realized or not). The reading of 'memoirs of the apostles' in church along with the Old Testament writings (to which Justin Martyr bears witness)[28] became an established practice which made it easy to accord to those 'memoirs' the same formal status as that accorded from the church's earliest days to the law and the prophets. If any church leader came along in the third or fourth century with a previously unknown book, recommending it as genuinely apostolic, he would have found great difficulty in gaining acceptance for it: his fellow-Christians would simply have said, 'But no one has ever heard of it!' (We may think, for example, of the widespread hesitation in accepting 2 Peter.) [29] Or, even if the book had been known for some generations, but had never been treated as holy scripture, it would have been very difficult to win recognition for it as such.

When William Whiston, in the eighteenth century, argued that the *Apostolic Constitutions* should be venerated among the New Testament writings, few if any took him seriously.[30] For one thing, Whiston's eccentricities were well known; for another thing, better judges than he had discerned its fourth-century date. But, even if Whiston had been a model of judicious sobriety, and even if strong reasons could have been adduced for dating the *Apostolic Constitutions* in the first century, there would have been no possibility of the work's being added to the canon: the tradition of all the churches would have been too strong.

INSPIRATION

For many centuries inspiration and canonicity have been closely bound up together in Christian thinking: books were included in the canon, it is believed, because they were inspired; a book is known to be inspired because it is in the canon.

How far was this so in the early church? One distinguished student of the early history of the canon has said that 'apostolicity was the

[28] See pp. 126f.

[29] *Cf* Eusebius, *Hist. Eccl.* 3.3.1: 'But the so-called second epistle [of Peter] we have not received as canonical ("intestamented"); nevertheless it has appeared useful to many, and has been studied with the other scriptures.'

[30] See p. 250.

principal token of canonicity for the west, inspiration for the east' —
not indeed in a mutually exclusive sense, since 'in the west apostolicity
to a certain extent includes inspiration, while in the east apostolicity
was an attendant feature of inspiration'. In Origen's view, for example,
'the crucial point . . . is not apostolicity but inspiration'.[31]

By inspiration in this sense is meant that operation of the Holy
Spirit by which the prophets of Israel were enabled to utter the word of
God. The vocabulary was theirs; the message was his. Only to certain
individuals, and only occasionally to them, was this enablement
granted. But in the New Testament age the situation was different.

On one occasion, when Moses was told that two men were
prophesying who had not received any public commission to do so, he
replied, 'Would that all the Lord's people were prophets, that the Lord
would put his spirit upon them!' (Num. 11:29). The New Testament
records the answer to Moses' prayer, telling how, on the first Christian
Pentecost, God initiated the fulfilment of his promise to pour out his
Spirit 'on all flesh' (Joel 2:28, quoted in Acts 2:17). All members of
the new community of believers in Jesus received the Spirit: 'any one
who does not have the Spirit of Christ', says Paul, 'does not belong to
him' (Rom. 8:9). This did not mean that all of them received the
specific gift of prophecy: the gift of prophecy — of declaring the mind
of God in the power of the Spirit — was but one of several gifts of the
Spirit distributed among members of the church.[32]

Only one of the New Testament writers expressly bases the authority
of what he says on prophetic inspiration. The Apocalypse is called 'the
book of this prophecy' (e.g., Rev. 22:19); the author implies that his
words are inspired by the same Spirit of prophecy as spoke through the
prophets of earlier days: it is in their succession that he stands (Rev.
22:9). 'The testimony of Jesus is the Spirit of prophecy' (Rev. 19:10):
the prophets of old bore witness to Jesus in advance, and the same
witness is still borne, in the power of the same Spirit, not only by a
prophet like John but by all the faithful confessors who overcome the
enemy 'by the blood of the Lamb and by the word of their testimony'
(Rev. 12:11). The readers of the seven letters at the outset of the book
are expected to hear in them 'what the Spirit says to the churches'
(Rev. 2:7, etc.). Whether the seer of Patmos was the son of Zebedee or

---

[31] Ellen Flesseman-van Leer, 'Prinzipien der Sammlung und Ausscheidung bei der
Bildung des Kanons', *ZTK* 61 (1964), pp.415f. For Origen see p. 195 above.
[32] See 1 Cor. 12:4, 7–11.

not, his appeal throughout the Apocalypse is not to apostolic authority but to prophetic inspiration.

It is plain that at the beginning of the Christian era the inspiration of the prophetic oracles of the Old Testament was believed to extend to the Old Testament scriptures as a whole. The writer to the Hebrews sees the Holy Spirit as the primary author not only of the warning of Psalm 95:7–11, 'Today, when you hear his voice...' (Heb. 3:7–11), but also of the structure and ritual of the Mossaic tabernacle (Heb. 9:8). Timothy is reminded, with regard to the sacred writings which he has known from childhood, that 'all scripture is inspired by God and profitable' for a variety of purposes (2 Tim. 3:15–17). When the New Testament writings were later included with the Old Testament as part of 'all scripture', it was natural to conclude that they too were 'inspired by God'. That they were (and are) so inspired is not to be denied, but most of the New Testament writers do not base their authority on divine inspiration.

Paul, for example, claims to have 'the mind of Christ'; his gospel preaching, he says, was attended by 'demonstration of the Spirit' (which was the secret of its effectiveness), and his instruction was imparted 'in words not taught by human wisdom but taught by the Spirit' (1 Cor. 2:14–16).[33] But when he needs to assert his authority—authority 'for building up and not for tearing down' (2 Cor. 13:10)—he rests it on the apostolic commission which he had received from the exalted Lord. In his exercise of this authority, he told the Corinthian Christians, they would find the proof which they demanded 'that Christ is speaking in me' (2 Cor. 13:3).

John the evangelist implies, by his report of the Lord's promises regarding the Paraclete in the upper-room discourses, that he himself in his witness experiences the Spirit's guidance 'into all the truth' as he brings to the disciples' remembrance what the Lord had said and makes its meaning plain (Jn 14:26; 16:12–15). Luke, for his part, claims no more than to give a reliable account in his twofold work, based on eyewitness testimony and on his own participation in the course of the events which he narrates (Lk. 1:1–4). The patristic idea that his Gospel owes something to the apostolic authority of Paul is

---

[33] Compare his semi-ironical remark, 'I think that I have the Spirit of God' (1 Cor. 7:40). But when he charges discerning Christians at Corinth to acknowledge that what he writes 'is a command of the Lord' (1 Cor. 14:37), this is an exercise of apostolic authority.

quite unfounded.[34] As for Mark, the tradition that his record is based (in part at least) on the preaching of Peter may have a foundation in fact,[35] but no appeal is made to Peter's authority in the course of the record. Neither is any appeal made to divine inspiration.

'If the writings of Mark and Luke are to be judged canonical', said N. B. Stonehouse, 'it must be because these evangelists were controlled by the Spirit of the Lord in such a manner that their writings, and not merely the apostolic message which they set forth, are divine. In other words, it is Mark's inspiration (which, to be sure, is not to be isolated from his historical qualifications), and not Peter's inspiration, which provides the finally indispensable ground for the acceptance of that work as canonical.'[36] On this be it said, again, that the divine inspiration of the Gospels of Mark and Luke is not to be denied, but these works were accepted, first as authoritative and then as canonical scripture, because they were recognized to be trustworthy witnesses to the saving events.

Clement of Rome acknowledges that Paul wrote 'with true inspiration'.[37] But he makes similar claims for his own letter. 'You will give us joy and gladness', he tells the Corinthians as he draws to a conclusion, 'if you are obedient to the things which we have written through the Holy Spirit.'[38] He is far from putting himself on a level with 'the blessed Paul the apostle',[39] but he and Paul had received the same Spirit. The high authority which he recognizes in Paul is his apostolic authority.

Similarly Ignatius claims to speak and write by the Spirit: he,

---

[34] See pp. 161, 257.

[35] Internal evidence in support of this tradition was presented in C. H. Turner, 'Marcan Usage', *JTS* 25 (1923–24), pp.377–386; 26 (1924–25), pp.12–20, 145–156, 225–240; 27 (1925–26), pp.58–62; 28 (1926–27), pp.9–30, 349–362; 29 (1927–28), pp.275–289, 346–361; and in *A New Commentary on Holy Scripture*, ed. C. Gore (London, 1928), Part II, pp.42–122; see also T. W. Manson, *Studies in the Gospels and Epistles* (Manchester, 1962), pp.28–45.

[36] N. B. Stonehouse, 'The Authority of the New Testament', in *The Infallible Word*, ed. N. B. Stonehouse and P. Woolley (Philadelphia, 1946), p.115.

[37] 1 Clem. 47.3.

[38] 1 Clem. 63.2; *cf* 59.1, where he describes the contents of his letter as 'words spoken by Christ through us'. The freedom with which the idea of inspiration was used by some of the church fathers is well illustrated by a letter from Augustine to Jerome, in which Jerome's biblical interpretation is said to be carried through 'not only by the gift but at the dictation of the Holy Spirit' (Augustine, *Epistle* 82.2 = Jerome, *Epistle* 116.2). See p.281 below with nn.36,37.

[39] 1 Clem. 47.1.

indeed, had the gift of (occasional) prophecy. 'It is not according to the flesh that I write to you', he tells the Roman church, 'but according to the mind of God.'[40] But, as bishop of another church, he has no thought of imposing his authority on the Romans, as he might have done on the Christians of Antioch. 'I do not command you like Peter and Paul', he says: 'they were apostles; I am a convict.'[41] Peter and Paul were also convicts at the end of their time in Rome, it might have been said; but the point is that, even as convicts in the eyes of Roman law, they were apostles in the eyes of the Roman church, and as such entitled to exercise the authority which the Lord had entrusted to them.

When the Muratorian list makes Paul follow the precedent of John in writing to seven churches, it may imply further that the precedent of John's Apocalypse, as a prophetic writing, validated the acceptance of Paul's letters as also prophetic. This has been argued in a well-known essay by Krister Stendahl.[42]

To those who argued that the apostles and evangelists spoke before they possessed 'perfect knowledge' (so that their works required gnostic amplification and interpretation) Irenaeus replied that they wrote after Pentecost: the power of the Holy Spirit with which they were invested then imparted the 'perfect knowledge' necessary for the execution of their commission.[43] The evangelists were the antitype of Ezekiel's four living creatures, animated by the same Spirit.[44]

Irenaeus in some degree, and Origen to a much greater extent, show their belief in the divine inspiration of the New Testament (as well as of the Old Testament) by their allegorical treatment of it. According to R. P. C. Hanson, 'Irenaeus is the first writer to allegorize the New Testament', and he feels free to do so 'because he is among the first writers to treat the New Testament unreservedly as inspired Scripture'.[45] Origen allegorizes both Testaments alike as liberally as his fellow-Alexandrian Philo allegorized the Old Testament two centuries earlier. This means that, instead of reading out of the inspired text what is actually there, he often reads into it what is not

[40] Ignatius, *To the Romans*, 8.3.   [41] *To the Romans*, 4.3.

[42] K. Stendahl, 'The Apocalypse of John and the Epistles of Paul in the Muratorian Fragment', in *Current Issues in New Testament Interpretation*, ed. W. Klassen and G. F. Snyder (New York, 1962), pp.239–245.

[43] Irenaeus, *Against Heresies*, 3.1.1.

[44] *Against Heresies*, 3.11.8 (see p.175 with n.29).

[45] R. P. C. Hanson, *Allegory and Event* (London, 1959), pp.112f.

there. With Origen, as with Philo, this allegorizing treatment was based on the conviction that the text under consideration was inspired word for word: only such an inspired text had a deeper meaning of a kind that allegorization alone could bring out.[46]

But at this stage inspiration is no longer a criterion of canonicity: it is a corollary of canonicity. 'It was not until the red ribbon of the self-evident had been tied around the twenty-seven books of the New Testament that "inspiration" could serve theologians as an answer to the question: Why are these books different from all other books?'[47]

OTHER ISSUES

There were other, more practical, corollaries of canonicity. As we have seen, it was helpful for church officials in times of persecution to distinguish between those books which might, as a last resort, be handed over to the police and those which must be preserved, if need be, at the cost of life itself.[48]

Then there was the question of those books which might properly be read in church. Those which were recognizably vested with the authority of the Lord and the apostles were prescribed for public reading; but in some churches at least other works were read which, although they lacked apostolic authority, were orthodox and edifying. Dionysius, bishop of Corinth, wrote to the bishop of Rome about AD 170 to express the thanks of his church for a letter and a gift which had been received from the Roman church. 'Today', he says, 'we observed the Lord's holy day, and we read out your letter, which we shall keep and read from time to time for our admonition, as we do also with the letter formerly written to us through Clement.'[49] So, between seventy and eighty years after it was sent, 1 Clement continued to be read at services of the Corinthian church. Neither it nor the more recent letter from Rome carried anything like the authority of the letters which the Corinthian church had received from Paul; but they were helpful for the building up of Christian faith and life.[50]

[46] See Hanson, *Allegory and Event*, pp. 187–209. Cf pp. 73, 195 above.
[47] K. Stendahl, 'The Apocalypse of John and the Epistles of Paul. . .', p. 243. See also P. Achtemeier, *The Inspiration of Scripture: Problems and Proposals* (Philadelphia, 1980); A. C. Sundberg, Jr., 'The Bible Canon and the Christian Doctrine of Inspiration', *Interpretation* 29 (1975), p. 352–371.
[48] See pp. 216f.   [49] In Eusebius, *Hist. Eccl.* 4.23.11.
[50] Compare Athanasius's commendation of the *Didachē* and the *Shepherd* (p. 209),

An issue of high importance for theologians in the church was the distinguishing of those books which might be used for settling doctrinal questions from those which were generally edifying. Only those books which carried apostolic authority (together with the Old Testament writings as interpreted in the New) were to be appealed to either for the establishing of truths to be 'most surely believed' in the church or for deciding disputed points in controversies with heretics. In such controversies it was naturally most satisfactory if appeal was made to those writings which both sides acknowledged in common. Tertullian in a legalistic mood might deny the right of heretics to appeal to the holy scriptures,[51] but when he himself engaged in controversy with them, it was on those scriptures that he based his arguments (he could do no other) and he expected his opponents to follow his arguments and admit their force. If the heretics refused to acknowledge the books to which orthodox churchmen appealed, or if they appealed to writings of their own, their error in these respects too had to be exposed; but the unique authority of the canonical writings must be preserved inviolable.

---

also what he and Jerome say about the use of the Old Testament Apocrypha (pp.79, 91f.), and the permission given by the Third Council of Carthage to read the accounts of martyrdoms on the appropriate saints' days (p.233).

[51] *On the Prescription of Heretics* (see p.151). Tertullian felt at times that there was no point in appealing to scripture when dealing with those whose allegorical interpretation was always able to extract from scripture the meaning they desired to find, in defiance of its plain sense. But the language of legal injunction was not the wisest course to adopt with them.

CHAPTER TWENTY-TWO

A CANON WITHIN
THE CANON?

THE 'INNER CANON'

In our survey of the canon of scripture thus far, occasional mention has been made of the idea of a 'canon within the canon'.[1] This is an idea that has received wider support and publicity in more recent times.

In a lecture delivered at Oxford in 1961 Professor Kurt Aland expressed the view that, as the Old Testament canon underwent a *de facto* narrowing as a result of the new covenant established in Christ, so also the New Testament canon 'is *in practice* undergoing a narrowing and a shortening,' so that we can recognize in the New Testament as in the Old a 'canon within the canon'.[2] This is a not unexpected attitude on the part of a scholar in the Lutheran tradition; it is common form, for example, for theologians in that tradition to pass a depreciatory judgment on those parts of the New Testament which smack of 'emergent catholicism' or 'incipient catholicism'.[3] The 'actual living,

---

[1] See pp.244, 251.

[2] K. Aland, *The Problem of the New Testament Canon*, E. T. (London, 1962), pp.27–29.

[3] German *Frühkatholizismus*, a term given to the tendency towards the institutionalizing of church belief and practice. It appears 'again and again in German theology of this century, and always as a term of reproach—a curious example of the way in which we are all influenced by our prepossessions—"Catholic" in English is not ordinarily a term of reprobation' (S. Neill, *The Interpretation of the New Testament 1861–1961* [Oxford, 1964], p.160, n.1).

effective Canon', as distinct from the formal canon, 'is constructed according to the method of "self-understanding".'[4]

But if it is suggested that Christians and churches get together and try to reach agreement on a common effective canon, it must be realized that the 'effective' canon of some groups differs from that of others. Professor Aland wisely spoke of the necessity to question one's own actual canon and take the actual canon of others seriously.[5]

If in the Lutheran tradition, and indeed in the evangelical tradition generally, the four chief Pauline epistles (Romans, 1 and 2 Corinthians, Galatians) play a leading part in the effective canon, there are other Christians for whom Paul's 'captivity epistles' are the New Testament documents most directly relevant to the present age.[6] Others would give the Synoptic Gospels pride of place, and yet others the Johannine writings.

The late Norman Snaith, in his day a distinguished Methodist Old Testament scholar, found pre-eminently in the great prophets of Israel those features of true religion which were to find their finest flowering in the Pauline gospel of justification by faith (later embraced and proclaimed by Luther and the Wesleys). But the message of the prophets had been encased in an iron binding of *habdalah*, 'separation', consisting of the priestly legislation of the Pentateuch at one end and the work of Ezra at the other, which (in his eyes) anticipated those elements in first-century Judaism which were inimical to the gospel of Christ (especially as expounded by Paul).[7] There are others, however, who find in the priestly legislation, especially in its sacrificial and other cultic ordinances, allegorically interpreted, the most wonderful adumbration of the gospel to be found anywhere in the Old Testament. The suggestion has even been made (more in popular Bible exposition than in serious exegesis) that, when the risen Lord on the Emmaus road opened to the two disciples 'in all the scriptures the things concerning himself' (Lk. 24:27), he took up the successive forms of sacrifice prescribed in the opening chapters of Leviticus—the burnt offerings, the cereal offerings, the peace offerings, the sin and guilt offerings—and showed them how each in its own way foreshadowed his own sacrifice.[8] To some of us such an idea seems incredibly

---

[4] Aland, *Problem*, p.29.   [5] Aland, *Problem*, pp.31f.

[6] This is the position taken, for example, by the *Berean Expositor* and publications of the Berean Publishing Trust, London.

[7] N. H. Snaith, *The Distinctive Ideas of the Old Testament* (London, 1944).

[8] Among those who have developed this christological typology of the levitical

far-fetched, but there are other Christians to whom it is self-evident, and if the priestly legislation belongs to their inner canon, it must be allowed its place within the church's canon.

There are those who see the difficulties inherent in the idea of an 'inner canon' and try to avoid them by using such an expression as 'material centre' (in German, *Sachmitte*). What they usually have in mind, however, is 'some passage or group of passages which "really" express and grasp this central matter; so that indirectly we are back again with a sort of inner canon'.[9] Such a 'material centre' might be compared to the 'rule of faith' to which the early Christian fathers appealed; but the rule of faith was not any kind of inner canon; it was rather a summary of the essence of scripture, properly interpreted. One may think of the Reformers' principle of biblical interpretation according to the 'analogy of faith'—the analogy of faith being the main thrust of scripture, as they understood it.[10]

MANY WITNESSES, ONE CHURCH, ONE LORD

'Does the canon of the New Testament constitute the unity of the church?' This was the title of a well-known essay by Ernst Käsemann; he gave his question the answer 'No'. He based his answer on the ample witness which the canon bears, in his view, to the *disunity* of the first-century church. If Galatians and Acts, Romans and James, the Fourth Gospel and the Apocalypse are brought together (as we have them) in one authoritative collection, then this collection 'provides the basis for the multiplicity of the confessions'. This multiplicity need not be accepted as binding: the New Testament canon imposes the duty of 'discerning the spirits', even within its own component writings. If justification by faith be taken as the criterion for such discernment, Käsemann implies, then 'emergent catholicism' will be recognized for the secondary development that it is.[11]

The gospel, that is to say, is contained in the canon, but is not

offerings are A. Jukes, *The Law of the Offerings* (London, 1854); H. Law, *Christ is All: Leviticus* (London, 1857); A. A. Bonar, *A Commentary on the Book of Leviticus* (London, [4]1861); C. H. Mackintosh, *Notes on the Book of Leviticus* (London, [2]1861).

[9] J. Barr, *The Bible in the Modern World* (London, 1973), pp.160–162.
[10] See p.249f.
[11] E. Käsemann, 'The Canon of the New Testament and the Unity of the Church', E.T. in *Essays on New Testament Themes* (London, 1964), pp.95–117.

coextensive with the canon. The canon, to adapt Luther's metaphor, is the cradle in which the gospel is laid.

To Käsemann's essay a reply was made by Hans Küng. Küng maintains that the catholicity of the canon is a good thing in itself. The multiplicity which Käsemann finds in the New Testament is a multiple expression of the gospel. 'The Catholic attitude is to be, in principle, open in every direction that the *New Testament* leaves open; not to exclude, either in principle or in practice, any line that belongs to the New Testament. . . . By including Paul along with Acts, Paul along with James; by, in short, making the *whole* New Testament canonical', the church carried out her duty of 'discerning the spirits'. As for 'the bold programme of "a Canon within the Canon",' it amounts to a demand to be 'more biblical than the Bible, more New-Testament-minded than the New Testament, more evangelical than the Gospel, more Pauline, even, than Paul'.[12]

It would be hazardous to try to name any part of scripture—even the genealogical tables!—in which some receptive reader or hearer has not recognized an effective and redeeming word from God. In the nineteenth century William Robertson Smith, called to account before a church court, affirmed his belief in the Bible as the Word of God and gave this as his reason: 'Because the Bible is the only record of the redeeming love of God; because in the Bible I find God drawing near to me in Jesus Christ, and declaring to me, in Him, His will for my salvation. And this record I know to be true by the witness of His Spirit in my heart, whereby I am assured that none other than God Himself is able to speak such words to my soul.'[13] This was expressed in the genuine tradition of Calvin and the Westminster divines. If Robertson Smith had been asked just where in the Bible he recognized this record and experienced this witness, he would probably not have mentioned every book, but he might well have said that the record of God's love and the witness of the Spirit were so pervasive that they gave character to the Bible as a whole. Others might bear the same testimony, but might think of other parts of the Bible than Robertson Smith had in mind.

If those who adhere to the principle of an inner canon concentrate on that inner canon to a point where they neglect the contents of the

---

[12] H. Küng, *The Living Church*, E.T. (London, 1963), pp.233–293; *Structures of the Church*, E.T. (London, 1965), pp.135–147.

[13] W. R. Smith, *Answer to the Form of Libel now before the Free Church Presbytery of Aberdeen* (Edinburgh, 1878), p.21.

'outer canon' (as they might call it), they deny themselves the benefits which they might derive from those other books. N.B. Stonehouse gave as his 'basic criticism' of Luther's viewpoint 'that it was narrowly Christocentric rather than God-centred, and thus involved an attenuation and impoverishment of the message of the New Testament. However significant *was Christum treibet* may be for the understanding of the New Testament, it lacks the breadth of perspective and outlook given by understanding it, for example, in terms of the coming of the kingdom of God'. But, 'formulating his criterion in narrow terms, and insisting upon the same manifestation of it in each writing of the New Testament', Luther 'missed much of the richness of the revelation of the New Testament organism of Scripture'.[14]

With a rather different emphasis, but to much the same effect, Ernest Best (probably with Rudolf Bultmann and other 'existential' exegetes in mind) has put it this way:

> The New Testament contains a variety of interpretations from a variety of contexts.... The Gospel of Luke and the Pastoral Epistles with their non-existentialist interpretation clearly met a need of the late first century and the beginning of the second and it can be argued that they have met the need of many Christians since then. They have sustained the church through many difficulties and have enabled it to take care of itself not only in time of persecution but also in time of heresy. Had we only the existentialist interpretation of Paul and John, supposing that their interpretations are purely existentialist, the church might well have lacked an essential element for its continued existence.[15]

The multiplicity of witness discernible in the New Testament is a multiplicity of witness to Christ. To quote the title of a helpful work by William Barclay, it presents us with 'many witnesses, one Lord'.[16] In his more academic work, *Unity and Diversity in the New Testament*, J. D. G. Dunn does not play down the diversity, but finds the unity which binds it together in the witness which it bears to the Jesus of

---

[14] N. B. Stonehouse, 'Luther and the New Testament Canon', in *Paul Before the Areopagus and Other New Testament Studies* (Grand Rapids, 1957), pp. 196f.

[15] E. Best, 'Scripture, Tradition and the Canon of the New Testament', *BJRL* 61 (1978–79), p. 286.

[16] W. Barclay, *Many Witnesses, One Lord* (London, 1963).

history who is identical with the exalted Lord of the church's faith and preaching.[17] What Jesus said of the Hebrew scriptures is equally applicable to the New Testament writings, 'outer canon' as well as 'inner canon': 'it is they that bear witness to me' (Jn. 5:39).

In short, it must be acknowledged that the churchmen of the age after Marcion were right when they insisted on a catholic collection of Christian scriptures in opposition to his sectarian selection.[18]

CRITERIA TODAY

Dr Ellen Flesseman-van Leer has argued that those who accept the traditional canon of scripture today cannot legitimately defend it with arguments which played no part in its formation.[19] She is supported by Hans von Campenhausen, who maintains nevertheless that 'the Scripture, read in faith and with the aid of reason, still remains the canon, the "standard". Without adherence to the Canon, which — in the widest sense — witnesses to the history of Christ, faith in Christ in any church would become an illusion.'[20] Of course it would, because the written testimony to Christ on which that faith is based would have disappeared.

This written testimony is enshrined in both Testaments, and both remain indispensable. 'Even an Old Testament read with critical eyes', says von Campenhausen, 'is still the book of a history which leads to Christ and indeed points toward him, and without him cannot itself be understood.'[21] Adolf von Harnack showed a strange insensitivity when he said that the Protestant church's continuing in his day to treasure the Old Testament as a canonical document was 'the result of a paralysis which affects both religion and the church'.[22]

Those who are interested in the Bible chiefly as historians of religious literature have naturally little use for the concept of a canon. Old Testament apocrypha and pseudepigrapha are as relevant to their studies as the contents of the Hebrew Bible; for them there is no

---

[17] J. D. G. Dunn, *Unity and Diversity in the New Testament* (London, 1977), pp. 205–216 *et passim*.

[18] See pp. 150–154.

[19] 'Prinzipien der Sammlung und Ausscheidung bei der Bildung des Kanons', *ZTK* 61 (1964), p. 419.

[20] *The Formation of the Christian Bible*, E.T. (London, 1972), p. 333.

[21] *Ibid.*

[22] Harnack, *Marcion: Das Evangelium vom fremden Gott* (Leipzig, 1921), p. 217.

distinction in principle between the New Testament writings and other early Christian literature from (say) Clement of Rome to Clement of Alexandria. But for theologians, and indeed for members of Christian churches in general, the principle of the canon is one of abiding importance.

Some may say that they receive the traditional canon as God's Word written because it has been delivered to them as such. Others will say that, if the traditional canon is indeed God's Word written, there will be recognizable criteria which mark it out as such. If the criteria which satisfied men and women in the early church are no longer so convincing to us as they were to them, on what grounds (apart from the bare fact that this is the canon which we have received) can we justify our acceptance of the traditional canon? It is not only legitimate but necessary to know what these grounds are and to state them.

So far as the Old Testament is concerned, this is a heritage with which the Christian church was endowed at its inception. Its contents meant much in the life of the church's Lord; they cannot mean less in the life of the church. 'What was indispensable to the Redeemer must always be indispensable to the redeemed.'[23] Differences may persist over matters of detail, such as the relation of the deuterocanonical books to those which belong to the Hebrew Bible, or the right of books like Esther, Ecclesiastes or the Song of Songs to be included in the canon. But these differences do not affect the main point—the essential place that the Old Testament has in the church's scriptures. And if questions arise about the inclusion of certain books which at one time were disputed, such questions may best be given a comprehensive answer. It is probable that the considerations which led to the inclusion of the Song of Songs in the canon would be dismissed by us as quite misguided. But with hindsight it is a matter for satisfaction that the Christian canon does include this exuberant celebration of the joy that man and woman find in each other's love.

Where the New Testament is concerned, the criterion of apostolicity can still be applied, but in a different way from its second-century application. Luke's Gospel, for example, does not seem to be in any way indebted to Paul, and has no need to be validated by his apostolic authority: Luke's access to the testimony of eyewitnesses and other primitive 'ministers of the word', with his own handling of the

[23] G. A. Smith, *Modern Criticism and the Preaching of the Old Testament* (London, 1901), p.11.

material he received, may well give the reader confidence that his record is based on the authentic apostolic preaching.[24] The letter to the Hebrews needs no apostle's name to certify its credentials as an original first-century presentation of the significance of the work of Christ as his people's sacrifice and high priest. 'Whether then it was I or they', says Paul, referring to others to whom the Lord appeared in resurrection, 'so we preach and so you believed' (1 Cor. 15:11)[25] — and his 'they' can properly be extended to include all the New Testament writers. With all the diversity of their witness, it is witness to one Lord and one gospel. There is a directness about the authority investing their words which contrasts with the perspective of Clement of Rome and his second-century successors, who look back to the apostolic age as normative. Not that a hard-and-fast line is drawn in this respect between the latest New Testament writings and the earliest of the Apostolic Fathers: the latest New Testament writings urge their readers to 'remember . . . the predictions of the apostles of our Lord Jesus Christ' (Jude 17; cf. 2 Pet. 3:2).[26] But the reasons which led to the overcoming of doubts once felt about these and other disputed catholic epistles were probably sound: in any case, the majority of the New Testament books, with their self-authenticating authority, can easily carry these, which form part of the same traditional canon.

It is sometimes said that the books which made their way into the New Testament canon are those which supported the victorious cause in the second-century conflict with the various gnostic schools of thought. There is no reason why the student of this conflict should shrink from making a value-judgment: the gnostic schools lost because they deserved to lose. A comparison of the New Testament writings with the contents of *The Nag Hammadi Library* should be instructive, once the novelty of the latter is not allowed to weigh in its favour against the familiarity of the former. Diverse as the gnostic schools were from one another, they all tended to ascribe creation and redemption to two separate (not to say opposed) powers. They fostered an individualist rather than a social form of religion — 'he travels the

---

[24] See I. H. Marshall, *Luke: Historian and Theologian* (Exeter, 1970).

[25] Paul's repeated 'so' refers to the foundation of the gospel in the death, burial and well attested resurrection of Christ.

[26] In the similar language of Eph. 3:5 'the mystery of Christ . . . has *now* been revealed to his holy apostles and prophets by the Spirit'; they are not yet figures of a past generation. See p.59.

fastest who travels alone'. They not only weakened a sense of community with other contemporaries but a sense of continuity with those who went before. True Christianity, like biblical religion in general, looks to one God as Creator and Redeemer, knows nothing of a solitary religion, and encourages among the people of God an appreciation of the heritage received from those who experienced his mighty acts in the past. And the documents which attest this true Christianity can claim, by the normal tests of literary and historical criticism, to be closer in time and perspective to the ministry of Jesus and the witness of his first apostles than the documents of the gnostic schools. Gnosticism was too much bound up with a popular but passing phase of thought to have the survival power of apostolic Christianity.[27]

The New Testament writings provide incontrovertibly our earliest witness to Christ, presenting him as the one in whom the history of salvation, recorded in the Old Testament, reached its climax.[28] What Hans Lietzmann said of the four gospels in the early church may be said of the New Testament writings in general: 'the reference to their apostolic authority, which can only appear to us as a reminder of sound historical bases, had the deeper meaning that this particular tradition of Jesus—and this alone—had been established and guaranteed by the Holy Spirit working authoritatively in the Church.'[29] Within 'this particular tradition' different strands of tradition may be recognized, but the church, in earlier and in more recent days, has been more conscious of the overall unity than of the underlying diversity, and has maintained 'this particular tradition' over against others which conflict with the New Testament witness but cannot establish a comparable title to apostolic authority.[30]

WHAT IF . . . ?

What would happen if a lost document from the apostolic age were to be discovered, which could establish a title to apostolic authority

[27] See P. Henry, *New Directions in New Testament Study* (London, 1980), pp.93–119.

[28] See H. von Campenhausen, *The Formation of the Christian Bible*, pp.327–333.

[29] H. Lietzmann, *The Founding of the Church Universal*, E.T. (London, 1950), p.97.

[30] See also E. Best, 'Scripture, Tradition and the Canon of the New Testament', *BJRL* 61 (1978–79), pp.258–289 (especially pp.288f.) for the sense in which the New Testament is both primary and essential: 'Every understanding of God through Christ is funnelled back through scripture to God and then forward again to us.'

comparable with that of the New Testament writings? Some years ago
a piece of writing was discovered in a Palestinian monastery which
purported to be a copy of part of a letter written by Clement of
Alexandria.[31] Some well-known students of Clement's work examined
this piece of writing and agreed that it might well be a genuine
fragment of his. Suppose a piece of writing were discovered somewhere
in the Near East which purported to be part of a letter of Paul's — say
his lost 'previous' letter to the Corinthian church (to which he refers in
1 Cor. 5:9). Suppose, too, that students of the Pauline writings who
examined it were agreed for the most part that it was genuine, that it
really was what it purported to be.[32] What then? Should it be
incorporated in the New Testament forthwith?

The criteria which lead scholars to conclusions about the date and
authorship of a document are different from the criteria leading to
canonical recognition. A newly discovered document could not be
treated as something accepted 'everywhere, always, by all' and so,
initially, could satisfy the criteria neither of catholicity nor of tradition.
Moreover, who is there today who could make a pronouncement on its
canonicity with such authority as would be universally followed? Even
if the Pope, the Ecumenical Patriarch and the Presidents of the World
Council of Churches were to issue a joint pronouncement, there are
some people of independent temper who would regard such a
pronouncement as sufficient cause for rejecting this candidate for
canonicity. Unless and until such a discovery is made, it is pointless to
speculate. But the precedent of earlier days suggests that it would first
be necessary for a consensus to develop among Christians in general;
any papal or conciliar pronouncement that might come later would be
but a rubber-stamping of that consensus.

ORTHODOXY

The time has long since gone by when the contents of the Bible could
be judged by an accepted 'rule of faith'. No doubt a hypothetical
document such as has just been discussed would be judged, among
other things, by its consistency with the existing canon — some
would add, by its consistency with the 'inner canon' (whatever their

[31] See pp. 298–315.

[32] The delicate nature of proof in such a matter may be illustrated by the
publication in recent years of what purported to be Hitler's diaries — a fabrication
which for a short time deceived one of our most eminent modern historians.

criteria for the inner canon might be). Oscar Cullmann has maintained that 'both the idea of a canon and the manner of its realization are *a crucial part* of the salvation history of the Bible'. It is in its recording of the history of salvation that he finds the unity of the biblical message (in Old and New Testaments together); 'through the *collection together* of the various books of the Bible, the whole history of salvation must be taken into account in understanding any one of the books of the Bible.'[33] The history of salvation was consummated in the once-for-all saving event; but that event can be appreciated only when one considers the process of which it is the fulfilment (documented in the Old Testament) and the unfolding of its significance (in the writings of the New Testament). Cullmann may press his thesis too far, but in his exposition of the principle of salvation history he presents a very attractive account of the coherence of the canon of scripture. This coherence is specially to be found in the witness borne to the author of salvation, the way of salvation, and the heirs of salvation. Even those parts of the Bible in which salvation is not so central as it is in others make their contribution to the context in which the history of salvation can be traced.

INSPIRATION

Inspiration—more particularly, prophetic inspiration—was identified by many as the distinguishing feature of the Old Testament collection when once it was reckoned to be complete. The collection was complete in principle, according to Josephus, when 'the exact succession of prophets' came to an end in Israel.[34] The rabbis assigned prophets as authors for the principal historical books (Joshua, Judges, Samuel, Kings) as well as for the Pentateuch and the Psalms.[35] According to the later books of the New Testament, the whole of Hebrew scripture (whether the original text or the Greek version) 'is inspired by God' (2 Tim. 3:16), for 'men moved by the Holy Spirit spoke from God' (2 Pet. 2:21).

Christians have been right in discerning the Holy Spirit similarly at work in the New Testament scriptures, although (as has been said) only one book of the New Testament explicitly claims prophetic

[33] O. Cullmann, *Salvation in History*, E.T. (London, 1967), pp. 294, 297.
[34] Josephus, *Against Apion*, 1.41 (see p. 33).
[35] See p. 30. Ezra and Job also ranked as prophets.

inspiration. But there has been a tendency to isolate the work of the Spirit in the composition of the individual New Testament scriptures from his subsequent work in relation to them. The Christians of the early centuries did not think that inspiration had ceased with the last book of the New Testament; they continued consciously to enjoy inspiration themselves (albeit not in conjunction with the apostolic authority which puts the New Testament writings on a level all their own). The strong word 'God-breathed' (Greek *theopneustos*) which is used in 2 Timothy 3:16 was occasionally used of post-apostolic writings—of the metrical inscription of Avircius, for example (describing his visit to churches between Rome and Mesopotamia),[36] and even of the decision of the Council of Ephesus (AD 431) condemning Nestorius![37]

It is not the usage of words that is important, however, but the realities of the situation. The theological aspect of canonization has not been the subject of this book, which has been concerned rather with the historical aspect, but for those who receive the scriptures as God's Word written the theological aspect is the most important. The Holy Spirit is not only the Spirit of prophecy; he is also the witnessing and interpreting Spirit. In the fulfilment of Jesus' promise that the Spirit would be the disciples' teacher and bring his own words (with their significance) to their remembrance,[38] the scriptures have been, and continue to be, one of the chief instruments which the Spirit uses. That the promise was not understood as applying only to those who were actually present with Jesus in the upper room is plain from 1 John 2:20, 27, where Christians of a later generation are assured that the 'anointing' which they have received from 'the Holy One' teaches them about everything (guides them 'into all the truth', in the sense of John 16:13).

The work of the Holy Spirit is not discerned by means of the common tools of the historian's trade. His inner witness gives the assurance to hearers or readers of scripture that in its words God himself is addressing them; but when one is considering the process by which the canon of scripture took shape it would be wiser to speak of the providence or guidance of the Spirit than of his witness. It is unlikely, for example, that the Spirit's witness would enable a reader

---

[36] See p.22.
[37] E. Schwartz (ed.), *Acta Conciliorum Oecumenicorum*, I.1.2 (Berlin/Leipzig, 1927), p.70. See p.266 above with n.38.
[38] John 14:26.

to discern that Ecclesiastes is the word of God while Ecclesiasticus is not: indeed, we have seen how John Bunyan heard the reassuring voice of God in the latter book, although it was not one of the books which he had been taught to receive as 'holy and canonical'.[39] Certainly, as one looks back on the process of canonization in early Christian centuries, and remembers some of the ideas of which certain church writers of that period were capable, it is easy to conclude that in reaching a conclusion on the limits of the canon they were directed by a wisdom higher than their own. It may be that those whose minds have been largely formed by scripture as canonized find it natural to make a judgment of this kind. But it is not mere hindsight to say, with William Barclay, that 'the New Testament books became canonical because no one could stop them doing so'[40] or even, in the exaggerated language of Oscar Cullmann, that 'the books which were to form the future canon *forced themselves on the Church by their intrinsic apostolic authority*, as they do still, because the *Kyrios* Christ speaks in them'.[41]

A further point to be made on the criterion of inspiration is that, in the words of H. L. Ellison, 'the writing of the Scriptures was only the half-way house in the process of inspiration; it only reaches its goal and conclusion as God is revealed through them to the reader or hearer. In other words, the inbreathing of the Holy Spirit into the reader is as essential for the right understanding of the Scriptures as it was in the original writers for their right production of them.'[42] If his 'inbreathing' into the authors is called inspiration and his 'inbreathing' into the hearers or readers is called illumination, this verbal distinction should not obscure the fact that at both stages it is one and the same Spirit who is at work.

The suggestion is made from time to time that the canon of scripture might be augmented by the inclusion of other 'inspirational' literature, ancient or modern, from a wider cultural spectrum.[43] But

---

[39] See p. 100.

[40] W. Barclay, *The Making of the Bible* (London, 1961), p.78.

[41] O. Cullmann, 'The Tradition' in *The Early Church,* E.T. (London, 1956), p.91 (his italics). It would be difficult to give a precise definition of '*intrinsic* apostolic authority'.

[42] H. L. Ellison, 'Some Thoughts on Inspiration', *EQ* 26 (1954), p.214.

[43] B. M. Metzger reports that, shortly after Martin Luther King, Jr., was assassinated in 1968, a group of ministers seriously proposed that his 'Letter from a Birmingham Jail' (1964) should be added to the New Testament (*The Canon of the New Testament* [Oxford, 1987], p.271).

this betrays a failure to appreciate what the canon actually is. It is not an anthology of inspired or inspiring literature. If one were considering a collection of writings suitable for reading in church, the suggestion might be more relevant. When a sermon is read in church, the congregation is often treated to what is, in intention at least, inspirational literature; the same may be said of prayers which are read from the prayerbook or of hymns which are sung from the hymnbook. But when the limits of the canon are under consideration, the chief concern is to get as close as possible to the source of the Christian faith.

By an act of faith the Christian reader today may identify the New Testament, as it has been received, with the entire 'tradition of Christ'. But confidence in such an act of faith will be strengthened if the same faith proves to have been exercised by Christians in other places and at other times — if it is in line with the traditional 'criteria of canonicity'. And there is no reason to exclude the bearing of other lines of evidence on any position that is accepted by faith.

In the canon of scripture we have the foundation documents of Christianity, the charter of the church, the title-deeds of faith. For no other literature can such a claim be made. And when the claim is made, it is made not merely for a collection of ancient writings. In the words of scripture the voice of the Spirit of God continues to be heard. Repeatedly new spiritual movements have been launched by the rediscovery of the living power which resides in the canon of scripture — a living power which strengthens and liberates.

CHAPTER TWENTY-THREE

CANON, CRITICISM, AND INTERPRETATION

CANONICAL CRITICISM

When writings are gathered together into a collection with a unifying principle, some critical questions arise with regard to the collection as such, in the light of that unifying principle, which do not arise in the same way with regard to the individual writings which make it up. Where the canon of scripture is concerned, these critical questions have been comprehensively termed 'canonical criticism'.

One of the most important critical questions has been formulated thus: 'Which form of the text is canonical?'[1] The question is often asked in relation to the New Testament, and some of those who ask it are prepared themselves to give it a quite confident answer. But when it is asked in relation to the New Testament, it is helpful first to consider it in relation to the Old Testament.

Which form of the Old Testament text is canonical? If the question is put to orthodox Jews, their answer is not in doubt: it is the traditional form, the Masoretic text of the Hebrew scriptures. And many scholars, Jews and Gentiles alike, will agree that, of all the extant varieties of text, the Masoretic is most reliable. It is no doubt

---

[1] This question forms the heading of a section in the last chapter of B. M. Metzger, *The Canon of the New Testament* (Oxford, 1987), p. 267.

subject to correction here and there, but no rival variety of Hebrew text—for example, that which appears to underlie the Septuagint version—can hold a candle to it.

But which form of the Old Testament text was recognized as canonical, or at least authoritative, by our Lord and his apostles, or by the New Testament writers in general? No one form.

One might expect that writers in Greek would use an accessible Greek version of the ancient scriptures, that is to say, the Septuagint. The New Testament writers did this to a very considerable extent. Luke and the writer to the Hebrews in their biblical citations and allusions adhere quite closely to the Septuagint wording. But other New Testament writers exercise greater freedom.

In Matthew 12:18−21 there is a quotation from Isaiah 42:1−4 in a Greek form which is markedly different from the Septuagint. The Septuagint version of Isaiah 42:1 identifies 'my servant' as Israel,[2] which would not have suited Matthew's purpose. A New Testament writer may quote the Old Testament in a form closer to the Hebrew construction; he may even quote it in a form paralleled neither in the Septuagint nor in the traditional Hebrew text, but in an Aramaic paraphrase or targum. For example, both Paul and the writer to the Hebrews quote Deuteronomy 32:35 in the form 'Vengeance is mine, I will repay' (Rom. 12:19; Heb. 10:30). This follows neither the familiar Hebrew wording ('Vengeance is mine, and recompense') nor the Septuagint ('In the day of vengeance I will repay'), but it agrees exactly with the targumic version. Occasionally, indeed, there is evidence of the use of a text resembling the Samaritan edition of the Pentateuch.[3] It looks at times as if the New Testament writers enjoyed liberty to select a form of Old Testament text which promoted their immediate purpose in quoting it: certainly they did not regard any one form of text as sacrosanct.

In this they have provided a helpful precedent for us when we are told (especially on theological, not critical, grounds) that one form of New Testament text is uniquely authoritative. In the eighteenth century William Whiston maintained that what we call the 'Western'

---

[2] 'Jacob my servant, I will help him; Israel my chosen one, my soul has accepted him.'

[3] The statement in Acts 7:4 that Abraham left Harran for Canaan 'after his father died' agrees with the chronology of the Samaritan text of Gen. 11:26—12:4 rather than with that of the Masoretic text or Septuagint version. See p.54.

text was the true, 'primitive' form of the New Testament.[4] In the second half of the nineteenth century John William Burgon vigorously defended the exclusive right of the 'Byzantine' text (the text exhibited by the majority of Greek manuscripts from the fifth to the fifteenth century) to be recognized as authentic and 'inspired'.[5] There are some who continue to maintain this position.[6] In his day there were those who held, on the other hand, that the text established by a succession of leading scholars on the basis of the earliest manuscripts should displace the Byzantine or 'majority' text as 'canonical'. A Scots Bible teacher of a past generation used to affirm in public that 'where Lachmann, Tregelles, Tischendorf and Westcott and Hort agree, there you have verily what the Spirit saith'.[7] That viewpoint was widely shared; nowadays few would venture to speak so positively, even on behalf of such an excellent publication as K. Aland's revision of E. Nestle's edition of the Greek New Testament.[8]

In more recent times the topic of 'canonical criticism' has been introduced, especially by B. S. Childs.[9] In canonical criticism the techniques of critical study are practised in relation to the Old or New Testament canon as such, or to the form in which any one of the individual books was finally included in the canon. It is true that, for nearly all books of the Bible, the final canonical form is the only one directly accessible to us: any earlier form must be in some degree a matter of speculation or reconstruction. (Occasionally one can distin-

[4] W. Whiston, *The Primitive New Testament Restor'd* (London, 1745). The 'Western' text is represented by *Codex Bezae* (D) of the Gospels and Acts (see p. 12) and by *Codex Claromontanus* (D^P) of the letters of Paul (see p. 218), as well as by a variety of other witnesses.

[5] Burgon's best-known statement of this position is his learned work, *The Revision Revised* (London, 1883).

[6] E.g. E. F. Hills, *The King James Version Defended!* (Des Moines, 1956); J. van Bruggen, *The Ancient Text of the New Testament*, E.T. (Winnipeg, 1976); W. N. Pickering, *The Identity of the New Testament Text* (Nashville/New York, 1977).

[7] The Bible teacher was John Brown (1846–1938), once well known among Christian Brethren in Scotland. K. Lachmann, S. P. Tregelles, C. von Tischendorf, and (together) B. F. Westcott and F. J. A. Hort between 1831 and 1881 published successive editions of the Greek New Testament based on the text of the earliest witnesses then available.

[8] Nestle-Aland, *Novum Testamentum Graece* (Stuttgart, 1979). The critical apparatus of this edition is the work of K. and B. Aland; the text is practically identical with that of *The Greek New Testament* (United Bible Societies, ³1975).

[9] See B. S. Childs, *Introduction to the Old Testament as Scripture* (London, 1979), pp. 74–105; *The New Testament as Canon: An Introduction* (London, 1984), pp. 521–530.

guish two 'canonical' forms of a book, as in the book of Jeremiah: there is the longer form preserved in the Masoretic text and a shorter Greek form preserved in the Septuagint, and both were canonized.)[10]

It may be argued that the final canonical form is that which should be acknowledged as the valid standard of authority in the church. But the textual or historical critic will not be deterred from working back to the form in which the document first appeared, or as nearly as it is possible to get to that form. And it may equally be argued that, if apostolic authority is the chief criterion of canonicity in the New Testament, the form of the letter to the Romans (say) as Paul dictated it and Tertius wrote it down must be its most authoritative form. To be sure, where the Pauline letters are concerned, textual critics would be happy if they could establish the wording of the first edition of the Pauline corpus, but even that (if attainable) would be pre-canonical.[11]

'AS ORIGINALLY GIVEN'

It might be thought at first blush that insistence on the final canonical form stands at the opposite pole from insistence on the text 'as originally given', which finds expression in some present-day statements of belief. The Universities and Colleges Christian Fellowship, for example, confesses its faith in 'the divine inspiration and infallibility of Holy Scripture, as originally given, and its supreme authority in all matters of faith and morals'.[12] The phrase 'as originally given' does not imply that the qualities of inspiration and infallibility belong to some lost and irrecoverable stage of the biblical text; it implies rather that these qualities should not be ascribed to defects of transmission and translation.

In another context the phrase 'as originally given' might refer to earlier forms of a biblical book which have been discerned by the exercise of literary or historical criticism. For example, it has been argued persuasively by David Clines that the 'proto-Masoretic' book of Esther comprised the first eight chapters only; not only so, but he goes farther back and envisages a 'pre-Masoretic' form of the book.[13] Could one say that one or other of these forms should be identified with the

---

[10] The shorter form was originally a variant Hebrew edition, which is represented by a fragmentary manuscript from Qumran (4QJer[b]). As the Septuagintal form it was 'canonized' by the Greek-speaking church.

[11] See pp. 129f.   [12] See *Evangelical Belief* (Inter-Varsity, 1935; ³1961).

[13] D. J. A. Clines, *The Esther Scroll: The Story of the Story* (Sheffield, 1984).

book of Esther 'as originally given'? Or, to take a New Testament example, some scholars have held that, when Papias wrote of Matthew's compilation of 'the oracles in the Hebrew speech',[14] he referred not to our Gospel of Matthew but to an early collection of sayings of Jesus which constituted a major source for the evangelists Matthew and Luke (the source of the so-called 'Q' material).[15] If they are right, could one say that this collection should be identified with the Gospel of Matthew 'as originally given'? It is safe to say that such possibilities were not contemplated by the authors of the UCCF doctrinal basis. In fact, they had in view the canonical forms of the biblical books, with errors of transmission or translation removed. There is not so much difference as might appear at first blush between this position and that of Professor Childs (which is not to say, of course, that he takes the UCCF line on inspiration and infallibility).

In the 'received text' of the New Testament there are some passages which find no place in modern critical editions of the Greek Testament (or in translations based on these). Should such passages be recognized as canonical? There is no person or community competent to give an authoritative ruling on this question; any answer to it must be largely a matter of judgment.[16]

There is, for example, the text about the three heavenly witnesses which appears in AV/KJV at 1 John 5:7. This passage is a late intruder; it has no title to be considered part of the New Testament or to be recognized as canonical.[17]

What of the last twelve verses of Mark's Gospel (Mk. 16:9–20)? These verses — the longer Marcan appendix — were not part of Mark's work. That in itself would not render them uncanonical — as we have seen, canonicity and authorship are two distinct issues — but their contents reveal their secondary nature. They seem to present, in the main, a summary of resurrection appearances recorded in the other Gospels. Some readers may like to have in verse 18 canonical authority for snake-handling; the clause 'they will pick up serpents', however, is probably based on Paul's encounter with the viper on Malta (Acts

---

[14] See p. 125.

[15] So, e.g., T. W. Manson, *Studies in the Gospels and Epistles* (Manchester, 1962), pp. 68–104.

[16] At one time the Holy See reserved to itself the right of passing final judgment on such questions: little has been heard of this right since the issue of Pope Pius XII's encyclical *Divino afflante Spiritu* ('by the inspiration of the divine Spirit') in 1943.

[17] See F. F. Bruce, *The Epistles of John* (London, 1970), pp. 129f.

28:3–6). The following words about drinking poison without harmful consequences are reminiscent of a story which Philip's daughters are said to have told of Joseph Barsabbas, surnamed Justus (one of the nominees for the succession to Judas Iscariot, according to Acts 1:23).[18] The right of these twelve verses to receive canonical recognition is doubtful.[19]

Then there is the story of the woman taken in adultery (Jn. 7:53—8:11). This certainly does not belong to the Gospel of John. It is an independent unit of gospel material, of the same general character as the Holy Week incidents in the temple court recorded in Mark 12:13–37. 'The account has all the earmarks of historical veracity',[20] and as a genuine reminiscence of Jesus' ministry is eminently worthy of being treated as canonical.[21]

STAGES OF COMPOSITION

Even in its canonical form a biblical document may be better understood if account be taken of successive stages in its composition.

There can be no doubt, for example, of the canonical form of the Gospel of Matthew, nor yet of its canonical position. Ever since the fourfold gospel was brought together, the Gospel of Matthew has stood at its head. A few modern editors have displaced it—*The Twentieth Century New Testament,* for example, put Mark first and Ferrar Fenton put John first—but Matthew's traditional primacy has not been imperilled. That primacy is due not to chronological considerations but to Matthew's character: it is a proper catholic introduction to a catholic gospel collection and, in due course, to a catholic New Testament.[22]

If we had no other gospel than Matthew, we should have to exercise our critical faculties on its own internal evidence as best we might. Happily, however, we can compare it with the other gospels (especially Mark and Luke) and thus reach firmer conclusions about its composi-

---

[18] Eusebius, *Hist. Eccl.* 3.39.9f.

[19] Their authenticity has been defended by J. W. Burgon, *The Last Twelve Verses of the Gospel according to S. Mark* (London, 1871); *cf* W. R. Farmer, *The Last Twelve Verses of Mark* (Cambridge, 1974).

[20] B. M. Metzger, *A Textual Commentary on the Greek New Testament* (London/New York, 1971), p.220.

[21] See F. F. Bruce, *The Gospel of John* (Basingstoke/Grand Rapids, 1983), pp.413–418.

[22] See p.153.

tion. We may conclude, as many have done, that this evangelist used at least two written sources—one being the Gospel of Mark or something very like it, and the other being the sayings collection which underlies the 'Q' material ('Q' being a convenient shorthand symbol for the non-Marcan material common to Matthew and Luke). Other sources have been discerned behind Matthew's record: whether they were written or not is difficult to determine. One of these may have been a second collection of sayings of Jesus, preserved in a more conservative Jewish-Christian circle than the circle in which the other collection circulated. But, whatever sources lay at Matthew's disposal, he treated them as an independent author, arranging his sayings material so as to form five bodies of teaching, each prefaced by a narrative section; the whole was introduced with a nativity narrative and concluded with an account of the passion of Jesus and his resurrection appearances (the main outlines of this last account having been largely fixed at an early stage in the church's life). A consideration of the evangelist's probable sources and of his treatment of them thus helps one to appreciate his workmanship, together with the value of his distinctive witness to Jesus and his special contribution to the New Testament.[23]

VARIETY IN UNITY

When all the books of the Bible are brought together as parts of one canon, bound in one volume and recognized as the product of one divine Spirit, there is an inevitable tendency to emphasize the unity of the whole in such a way that differences of idiom and perspective between one writer and another are overlooked. This is the tendency that Harnack had in mind when he remarked that the process of canonization 'works like whitewash; it hides the original colours and obliterates all the contours'.[24] But there is no good reason for allowing canonicity to efface differences of date, authorship, outlook and so forth. Critical and exegetical study can be pursued as intensively with canonical literature as with uncanonical; indeed, the fact that a body of literature is acknowledged as canonical should serve as a specially powerful incentive to such study.

However, it is not always so. The danger of failing to give sufficient

[23] See R. H. Gundry, *Matthew: A Commentary on his Literary and Theological Art* (Grand Rapids, 1982).

[24] A. von Harnack, *The Origin of the New Testament*, E.T. (London, 1925), p.141.

weight to such differences between one writer and another is one against which exponents of the theology of the New Testament should be on their guard, not to speak of exponents of biblical theology as a whole. Indeed, even a work on the theology of Paul may fail to do justice to the progress of Paul's thought as it finds expression in his chief epistles, read in chronological order. Similarly, any one who would write on the teaching of Jesus must remember that his teaching, as we have it, is mediated through several witnesses. Quite apart from the issues raised by differences of emphasis among the synoptic evangelists, the difficulty of weaving his teaching according to them and his teaching according to John into a coherent whole makes most writers on the subject decide to concentrate on the synoptists' testimony and leave John's on one side—at least for the time being.[25]

CANONICAL EXEGESIS

Canonical exegesis may be defined as the interpretation of individual components of the canon in the context of the canon as a whole.

Even in the pre-canonical period evidence of intra-biblical interpretation is not lacking. In the Old Testament it can be seen how later law-codes took over the provisions of earlier codes and applied them to fresh situations, or how later prophets took up and reinterpreted the oracles of their predecessors. Ezekiel, for example, makes it plain that Gog (under other names) was the subject of earlier prophecy in Israel (Ezek. 38:17): what had been said about him before was repeated and given fresh point with regard to a new situation. In Daniel's visions especially one can see oracles of Isaiah, Jeremiah and Ezekiel reinterpreted. Jeremiah's prediction of seventy years' desolation for Jerusalem (Jer. 25:11f.; 29:10) is reinterpreted to cover a period seven times as long (Dan. 9:2, 24−27)—for Daniel, Jeremiah belongs to a collection called 'the books'. The forecast of the decline and fall of Antiochus Epiphanes in Daniel 11:40−45 is a re-presentation of the downfall of the Assyrian invader as foretold by Isaiah (Is. 14:24−27; 31:8f.) and

---

[25] Because 'the modern student cannot but feel that to turn from the Synoptics to the Fourth Gospel is to breathe another atmosphere, to be transported to another world' (H. Latimer Jackson, *The Problem of the Fourth Gospel* [Cambridge, 1918], p.82), words which would still be widely echoed. But now that the tradition of Jesus' ministry preserved by John is increasingly recognized to be parallel to the synoptic traditions, although independent of them, it cannot properly be left out of account in any presentation of Jesus' life and teaching.

of Gog as foretold by Ezekiel (Ezek. 39:1–8).

In the New Testament writings many Old Testament texts are adduced and interpreted in the light of their fulfilment in the work of Christ and its sequel. Within the New Testament itself we find earlier gospel material reinterpreted by later evangelists, and we can see 2 Peter revising and reapplying Jude, omitting its allusion to the *Assumption of Moses* and its quotation from 1 Enoch, but retaining the reference to the fallen angels (Jude 6) who provide the main theme of the relevant section of 1 Enoch.[26] Moreover, 2 Peter (as has been mentioned before) refers to a collection of letters of Paul, which are associated with 'the other scriptures', and warns against their misuse (2 Pet. 3:15f.).[27]

If this tendency is visible even before the documents finally formed part of a canonical collection, it is intensified after the completion of the canon, or even after the formation of smaller collections, such as the fourfold gospel or the Pauline *corpus*.

An individual gospel might have been designed as *the* gospel for a particular community, but when it was included in a collection with other writings of the same *genre*, the individual writings were viewed as complementary one to another, each presenting a distinctive aspect of the ministry of Jesus. Each was then interpreted in the light of the others. In the course of copying them, scribes tended to conform the text of the less frequently read to that of the more frequently read.[28] Uncritical readers or hearers might be unaware of any problems raised by the coexistence of the four accounts: the impression left on their minds would take the form of a composite picture of Jesus and his ministry. Those who discerned the problems were moved to give some explanation of them. Clement of Alexandria explained the differences between the synoptic records and John's by saying that the first three evangelists set forth the 'bodily' facts whereas John composed a 'spiritual' gospel.[29]

Others tackled the problem of harmonization in different ways. Tatian tackled it by weaving the material of all four records into a continuous narrative. Eusebius and Augustine addressed themselves

---

[26] See p. 85.   [27] See p. 120.

[28] In particular, there was a tendency to conform the text of Mark and Luke to that of Matthew; compare the wording of the Lord's Prayer in Lk. 11:2–4, AV/KJV (where it is conformed to the wording of Mt. 6:9—13a), with the original Lucan wording preserved in RSV, NEB, NIV and other modern versions.

[29] Quoted by Eusebius, *Hist. Eccl.* 6.14.7 (see p. 189).

to the issue of detailed discrepancies, and endeavoured to solve them by chronological and other arguments. Eusebius, for example, points out that the ministry of Jesus in the synoptic accounts includes only what happened after John's imprisonment (cf Mk. 1:14, etc.), while John relates much that Jesus did before that event (cf Jn. 3:22).[30] Augustine deals seriously, among other things, with the chronology of the resurrection appearances reported by various evangelists.[31]

Another kind of harmonization was achieved by means of the allegorical method of Origen and others. Convinced as he was of the divine inspiration of the four gospels (as of all scripture), Origen concluded that spiritual allegorization was the only worthy means of bringing their full meaning to light. But when discrepancies were allegorized, they ceased to be discrepancies: they were seen to be complementary aspects of higher truth.

But it was the formation of the fourfold gospel that made these harmonizing exercises necessary: Christians who used only one gospel had no such problems to concern themselves with.

Similarly, when the letters of Paul were gathered into one *corpus,* each of them began to be read in the context of the whole *corpus.* At one time the only letters of Paul known (say) to the church of Corinth were those which it received from him—four or five, probably, within the space of two or three years. Not all of these have come down to us, and at certain points in the surviving Corinthian correspondence there are problems of interpretation which might be solved without more ado if we could consult the missing letters or parts of letters. For example, the letter which Paul says he wrote 'with many tears' (2 Cor. 2:4) seems to have been lost; if it were still available, there are passages in 2 Corinthians which we should understand better than we do. But when Paul's surviving Corinthian correspondence formed part of the same *corpus* as his letters to the Thessalonians, Galatians, Romans, Philippians and others, fresh problems began to appear. Some readers have felt that the ethical guide-lines set out in (say) 1 Corinthians are in tension with the more libertarian tone of (say) Galatians.[32] This tension is fairly easily resolved when the different occasions of the two letters are taken into account; but if both are read as holy scripture on one undifferentiated level, without regard to their historical back-

---

[30] *Hist. Eccl.* 3.24.7–13.
[31] *On the Consensus of the Evangelists,* 3.70–86 (see also p.232).
[32] See J. W. Drane, *Paul: Libertine or Legalist?* (London, 1975).

ground, problems are created with which the Corinthians and Galatians themselves did not have to cope. The injunctions in such occasional documents as Paul's letters were never intended to be applied as canon law to personal or communal Christian life at all times and in all places.

Such tensions were multiplied when the earlier *corpus* of ten letters was enlarged to accommodate the Pastoral Epistles, because these three documents share a distinctive ethos and range of interest which is not found in the other letters. They were multiplied still more when, toward the end of the second century, the *corpus* was further enlarged to take in the letter to the Hebrews, a document which did not originally belong to the Pauline tradition.

'ALL SCRIPTURE'

When the New Testament collection was received as a whole, whether in twenty-two or in twenty-seven books, further exegetical adjustments were made. When the Acts of the Apostles preceded the epistles, it was natural that the epistles, especially Paul's earlier ones, should be read in the light of Luke's narrative — although, when it is considered that Acts is later than Paul's epistles, a strong case can be made out for reading Acts in the light of Paul's epistles and testing its historical value by means of their evidence.[33]

When the New Testament collection was read as part of the same Bible as the Old Testament writings, especially when both Testaments were bound together in one codex, 'all scripture' provided a still wider context within which 'every scripture' was to be understood.

For example, since New Testament times Christians have been familiar with what we have come to call the 'Servant Songs' of Isaiah 40–55, and in particular with the fourth Servant Song (Is. 52:13–53:12), and have without further thought identified the Servant whom they portray with Jesus. Why should they do this? Because, from the beginnings of the Christian faith — indeed, from the teaching of Jesus himself[34] — this identification has been standard in the church. One would not expect it to be standard in the synagogue: indeed, the synagogue seems to have reacted vigorously against it. At one time an

---

[33] See F. F. Bruce, *The Acts of the Apostles* (Grand Rapids/Leicester, [3]1989), Introduction ('Acts and the Pauline Epistles').

[34] But see M. D. Hooker, *Jesus and the Servant* (London, 1959).

acceptable Jewish interpretation identified some at least of the Servant references with the expected Messiah,[35] and this could well have been in line with the prophet's intention.[36] But, because the church adopted this interpretation (with the corollary that the Messiah was Jesus), the messianic interpretation of the Servant Songs fell out of favour with the synagogue.[37]

When both Testaments are read together as part of holy scripture, the importance for the church of reading the Old Testament in the light of the New might be regarded as axiomatic, but at some times and in some places it has been admitted only with qualifications. The abolition of animal sacrifices by the work of Christ has been almost universally taken for granted, but the New Testament teaching about food restrictions and the observance of special days still meets with some resistance. The law of exact retaliation, 'life for life, eye for eye, tooth for tooth. . .' (Ex. 21:23–25), was replaced for Jesus' disciples by his principle of turning the other cheek and going the second mile (Mt. 5:38–42); but many of his disciples still invoke the law of retaliation when it seems appropriate: after all, Moses' law and Jesus' teaching are both in the Bible, are they not?

This is not to imply an incompatibility between Moses' law and Jesus' teaching: Jesus himself affirmed that his teaching did not abrogate but fulfilled 'the law and the prophets' (Mt. 5:17). It does imply the importance of the historical dimension in biblical interpretation. When this is borne in mind, it will be realized that even the law of exact retaliation marked an ethical advance on the earlier principle of vendetta or blood-feud, demanding as it did one life, and no more, for a life; one eye, and no more, for an eye, and so forth. Moreover, for an eye or some other part of the body monetary compensation was acceptable; only for a life deliberately taken could

---

[35] For example, in the Targum on the Prophets, those passages in Is. 52:13–53:12 which speak of the Servant's triumph are applied to the Messiah.

[36] See C. R. North, *The Suffering Servant in Deutero-Isaiah* (Oxford, [2]1956).

[37] According to H. Loewe, it was sensitiveness to the Christian application of Is. 52:13–53:12 that was responsible for the non-inclusion of this passage in the regular synagogue readings from the Prophets, although the passages immediately preceding and following are included (C. G. Montefiore and H. Loewe, *A Rabbinic Anthology* [London, 1938], p.544). In general it may be said that the combination of the Old Testament with the New (first as oral teaching and ultimately as a literary canon) made all the difference between the church's understanding of the Old Testament and the synagogue's (see pp.63–67 above).

there be no such redemption (*cf* Deut. 19:13).

It is not enough to say 'the Bible says. . .' without at the same time considering to whom the Bible says it, and in what circumstances. One sometimes meets people who, in discussing the life to come, quote Ecclesiastes 9:5, 'the dead know nothing', as though that were the Bible's last word on the subject, as though Jesus' death and resurrection had not given his people a new and living hope to which the author of Ecclesiastes was a stranger.

Canonical exegesis does not absolve the reader from the duty of understanding the scriptures in their historical setting. Indeed, it reinforces that duty. Each part of the canon makes its contribution to the whole, but that contribution cannot be properly appreciated unless attention is paid to the historical setting of each part in relation to the whole. Historical criticism, rightly applied, is as necessary for canonical exegesis as it is for the exegesis of the separate biblical documents. Each separate document may take on fuller meaning in the context of the wider canon to which it now belongs, but that fuller meaning cannot be logically unrelated to its meaning in the original (uncanonical) context. A study, for example, of the biblical doctrine of election[38] could not be undertaken if there were no Bible, no canon of scripture; but it would be worthless unless it took into account the historical sequence of the relevant subject-matter.

This is bound up with what is often called progressive revelation. That the biblical revelation is progressive is obvious when one considers that it was given in the course of history until, 'when the time had fully come, God sent forth his Son' (Gal. 4:4). To call it progressive, however, may be misleading if that adjective suggests that every stage in the revelation is more 'advanced' than the stages which historically preceded it. If one thinks again of the doctrine of election, the principle of election implied in God's call of Abraham, according to the narrative of Genesis 12:1–3, is more ethically and religiously 'advanced' than many of the ideas on the subject cherished by some of Abraham's descendants at later stages in their history. (The principle revealed in the call of Abraham, that some are elected in order that others through them may be blessed, has not always been borne in mind by those who thought of themselves as the elect of God.)

To adapt words of Paul, the reader of scripture should say, 'I will

[38] Such a study is found in H. H. Rowley, *The Biblical Doctrine of Election* (London, 1950).

read with the Spirit and I will read with the mind also.'[39] The inclusion of each scripture in the canon of all scripture helps one in the understanding of each scripture, but at the same time, since each scripture makes its contribution to all scripture, the understanding of all scripture is impossible without the understanding of each scripture.

[39] *Cf* 1 Cor. 14:15.

APPENDIX I

THE 'SECRET' GOSPEL
OF MARK

Ethel M. Wood Lecture, 1974

SECRET WRITINGS

All the world loves a mystery, and there is something about the announcement of a 'secret' Gospel which attracts instant attention.

In Judaism of the closing centuries BC and early centuries AD there was a number of apocalyptic writings, bearing the names of authors long since deceased—Enoch, Noah, the Hebrew patriarchs, Ezra and so forth. If it was asked why there was such a time-lag between their alleged date of composition and their publication, the answer was that the works were 'sealed', kept secret by heavenly direction, until the time to which they pointed forward had arrived; then their contents might be divulged. A New Testament example of this is the sealed scroll in the Apocalypse, containing a record of the divine purpose for the world, which could not be put into effect until someone appeared with the requisite authority to break the seals and expose the contents.

In Judaism, again, by contrast with those works which were suitable for public reading in synagogue (the canonical books of the Hebrew Bible) there were others which were 'hidden', withdrawn from public circulation, and reserved for the eyes of those with sufficient maturity to profit by them. According to one rabbinical tradition, the canonical book of Ezekiel was at one time in danger of being 'hidden', in this sense of being withdrawn from public currency, because of theological difficulties raised by some of its contents.[1]

The Greek adjective *apokryphos,* which was used for such 'hidden' or 'secret' books, is the word from which our adjective 'apocryphal' is derived. We, however, have come to use this adjective of those Old Testament books which, while they were not included in the Hebrew Bible, came to be recognized as canonical or deutero-canonical over wide areas of the Christian church. This usage goes back to Jerome, who used the Latin adjective *apocryphus* to denote those books which were suitable for reading in church to inculcate ethical lessons but were not to be used for the establishment of doctrine.[2] But there was never anything 'hidden' or 'secret' about most of those books.

In Gnosticism, however, the idea of secret writings, containing truth for the spiritual *élite,* enjoyed a fresh and vigorous lease of life. In addition to his public teaching, preserved in the church's gospel tradition, it was maintained that Jesus had imparted private teaching to his disciples which was not to be blazed abroad to the world at large but communicated to a minority of favoured souls who had proved themselves worthy to receive it. If New Testament writers like Paul and John refuse to countenance the idea that there is any Christian teaching which may not be imparted to Christians as a whole, this simply proves that already in the first century the idea of an esoteric teaching for the spiritual *élite* was gaining currency.

If, as Luke says, Jesus spent the interval of forty days between his resurrection and ascension telling his disciples 'the things concerning the kingdom of God' (Acts 1:3), what were those things? The New Testament writings do not go into much detail about them, but the second century was very willing to make good the deficiencies of the first. The gnostic compilation *Pistis Sophia,* for example (known only from a fourth-century Coptic manuscript), purports to record teaching given by Jesus to his disciples over a period of *twelve years* between his resurrection and final ascension. The *Secret Book (Apocryphon) of John* tells how the exalted Christ appeared to John some time after his ascension, in the role of the gnostic Redeemer, and promised to be with John and his fellow-disciples always (*cf* Mt. 28:20). The same literary device could be used quite early in anti-gnostic circles, as is seen possibly in the *Didache* ('The Teaching of the Lord through the Twelve Apostles to the Gentiles') and certainly in the *Epistle of the*

---

[1] TB *Shabbat* 13b. See p.35 above.
[2] Prologues to Samuel and to the Solomonic books (see pp.89–92 above).

Apostles, a second-century treatise extant in Coptic and Ethiopic versions.

The gnostic library from near Nag Hammadi in Upper Egypt, discovered about 1945, includes among its fifty-two treatises (contained in thirteen leather-bound papyrus codices) several whose titles proclaim their 'secret' character. Such are the *Secret Book (Apocryphon) of John* already mentioned, the *Secret Book (Apocryphon) of James* and (best known of all) the compilation called in its colophon the *Gospel according to Thomas,* which begins: 'These are the secret words which Jesus the Living One spoke and Didymus Judas Thomas wrote down'. Despite the designation of the following contents as 'secret words', there is nothing particularly secret about the 114 real or alleged sayings of Jesus which this work comprises; perhaps it was their interpretation that was secret. When the first popular English edition of the *Gospel of Thomas* was published—the excellent edition by R. M. Grant and D. N. Freedman—its public appeal was no doubt enhanced by its title: *The Secret Sayings of Jesus.*[3]

Irenaeus speaks of his gnostic opponents as adducing 'an indescribable multitude of apocryphal and spurious scriptures'[4] and elsewhere says that 'those who separate Jesus from the Christ, holding that the Christ remained impassible, while Jesus suffered, prefer the Gospel according to Mark'[5]—from which his editor W. W. Harvey inferred that another Gospel assigned to Mark, in addition to the well-known one, was current in Alexandria, although Harvey was disposed to identify this other Gospel with the *Gospel of the Egyptians* (to which reference will be made later).[6]

It is in the context of this wealth of esoteric gospel-literature that we have to evaluate the 'secret' Gospel of Mark to which our attention has been drawn in recent years by Professor Morton Smith, of the Department of History in Columbia University, New York City.

THE CLEMENTINE LETTER AND
THE EXPANDED GOSPEL

In 1958 Professor Smith was engaged in cataloguing the contents of the library of the ancient monastery of Mar Saba, in the wilderness of

[3] London: Collins, 1960.   [4] *Against Heresies,* 1.20.1.
[5] *Against Heresies,* 3.11.7.
[6] W. W. Harvey (ed.), *Sancti Irenaei...libros quinque adversus haereses,* II (Cambridge, 1857), p.46. See p.189.

Judaea, some twelve miles south of Jerusalem, when he came upon a copy of Isaac Voss's edition of six letters of Ignatius, printed and published at Amsterdam in 1646.[7] On the end-papers of this volume was a copy, in what seemed to be a mid-eighteenth-century hand, of a Greek letter, purporting to be the work of Clement the *stromateus*, meaning the author of the *Stromateis* ('Miscellanies')—i.e. Clement of Alexandria (who flourished between AD 180 and 200).[8] The letter launched an attack on the followers of the heretic Carpocrates and embodied an account (unfortunately broken off short at the end) of an expanded text of part of the tenth chapter of the Gospel of Mark.

Professor Smith reported his discovery to the Society of Biblical Literature at its ninety-sixth meeting in December 1960. He indicated that he was disposed to accept the ascription of the letter to Clement of Alexandria, but he submitted the text to the judgment of a few other scholars, specially competent in the Greek patristic field, some of whom agreed with him while others preferred a different origin. A. D. Nock was moved by 'instinct' to disagree with the ascription, although he wished to date the letter not later than the fourth century;[9] J. Munck argued that the letter showed dependence on Eusebius and therefore could not be earlier than the fourth century. But the majority of the scholars consulted accepted the ascription to Clement; these included H. Chadwick, R. M. Grant and G. W. H. Lampe.[10] We too may accept it as a working hypothesis.

The text of the letter was not published until the summer of 1973; it appeared, together with a translation and an exhaustive treatment of its literary, historical and religious implications, in Professor Smith's book *Clement of Alexandria and a Secret Gospel of Mark*.[11]

[7] I. Vossius, *Epistolae Genuinae S. Ignatii Martyris* (Amstelodami, 1646).

[8] See p. 187 above.

[9] Nock, in a letter of September 20, 1962, quoted by M. Smith (*Clement of Alexandria and a Secret Gospel of Mark*, p. 88, n. 1), suggested that the whole thing was a piece of 'mystification for the sake of mystification'. A similar conclusion was proposed by Q. Quesnell in 'The Mar Saba Clementine: A Question of Evidence', *CBQ* 37 (1975), pp. 48–67, except that he thought not of a fourth-century but of a twentieth-century mystification—to be dated, more precisely, between 1936 and 1958. See M. Smith's response to Quesnell in 'On the Authenticity of the Mar Saba Letter of Clement', *CBQ* 38 (1976), pp. 196–199.

[10] To these names must be added that of R. P. C. Hanson; see his review of *Clement of Alexandria and a Secret Gospel of Mark* in *JTS*, n.s. 25 (1974), pp. 513–521.

[11] Cambridge, MA: Harvard University Press, 1973. This was followed by his more popular treatment of the same subject: *The Secret Gospel* (London: Gollancz, 1974).

To evaluate Professor Smith's conclusions would take us far beyond the limits of an hour's lecture. Suffice it here to present an English translation of the document, based on Professor Smith's *editio princeps* of the Greek text, and discuss some of the issues which it raises.

The letter runs as follows:

> From the letters of the most holy Clement, author of the *Stromateis.*
> To Theodore:
> You have done well in muzzling the unmentionable doctrines of the Carpocratians. It is they who were prophetically called 'wandering stars' [Jude 13], who stray from the narrow way of the commandments into the fathomless abyss of fleshly sins committed in the body. They have been inflated with the knowledge, as they say, of 'the deep things of Satan' [Rev. 2:24]. They cast themselves unawares into the gloom of the darkness of falsehood [*cf* Jude 13]. Boasting that they are free, they have become the slaves of lusts that bring men into bondage. These people must be totally opposed in every way. Even if they were to say something true, not even so would the lover of truth agree with them; everything that is true is not necessarily *truth*. Nor should one prefer the apparent truth which is according to human opinions to the real truth which is according to faith. But of the matters under dispute concerning the divinely-inspired Gospel of Mark, some are utterly false and some, even if they contain certain things that are true, are not so truly delivered; for the things that are true are corrupted by those that are fictitious, so that, as it is said, 'the salt has lost its savour' [Mt. 5:13//Lk. 14:34].
> Mark, then, during Peter's stay in Rome, recorded the acts of the Lord, not however reporting them all, for he did not indicate the mystical ones, but selected those which he thought most useful for the increase of the faith of those undergoing instruction.
> When Peter had borne his witness (i.e. suffered martyrdom), Mark arrived in Alexandria, taking his own and Peter's memoirs. From these he copied into his first book the things appropriate for those who were making progress in knowledge but compiled a more spiritual Gospel for the use of those who were attaining perfection. Yet not even so did he divulge the unutterable things themselves, nor did he write down the Lord's hierophantic teaching. But adding to the previously written acts others also, he presented, over and above these, certain oracles whose

interpretation he knew would provide the hearers with mystical guidance into the inner shrine of the seven-times-hidden truth. Thus, then, he made advance preparation—not grudgingly or incautiously, as I think—and on his death he left his composition to the church in Alexandria, where even until now it is very well guarded, being read only to those who are being initiated into the great mysteries.

But abominable demons are always devising destruction for the human race, and so Carpocrates, having been instructed by them, used deceitful devices so as to enslave a certain elder of the church in Alexandria and procured from him a copy of the mystical Gospel, which he proceeded to interpret in accordance with his own blasphemous and carnal opinion. Moreover, he polluted it further by mixing shameless falsehoods with the holy and undefiled sayings, and from this mixture the dogma of the Carpocratians has been drawn out. To these people, then, as I have said already, one must never yield, nor must one make any concession to them when they pretend that their tissue of falsehoods is the mystical Gospel of Mark, but rather deny it with an oath. It is not necessary to speak *all* the truth to everyone; that is why the wisdom of God proclaims through Solomon: 'Answer a fool according to his folly' [Prov. 26:5]—meaning that from those who are spiritually blind the light of the truth must be concealed. Scripture also says, 'From him who has not will be taken away' [Mk. 4:25] and 'Let the fool walk in darkness' [Eccles. 2:14]. But we are sons of light, having been illuminated by 'the dayspring from on high' of the Spirit of the Lord [*cf* Lk. 1:78], 'and where the Spirit of the Lord is', Scripture says, 'there is liberty' [2 Cor. 3:17]; for 'to the pure all things are pure' [Tit. 1:15]. To you, then, I will not hesitate to give an answer to your questions, exposing those people's falsehoods by the very words of the Gospel.

Thus far Clement's preamble (to some points in which we must come back); from now on he gives an account of the expanded text of Mark 10:32ff. in the second edition of the Gospel to which he has referred:

Immediately after the section which begins *And they were on the road, going up to Jerusalem* and continues to *after three days he will rise* [Mk. 10:32–34], there follows, as the text goes: 'And they come to Bethany, and there was a woman there whose brother had died. She came and prostrated herself before Jesus and says

303

to him, "Son of David, pity me." The disciple rebuked her, and Jesus in anger set out with her for the garden where the tomb was. Immediately a loud voice was heard from the tomb, and Jesus approached and rolled the stone away from the entrance to the tomb. And going in immediately where the young man was, he stretched out his hand and raised him up, taking him by the hand. The young man looked on him and loved him, and began to beseech him that he might be with him. They came out of the tomb and went into the young man's house, for he was rich. After six days Jesus laid a charge upon him, and when evening came the young man comes to him, with a linen robe thrown over his naked body; and he stayed with him that night, for Jesus was teaching him the mystery of the kingdom of God. When he departed thence, he returned to the other side of the Jordan.'

After this there follows *And James and John came forward to him* and all that section [Mk. 10:35–45]. But as for 'naked to naked' and the other things about which you wrote, they are not to be found.

After the words *And he comes to Jericho* [Mk. 10:46a] it adds only: 'And there was the sister of the young man whom Jesus loved and his mother and Salome; and Jesus did not receive them.' But as for the many other things which you wrote, they are falsehoods both in appearance and in reality. Now the true interpretation, which is in accordance with the true philosophy...

— and there the writing breaks off. Probably the scribe who copied the text on to the end-papers of the Ignatius volume found that his exemplar failed him at that point, so he could copy no more.[12]

CLEMENT AND THE GOSPEL TEXT

That, then, is the text: what are we to make of it?

No letters by Clement of Alexandria have been preserved, but two or three citations from letters ascribed to him appear in the compilation of biblical and patristic maxims called *Sacra Parallela*, traditionally attributed to John of Damascus (c 675-c 749)—who himself, coincidentally, spent some time at Mar Saba. (Even if the *Sacra Parallela* be not his, some letters ascribed to Clement were apparently

[12] About one third of the final and end-paper is left blank.

known to the real author, whoever he was.)

Towards the end of the newly-published document the letter-writer quotes the opening words of Mark 10:46 in the form 'And he comes to Jericho'. This is the Western reading, in place of the majority text 'And they come to Jericho'. It is not unusual to find readings characteristic of the Western text in the Gospel citations of Clement of Alexandria.

The letter-writer commences his account of the expanded text by saying that it comes immediately after the section which begins, 'And they were on the road, going up to Jerusalem...' (Mk.10:32). Immediately before that section comes the incident of the rich man who asks Jesus what he must do to inherit eternal life (Mk. 10:17–31). This incident provides the subject-matter for Clement's homily, *The Salvation of a Rich Man*—a homily which includes a quotation *in extenso* of these fifteen verses of Mark.[13] This quotation contains no esoteric or other expansion, but presents some textual peculiarities, on which the redoubtable J. W. Burgon animadverted in a famous passage:

> I request that the clock of history be put back seventeen hundred years. This is AD 183, if you please; and—(indulge me in the supposition!)—you and I are walking in Alexandria. We have reached the house of one Clemens,—a learned Athenian, who has long been a resident here. Let us step into his library,—he is from home. What a queer place! See, he has been reading his Bible, which is open at S. Mark x. Is it not a well-used copy? It must be at least 50 or 60 years old. Well, but suppose only 30 or 40. It was executed therefore *within fifty years of the death of S. John the Evangelist.* Come, let us transcribe two of the columns... as faithfully as we possibly can, and be off... We are back in England again, and the clock has been put right. Now let us sit down and examine our curiosity at leisure... It proves on inspection to be a transcript of the 15 verses (ver. 17 to ver. 31) which relate to the coming of the rich young Ruler to our LORD.
>
> We make a surprising discovery... *It is impossible to produce a fouler exhibition of S. Mark x. 17–31 than is contained in a document full two centuries older than either B or Aleph,—itself the property of one of the most famous of the ante-Nicene Fathers...* The foulness of a text which must have been penned within 70 or 80 years of the

[13] See p. 187 above.

death of the last of the Evangelists, is a matter of fact,—which must be loyally accepted, and made the best of.[14]

Dean Burgon was concerned to make the point that the most ancient manuscripts of the New Testament are not necessarily the purest. The text of Mark 10:17−31 as quoted by Clement in this treatise is rather heavily contaminated by the texts of the Matthaean and Lukan parallels. But it is not at all certain that, if we could visit Clement's study and look at his scroll (or, more probably, codex) of the Gospel of Mark open at this place, we should find the text which is reproduced in his treatise. He may have quoted it in part from memory, and when we depend on memory for a text which appears in all three Synoptic Gospels we are apt to produce a very mixed text, as Clement does here. (Dean Burgon himself gives evidence of such reliance on his memory when he speaks of 'the rich young Ruler'; it is Matthew, not Mark, who says that he was young, and Luke who says that he was a ruler.) Clement gives evidence of memory quoting later in the same treatise when he comments on the words of verse 21, 'sell what things you have' (*hosa echeis*), which he has quoted above in their Marcan form, quoting them the second time in the more familiar form of Mt. 10:21, 'sell your property' (*ta hyparchonta*). If one Alexandrian writer was able to produce such a contaminated Gospel text, we need not be surprised if the author of the additional pericope quoted by our letter-writer amplifies his Marcan phrases occasionally by means of their Matthaean parallels.

THE EXPANDED TEXT

The pericope inserted between verses 34 and 35 of Mark 10 is Marcan in diction, for the simple reason that it is largely a pastiche of phrases from Mark ('contaminated' by Matthaean parallels), coupled with some Johannine material. The story of Jesus' raising the young man of Bethany from the tomb at his sister's entreaty is superficially similar to the incident of the raising of Lazarus in John 11:17−44; but our present story, far from presenting the features of an independent Marcan counterpart to the Johannine incident, is thoroughly confused: in view of the loud voice which was heard from the tomb as Jesus approached, it is doubtful if the young man was really dead. In this

---

[14] *The Revision Revised* (London, 1883), pp. 326−329.

story Jesus himself rolls away the stone from the entrance to the tomb, whereas in John 11:39 he commands the bystanders to remove the stone which covered the tomb of Lazarus.

The young man's sister makes her plea to Jesus after the example of the Syrophoenician woman who fell at Jesus' feet (Mk. 7:25), saying, 'Pity me, son of David' (Mt. 15:22), and like her she incurs the disciples' disapproval (Mt. 15:23). (We may compare the similar plea of blind Bartimaeus in Mark 10:47f., and his refusal to be silenced by the rebuke of those around.) Jesus' anger is matched by his reaction to the leper's plea in the Western text of Mark 1:41, and by his indignation at the tomb of Lazarus (Jn. 11:33, 38). 'The garden where the tomb was' is a detail borrowed from John's account of the burial of Jesus (Jn. 19:41).

Jesus' action in taking the young man by the hand and raising him up comes not from the account of the raising of Lazarus but from the raising of Jairus's daughter (Mk. 5:41) or, even more closely, from the healing of Simon Peter's mother-in-law (Mk. 1:31). The statement that 'the young man looked on him and loved him' reverses that of Mark 10:21, where Jesus looked on the rich man and loved him. The young man who is here raised from the tomb was also rich. When he began to beseech Jesus that he might be with him, he followed the example of the cured Gerasene demoniac (Mk. 5:18). The time-note 'after six days' was the interval between the Caesarea Philippi incident and the transfiguration (Mk. 9:2). The linen robe thrown over the young man's naked body reminds us of the young man similarly attired at the scene of Jesus' arrest (Mk. 14:51). The statement that 'he stayed with him that night' may recall John 1:39, 'they stayed with him that day.'

The reference to the young man's sister and mother in the amplified form of Mark 10:46 is probably meant to integrate the incident of the young man with its general context. Curiously, however, the young man is now identified as the one 'whom Jesus loved'; we have reverted to the situation of Mark 10:21 — although, since the verb 'loved' is in the imperfect tense here *(ēgapa)*, in contrast to the aorist *(ēgapēsen)* of Mark 10:21 and of the earlier statement in our pericope that the young man 'loved' Jesus, we may detect the influence of the Johannine references to 'the disciple whom Jesus loved' (Jn. 13:23, etc.). It is not clear what Salome is doing in the company, but she figures as a somewhat self-assertive disciple of Jesus in a number of gnostic texts; we may recall, too (if she is to be identified with the mother of the sons of Zebedee, as a comparison of Mk. 15:40 with Mt. 27:56 might suggest), that she figures in the Matthaean counterpart to the incident of Mark 10:35–45, for in Matthew 20:20f. it is the mother of James and John who takes the initiative in asking for them the places of highest honour in the coming kingdom. Jesus' declining to grant this request may lie behind the statement at the end of our writer's quotation that he 'did not receive' the three women who met him at Jericho.

The fact that the expansion is such a pastiche (as it seems to me), with its internal contradiction and confusion, indicates that it is a thoroughly artificial composition, quite out of keeping with Mark's quality as a story-teller. Morton Smith indeed argues that it is no mere pastiche or cento,[15] but I find his arguments unconvincing. That the letter-writer was disposed to acknowledge it as part of a fuller edition of Mark's Gospel, written by the evangelist himself, is quite in line with evidence which we have of Clement's credulity in face of apocryphal material. He treats the work entitled the *Preaching of Peter* as a genuine composition of the apostle Peter, and he similarly accepts the authenticity of the *Apocalypse of Peter*.[16] We shall see, too, how readily he acknowledges as dominical sayings ascribed to Jesus in the *Gospel according to the Hebrews* and the *Gospel of the Egyptians*, explaining them in terms of his own philosophy.

MARK AND ALEXANDRIA

The information that Mark came from Rome to Alexandria is otherwise known to us from Eusebius. Johannes Munck concluded for this reason that our letter could not be earlier than Eusebius.[17] But Eusebius did not originate the story of Mark's coming to Alexandria; he received it from others. After telling of Mark's association with Peter in Rome, he goes on: 'They say that this man [Mark] was the first to be sent to Egypt to preach the gospel, which he also put together in writing, and that he was the first to establish churches in

---

[15] *Clement of Alexandria and a Secret Gospel of Mark*, pp. 141–144.

[16] For the *Preaching of Peter* cf. *Strom*, 2.15.68; 6.5.39ff. (see p. 191 above). According to Eusebius, *Hist. Eccl.* 6.14.1, Clement included the *Apocalypse of Peter* among the writings interpreted in his *Hypotypōseis*.

[17] J. Munck, quoted in M. Smith, *Clement of Alexandria and a Secret Gospel of Mark*, p. 33.

Alexandria itself.'[18] Then he says that the success of Mark's preaching may be gauged by the quality of the Therapeutae described by Philo,[19] whom he takes—quite wrongly and indeed anachronistically—to have been a Christian community.[20] Later he says that in Nero's eighth year (AD 61/62) Mark was succeeded by one Annianus in the ministry of the Alexandrian church.[21]

We can but guess the source from which Eusebius derived this information—or misinformation—but some awareness of the situation in the church of Alexandria keeps him from using the term *episkopos* of its leading minister in earlier days.

At any rate the story of Mark's founding the church of Alexandria is of most questionable authenticity. If it has any historical basis, that may be found in the coming of a codex of the Gospel of Mark to Alexandria, soon after its publication in Rome.[22] Even more questionable is the whole succession-list of the Alexandrian church leaders from Mark and his alleged successor Annianus on to the last decade or two of the second century. The first bishop of Alexandria of whom we can speak with confidence is Demetrius (*c* 190–233), first the friend and then the enemy of Origen. Many have been persuaded by the argument of Walter Bauer that Alexandrian Christianity in its earliest generations was predominantly gnostic or gnosticizing, and that not until the last quarter of the second century did the 'orthodox' interpretation of the gospel begin to gain the upper hand.[23] (The study of early Christian papyri has placed a question-mark against Bauer's case.)[24] In the 'orthodox' interpretation of the gospel the catechetical school founded at Alexandria by Pantaenus, Clement's teacher, played an important part. It may not be without significance that Pantaenus was a Sicilian by birth, while Clement probably came

---

[18] Eusebius, *Hist. Eccl.* 2.16.1.   [19] Philo, *On the Contemplative Life,* 2–90.
[20] *Hist. Eccl.* 2.17.2–24.   [21] *Hist. Eccl.* 2.24
[22] *Cf* C. H. Roberts, 'The Christian Book and the Greek Papyri', *JTS* 50 (1949), pp. 155–168; L. W. Barnard, 'St. Mark and Alexandria', *HTR* 57 (1964), pp. 145–150.
[23] W. Bauer, *Orthodoxy and Heresy in Earliest Christianity,* E.T. (Philadelphia, 1971), pp. 44–60. *Cf* R. M. Grant, 'The New Testament Canon', *CHB* I (Cambridge, 1970), p. 298: 'in the second century, as far as our knowledge goes, Christianity in Egypt was exclusively "heterodox".'
[24] The papyrus evidence 'points to more than a few scattered individuals holding orthodox beliefs' among second-century Christians in Egypt (C. H. Roberts, *Manuscript, Society and Belief in Early Christian Egypt* [London, 1979], p. 53). See p. 187 above.

from Athens. But even the orthodoxy of the catechetical school was suspect in the eyes of some later theologians; its leaders indulged too daringly in speculation.

The picture of Mark as the founder of Alexandrian Christianity represents an attempt to provide the church of that city with an orthodox pedigree, one moreover which linked it closely with the Roman church, the pillar and ground of orthodoxy, and incidentally gave it quasi-apostolic status. For if Mark's association with Peter gave apostolic authority to the gospel which he penned, it equally gave apostolic lineage to the church which he founded.

In the New Testament, however, Alexandria figures as the home of the associate of another apostle—Apollos, the friend and colleague of Paul, who (according to the Western text of Acts 18:25) had been instructed in Christianity in his native city. Could Apollos not have provided the church of Alexandria with apostolic prestige? Evidently not—perhaps because it is made so plain in Acts 18:24–26 that Apollos's original understanding of Christianity was defective, so that he had to be taken in hand by Priscilla and Aquila (foundation-members, perhaps, of the Roman church) and taught the way of God more accurately. (Not all Alexandrian Christians were Gnostics or gnosticizers, of course; the Letter to the Hebrews and the *Letter of Barnabas* may both have been written by Alexandrian Christians, and neither of them bears a gnostic stamp.)

Our letter, however, does not say that Mark planted the church of Alexandria, but that he came to Alexandria after Peter's martyrdom (not several years before it, as Eusebius implies) and continued there the literary activity which he had begun in Rome. This is possibly an earlier form of the story of his connexion with Alexandria than that reported by Eusebius, but if so it may have provided a basis for Eusebius's account. Eusebius probably derived his account from the *Chronicle* of Sextus Julius Africanus, who visited Alexandria when Demetrius was bishop and Heraclas, Origen's successor, was head of the catechetical school, and may well have learned it from them.

The kind of gospel literature that was current in Egypt in the generation before Clement is exemplified by the *Gospel according to the Hebrews* and the *Gospel of the Egyptians*, which Bauer supposed were used respectively by the Jewish Christians and Gentile Christians of Alexandria.[25] Clement was acquainted with both of these documents.

[25] W. Bauer, *Orthodoxy and Heresy in Earliest Christianity*, p.52.

From the *Gospel according to the Hebrews* he quotes the logion, 'He who seeks shall not desist until he finds; when he has found he will marvel; when he has marvelled he will attain the kingdom; when he has attained the kingdom he will rest.'[26] Another form of this Greek logion appears in the Oxyrhynchus Sayings,[27] and, in a Coptic version, as the second logion in the *Gospel of Thomas*. Clement characteristically interprets the saying of the true (Christian) philosopher.

From the *Gospel of the Egyptians* Clement quotes an alleged saying of Jesus, 'I came to destroy the works of the female', and illustrates it with a conversation between Jesus and Salome. In reply to Salome's question, 'How long will death prevail?' he said, 'As long as you women give birth to children.' 'Then', said she, 'I have done well in bearing none.' (In this tradition obviously Salome is not the mother of James and John.) 'Eat every herb', said Jesus, 'except that which has a bitter fruit.' When she pressed her original question again, he replied more fully, 'When you tread underfoot the garment of shame, when the two become one and the male with the female neither male nor female'.[28] This expresses a Valentinian theme, that death entered into human life with the separation of the female from the male—death being included, along with conception and birth and the other phases of the biological cycle, among 'the works of the female'—and that the state of perfection and immortality would be attained when the female was reabsorbed with the male into the complete human being. This view was unacceptable to Clement but, as he did not wish to give up Jesus' reported words to Salome as unauthentic, he replaced their proper gnostic sense with an ethical allegorization, in which the 'female' whose works are to be destroyed is concupiscence and 'neither male nor female' means neither anger nor concupiscence.

When the author of the letter says that Mark, after publishing his first book, 'compiled a more spiritual Gospel', it is impossible not to be reminded of Clement's statement that, after the first three evangelists had published their works, 'John last of all, conscious that the "bodily" facts had been set forth in those Gospels, urged by the disciples and divinely moved by the Spirit, composed a "spiritual" Gospel'.[29] By the 'bodily' facts in the synoptic record Clement appears to mean the outward historical details, whereas John's Gospel is 'spiritual' in the sense that it brings out their allegorical significance.

[26] *Strom.* 2.9.45; 5.14.96.   [27] *P. Oxy.* 654.2.
[28] *Strom.* 3.6.45; 3.9.63ff.; 3.13.91ff. See p. 189 above.
[29] In Eusebius, *Hist. Eccl.* 6.14.7; see p. 189 above.

Presumably Mark's 'more spiritual Gospel' was one which brought out the allegorical significance of his first edition, but we are not told what might be the allegorical significance of the extract we are given from the amplified edition. If the letter-writer is Clement, he may well have given it a moralizing interpretation such as he gives to the conversation with Salome in the *Gospel of the Egyptians,* and he might be just as far from the true sense.

In fact we might ask what there is of a 'secret' or 'hierophantic' character about the pericope quoted by the letter-writer from the amplified Gospel of Mark—unless, as with the *Gospel of Thomas,* it was the interpretation and not the written text that was regarded as esoteric. And this brings us to what the letter says about Carpocrates and his followers.

THE CARPOCRATIANS AND THE 'SECRET' GOSPEL

Carpocrates was an Alexandrian Platonist of the earlier part of the second century; he flourished two generations before Clement. According to Irenaeus,[30] he taught that the world was created by angel-archons, not by the supreme God, and (like the Ebionites) held that Jesus was a man, the son of Joseph by natural generation, on whom the divine power descended. The same power might be received by the souls of all who, like Jesus, set the archons at naught and conquered the passions which exposed men to their penalties. He also appears to have taught metempsychosis for all who were enslaved to the archons; only by defying and overcoming them, as Jesus did, could men be released from the necessity of successive reincarnations. Pythagorean influence may be indicated here, and it is perhaps relevant that, according to Irenaeus, the Carpocratians venerated images of Pythagoras, Plato and Aristotle along with images of Jesus.[31]

The followers of Carpocrates are charged by Irenaeus and Clement[32] with ethical neutralism and specifically with the practice of sexual promiscuity at their love-feasts—with the same kind of conduct, in fact, as was alleged in a number of pagan circles against Christians in general (*cf* the 'Oedipodean intercourse' of which the churches of the Rhône valley were accused, according to their letter of AD 177

---

[30] Irenaeus, *Against Heresies,* 1.25.1f.   [31] *Against Heresies,* 1.25.6.
[32] Irenaeus, *Against Heresies,* 1.25.3–5; Clement, *Strom.* 3.2.5–11.

preserved by Eusebius).[33] While we should not swallow uncritically what is said of the Carpocratians by their orthodox opponents, it is to be observed (i) that such charges are not levelled against all gnostic groups indiscriminately and (ii) that a philosophical defence of promiscuity by Epiphanes, the son of Carpocrates by a Cephallenian woman, is quoted by Clement.[34] Cardinal Daniélou, who regarded Carpocrates himself as an exponent of what he identified as Jewish Gnosticism, held that Epiphanes hellenized his father's system, 'just as Valentinus did Samaritan Gnosticism and Justin the orthodox gnosis of the same period'.[35]

Whereas Tertullian could say, 'we have all things in common, except our wives'[36] (probably implying that private property was a sign of sinful covetousness), Epiphanes and the Carpocratians appear to have gone farther and said, 'we have all things in common, including our wives.' Epiphanes justified this policy by an appeal to the principles of divine righteousness or equity as embodied not in the law of Moses but in the law of nature. He pointed to the example of the animal creation, and thus incurred the rebuke of Jude: 'by those things that they know by instinct, as irrational animals do, they are destroyed' (Jude 10). It was evidently predecessors of the Carpocratians, if not the Carpocratians themselves, whom Jude denounced so unsparingly for following the precedent of the disobedient angels and the men of Sodom. Indeed, Clement himself, in his account of the Carpocratians, expresses the opinion that 'it was of these and similar heresies that Jude spoke prophetically in his epistle'.[37] He further links them with the Nicolaitans of Revelation 2:6, 14f., and the author of our letter links them with those who explore 'the deep things of Satan'—i.e. the adherents of 'that Jezebel of a woman', denounced in the letter to the church of Thyatira, whose tenets were practically identical with those of the Nicolaitans (Rev. 2:20–23).

For our present purpose it is particularly interesting that, on the testimony of Irenaeus, the Carpocratians emphasized the statements of Mark 4:11, 34, that Jesus explained the mystery of the kingdom of God privately to his disciples, while speaking to the general public in parables; they claimed also that the disciples were authorized to deliver this private teaching 'to those who were worthy and who

[33] *Hist. Eccl.* 5.1.14.   [34] *Strom.* 3.2.6.
[35] J. Daniélou, *The Theology of Jewish Christianity,* E.T. (London, 1964), pp.84f.
[36] Tertullian, *Apology,* 39.11.   [37] Clement, *Strom.* 3.2.11.

assented to it'.[38] They themselves, in other words, were the custodians of Jesus' private teaching—of the 'messianic secret', so to speak. But whereas the historical 'mystery of the kingdom' or 'messianic secret' was concerned with the nature of the kingdom, of the God whose kingdom it was and of the messianic ministry by which it was being inaugurated, it was reinterpreted—or rather misinterpreted—among the Carpocratians and in other gnostic schools in terms of mystical initiation. The letter-writer himself uses the language of mystical initiation with regard to the mature Christian (as Clement does with regard to his 'true Gnostic'),[39] but with him (as with Clement) this is but a figure of speech.

It was evidently the Carpocratians' claim to be the transmitters of Jesus' esoteric doctrine that moved Theodore to write to Clement (if we accept the attribution of the letter). They appealed to an edition of Mark's Gospel which, they maintained, vindicated their assertion that Jesus taught conventional morality in public but communicated a more uninhibited ethic to select souls in private. Theodore evidently asked Clement about this 'secret' Gospel of Mark. 'Clement' knows about it, but denies that it supports Carpocratian doctrine: Carpocrates procured a copy, he says, by underhand means, and his followers have perverted its interpretation, putting a libertine construction, for example, on the incident of the young man 'with a linen robe thrown over his naked body', as though the impartation of the mystery of the kingdom of God involved complete physical contiguity. When 'Clement' says that the phrase 'naked to naked', about which Theodore had asked, is not found in the text of the 'secret' Gospel, we may reasonably infer that this phrase summed up the Carpocratians' interpretation of the incident, which they probably invoked in defence of their own 'sacramental' practice.

That there was an extreme libertine tradition in early Christianity as well as an extreme ascetic tradition is plain to readers of the New Testament, especially of the Pauline letters. Paul himself, like Jesus before him, taught a way of holiness which did not belong to either of these extreme traditions. As for the libertine tradition, Professor Smith finds it so firmly embedded in early Christianity that he concludes it must have gone back to Jesus' esoteric teaching, as the more ascetic tradition went back to his public teaching. But such evidence as we have points to a Gentile origin for the libertine

[38] Irenaeus, *Against Heresies*, 1.25.5.
[39] Clement, *Strom*. 7.1–16. See p. 187 above.

tradition. We cannot be sure about the Nicolaitans of the Apocalypse, whether or not they were called after Nicolaus the proselyte of Antioch (Acts 6:5), as Irenaeus believed:[40] perhaps they and kindred groups simply wished to relax the terms of the apostolic decree of Acts 15:28f. But Paul's Corinthian correspondence gives us a clear enough line: the libertines in the Corinthian church were the 'spiritual' men who had come to regard all bodily activities as morally indifferent, and devised a theological defence of their continued indulgence in the besetting sin of Corinth, even after their conversion to Christianity. They probably maintained that they were carrying to its logical conclusion Paul's gospel of freedom from the law. It was men of this outlook who regarded the cohabitation of one of their number with his father's wife as a fine assertion of Christian liberty (1 Cor.5:1–13). Epiphanes, whose father had taught him Platonism with a dash of Pythagoreanism, devised a more sophisticated theological defence for this kind of conduct.

As for the 'secret' Gospel of Mark, it may well have come into being within the Carpocratian fellowship, or a similar school of thought. That 'Clement' thought it went back to Mark himself is neither here nor there, in view of the historical Clement's uncritical acceptance of other apocrypha. The raising of the young man of Bethany is too evidently based—and clumsily based at that—on the Johannine story of the raising of Lazarus for us to regard it as in any sense an independent Marcan counterpart to the Johannine story (not to speak of our regarding it as a *source* of the Johannine story). Since this conclusion is so completely at variance with Professor Smith's carefully argued case, one must do him the justice of giving his case the detailed consideration which it deserves. But this lecture presents my initial assessment[41] of the document which he has discovered and published.[42]

[40] *Against Heresies,* 1.26.3.

[41] My assessment of the document remains substantially the same fifteen years later.

[42] This lecture was first published by the Athlone Press, University of London, in 1974.

APPENDIX II

PRIMARY SENSE
AND PLENARY SENSE

Peake Memorial Lecture, 1976

Any biblical student might well feel honoured in being invited to deliver a lecture in the series dedicated to the memory of Arthur Samuel Peake, but it is with a sense of double honour that the invitation is accepted by one who is already honoured by holding the academic position which was first held—and with rare distinction—by Dr Peake.[1]

A. S. PEAKE AND BIBLICAL EXEGESIS

For the last twenty-five years of his life (1904–1929), Dr Peake occupied the Rylands Chair of Biblical Exegesis in the University of Manchester. For most of his incumbency that was the designation of the Chair: only towards the end of the twenty-five years was the wording amplified to 'Biblical Criticism and Exegesis'. Dr Peake was, of course, a practitioner and teacher of biblical criticism as well as exegesis, but the original designation of the Chair perhaps implies that criticism, whether lower or higher, is a means to an end. As Dr Peake himself said, 'criticism has never attracted me for its own sake. The all-important thing for the student of the Bible is to pierce to the

[1] The lecture was delivered during the lecturer's incumbency of the Rylands Chair of Biblical Criticism and Exegesis in the University of Manchester.

316

core of its meaning.'[2] When criticism has done its perfect work, the important question remains: What does the text mean? Critical study will help very considerably to find the answer to this question, but the meaning of scripture—its meaning for those to whom it came in the first instance, and its meaning for readers today—is what matters most.

Dr Peake was well aware of this, and he taught the principles of biblical interpretation not only to his students in the lecture-room but to the rank and file of his fellow-Christians also. *The Bible: Its Origin, its Significance and its Abiding Worth*—a book which I found particularly helpful in my formative years—was written for a wider public, consisting, to begin with, of readers of *The Sunday Strand*. His *Plain Thoughts on Great Subjects,* a collection of more popular articles and addresses, illustrates his concern that Christians should free their minds from time-honoured interpretations which had no basis in the proper meaning of the biblical text. The 'wayfaring men, yea fools', who 'shall not "err"' in the way of holiness, he pointed out, are reprobates who may not trespass on the path reserved for 'the ransomed of the LORD' (Is. 35:8, 10);[3] the blood-stained figure who comes from Edom, 'with dyed garments from Bozrah', having 'trodden the wine-press alone', is as far as can well be imagined from our Lord, fresh from the scene of his passion; the blood which reddens the apparel of the warrior of Isaiah 63:1–6 is that of the slaughtered sons of Esau.[4] (I am bound to add that I suspect that the seer of Patmos made an early contribution to the christological interpretation of this oracle; but he could bend the most recalcitrant material to serve his purpose.)[5]

The distinction between the primary and plenary sense of scripture is not one that I recall coming across in Dr Peake's writings. He does draw attention to the distinction between the primary and secondary sense,[6] but that is not always the same distinction. The plenary sense, I suppose, is always secondary, but the secondary sense need not be plenary.

Dr Peake distinguished, for example, between the primary and the

---

[2] A. S. Peake, *The Bible: Its Origin, its Significance and its Abiding Worth* (London, 1913), p.455.

[3] A. S. Peake, *Plain Thoughts on Great Subjects* (London, 1931), pp.175–180.

[4] *Plain Thoughts,* pp.170–174.

[5] *Cf* Rev. 19:13, with G. B. Caird, *The Revelation of St John the Divine* (London/New York, 1966), pp.242–244.

[6] *The Bible,* pp.452, 455.

secondary sense of the Servant Songs of Isaiah 42—53. He was convinced that 'the collective judgment of Christendom has been right in finding the fulfilment of these prophecies in Christ' because 'the prophet's language is fulfilled in Jesus as in no other'.[7] In saying this, he attaches what we should call a plenary sense—*the* plenary sense—to the Songs, pointing out that 'we often find meanings in great works of Art which were probably not intended by the authors themselves' and that 'when inspiration works at so high a level as it often does in the Bible we may not unnaturally expect to find deeper senses than that of which the original author was aware.'[8] But such a deeper sense, even if it be acknowledged as plenary, is chronologically secondary; the sense of which the biblical author was aware is the primary sense. As it happens, the primary sense of the Servant Songs is not so readily ascertainable: the Ethiopian's question to Philip, 'About whom, pray, does the prophet say this, about himself or about someone else?' (Acts 8:34), is still a suitable question to be set in an examination paper. In my own view, Dr Peake's estimate of the primary sense of these particular scriptures was not so near the mark as that of another great Methodist scholar, the late Christopher North.[9]

'SPRINGING AND GERMINANT ACCOMPLISHMENT'

When we speak of primary sense and plenary sense we may imagine that primary sense is a straightforward matter by contrast with the complexities of plenary sense. Primary sense is the sense which the author intended by his words, the sense which he expected his readers or hearers to understand by his words. Plenary sense is a richer thing than that. It can best be defined and described, perhaps, in a passage which I quote from Dorothy L. Sayers:

> A phrase used by Dante not only contains and is illuminated by the meanings it derived from Virgil or the Vulgate: it, in its turn, illuminates Virgil and the Vulgate and gives new meaning to them. It not only passes on those meanings, supercharged with Dante's own meaning, to Tennyson and Landor, to Rossetti and Yeats, to Williams and Eliot and Pound, but it receives

---

[7] *The Bible*, p.453.   [8] *The Bible*, p.452.
[9] *Cf* C. R. North, *The Suffering Servant in Deutero-Isaiah* (Oxford, [2]1956).

back from them the reflected *splendore* of their own imaginative
use of it.[10]

Thomas Aquinas, in the thirteenth century, put it this way:

> Prophecies are sometimes uttered about the things which existed
> at the time in question, but are not uttered primarily with
> reference to them, but in so far as these are a figure of things to
> come. Therefore the Holy Spirit has provided that, when such
> prophecies are uttered, some details should be inserted which go
> beyond the actual thing done, so that the mind may be raised to
> the thing signified.[11]

St Thomas was referring to the interpretation of one particular area of
biblical literature—predictive prophecy. He used the word 'primarily'
where we should say 'plenarily', when he said that the contemporary
reference of biblical prophecies was not their primary reference.[12] As
we are now using the words, their contemporary reference *was* their
'primary' reference, the 'things' to come' of which the contemporary
reference was a figure belonging to the plenary sense, in so far as they
are genuinely relevant to the scripture in question. Thus the primary
sense of Isaiah's virgin oracle related to a prince about to be born in the
near future; Matthew's application of the oracle to the birth of Jesus
can be said to set forth the plenary sense, not least because the idiom of
the original oracle (although Matthew need not have known this) was
already a well-established form of words for the annunciation of the
birth of a coming deliverer,[13] and was therefore appropriate for
heralding the nativity of the Messiah.

To the same effect Francis Bacon at a later date spoke of the
necessity of 'allowing . . . that latitude which is agreeable and familiar
unto Divine prophecies; being of the nature of their Author with
whom a thousand years are but as one day, and therefore are not
fulfilled punctually at once, but have springing and germinant
accomplishment throughout many ages, though the height or fulness

---

[10] D. L. Sayers, *The Poetry of Search and the Poetry of Statement* (London, 1963),
p.272.

[11] Thomas Aquinas, *Commentary on Psalms,* preface.

[12] What we here call the primary sense he called the literal sense.

[13] See the Ugaritic poem, 'The Wedding of Nikkal and Yarih', lines 5, 7, in C. H.
Gordon, *Ugaritic Handbook* (Rome, 1947), p.152; *Ugaritic Literature* (Rome, 1949),
pp.63f.

of them may refer to some one age.'[14] What Bacon here argues for is sufficient scope to accommodate not only the primary reference but further provisional fulfilments as well, until at last their 'height or fulness', their plenary sense, is manifested.

A biblical scholar of the present century, the late Cuthbert Lattey, attached high value to this interpretative approach in what he called the principle of 'compenetration'.[15] He found this principle helpful in the exegesis of such a passage as Isaiah's virgin oracle and of larger literary units.[16] An adequate exegesis of the visions of Daniel, he believed, 'must take into account, as it were, three historical planes, that of the persecution of Antiochus IV Epiphanes, and of the first and second comings of Christ'.[17] Whether or not this three-dimensional perspective is necessary for the exposition of Daniel, it must be insisted that the exegete's first responsibility is to establish the primary historical reference of the author and his original readers, and then to decide how far visions or oracles whose primary sense is thus ascertained can be related, by implication or in principle, to later situations.

There is a similarity between the idea of 'springing and germinant accomplishment' and the idea of Christian tradition as expounded in our time, for example, by Père Y. M. -J. Congar. Tradition, he says, is another mode by which the truth embodied in scripture, the apostolic heritage, is communicated to us. 'Scripture has an absolute sovereignty',[18] whereas tradition is a *thésaurisation* or constant accrual of meditation on the text of scripture in one generation after another, 'the living continuity of faith quickening God's people'.[19] The reality of such tradition cannot be doubted: many parts of scripture have a richer meaning for Christians today than they had for Christians in the early centuries AD because of what they have meant for intervening genera-tions of Christians. (It is equally true that many parts of scripture had a meaning for Christians in other centuries that they cannot have for us today, but that is another story.) However, such tradition is derivative and dependent: the interpretation of scripture, even if it

---

[14] F. Bacon, *Advancement of Learning*, II (*Ecclesiastical History* 2.2: 'History of Prophecy') in *Works*, ed. B. Montagu, II (London, 1825), p.117.

[15] C. C. Lattey, S.J., *Back to Christ* (New York, 1919), pp.64ff.

[16] C. C. Lattey, 'The Emmanuel Prophecy (Is. 7:14)', *CBQ* 8 (1946), pp.369–376.

[17] C. C. Lattey, *The Book of Daniel* (Dublin, 1948), p.vii.

[18] Y. M. -J. Congar, O.P., *Tradition and Traditions*, E.T. (London, 1966), p.422.

[19] *Tradition and Traditions*, p.4.

accrues at compound interest from generation to generation, cannot get more out of scripture than is there already—implicitly if not expressly. This, I am sure, was Dr Peake's view (it is equally mine), but is it valid? I know some theologians who would suggest that the Holy Spirit may bring forth from scripture today truth which bears little relation to that conveyed by the text in its historical setting, but I cannot think they are right. Even the devotional application of scripture, which is specially impatient of strict exegetical controls, must be reasonably deducible from what scripture says; otherwise, why base a 'blessed thought' on one text rather than another, or why base it on a text of scripture at all?

One example of the way in which a new and widely accepted interpretation can be attached to an ancient scripture is provided by the lament of the desolate city of Jerusalem, after the siege and devastation endured at the hands of the Babylonian army: 'Is it nothing to you, all you who pass by? Look and see if there is any sorrow like my sorrow which was brought upon me, which the LORD inflicted on the day of his fierce anger' (Lam. 1:12).

It is safe to say that many English-speaking Christians, perhaps the majority of them, when they hear these words, do not think of the sack of Jersualem in 587 BC but of the passion of our Lord. We recognize that Charles Wesley and Sir John Stainer between them bear considerable responsibility for this; but neither Wesley nor Stainer originated this passion interpretation: it goes back to the traditional employment of the language of Lamentations in the church's Holy Week commemoration.

Yet the application of these words to our Lord's passion may be acknowledged as a valid instance of the 'plenary sense' of scripture if (as Norman K. Gottwald has argued) the expression of communal disaster found in Lamentations draws on various categories of individual lament, constituting a 'deliberate fusion of hitherto comparatively separate types'—a process which reached a climax in the fourth Isaianic Servant Song (Is. 52:13—53:12).[20] If, then, the distinctively Christian interpretation of the Servant of Yahweh is as justified as Dr Peake held (and with good reason), the plenary sense of the fourth Servant Song (or something very like it) can legitimately be read out of certain passages of Lamentations, like Lamentations 1:12, where the language lends itself to this extended application.

[20] N. K. Gottwald, *Studies in the Book of Lamentations* (London, 1954), p.46.

THE COMPLEXITY OF 'PRIMARY SENSE'

To this matter of extended application we shall return. But, having provided one illustration of what is meant by 'plenary sense' in relation to the Bible, we must look more closely at what is involved in 'primary sense'.

I recall some correspondence in a leading literary journal several years ago which was started by someone's taking a passage from a poem by Roy Fuller and drawing certain inferences from it. Roy Fuller in due course wrote to the editor and said that the first writer had misunderstood the passage: that was not what he had meant at all. This brought an indignant rejoinder: what business was it of the author of a poem to say what his poem meant? Once the poem had become public property, the sense in which the reader understood it was as valid as the sense which the author claimed to have had in mind when he composed it. The terms 'primary sense' and 'plenary sense' were not used, so far as I can remember; but from the tone in which the reader wrote I doubt if he would have conceded that the author's interpretation had any greater right to be called 'primary' than his own. As we are using the terms now, however, the author's meaning would be 'primary' and the reader's interpretation, whether legitimate or not, would be 'secondary'—not, I think, 'plenary'. The reader's protest reminded me too forcibly of the attitude of those whose main exegetical criterion in Bible study is '*I* like to think that it means this.'

But the establishment of the primary sense of a passage of scripture is not always such a straightforward matter as is commonly supposed. Take, for example, a gospel parable in which the intention of Jesus may have been one thing and the evangelist's interpretation something else. You may recall C. H. Dodd's remark on Matthew's interpretation of the parable of the tares: 'We shall do well to forget this interpretation as completely as possible.'[21] What he meant was, that we ought to forget this interpretation if we are concerned to discover the original point of the parable—which he took (rightly, I think) to be essentially dominical. But if we are speaking of biblical exegesis in the strict sense—in this instance, the exegesis of the Gospel according to Matthew—then the Matthaean interpretation is of the first importance. If Jesus meant to teach a different lesson from that which the evangelist inculcates, which of the two is primary? Jesus' meaning, of course, both in regard to historical order and in regard to our under-

---

[21] C. H. Dodd, *Parables of the Kingdom* (London, 1935), p. 184 (on Mt. 13:36–43).

standing of his teaching; but so far as biblical exegesis is concerned, it is the Gospel of Matthew, not the tradition lying behind it, that is part of holy writ, and a case could be made out in this context for regarding Matthew's interpretation as 'primary'. Admittedly, important as the four evangelists' theology and presentation may be, their primary value resides in the witness which they bear to Jesus and his ministry, so that, absolutely, it is the intention of Jesus that is of primary importance. (Let it not be forgotten that our knowledge of his intention must be derived from the witness of the evangelists.) But, when we are dealing with the Gospels and other biblical writings as literary documents, then the intention of the authors is of primary importance for the interpretation of their writings.

A further complication is introduced into our study of Matthew's Gospel from this point of view when we have documentary evidence of an intermediary stage between the teaching of Jesus and the literary activity of the evangelist. There is no other version of the parable of the tares in the New Testament, but there are some parables in the same Matthaean context which appear in an earlier form in Mark's Gospel. There we may have to distinguish between the intention of Jesus, the intention of Mark and the intention of Matthew, and to which of these we accord 'primary' status will depend on the primary purpose of our study — the exposition of the teaching of Jesus or the interpretation of one or the other of the two gospels in question.

Even if we concentrate on the earliest gospel writing and study (say) the parable of the sower (Mk. 4:3–20), we may trace three successive stages in the growth of the tradition: (a) the parable itself, (b) the interpretation of the parable with its explanation of the four kinds of soil into which the good seed fell and (c) the appended statement about the purpose of parables with its allusion to the Isaianic passage about unresponsive hearts, deaf ears and unseeing eyes. The primary sense of a biblical text may thus be quite a complex thing.

To take an example from the Old Testament: the primary sense of Psalm 51 was the sense intended by the penitent who first made it his prayer of confession. It is traditionally ascribed to David, as though it were an expansion of his response to the prophet Nathan: 'I have sinned against Yahweh' (2 Sam. 12:13). In any case, it belongs originally to the period of the monarchy, as probably do most of the individual psalms. The penitent knows that, where the soul has direct dealings with God in the way of repentance and forgiveness, ritual performances are irrelevant:

Thou hast no delight in sacrifice;
were I to give a burnt offering,
    thou wouldst not be pleased.
Thy sacrifice, O God, is a broken spirit;
    a broken and contrite heart, O God,
    thou wilt not despise.

But the time came when this psalm was included in a collection of hymns designed for liturgical use in the Second Temple. This liturgical use implied a sacrificial context, so something had to be added which modified the sense of the psalmist's words about sacrifice. The editor who adapted the psalm to its new setting suggested that the psalmist's omission of sacrifice was due not so much to his conviction that Yahweh had no pleasure in any such thing as to the conditions of exile, when no sacrifice was possible. Hence his supplement runs:

Do good to Zion in thy good pleasure;
    rebuild the walls of Jerusalem,
then wilt thou delight in right sacrifices,
    in burnt offerings and whole burnt offerings;
    then bulls will be offered on thy altar.

If the editor or compiler lived toward the end of the exile, this may have been his prayer, although it was not the prayer of the original suppliant. But in the exegesis of the psalm, do we concentrate on what appears to have been its original text, or accept it in its fuller canonical form? We must certainly pay attention to the canonical form, in order to ascertain the significance of the composition for worshippers who made it the vehicle of their devotions in the post-exilic age. But, where the fuller form conflicts with the meaning of the earlier form, we cannot say that the fuller form gives the plenary sense, for the plenary sense must preserve, even when it amplifies, the primary sense.

Similar considerations apply to almost every part of the Old Testament. We have to ask what each part meant in its original form and setting, what it meant when it was embodied in a larger *corpus,* and what it meant in the completed Hebrew Bible. Then, if we are Christians, we have to take a further step and ask what it means in the total volume of Christian scripture, Old and New Testaments together. An examination of the use of the Old Testament in the New, as bearing witness to Christ, helps to answer this last question.

When we come to the use of the Old Testament in the New, we have left the primary sense and reached the plenary sense, as has been seen in relation to the Servant Songs and their Christian application. But we find a halfway house between primary and plenary sense within the Old Testament itself, when earlier texts are taken up and reapplied in later books. Some of these reapplications are instances of transferred rather than plenary sense, as when (say) Habakkuk applies to the Chaldaean invaders the language which Isaiah had used of their Assyrian predecessors.[22]

In the visions of Daniel, however, we find something that does belong more recognizably to the category of plenary interpretation. For example, describing the rebuff which Antiochus Epiphanes received, during his second invasion of Egypt, from the Roman delegation under Popilius Laenas which was put ashore by the Roman flotilla anchored in the harbour of Alexandria, the interpreting angel tells Daniel that 'ships of Kittim shall come against him' (Dan. 11:30). This reference to the Roman vessels as 'ships of Kittim' established a precedent which was to be followed in the Qumran texts, where *Kittim* is a regular code-word for 'Romans'. But why should 'ships of Kittim' appear here in the book of Daniel? Almost certainly the expression harks back to Balaam's oracle about the latter days which foretold how 'ships shall come from Kittim and shall afflict Asshur and Eber' (Num. 24:24). The original historical reference of this oracle is a question in its own right: few will suppose that Balaam had Antiochus Epiphanes in mind. But the implication of Daniel 11:30 is that the incident of 168 BC was the true fulfilment of Balaam's oracle. An interpretative tradition was thus set up which finds independent attestation centuries later in the Targum of Onqelos, where Numbers 24:24 is rendered 'ships will come from the Romans', and in Jerome's Vulgate, which renders the same clause, 'they will come in triremes from Italy'.

Here, then, within the Hebrew Bible itself are two levels of exegesis. Balaam's oracle had one distinct primary sense: it is the task of historical interpretation to determine what it was—whether the invasions of the sea peoples at the end of the thirteenth century BC or some later occasion, perhaps in the period of the monarchy. But when we come to Daniel and his successors we recognize the beginning of a new exegetical tradition which in their eyes represented the definitive sense of the oracle. We may classify it under the heading of plenary

[22] Compare Hab. 1:5 with Is. 29:14.

325

sense (although they themselves might have maintained that it was the *primary* sense, meaning that it was to this that the oracle pointed from the outset).

Again, the sequel to Antiochus's rebuff is described in Daniel 11:30–39 in terms which can be checked, point by point, against the available historical evidence. But there comes a moment when the historical outline fails; yet the remaining career of Antiochus must be traced until his final downfall. The apocalyptist is not thrown back on his unaided imagination: the last stages in the oppressor's career had been foretold by the prophets. Isaiah had told how the Assyrian, invading the holy land from the north, would fall with a mighty crash at the peak of his arrogance, in the very act of shaking his fist at Jerusalem, and how he would be devoured by no human sword (Is. 10:27b–34; 31:8). In more explicit detail, Ezekiel had told how Gog, the invader from the north, would be turned round in his tracks, be forced to go back by the way that he came, and be overthrown on the mountains of Israel (Ezek. 39:1–6). With this wealth of information about the fate of the last Gentile invader, all that was necessary for Daniel was that it should be reworded in accordance with the idiom of the preceding part of the vision.

'WRESTLING JACOB'

We come back now to the matter of extended application accruing to the development of a plenary sense well beyond the biblical period. This time a well-known patriarchal narrative will serve as an example.

The story of Jacob's wrestling with the angel at the ford of Jabbok (Gen. 32:22–32) is one that is capable of being interpreted at several levels. We know it as an incident in the life of Jacob as recorded in Genesis, but it may have had an earlier currency—earlier even than its inclusion in an oral or documentary source underlying the Pentateuchal record. Sir James Frazer suggested that 'we may, perhaps, provisionally suppose that Jacob's mysterious adversary was the spirit or jinnee of the river, and that the struggle was purposely sought by Jacob for the sake of obtaining his blessing'; he compared Menelaus's grappling with the sea-god Proteus.[23] Well, perhaps; Frazer acknowledged that any explanation of the story 'must be to a great extent conjectural', and one might equally well conjecture that the river-god was disputing

[23] J. G. Frazer, *Folk-lore in the Old Testament* (London, 1923), pp.251–258.

passage with this intruder into his domain.[24] But neither of these conjectures belongs to the realm of biblical interpretation. Biblical interpretation is concerned with the meaning of the passage in its literary context; in this context the primary sense of the story is the sense intended by the biblical author.

If we were examining the significance of an episode in Shakespeare's *Macbeth,* it would not be deemed sufficient to look up Raphael Holinshed's *Chronicle,* from which Shakepeare evidently derived the plot, and conclude that the primary sense of the episode was the sense which it bears in that compilation of historical fiction, or even in some oral tradition antedating Holinshed. For the student of Shakespeare, the primary sense is that which Shakespeare intended the episode to bear. So, for the student of scripture, the primary sense of the incident of wrestling Jacob is that intended by 'the author of Genesis' (to quote a form of words from the 1962 edition of Peake's *Commentary* which one would not expect to find in the original edition.)[25] For our present purpose it makes little difference whether we think of the Yahwist or of the final author: for the one as for the other, the significance of the incident is that which it has in the context of the story of Jacob, his dealings with God and the development of his character. It is not, I think, reading into the narrative something which the author did not intend if we consider that Jacob's experience at the ford of Jabbok crystallizes the whole tenor of his life up to that point. Only when his strength and his self-confidence were drained away, when he was disabled by one stronger than himself and could do nothing but cling for dear life and refuse to let the stranger go until he received his blessing, was that blessing actually given. Jacob received the name Israel there because he had 'striven with God and man, and had prevailed'; he left the place empowered and enriched because, as he said, 'I have seen God face to face, and my life is preserved' (Gen. 32:30). There is no need to import this language into the narrative, because it is there already, and points to the sense which the author intended — the primary sense.

For various forms of the plenary sense of the narrative we go to later writers. Hosea, like the author of Genesis, uses the incident (which he

---

[24] *Cf* A. S. Peake in *Peake's Commentary on the Bible* (London, [1]1919), p.160, where the exposition of the incident seems to refer to a pre-literary stage of its transmission (like the exposition of the serpent's rôle in Gen. 3:1–15, *ibid.,* p.140).

[25] S. H. Hooke in *Peake's Commentary on the Bible* (London, [2]1962), p.175.

may have known in a slightly different form) to illustrate the progress of Jacob's experience of God (Hos. 12:3f.):

> In his manhood he strove with God;
> he strove with the angel and prevailed,
>   he wept and sought his favour.

Centuries later, the author of the book of Wisdom says that Wisdom acted as umpire at Jacob's wrestling-match (Wisdom 10:12):

> In his arduous contest she gave him the victory,
> so that he might learn that godliness
>   is more powerful than anything else.

This is a pardonable moralization, not so remote from the primary sense as the lesson drawn by Philo—that 'to win honour in both spheres, in our duty towards the uncreated and the created, calls for no petty mind, but for one which in very truth stands midway between the world and God'.[26]

With the coming of Christ, and the new understanding of the Old Testament scriptures as bearing witness to him, a new dimension of biblical interpretation was opened up. But the Christian interpretation of the Old Testament in the New Testament is restrained and disciplined by contrast with what we find in the post-apostolic period. There is no reference to wrestling Jacob in the New Testament nor yet in the Apostolic Fathers. But Justin Martyr, in his *Dialogue with Trypho the Jew*, asserts confidently that the mysterious wrestler, whom the narrator describes as 'a man', and of whom Jacob speaks as 'God', must be the one whom Christians acknowledge as both God and man. Trypho is increasingly bewildered as he listens to the flow of Justin's argument: such application of sacred scripture is quite foreign to him, and he cannot comprehend how any one can understand it in such a sense as Justin expounds.[27] But to Justin this understanding of the incident is all of a piece with his understanding of other Old Testament incidents in which God, or his angel, appears or speaks to human beings in the form of a man. The christological exposition of such incidents is hardly attested, if at all, in the New Testament documents; but it was a well-established tradition by Justin's time, for Justin can

---

[26] Philo, *On Drunkenness*, 82f.
[27] Justin, *Dialogue with Trypho*, 58, 126.

scarcely be supposed to have initiated it. Once established, the tradition was actively maintained.

The story of wrestling Jacob, says Dr Peake in the original edition of his *Commentary*, 'has been so filled with deep, spiritual significance (Charles Wesley's "Come, O Thou traveller unknown" is a classic example) that it is difficult for the modern reader to think himself back into its original meaning.'[28] But in fact 'Come, O Thou traveller unknown' is a superb example of what is meant by the plenary sense of scripture.

It has occurred to me from time to time that it would be an agreeable exercise to write a thesis, or at least to supervise one, on 'Biblical Interpretation in the Hymns of Charles Wesley'. One does not go to Wesley's hymns for historical exegesis or the primary sense of scripture, but time and again one finds in them the plenary sense. The twelve stanzas of 'Come, O Thou traveller unknown' present a thorough-going transmutation of the story of wrestling Jacob into something akin to Paul's mysterious experience recounted in 2 Corinthians 12:2–10, which taught him the lesson: 'when I am weak, then I am strong'. But, so far as the author of Genesis is concerned, this (in my judgment) is the lesson which he intends to be drawn from the story of wrestling Jacob; and Charles Wesley, in drawing out and developing this lesson, does no injustice to the primary intention; rather, he lays bare the plenary sense in a Christian idiom:

> And when my all of strength shall fail,
> I shall with the God-Man prevail.

PRESENT APPLICATION

At the beginning of the nineteenth century, when new critical methods were being applied to the biblical records, F. D. E. Schleiermacher manifested a hermeneutical concern as well as a critical interest. Granted that the new methods disclosed the intention of the biblical writers in their contemporary context, what did their message mean to readers in the different context of Schleiermacher's day? How could the new critical contributions enrich the present understanding and application of that message?[29]

[28] *Peake's Commentary on the Bible*, p.160.
[29] F. D. E. Schleiermacher, *The Christian Faith*, E.T. (Edinburgh, 1928), pp.591ff. et passim.

Similar questions are asked today and fresh attempts are made to answer them by interpreting scripture as an integral and controlling element in the continuing life of the people of God, or as the locus of that life-giving and active word which awakens the hearers' faith, helps them to understand their existence and thus transforms it and imparts 'authenticity' to it, liberating them from their bondage to the past and enabling them to be 'open' toward the future. This is the idiom of the 'new hermeneutic'.[30]

An example on the grand scale of what is involved in interpreting an Old Testament book as 'scripture of the church', as an integrating element in the Christian canon, is provided by Brevard Childs' magisterial commentary on Exodus which has replaced the earlier commentary by Martin Noth in the Old Testament Library of the SCM Press.[31] Here is a work which takes fullest account of all that historical-critical exegesis can say about the text, but goes on to maintain that the church's canon, and indeed the church's life, constitute the context within which the text is most fully to be understood. The theme which gives the book of Exodus its Greek name, Israel's departure from Egypt, is of course a *Leitmotiv* in Old Testament thought about God and reflection on Israel's history from that time forth, and supplies a pattern for the unfolding of that later redemptive act in which Christians find supreme significance. But does the New Testament treatment of the Exodus theme or the New Testament application of the story of Moses make a contribution to our understanding of the book of Exodus? Yes, if we are thinking of the plenary sense. The primary sense of Exodus is to be sought within the context of that Old Testament book itself, or at least within the context of the Pantateuch; but the later Christian interpretation brings out a deeper sense in so far as it uncovers layers of meaning implicit in the primary sense. One obvious criticism is forestalled by Professor Childs: to those who point out that Jewish tradition as well as Christian tradition has its 'plenary' interpretation of the Exodus story he replies that he is well aware of this, and that the Jewish tradition also must have its place in the full exposition of the text.[32]

Professor Childs has shown a measure of courage remarkable in an academic theologian, because he knows how vigorously he must be

---

[30] *Cf* J. M. Robinson and J. B. Cobb, *The New Hermeneutic* (New York, 1964).

[31] B. S. Childs, *Exodus: A Commentary* (London, 1974). p.ix.

[32] *Cf* his inclusion of 'Calvin and Drusius, Rashi and Ibn Ezra' among the 'giants' who 'need to be heard in concert with Wellhausen and Gunkel' (p.x).

critized by fellow-exegetes and theologians for importing 'irrelevant' considerations into the interpretation of an ancient Hebrew text. Some of the criticisms already voiced must be recognized to have some substance.[33] But Professor Childs' *Exodus* is a pioneer work, so far as the production of a full-scale scholarly commentary along these lines is concerned. It is not to be compared with the undisciplined puerilities of Wilhelm Vischer a generation ago.[34] In a day when it is proclaimed that 'historical biblical criticism is bankrupt'[35] — a proposition with which I disagree, while I can understand the mood which lies behind it — Professor Childs' 'canonical' exegesis might point a way forward. But if it does, the way forward will be in essence the way of plenary interpretation — that is to say, a way which does not break loose from the primary sense, but expounds the text so as to reveal its relevance to human life today, just as the successive generations intervening between the original readers and ourselves have heard it speak to their varying conditions.

THE HERMENEUTICAL CIRCLE

Frequent reference is made nowadays to the 'hermeneutical circle', an expression which bears more than one meaning. It may denote the circular movement from exegesis to theology and back from theology to exegesis; or it may denote the interpretative process flowing from subject to object (i.e. from the reader to the text), or indeed from object to subject, and then back again, as the one interacts with the other.[36] Any such circular motion must be treated circumspectly.

Naturally, the more one studies (say) Paul, the more one's understanding of Paul's thought grows, so that it becomes easier to determine what Paul means in any one passage of his correspondence. Yet we should remember that Paul was accused of vacillation by some of his critics, and that he himself speaks of being 'all things to all' (1 Cor.

[33] The review by a Christian scholar, J. A. Wharton ('Splendid Failure or Flawed Success?') in *Interpretation* 29 (1975), pp.266–276, is more critical than that by a Jewish scholar, J. Neusner, in *Journal of Jewish Studies* 27 (1976), p.91.

[34] *Cf* W. Vischer, *The Witness of the Old Testament to Christ*, I, E.T. (London, 1949); see also p.101, n.9.

[35] W. Wink, *The Bible in Human Trans-formation* (Philadelphia, 1973), p.1.

[36] *Cf* H. Diem, *Dogmatics*, E.T. (Edinburgh, 1959), pp.236ff.; M. Heidegger, *An Introduction to Metaphysics*, E.T. (Oxford, 1959), pp.146ff.; E. Fuchs, *Marburger Hermeneutik* (Tübingen, 1968), pp.79ff.

9:22). While, then, there is a reasonable presumption that he will not be wildly or radically inconsistent with himself, we must be prepared to find some places where he expresses himself atypically, and these cannot simply be interpreted in terms of our reconstruction of 'Paulinism'. The need for caution is all the greater when the attempt is made to construct a system of biblical theology on the exegesis of several biblical authors and then to use that system as an exegetical tool.

Such attempts were commonplace in the generations before Peake, but in more recent times we have to deal with a tendency which lays itself open to the same objection. Rudolf Bultmann insisted that exegesis without presuppositions is impossible, and his own work illustrates that proposition.[37] He set out on the exegetical enterprise with the presuppositions of Heideggerian existentialism and found those presuppositions confirmed in the biblical text. It must be conceded that, when one attempts in this way to simplify or summarize Professor Bultmann's hermeneutical procedure, it is all too easy to do him injustice: this I should be very sorry to do. His name is one that ought never to be mentioned without profound respect. But he himself affirmed as explicitly as possible that Martin Heidegger and other existential philosophers 'are saying the same thing as the New Testament and saying it quite independently'.[38]

But whether the hermeneutical circle moves in the realm of the older scholasticism or in that of the newer existentialism, it can very readily become what logicians call a vicious circle, in which, by virtually assuming what requires to be proved, one arrives at the point from which one set out.

I think we can tell where Dr Peake would have stood on this issue, and I am sure I should gladly take my place beside him. Inevitably we come to the Bible with our presuppositions. But the wise course is to recognize those presuppositions, to make allowance for them, to ensure that they do not exercise an undue influence on our understanding of what we read. It is the unconscious and unsuspected presuppositions that are harmful. There are, indeed, some people who say, 'Yes, I have my presuppositions, but then, you have yours; if you read the Bible in the light of your inadequate presuppositions, I am

[37] R. Bultmann, 'Is Exegesis without Presuppositions Possible?' E.T. in *Existence and Faith,* ed. S. M. Ogden (London, 1964), pp.342–351.
[38] R. Bultmann, 'New Testament and Mythology' in *Kerygma and Myth,* ed. H. W. Bartsch, E.T., I (London, 1953), p.25.

entitled to read it in the light of my much more adequate ones.' But if I suspect that someone's false conclusions are due to the false presuppositions with which he started, that does not justify me in letting my own assumptions, true though I may believe them to be, play a part in my exegetical work which they have no right to play.

Dr Peake was widely criticized in his day by people who believed that his conclusions were incompatible with biblical inspiration. What they often meant was that his conclusions were incompatible with what they understood biblical inspiration to involve. Let biblical inspiration or any other aspect of biblical authority be stated in the most emphatic and all-embracing fashion: any such statement is devoid of real content unless one discovers, by critical and exegetical study, what the biblical text says and means. Our biblical theology must depend on our exegesis, not *vice versa*. It we allow our exegesis to be controlled by *theologoumena*, we shall quickly find ourselves involved in circular reasoning. I have friends who say, 'Well, yes; but then all theological reasoning is circular; let us simply make sure that we get into the right circle.' I have no wish to accompany them on this magic roundabout.

To approach the exegetical task with unchecked theological assumptions is to find those assumptions reflected back to us from the text. There was a time when Paul and John and the writer to the Hebrews could not be allowed to express their independent insights: they had to say virtually the same thing and be fitted into a comprehensive theological system.[39] Today indeed there has been a tendency to go to the opposite extreme: to emphasize the differences among the New Testament writers to a point where their common and fundamental witness to Jesus as Lord has been overlooked. But this unity of witness is a unity in diversity, and it is the province of exegesis to bring out the diversity within the comprehensive unity.[40] Even in the works of one writer some diversity may be discerned: there is a danger, for example, of missing the distinctive emphases of Galatians and 1 Corinthians if both documents are accommodated to a single corpus of teaching called Paulinism.[41]

It is not given to mortals to attain complete objectivity — not even

[39] *Cf* A. S. Peake, *The Bible,* p.440.

[40] *Cf* J. D. G. Dunn, *Unity and Diversity in the New Testament* (London, 1977).

[41] *Cf* J. W. Drane, *Paul: Libertine or Legalist?* (London, 1974), which discerns a dialectic process in Paul's capital epistles; also H. Hübner, *Law in Paul's Thought,* E.T. (Edinburgh, 1984), for differences in emphasis between Galatians and Romans.

to mathematicians. But one can at least acknowledge objectivity as an ideal and endeavour to approach it as nearly as possible, instead of decrying it as a misleading will o' the wisp. Theology is more than the application of grammar to the text, but it cannot dispense with the application of grammar to the text as a basic procedure.

I have known classical teachers and colleagues to engage occasionally in biblical exegesis. They may have been Christians; they may have been agnostics. But when, without theological *parti pris,* they applied to the New Testament documents the interpretative skills acquired in their classical studies, their contributions, in my experience, have always been illuminating. And why? Because they helped to uncover the primary sense of the documents.

The conclusion of the whole matter, as I see it, is this: the way to ensure that the extended interpretation or existential application of the text does not get out of hand is to determine the primary sense (even when it is complex) and keep it constantly in view. The plenary sense, to be valid, must be the plenary sense *of the biblical text:* it will remain that if its relationship and consistency with the primary sense be maintained. Hermeneutic must never be divorced from exegesis. This was something on which Dr Peake insisted in his own time and in his own way: we shall do well if we follow his example.[42]

[42] This lecture was first published in *Epworth Review* 4 (1977), pp.94–109.

BIBLIOGRAPHY *

ACHTEMEIER, P., *The Inspiration of Scripture: Problems and Proposals* (Philadelphia, 1980).

ALAND, K., *The Problem of the New Testament Canon* (London, 1962).

ANDERSON,G.W. (ed.), *Tradition and Interpretation* (Oxford, 1979).

APPEL, N., *Kanon und Kirche* (Paderborn, 1964).

BARCLAY, W., *The Making of the Bible* (London/New York, 1961).

BARR,J., *Holy Scripture: Canon, Authority, Criticism* (Oxford, 1983).

BARTON, J., *Oracles of God: Perceptions of Ancient Prophecy in Israel after the Exile* (London, 1986).

BECKWITH, R. T., *The Old Testament Canon of the New Testament Church* (London, 1985).

BLACKMAN, E. C., *Marcion and his Influence* (London, 1948).

BLENKINSOPP, J., *Prophecy and Canon* (South Bend, Indiana, 1986).

BUHL, F. P. W., *Canon and Text of the Old Testament,* E.T. (Edinburgh, 1892).

CAMPENHAUSEN, H. von, *The Formation of the Christian Bible,* E.T. (London, 1972).

CARSON,D.A., and WOODBRIDGE, J. D. (ed.), *Hermeneutics, Authority and Canon* (Leicester, 1986).

CHARTERIS, A. H., *Canonicity: Early Testimonies to the Canonical Books of the New Testament* (Edinburgh, 1880).

CHILDS, B. S., *Introduction to the Old Testament as Scripture* (London, 1979).

CHILDS, B. S., *The New Testament as Canon: An Introduction* (London, 1984).

---

* This bibliography lists books only. Many important articles are cited above in the footnotes.

CORNILL, C. H., *Introduction to the Canonical Books of the Old Testament*, E.T. (London, 1907).

CROSS, F.M., *The Ancient Library of Qumran and Modern Biblical Studies* (Grand Rapids, ³1980).

DAVIDSON, S., *The Canon of the Bible* (London, ³ 1880).

DIEM, H., *Das Problem des Schriftkanons* (Zollikon-Zurich, 1952).

EISSFELDT, O., *The Old Testament: An Introduction*, E.T. (Oxford, 1965).

EVANS, C.F., *Is 'Holy Scripture' Christian? and Other Questions* (London, 1971).

FARMER, W. R., *Jesus and the Gospel: Tradition, Scripture and Canon* (Philadelphia, 1982).

FARMER, W. R., and FARKASFALVY, D. M., *The Formation of the New Testament: An Ecumenical Approach* (New York, 1983).

FILSON, F. V., *Which Books Belong in the Bible?* (Philadelphia, 1957).

FLESSEMAN-VAN LEER, E., *Tradition and Scripture in the Early Church* (Assen, 1955).

GAMBLE, H. Y., *The New Testament Canon: Its Making and Meaning* (Philadelphia, 1985).

GAUSSEN, L., *The Canon of the Holy Scriptures*, E. T. (London,³ 1863).

GOODSPEED, E.J., *The Formation of the New Testament* (Chicago, 1926).

GRANT, R. M., *The Earliest Lives of Jesus* (London, 1961).

GRANT, R. M., *The Formation of the New Testament* (London, 1965).

GREGORY, C. R., *Canon and Text of the New Testament* (Edinburgh, 1907).

HALDANE, R., *The Books of the Old and New Testament Proved to be Canonical* (Edinburgh, ⁷1877).

HANSON, R. P. C., *Origen's Doctrine of Tradition* (London, 1954).

HANSON, R. P. C., *Allegory and Event: A Study of the Sources and Significance of Origen's Interpretation of Scripture* (London, 1959).

HANSON, R. P. C., *Tradition in the Early Church* (London, 1962).

HARNACK, A. von, *The Origin of the New Testament*, E. T. (London, 1925).

HARNACK, A. von, *Marcion: Das Evangelium vom fremden Gott* (Leipzig, 1921, ²1924).

HARRIS, R. L., *Inspiration and Canonicity of the Bible* (Grand Rapids, 1957).

HAWTHORNE, G. F., and BETZ, O. (ed.), *Tradition and Interpretation in the New Testament* (Grand Rapids, 1987).

HENNECKE, E., and SCHNEEMELCHER, W., *New Testament Apocrypha*, E. T. edited by R. McL. Wilson, I, II (London, 1963, 1965).

KÄSEMANN, E. (ed), *Das Neue Testament als Kanon* (Göttingen, 1970).

KATZ, P., *Philo's Bible* (Cambridge, 1950).

KELLY, J. F., *Why is there a New Testament?* (London, 1986).

KLINE, M. G., *The Structure of Biblical Authority* (Grand Rapids, 1972).

KNOX, J., *Marcion and the New Testament* (Chicago, 1942).

LEIMAN, S. Z. *The Canonization of Hebrew Scripture: The Talmudic and Midrashic Evidence* (Hamden, CT, 1976).

LEIPOLDT, J., *Geschichte des neutestamentlichen Kanons*, I, II (Leipzig, 1907, 1908; reprinted 1974).

LIGHTFOOT, J. B., *Essays on the Work Entitled 'Supernatural Religion'* (London, 1889).

LÖNNING, I., *Kanon im Kanon: Zum dogmatischen Grundlagenproblem des neutestamentlichen Kanons* (Oslo, 1972).

MARCH, W. E. (ed.), *Texts and Testaments: Critical Essays on the Bible and the Early Christian Fathers* (San Antonio, TX, 1980).

MARSHALL, I. H. (ed.), *New Testament Interpretation* (Leicester, 1977).

MARXSEN, W., *The New Testament as the Church's Book*, E. T. (Philadelphia, 1972).

MEADE, D. G., *Pseudonymity and Canon* (Tübingen/Grand Rapids, 1986/7).

METZGER, B. M., *The Canon of the New Testament* (Oxford, 1987).

MITTON, C. L., *The Formation of the Pauline Corpus of Letters* (London, 1955).

MOULE, C. F. D., *The Birth of the New Testament* (London, [3]1981).

NEUSNER, J., *Christian Faith and the Bible of Judaism: The Judaic Encounter with Scripture* (Grand Rapids, 1988).

OHLER, A., *Studying the Old Testament from Tradition to Canon* (Edinburgh, 1985).

OHLIG, K.-H., *Die theologische Begründung des neutestamentlichen Kanons in der alten Kirche* (Düsseldorf, 1972).

OPPEL, H., *KANŌN: Zur Bedeutungsgeschichte des Wortes und seiner lateinischen Entsprechungen (Regular-Norma)* = *Philologus*, Supp.-Band 30.4 (Leipzig, 1937).

OVERBECK, F., *Zur Geschichte des Kanons* (Chemnitz, 1880, reprinted 1965).

REGUL, J., *Die antimarcionitischen Evangelienprologe* = Aus der Geschichte der lateinischen Bibel, 6 (Freiburg, 1969).

REUSS, R. E., *The History of the Canon of the Holy Scriptures in the Christian Church*, E. T. (Edinburgh, 1891).

ROBINSON, D. W. B., *Faith's Framework: The Structure of New Testament Theology* (Exeter, 1985).

ROWLEY, H. H., *The Growth of the Old Testament* (London, 1950).

RYLE, H. E., *The Canon of the Old Testament* (London, [2]1904).

SANDAY, W., *The Gospels in the Second Century* (London, 1876).

SANDERS, J. A., *Torah and Canon* (Philadelphia, 1972).

SANDERS, J. A., *Canon and Community* (Philadelphia, 1984).

SANDERS, J. A., *From Sacred Story to Sacred Text: Canon as Paradigm* (Philadelphia, 1987).

SMITH, W. R., *The Old Testament in the Jewish Church* (London, [2]1895).

SOUTER, A., *The Text and Canon of the New Testament* (London, 1913, revised by C. S. C. Williams, 1954).

SPARKS, H. F. D., *The Growth of the New Testament* (London, 1952).

STONEHOUSE, N. B., *The Apocalypse in the Ancient Church* (Goes, 1929).

SUNDBERG. A. C., Jr., *The Old Testament in the Early Church* = Harvard Theological Studies, 20 (Cambridge, MA, 1964).

THERON, D. J., *The Evidence of Tradition* (London, 1957).

WEINGREEN, J., *From Bible to Mishna* (Manchester, 1976).

WESTCOTT, B. F., *The Bible in the Church* (London, 1864, [9]1885)

WESTCOTT, B. F., *A General Survey of the History of the Canon of the New Testament* (London, [4]1874).

WILDEBOER, G., *The Origin of the Canon of the Old Testament*, E. T. (London, 1895).

ZAHN, Th. von., *Geschichte des neutestamentlichen Kanons*, I, II (Erlangen, 1888–92).

ZAHN, Th. von., *Grundriss der Geschichte des neutestamentlichen Kanons* (Leipzig, [2]1904).

INDEX